Rethinking the World

A volume in the series

CORNELL STUDIES IN SECURITY AFFAIRS

edited by Robert J. Art, Robert Jervis, and Stephen M. Walt

A list of titles in the series is available at

www.cornellpress.cornell.edu.

Rethinking *the* World

GREAT POWER STRATEGIES
AND INTERNATIONAL ORDER

JEFFREY W. LEGRO

Cornell University Press

ITHACA AND LONDON

First published 2005 by Cornell University Press
First printing, Cornell Paperbacks, 2007

Printed in the United States of America

Library of Congress Cataloging–in–Publication Data

Legro, Jeffrey
    Rethinking the world : great power strategies and international
order / Jeffrey W. Legro.
        p. cm. — (Cornell studies in security affairs)
    Includes bibliographical references and index.
    ISBN–13: 978–0–8014–4272–8 (cloth : alk. paper)
    ISBN–13: 978–0–8014–7383–8 (pbk. : alk. paper)
    1. International organization.   2. International relations.   I. Title.
    II. Series.
    JZ1308.L44 2005
    327.1'01—dc22
2005008834

Cornell University Press strives to use environmentally responsible
suppliers and materials to the fullest extent possible in the publishing
of its books. Such materials include vegetable-based, low-VOC inks
and acid-free papers that are recycled, totally chlorine-free, or partly
composed of nonwood fibers. For further information, visit our
website at www.cornellpress.cornell.edu.

Cloth printing   10 9 8 7 6 5 4 3 2 1
Paperback printing   10 9 8 7 6 5 4 3 2 1

To the Reverend Janet Hatfield Legro

Contents

List of Figures and Tables   ix

Acknowledgments   xi

1. Great Power Ideas and Change   1

2. Explaining Change and Continuity   24

3. The Ebb and Flow of American Internationalism   49

4. Germany, from Outsider to Insider   84

5. Overhaul of Orthodoxy in Tokugawa Japan and
    the Soviet Union   122

6. The Next Century   161

    Appendix 1: The Transformation of Economic Ideas   189

    Appendix 2: Analysis of Presidential Discourse   199

    Notes   201

    Index   248

Figures and Tables

FIGURES

1.1	Conventional explanation of change	14
1.2	Two-stage model of change	14
3.1	American foreign policy ideas, 1908–1950	54
5.1	Map of Japan about 1850	129
5.2	Daimyo opinion on seclusion versus openness, 1853	130
5.3	Crude oil prices, 1949–2004	150

TABLES

1.1	A typology of national ideas about international society	10
2.1	Collapse: Ideas and events	33
2.2	Consolidation: Oppositional ideas and efficacy	36
3.1	American foreign policy ideas transformed	59
3.2	United States international agreements	60
5.1	The development of Japan's foreign policy	126
6.1	A foreign policy revolution?	167

Acknowledgments

Moving from old to new ideas is not easy. To the extent I have done so in my own thinking, it is due to help from colleagues, friends, and family. I should probably be embarrassed to list all those who have generously pitched in, but it is actually a pleasure to recall all their quips, critiques, guffaws, brilliant insights, and priceless encouragement.

Thanks to Gerard Alexander, Michael Barnett, Sheri Berman, Kurt Campbell, Mike Desch, Andrew Erdmann, Matthew Evangelista, Peter Feaver, Martha Finnemore, Paul Freedman, Joseph Grieco, John Ikenberry, Iain Johnston, Robert Keohane, David Lake, Melvyn Leffler, Kate McNamara, Andrew Moravcsik, Ido Oren, Richard Price, Dan Reiter, Len Schoppa, Peter Trubowitz, David Waldner, Alexander Wendt, William Wohlforth, and Brantly Womack for their contributions.

Going beyond the call of duty and reading large chunks of some version of the manuscript, sometimes more than once, Dale Copeland, Erica Gould, Peter Katzenstein, John Owen, Herman Schwartz, Arthur Stein, and Stephen Walt (as series editor at Cornell) provided critical feedback that inspired and sometimes infuriated me. I could not hope for more.

Talented students here at the University of Virginia helped with tasks big and small throughout the project. I am grateful to Spencer Bakich, Monica Black, Kelly Erickson, Jennifer Johnson, Travis Larrabee, Rob Martin, Mindy Martin, Haiyan Qu, Justin Tomlinson, Alesia Walker, Hiro Yamamoto, and Daniel Weir.

I benefited from comments received on various parts of the manuscript in talks given at the University of Chicago, Duke University, the George Marshall Foundation, George Washington University, the University of Minnesota, Princeton University, Stanford University, and the University of Texas. This project had its origins while I was a fellow at the John M. Olin

[xi]

Center for Strategic Studies at Harvard University under the valuable guidance of Samuel Huntington and Stephen Rosen. Portions of chapters 2 and 3 first appeared in "The Transformation of Policy Ideas," *American Journal of Political Science* 44, no. 3 (2000): 419–22 and in "Whence American Internationalism," *International Organization* 54, no. 2 (2000): 253–89. I am grateful to Blackwell Publishing and MIT Press for permission to use that material here. The University of Virginia has provided several summers of research funds. Roger Haydon has again worked his magic at Cornell University Press and kept me smiling, even when the answer was no. Karen Laun and Katy Meigs edited masterfully and saved me from an array of embarrassments.

My siblings did little on this project except heckle me—but since they love to see their name in print, I thank Bonnie Legro, Sherrie Legro Round, and Dr. Richard Legro for their wit and the enduring lessons they gave their younger brother. We all follow the wisdom of the matriarch—Janet Wenner Legro—and still do not know if she views her use of a BA in child psychology on her own children as a failed experiment. My in-laws Doug and Judy Hatfield helped in ways they did not know but which were deeply appreciated.

The heavy lifting was done at home. Our spectacular daughters, Maddie and Meg, have been an endless source of fresh insight, joy, and love—a big help when the slogging was tough. Last, and first, is my *airen*, Janet. She has done everything to make the book happen except write or read it—reminding me again that the best of my life has always been beyond its pages. Thank you Hattie, this is for you.

Rethinking the World

[1]

Great Power Ideas and Change

In world politics, leaders look ahead for signs of the next wildfire. Not surprisingly, they often focus on the foreign policy ideas of major states. Will Japan adhere to its post–World War II pacifism or take a turn toward militarized autonomy? Is China bound for integration in the international system, or for a Qing-era isolationism, or a rebellion against the existing order? Might Germany one day leave behind its integrationist mind-set and revive a revisionist foreign policy, one that seeks to overturn the dominant international norms? Perhaps most important, some wonder whether the United States will persist in turning its back on the international institutions and political-military commitments built over the past sixty years in favor of a new Pax Americana.

Such enduring great power ideas matter because they guide foreign policy and are a building block of international life.[1] Yet sometimes they radically change, usually with earthquake-like effects. Consider, for example, how Mikhail Gorbachev's "new thinking" fundamentally altered both the Soviet Union's actions and the cold war dynamic that had dominated world politics for forty-five years. Other seismic shifts have similarly marked international life over the past two centuries. When Japan emerged from two hundred years of isolation in the 1860s, a new era of great power relations in Asia began. And when the United States adopted an internationalist outlook after World War II, it spearheaded an unprecedented level of development in the institutional texture of world politics.

Yet, just as international order is made by national ideas, so is it unmade. Ideas do not always shift in the direction of harmonious engagement. When Soviet Russia rejected the dominant ethos of the international arena in 1917, a new source of tension and division frayed global politics. Similarly, when the United States reverted to aloofness from major power commitments after World War I, the nascent League of Nations was disabled and the seeds of the Great Depression were sown. And when Germany once again embraced continental domination in the interwar period, a second world war took wing. In some instances states turn toward integration in international order—what Hedley Bull called "international society"—the dominant rules, institutions, and norms that characterize the international system.[2] In other situations, nations understand their interests as best served by separating themselves from that society, or even by dramatically revising it. This variation begs for analysis.

Despite the importance of these ideational transformations, scholars and policymakers have few tools with which to understand and anticipate them. Those who have paid the closest attention to the importance of the international system have paid less attention to the sources of change in that system.[3] Hedley Bull and his associates, for example, focused on the nature and different forms of international society, not on its dynamic transformation. They ignored one of the primary sources of change in international life—the collective ideas of major powers. What is clear is that states have often differed in their reactions to international rules—some accepting them, others not. Such attitudes can enhance or undermine overall order.[4] International relations specialists since World War II have explored in detail the importance of power, the influence of institutions, and the role of domestic politics in world politics.[5] In these studies, the collective ideas of nations are often pushed to the wings: they are marginalized as "cheap talk," a side product of more central causes, or post hoc justifications.

Starting in the 1980s, however, some scholars have devoted considerable effort to correcting this oversight by intensive study of the way ideas (norms, beliefs, identity, etc.) at the international, national, and subnational levels have affected politics.[6] What remains a puzzle, despite the volume of this literature, is why collectively held (or group) ideas sometimes radically *change*. Max Weber compared ideas to "switchmen" who work the railroads: they point actors, like trains, down tracks in some directions and divert them from others. This famous metaphor, however, begs a critical question: What decides the direction of the switch?

Adherents of psychological and constructivist approaches have paid serious attention to ideas, yet they also illustrate the problem. The psychology literature in international relations has illuminated the dynamics of change in the ideas that individuals hold. Not surprising, given its focus on the human mind, psychology has been less helpful in explaining how individual ideas come together to affect (or in many cases *not* affect) national ideas, such as those that guide foreign policies.[7] Constructivists, by contrast, have focused on collective ideas and illuminated their influence theoretically and empirically in a variety of national and international settings. They have also shown how ideas have played a role in periods of political change.[8] Yet general explanations of change in the ideas themselves are rare. And to push the issue one step further, how ideas shape their own transformation, if they even do, remains an enigma.

Given this lacuna in the academy, policymakers—and those who would try to influence officials—face a challenge. In the absence of some general notion about the transformation of ideas, we cannot begin to think about likely outcomes in ongoing specific cases. For example, consider two big contemporary phenomena in world politics: the "rise of China" and the Bush "foreign policy revolution."

China's rapid economic growth and prominence has naturally been a focus of research.[9] Considerable analysis, and much of the debate, has high-lighted questions that link power to behavior. Will China's emerging power lead to revisionist goals? Will it produce armed conflict as China ascends in power and other countries (e.g., Japan and the United States) decline in relative terms?[10] As important as these questions are, what they miss is the way that international relations are shaped not just by the power states have but the *ideas* the states hold about how that power should be used.[11] Power, of course, is a tool, and ideas about the uses of tools vary considerably.[12] Power does not determine ideas nor do power transitions among states inevitably lead to conflict. After World War I, the United States emerged as the most powerful country on earth, but U.S. government involvement did *not* expand during the interwar period. China's power has been growing since World War II, but it has adopted a range of different ideas toward the international system. And in terms of power trajectories, Britain and the United States *did not* go to war with each other at the turn of the twentieth century, even as the United States surpassed Britain as the dominant international power.[13] In these cases enduring ideas (e.g., how much to integrate into the extant international order, which states to align with) played a central role. Positing such a role for ideas does not explain their sources, however. Lacking such an explanation, we are handcuffed in considering, for example, how China's power trajectory will shape world politics.

Perhaps even more important is whether the United States is currently undergoing a foreign policy revolution. Since the end of World War II the United States has systematically favored active engagement in world affairs, a commitment to a liberal and open international order, and the development of multilateral practices and institutions. Many believe that in the wake of the 9/11 terrorist attacks the United States adopted a new and fundamentally different compass for navigating in the world arena.[14] The new orientation features accentuated American unilateral action, the preventive use of force, and an expanded geographical vision of the areas appropriate for aggressive democratization (e.g., moving beyond the Western hemisphere into the Middle East). Clearly, if such a transformation becomes orthodoxy, it will have huge implications for the United States and the world. Thinking about such a possibility demands a broad framework.

[3]

How do we account for the transformation—or continuity—of national ideas about international politics? Where do we even begin?

My short answer is that we start where we want to end—with ideas. New foreign policy ideas are shaped by preexisting dominant ideas and their relationship to experienced events, sometimes reinforcing the continuity of concepts and infrequently leading to their radical change. Yet that is still only the beginning of the story. To explain this complex variation means assessing not only ideas but how ideas interact in regular ways with the demands of strategic circumstances and domestic political pressures. Ideas, strategic circumstances, and domestic politics are typically treated as logically exclusive alternative approaches to explaining change or stability. Here I attempt to develop a synthetic explanation that captures their interactive effects. Why and how this happens is the longer account that follows.

My aim, then, is to gain some insight into the general determinants of the foreign policy concepts of various nation-states. By unraveling the general sources of foreign policy conceptual change we may also see new possibilities for future diplomacy and social action. In this chapter I lay the foundation by clarifying what it is I hope to explain, the conceptual and historical puzzles involved, the broad outlines of the argument, and why it matters.

The End of the Chain

A good starting point is clarity as to what exactly is being explained— that is, continuity and change in the ideas of nation-states about how to relate to international society. The term "ideas" inevitably invokes a wide range of images. My concern is with foreign policy ideas that can be differentiated from others in three basic ways that relate to their level, type, and content; such ideas (1) are collectively held; (2) involve beliefs about effective means; and (3) refer specifically to national conceptions about international society. Each dimension deserves brief discussion.

Level

First, the ideas to be explored are a property of groups (i.e., states, and are therefore inherently collective and institutional, not individual and "mental.")[15] We commonly use "ideas" (or "beliefs," "attitudes," "views," etc.) to refer to things people have in their head. Following this usage, a vibrant series of studies have drawn from the psychological literature for its insights on the human mind and its implications for international politics.[16] From this perspective, national ideas are studied as if they are (1) a reflection of individual leaders who cause national policies, or (2) the property of states with the same psychological biases as humans, or (3) are a summation of individual ideas that somehow "add up" to cause national policy.[17]

The seminal work of Robert Jervis on psychology and international relations uses all these techniques. For example, he argues that "when an event affects the perceptual predispositions of many members of an organization we can speak of organizational learning."[18] In this view, collective outcomes are mostly conceptualized as the summation of individual minds.

Two broad literatures suggest that some types of ideas have to be considered as properties that are not reducible to individual minds. One comes from the classic sociological tradition and is based on the work of scholars such as Emile Durkheim and Max Weber, who have attempted to demonstrate how social beliefs and concepts shape both individuals and group policy.[19] Modern philosophers such as Charles Taylor, John Searle, and Margaret Gilbert speak to the collective properties of ideas that are intersubjective and thus distinct from the subjective ideas—personal beliefs, attitudes, and opinions—that individuals hold.[20] "Far from being the product of our own will," Durkheim notes, social facts (i.e., collective ideas and representations) determine it from without. They are like moulds unto which we are forced to cast our actions."[21] An example (borrowed from Wittgenstein) is the way that language is not reducible to physical voice capacity or individual perception. Individuals may speak a language and use it for their own purposes, but the language itself is a preexisting entity to which they must adapt. Similarly, dominant ideas are often embedded in public discourse and symbols that also represent intersubjective phenomena that attach to group, not individual, orientation. Japanese leaders at the beginning of the nineteenth century did not choose to seclude Japan from the world. It was a tradition they were born into—it was as natural to them as "Japan" itself. To say that tradition was a product of individual opinion or even public opinion would be to misstate cause and effect.

Human biology lends support to the sociological view. Humans are adapted to living in groups and to understanding group dynamics. We have lived in groups for thousands of years and have been selected to think in terms of group interests and ideas, not just self-interest.[22] Our biology invites social influence. Three-quarters of the human brain develops outside of the womb, which is unique among primates. The brain grows at fetal rates for some two years after birth, and full development is not completed until puberty. We have an "ecological brain."[23] This means that humans to an important degree are not "knowledge-wired" at birth. Our postpartum social environment has a massive impact. A variety of work has begun to document the social roots of the "self," including human cognition.[24] Thus, the collective attributes of groups—for example, the ideas that characterize them—can matter both for individuals and society.

Scholars of organizations have developed a second literature that documents the way that collective ideas, that is, "organizational cultures," mold the behavior of firms and bureaucracies in a variety of different areas.[25] Organizational beliefs are a collective phenomenon that shapes the people who work within the organizations. This is not to say all individuals accept a predominant culture. Many organizations, in fact, are characterized by several cultures that compete for dominance or that give the organization a multifaceted character.[26] Nonetheless, to act coherently, large organizations require dominant themes for reasons of efficiency and identity. Culture provides a set of principles regarding collective identity and appropriate behavior, and by doing so it produces more coherent coordinated behavior among the many individuals involved in the planning and conduct of, say, foreign policy.[27] Organizations are certainly created and run by people, but such organizations can also constrain and shape individual ideas.

The literature on broad societies and the literature on organizations come together in the collective body that is central to this study: the modern nation-state, itself both society and organization. As large societies, nations require ideas that signify to their members what they stand for; as large organizations they require ideas to guide them in their interactions in the international arena. Ideas are not so much mental as symbolic and organizational; they are embedded not only in human brains but also in the "collective memories," government procedures, educational systems, and the rhetoric of statecraft.[28] To stress the collective nature of ideas should not imply that they are unrelated to human reflection and action. States do not have brains and inherent cognitive capacity, people do. People guide states (and social groups) and likewise struggle over collective ideas. Acknowledging this mutual effect underscores the difference between individual and social ideas. As Marx famously noted, "Men make their own history, but they do not make it just as they please . . . but under circumstances transmitted from the past. The tradition of all dead generations weighs like a nightmare on the brain of the living."[29] The tension Marx highlights exists today in contemporary foreign policy debates: When can creative human agency overturn tradition, and when is it unable to do so?[30]

Although the collective ideas examined here may be "dominant" in a particular group, they are nonetheless typically challenged by individuals offering different ideas. Collective ideational change, therefore, is inherently political and conflictual. Dominant ideas are almost never monolithic entities, reproduced and accepted in the mind of each and every citizen. While they may serve as the touchstone for the collectivity, and have the status of "tradition," they are also often questioned and politically contested by at least some individuals or subgroups. In most countries, most of the time, there is rarely just one opinion of what policy is appropriate; there are always defenders and critics of any single position. For example, in the interwar period in the United States, the dominant view was to avoid entanglement in great power security politics. Many individuals, however, supported a different, and largely ignored, vision of the United States actively making commitments to calm European instability in the 1920s and

1930s. These internationalists nonetheless had to operate within the dominant "no entanglement" orthodoxy even as they tried to change it.[31] It is possible therefore to talk about collective ideas located at the level of the nation-state, even though individuals and subgroups may challenge them.

A focus on enduring collective ideas can be found in various guises in the social science literature. Margaret Weir and Theda Skocpol highlight the importance of "policy legacies." Peter Hall uses the notion of "policy paradigm" to describe a "framework of ideas and standards that specifies not only the goals of policy and the kind of instruments that can be used to attain them, but also the very nature of the problems they are meant to be addressing." Stephen Ellingson employs the term "discourse" similarly to refer to a "set of arguments organized around a specific diagnosis of and solution to some social problem." Frank Dobbin refers to "industrial cultures" as "economic customs that structure . . . the means-ends designations." Finally, Sheri Berman studies "programmatic beliefs." In each of these cases, the author pays attention to dominant social concepts that shape policy but that are nonetheless politically contested.[32]

Type

There are, of course, different types of collective ideas. One type involves the way outsiders and citizens see the nation (identity). Another considers what a nation desires (interests). Still others refer to what a society believes is morally principled (ethics), or how it views others (images). In this book I examine beliefs about effective means for achieving interests or how states think about achieving their ends ("instrumentality").[33] One study has termed these "causal beliefs."[34] Barry Posen evokes a similar focus in defining "grand strategy" as "a theory states develop about how to cause security for themselves."[35]

Such ideas are sometimes wrongly portrayed as mere "tools" that are easily adopted or abandoned. Although these ideas may start as concepts to guide action, over time they may take on a value of their own. Under the influence of habit, and by the actions of those who benefit from them, they can become institutionalized. As organization theorists point out, particularly when groups have intangible goals such as that in the mission statement of the United States Department of State, to "create a more secure, democratic, and prosperous world for the benefit of the American people and the international community," organizations will focus their efforts on modes or methods of output, rather than actual goals.[36] Such ideas can even become what Ernest May has called "axiomatic"—formulations derived from history that become accepted assumptions of foreign policy.[37]

Naturally, state leaders make calculations about their actions based on the situation, but they often do so against a backdrop of certain entrenched national ideas about what general behavior is appropriate. Such ideas are typically not the often unassailable beliefs of religions. Nor are they the ideas that characterize action in realms where assessment is and can be made based on plentiful data and reliable feedback. They are in a middle ground between the unassailable and the easily assessable, where evaluation takes place, but it largely occurs in the absence of reliable data or testing by trial and error. It is hard to rerun an experiment on whether "empire" or "isolationism" is the best approach to world order. Yet as May suggests, such ideas are nonetheless vulnerable to transformation "as history grows" and countries "see the past in a new light."[38] I hope to illuminate exactly how and when this happens.

Content

A final distinction concerns the substance or issue area of the ideas to be examined. We might classify collective ideas by varying levels of analysis (systemic vs. national), varying issues (economic vs. foreign policy), and even by varying scope (regional vs. global). In short, there are a variety of different ideas one might choose to examine. Alastair Iain Johnston discusses "strategic culture" as a set of preferences for particular actions and uses it to account for the conflict behavior of Ming China. Charles Kupchan has also used the phrase "strategic culture" but in reference to ideas about the relationship between national security and empire. Judith Goldstein focuses on "beliefs about the efficacy of particular strategies for obtaining objectives" in explaining American trade policy. I have explored how dominant ideas in German, British, Soviet, and American military organizations affected whether those states used "unthinkable" weapons that they had agreed not to use.[39]

My focus here is on ideas related to a neglected dimension of foreign policy, specifically, national ideas about how to approach international society. Most studies of "grand strategy" have tended to focus on the military aspects of national security or the economic dimension of decline.[40] Those studies that have gone beyond a military focus have tended to give short shrift to the important role played by national ideas about the desirability of joining and sustaining the extant international order.[41] This is a large target and it necessarily means forgoing other types of ideas, for example, those that concern how to fight wars or those that relate to a specific region (for example, the United States's "containment" policy toward the Soviet Union).[42] National attitudes toward international society obviously affect the orientation of foreign policy and, when great powers are involved, the degree of consensus versus conflict in world politics. Such ideas deserve study in their own right.

States have encountered international society in many different ways, and each nation has had its own unique notions of how to relate to the rest of the world. We can categorize and compare these notions in a rough fashion, however, according to the degree to which a state sees its interests as served by one of three ideal (i.e., abstract or pure) positions—integrationism, separatism, and revisionism—that is, by joining, remaining outside of, or overturning the extant international society.

One ideal position is integration, defined here as an acceptance of and cooperative participation in the prevailing international society. Germany or Canada in the past several decades lean toward this position. China has moved in this direction since 1979. Integrationism in this sense is not the opposite of nationalism or opposed to national interests, in that either greater or lesser integration in international society might serve national well-being. Integrationism as used here should also not be conflated with a state's level of international activity. A country may be very involved in the global political arena but remain aloof from or resistant to extant institutions and norms. Generally, integration implies a cooperative or collaborative approach toward the Great Powers that define the system. It does not necessarily mean the absence of violence or coercion. Imperialism, for example, was part and parcel of nineteenth-century international society. War itself has also not been outlawed by prevailing norms. Like boxers, states may mutually agree to pummel one another.

A second ideal position, separatism, reflects a desire to remain aloof from the extant system. Separatism refers to states that resist the norms of the extant international society and prefer to remain largely uninvolved in it. An example of the rejection of that society is apparent in the policy of seclusion practiced by Japan's Tokugawa shogunate from 1640 to 1868, when relations with outside (especially European) powers were largely prohibited and even the Chinese tributary system was resisted. The United States for more than half of its history favored distance from European norms. Bhutan and North Korea are contemporary cases close to this extreme.

A third position is revisionism. This refers to states that reject the dominant norms of interaction in a given international society and believe that active involvement in overturning that order serves national interests. Historical examples of such revisionist states include Napoleonic France and Hitler's Germany. The Soviet Union initially thought the overthrow of the existing international system was the best way to pursue its interests. That notion faded after Stalin established the viability of "socialism in one country." The Soviet Union became very involved in international affairs, but it never accepted the rules of the Western capitalist–dominated international society. There is of course an active contemporary debate as to whether the United States itself has become a revisionist power in the wake of the terrorist attacks of September 2001.

The specific meaning of integrationism, separatism, and revisionism varies with the geographical, historical, and cultural context of international society.[43] Integrationism in the nineteenth century, for example, embraced imperialism. In contrast, in the late twentieth century, prevailing international norms rejected the formal practice of imperialism. The use of force could be related to an integrationist, separatist, or revisionist position, depending on the particular rules of an international order in a particular period.[44] The use of the most violent weapons has been acceptable in some periods (e.g., cannons in medieval times) but not in others (nuclear weapons today). This triangle of ideal alternatives allows consideration of different approaches throughout history in a broadly comparable conceptual framework (see table 1.1). It also encourages us to consider similar and dissimilar aspects of shifts that nations have taken in a particular direction at different times in relation to specific unique national contexts. Of course no country represents one ideal position, and typically every country embodies some element of each.

Why do the foreign policy ideas of specific nations show continuity in some instances and change in others? "Change" in this study refers to a significant shift in the way a state conceives of its relations with the world. "Continuity" refers to a basic uniformity of such concepts over time. My aim is not to categorize a country as exclusively integrationist, separatist, or revisionist, or to argue the normative value of any of the ideal positions, or merely to describe switches from one ideal position to another. I aim to ex-

Table 1.1 A typology of national ideas about international society

Ideas	Indicators	Examples
Revisionist	National rhetoric and doctrines that aspire to different international ordering principles; aggressive critiques of, and challenges to, existing norms and rules.	Napoleonic France, Nazi Germany, post-revolution USSR, early Maoist China.
Separatist	National rhetoric and doctrines that critique involvement with the dominant rules. Withdrawal or distance from important practices or institutions of the existing order.	Tokugawa Japan, United States before World War II, Cultural Revolution era China.
Integrationist	National rhetoric and doctrines that value engagement with the extant norms and rules. Efforts to join or sustain extant institutions.	Meiji Japan, Germany and the United States after World War II, Deng's China.

plain why states have (or have not) made notable conceptual moves away from their existing integrationist-separatist-revisionist ideas.

PUZZLES, ANALYTICAL AND HISTORICAL

Change is a fundamental site of intellectual debate about what shapes politics, and it is a difficult area for studying the influence of ideas. Skeptics of the causal role of ideas, even those who might concede ideas have some influence, still assert that ideas themselves are primarily the result of more fundamental forces. Scholars of world politics have traditionally viewed international relations as a product of strategic national behavior, the results of which are determined by interests, relative power, and institutional settings. Such work has offered powerful insights, but it is also incomplete because it ignores a necessary component—how nations *believe* they can achieve their desired outcomes.[45] We may know what societies desire, we may know the balance of power among them, and we may know the prevailing domestic and international rules. Yet, unless we also understand how states conceive of appropriate action—and when such conceptions are likely to change—we cannot understand how interests will be achieved, how power will constrain or enable such efforts, and which rules are likely to be heeded or violated. The point is not that rational accounts of politics lack utility. Rather it is that such models of unitary state behavior depend on collective ideas and under certain conditions (see chapter 2) require an exogenous theory of the sources of those ideas.[46]

If there is a default explanation for discontinuous shifts in social ideas it is "external shock"—typically such big events as war, revolution, or economic crisis. State notions, so this wisdom implies, tend to change with dramatic events. These arguments typically portray a *stasis-shock-change-stasis* cycle of conceptual development, one that is also familiar in the literature on institutional change.[47] Embedded mind-sets endure for relatively long periods of time, but then they change under the pressure of dramatic events, giving way to new ideas that last until the next crisis. Yet there is a problem with this formula. While crises are often related to change, exogenous shock remains an indeterminate explanation. Similar shocks seem to have different effects: some lead to change, some do not. Why?

We have poor answers to this question in part because we tend to look only at shocks that caused change (and not those where change did not occur), thus allowing wide room for misleading "causes." The answer implicit in the shock approach is that certain events somehow show extant beliefs to be wrong and that change is therefore unavoidable. But it is not clear which events are likely to have such an effect.[48] In the study of politics, no shock is more often cited as a source of national change than war. Yet comparable wars often seem to have different effects, regardless of whether the outcome was victory or defeat. Some cases that have been central to the history of international relations over the past two centuries illustrate this puzzle.

After World War I, the United States remained largely aloof from power politics and the institutions of European-dominated international society, despite its victory and predominant power status. The refusal of the United States to lead, or even follow, after World War I is interesting because it turned its back on the many incentives to play a major role. The United States enjoyed a newfound dominance in the international hierarchy and could use its leverage to shape global economic and security affairs to its own benefit. In Europe, countries welcomed U.S. involvement, and after the war U.S. citizens and corporations did resume engagement in international commerce and culture.[49] Yet the U.S. government clung to the tradition that national well-being was best preserved by remaining aloof from foreign entanglement in major power relations, especially treaty commitments to use military force.

In contrast, during World War II, the dominant U.S. thinking about how to conduct international affairs underwent a revolutionary change. The choice between aloofness and joining major power alliances and international institutions was relatively clear-cut: The United States saw the latter path as optimal, embracing a new view of how best to pursue its interests, one founded on the necessity of actively initiating, participating in, and remaining militarily committed to international relationships and institutions. Most important, this change predated the cold war and cannot be attributed to the rise of the Soviet threat or the bipolar standoff. U.S. attitudes toward international affairs had a large impact on international politics throughout these eras, both in what was done and what was left undone.

The shaping of international society in the twentieth century demands a look at countries other than the United States.[50] Few stand out as more central and provocative than Germany. The initiator of two world wars, Germany was soundly defeated in both. Yet it was only after the second conflict that it changed its basic notions of engagement with the world. In the first half of the twentieth century, Germany saw its security as being served by challenging international society and by expanding its homeland at the expense of other nations. Yet after World War II, West Germany embraced a completely different understanding of how to provide for its security—one that accepted and encouraged the emergent multilateral regimes by acting as a model of integration in an increasingly institutionalized global order.

This change defies simple answers. It was not, for example, foreordained by the cold war—as demonstrated by the intense debate in West Germany after the war about what its foreign policy should be. Likewise the shock of war, and especially defeat, also cannot explain the change. If that were true, why didn't Germany alter its views after defeat in World War I? Beaten by the Allies, Germany underwent a revolution in 1918. Yet soon thereafter, it again took up ideas about international relations similar to those it held before World War I. How can we best account for this puzzling continuity after World War I in contrast to the change after World War II—a change that has outlived the end of the cold war?

Other periods in history also offer puzzling cases of continuity and change in national ideas that have importantly affected international society. From about 1640 on, Japan isolated itself from almost all interaction with Western international society. It expelled most Westerners, strictly isolated those few allowed to remain, and passed laws that prohibited Japanese from traveling abroad. This self-seclusion attempted to keep Japan outside of the increasing presence of European international society. Yet in 1868, Japan dramatically reversed that position, opening itself to the external world and accepting the rules of engagement of Western-dominated order. Why did Japan separate itself for so long and why did it switch to integration in the international system in 1868?

In the late hours of the twentieth century, the Soviet Union, a country that had also cut itself off from "normal" engagement, likewise radically changed its orientation toward the international system, broadly accepting the prevailing Western capitalist rules and norms of international society. Despite our temptation to see that shift as inevitable due to declining Soviet power and economic vitality, there was no overwhelming reason it had to occur in the 1980s. Some of the same conditions that allegedly provoked the new thinking existed in earlier decades as well, but change did not occur then. And there is little doubt that the Soviet Union could have managed for years beyond 1985 with its existing system and ideas; yet it opted to change. Indeed the new foreign policy ideas were a cause, not a consequence, of the rapid dismantlement of the USSR. Why did this shift occur? And, as with Japan, why did it not occur earlier . . . or later?

AN OVERVIEW OF THE ARGUMENT

Foreign policy idea change (and continuity) depends on preexisting ideas. Collective ideas fundamentally shape their own continuity or transformation (1) by setting the terms and conditions of when change is appropriate and (2) constituting the most likely option(s) for the new orthodoxy. This impact has been relatively ignored because it is *correctly* assumed that something more than ideas has to be involved in major foreign policy transformations. Otherwise, the explanation risks tautology.[51]

My aim therefore is not to show that ideas "trump" other traditional factors—specifically power or interest groups—in explaining foreign policy change and continuity, but instead to make sense of how *ideas interact with other factors in specific ways* to cause outcomes. In short, the explanation I find most persuasive is a synthesis of factors typically treated as logical alternatives. Metaphorically, the analysis is similar to explaining how your arm might lift a coffee cup. Instead of simply asking whether the brain (ideas) or muscles (power) or hand (interest groups) does more, I explore how the brain, muscles, and hand work together to lift the cup in some instances but not others. The central emphasis is on the role of ideas (simply because it is the least understood), but the importance of power and interest groups will also be clear.

A necessary starting point is reconceptualizing collective-idea change. Typically, big shifts in national ideas are represented as a single sweeping phenomenon. Yet these changes are more usefully visualized as two distinct stages, which in practice are often difficult to disentangle (see figures 1.1 and 1.2). First, societal members must somehow concur, explicitly or tacitly, that the old dominant orthodoxy is inadequate, thus causing its collapse. Second, members must consolidate some new replacement set of ideas, lest they return to the old simply by default.[52] Neither stage is effortless. By definition, orthodoxies enjoy the favor of tradition and are defended by their partisans. Undermining them is not a trivial feat. Likewise, the institutionalization of new ideas breeds strife and uncertainty because particular orientations may favor some members over others and parties can disagree as to which, if any, new direction is more desirable.

Both collapse and consolidation, therefore, invoke *collective ideation problems* that make coordination difficult and/or give individuals incentives to shirk efforts to challenge and change dominant social beliefs. It is often hard for individuals to know whether others desire change and, if they do, how much they are willing to risk or contribute. Lacking such information, they cannot be sure whether their own desire and efforts for change (should they exist) will have any effect. Yet in some instances people do effectively transcend collapse and consolidation barriers, thus allowing na-

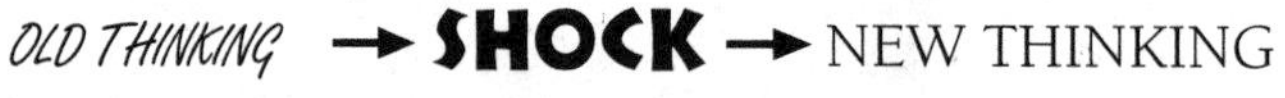

OLD THINKING
SHOCK
NEW THINKING

Fig. 1.1 Conventional explanation of change

OLD THINKING
SHOCK
1. Collapse
No (OLD THINKING)
Yes
2. Consolidation
No
NEW THINKING

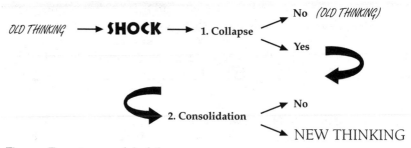

Fig. 1.2 Two-stage model of change

tions to alter their dominant foreign policy orthodoxies. How do they do this?

Both collapse and consolidation are affected by ideas, which in predictable ways, in conjunction with other factors, shape outcomes. In the *collapse* stage, the *interaction* between ideas and the consequences of experienced events is central. As explained in the next chapter, in most circumstances the interaction of expectations and events helps to reinforce the existing orthodoxy. Yet when events generate consequences for societies that deviate from their collective expectations *and* the consequences are starkly undesirable, change is more likely.

Considered in this light, change need not occur, indeed is not likely to occur, in circumstances where we might otherwise expect it. Consider the standard explanation of change: external shock. The problem is that shocks do not always lead to change—largely for reasons linked to either expectations or consequences. Take, for example, the continuity in U.S. foreign policy thinking ("Don't get entangled in Europe") both before and after the "shock" of World War I. Shocks are only a potential occasion for change depending on preexisting expectations. When a setback is anticipated by the existing orthodoxy, that mentality is not challenged but is sustained by the setback. Thus despite U.S. victory in World War I and the incentives it had to shape international relations based on its dominant power position, U.S. "disillusionment" (i.e., unmet expectations) with the intervention in the war led to America's return to nonentanglement. Losses and disasters alone, likewise, are also not sufficient to cause societal readjustment. Consider for example the case of the Weimar Republic, when Germany returned to the same expansionary ideas offered by its Wilhelmine predecessor despite ruinous defeat in World War I.

Consolidation, like collapse, invites collective ideation problems. Individuals may agree that the old view has to go but may not be able to agree or coordinate on what new orthodoxy should be the guide. Such a dynamic has been systematically charted in the study of revolution, but it also exists in policy disputes and debates.[53] The consolidation of a new approach in a society depends not only on the collapse of the old ideas but also on the existence of a leading replacement concept that has social support. Hence consolidation depends in part on the number and nature of alternative ideas.

The relationship between a dominant idea and its challenger(s) can take different forms or "structures" that provide different incentives for consolidation. Often such a structure is binary, involving one dominant and one main opposing idea. To the extent a unified opposition exists, consolidation will be easier. Efforts to overturn the old orthodoxy will not fracture over disagreement on what replacement idea to promote. When structures involve multiple alternative ideas, efforts to replace the old thinking may be hindered by infighting: such a standoff can encourage a return to tradition. Similarly, consolidation will be difficult when an orthodoxy is so dominant that there is no significant alternative. This was the case in Japan when the American Matthew Perry arrived in 1853—no established Japanese voices suggested abandoning the prevailing Tokugawa seclusion concept. In contrast, in the Soviet Union in the 1980s, "new thinking" already had a cadre of supporters when Gorbachev became general secretary in 1985. Consolidation, thus, was much easier in the latter case than the former one.

The sustainability of a new orthodoxy often hinges on some demonstration of its efficacy. Ideas that endure seem to do so because they appear to generate desirable results. When they do not, revanchists can use the shortfall to rally support for a return to the old ideas. Thus, immediately after World War I, the nascent shift toward international society in Germany was crippled by the results at Versailles, whereas after World War II, West Germany's new integrationism was sealed by the success of its economic "miracle" as part of the Western community. The point is not that there is always some "true knowledge" that shows certain ideas to be correct. The ideas must *appear* to be correct. In the political arena, correlation speaks louder than causation. Luck and timing are often decisive.

My argument features ideas as a pivot, but it explicitly acknowledges that multiple factors shape the transformation or continuity of foreign policy patterns. To invoke multicausality, however, is not to suggest "everything matters" or a laundry list of variables. What I offer is a framework that explains how ideas come together in particular and regular ways with other factors (e.g., power, domestic coalition pressure) to influence continuity or change in foreign policy. Strategic circumstances and relative power, for example, frequently matter in shaping negative and positive feedback to prevailing ideas. Dominant concepts that ignore such factors can lead to disappointing results that contribute to their overthrow. Likewise, the number and nature of alternatives that is so central to consolidation is shaped by the agency of interest groups and individuals that promote replacement ideas. As we will see, the rhetoric and justifications leaders employ are not simply instrumental tools; they can also either expand or deflate social expectations about dominant ideas, producing political dynamics unexpected by the leaders themselves.

Overall, these mechanisms have applicability across a range of historical cases and issue contexts. They should be useful in understanding a range of policy areas (see appendix 1). But the heart of the analysis concerns foreign policy. It suggests that the future of international relations depends on the contingent change and continuity of the dominant foreign policy ideas of states, especially the more powerful states. To stress contingency is not to forgo explanation. We can posit, at least in a probabilistic sense, that national changes will occur to the degree to which the expectations of particular dominant ideas are defied by events, negative consequences result, and some socially viable alternative exists. This general formulation deserves unpacking and I do so in the next chapter. First, however, it is useful to summarize why it matters.

THE STAKES: THEORY AND POLICY

In the study and practice of international relations, scholars and policymakers have tended to focus on particular types of factors in explaining and managing international politics. Such factors do indeed matter, but they matter only in conjunction with ideational dynamics, coming together in patterned ways to bring about change in some instances and maintain continuity in others. Absent this ideational influence, these potent sources of international politics are less compelling. My argument, therefore, builds on extant scholarship on ideas by clarifying the structural dynamics of change. The rest of the section examines how my argument relates to various schools in the study of international relations and the practical conduct of foreign policy.

Scholarship

The canon in international relations is that states are shaped by three basic types of forces. Realist studies give pride of place to the strategic (especially power) circumstances that states face. Liberal and Marxist studies often highlight the dominant interest groups within societies or the influence of individual leaders. A third group, "constructivist" writings, has featured ideas.

Some of the great works of modern social science emphasize the important role systemic imperatives play in shaping nation-states.[54] The prominent grand strategy approach, for example, depicts states as rational actors instrumentally reacting to international conditions to maximize security.[55] The problem is that grand strategy predictions and actual state thinking and behavior often seem to diverge. After World War I, the policy of the United States was not determined by its international position. Indeed, many believe that its isolationist turn contributed to the Great Depression, the rise of fascist regimes, and the United States's own lack of readiness to deal with the strategic threats that materialized in World War II.[56] Germany pursued disastrous wars of expansion twice within a generation, despite the counter-coalitions such efforts were likely to provoke. The Soviet Union in the 1970s *enlarged* the very geopolitical competition that helped undermine its ability to function. Tokugawa Japan after 1640 paid less attention to the development of military technologies abroad that would clearly one day threaten its standing. Adaptation to external challenges was simply not the highest priority for the Tokugawa leaders. States do not always read the markers of systemic incentives in a way that could be predicted from those conditions alone.[57] That is so because the search for security, based simply on circumstances, is a complex, difficult, and uncertain task. Clausewitz's "fog of war" is but one manifestation of the murky nature of international politics. Even if systemic conditions are clear they may not suggest a single optimal response. The practical implication is that we cannot understand and predict what states will do without knowing how they think about appropriate action. This necessarily involves attention to when such thinking is likely to change.

A second common approach views national ideas as the instruments of potent domestic interest groups within nations.[58] This approach suggests that when those group interests or power change, so too will the ideas. Such a dynamic alone, however, does not appear decisive in important situations. U.S. foreign policy did not change with the upheaval in the power and positions of interest groups brought on by the Great Depression; it took World War II to do that. Likewise, in Germany the reorganization of German politics after World War I and the 1918 revolution left the Social Democrats, not the conservative parties, in control of the government. Despite this fundamental disruption in the parties and interests that controlled the government, German foreign policy ideas quickly returned to their prior form.

Indeed in some instances the opposite influence is apparent: powerful interest groups may wield ideas, but the fate of ideas shapes the power of interest groups. The failure of the Weimar government's initial foreign policies at Versailles led to a major shift in power away from liberal integrationist groups and their supporters. In the United States the heavy burdens of "aloofness" thinking in the Great Depression and the specter of world war in Europe in the 1930s undermined isolationists and empowered internationalist groups. And in Gorbachev's USSR, the collective shift away from old foreign policy thinking brought to the fore new thinking groups that had lingered in the shadows for decades.

Some scholars have also explained national ideas by emphasizing leaders and their personal traits. Focusing on individuals is a mainstay of much historical scholarship. Such powerful personalities as Lenin, Stresemann, Roosevelt, Hitler, Mao, Adenauer, Deng, and Gorbachev were influential in the transformations of the twentieth century. If leaders are the source of ideational change and continuity, a focus on collective ideas is unnecessary and there are compelling reasons to investigate individual psychology and leadership traits.[59]

Yet even powerful leaders and their advisors, operate in a broader national setting that is characterized by ideas and symbols that often constrain and structure their individual preferences and attitudes. Franklin Delano Roosevelt articulated both isolationist and internationalist views in the run-up to World War II depending on what was politically possible in light of existing ideas. Gustav Stresemann, Weimar Germany's central foreign policy figure, displayed a similar leadership tendency: he put his thumb to the political wind and in many circumstances behaved as a kite would. He did not lack courage or ability—quite the opposite—but he did operate in a setting where certain broader ideas had to be heeded. The great councilors of the Bakumatsu period in Japan were hardly masters of their own fate, as they rapidly came and went, victims of Japan's turmoil related to its seclusion policy and Tokugawa legitimacy. Over a hundred years later, Gorbachev seemed to defy his circumstances. Through confidence and charisma, he helped remake Soviet foreign policy and the country. Yet Gorbachev himself was selected because he was a reformer, and he had few foreign policy plans of his own when he was chosen as executive. Indeed, his turn to "mutual security" has as much to do with the particular failures of old thinking and the ready supply of "new thinking" ideas as with his personal traits.

All of these leaders exercised influence within broader constraints and incentives, including ideational ones that affected when change was possible and what form it would take. I attempt to better specify the circumstances of such opportunities—ones that allow leaders and other social agents to shape their fates.

My emphasis on social processes here should not imply that human psychology is somehow irrelevant to continuity and change in collective ideas. After all, there is no group or national "mind" that can think the way the human mind can. At a basic level, idea change must involve individual psychology. What I want to suggest, however, is that change in *collective* ideas is as much a social process as it is a psychological one. As I explain in the next chapter there is no direct link between individual belief change and collective idea change. Even as individual beliefs remain constant, collective ideas can change, and even when individual beliefs change dramatically, collective ideas can remain the same. Some of the factors I point to as important also appear in Jervis's *Perception and Misperception*, which examines individual psychology and learning. While those factors may indeed have implications for the images in individual minds (which *may* be involved in collective change), I examine their role in social processes (which *must* be involved in change) central to the collective ideation problems. Jervis argues, for example, that when we see continuity in national strategy even though strategic circumstances change it is likely that "psychological difficulty" is involved. I want to suggest that such continuity may be due to the social properties of collective ideas rather than the cognitive attributes of individuals. Hence, my focus will be on the social dimensions of ideas and their change.

This line of argument is an outgrowth of a body of literature in international relations known as "constructivism" that has focused on social ideas.[60] Rich in concepts and evidence, constructivism has included a variety of works that have explored the role of social ideas at both the systemic level (e.g., the influence of international norms) and the national and subnational levels (e.g., strategic and organizational culture arguments). These studies have been strongest in theorizing and demonstrating the nature and effects of different types of collective ideas (identities, cultures, epistemes, norms, etc.). What has been relatively ignored is the problem of ideational change.[61] There have been nuanced studies of particular cases of change and continuity but little in the way of generalizable theory that elucidates when and why transformation versus continuity occurs.

What this literature does provide is a powerful image of social change, one that has led Emanuel Adler to claim, "If constructivism is about anything, it is about change."[62] Social ideas are conceptualized not as some sort of fossilized structure but as a dynamic thing—under formation or reformation as the agents that hold those ideas interact with others. Structures and agents mutually constitute one another and mutually shape one another over time.[63] Such an image opens up fruitful avenues for studying international relations, but it also raises difficulties for understanding change. It problematically cannot tell us when continuity or transformation is likely. As one scholar puts it, change "becomes an immanent but indeterminate possibility, equally likely or unlikely at any given moment and therefore unpredictable and inexplicable."[64]

Constructivists addressing change have tended to study enterprising social agents who are able to persuade others.[65] While there is much to these studies, ultimately they hinge on defining what is persuasive independent of the outcomes, that is, change in collective—not just in some or even many individual—ideas. To date this has been an elusive task.[66] In short, there has been a high degree of indeterminacy in explaining how and why individual idea change translates into collective idea change.[67] I try to reduce the indeterminacy in such accounts by demarcating the circumstances under which agentic arguments will be persuasive and when collective ideas are likely to be malleable (versus resilient) in the ongoing processes of mutual constitution and public argumentation.

My argument also has implications for how different types of ideas (identity, preferences, and causal beliefs) relate to one another. The general presumption seems to be that "identity" precedes the definition of interests and the formulation of particular actions in certain situations or interest areas.[68] Changing interests then are a part of changing identities and vice versa. But this vision slights a key category of ideas that can affect both identity and interests: the notions that actors have about how to enact their identity or achieve their interests. The logic and cases that follow suggest a reverse effect: states become what they do as much as they do what they are, they desire what they do as much as they do what they desire.[69] Change in national ideas about how to interact in the international arena often seems to be the instigator of the reformulation of national identities and interests.

This proposition supports a view of identity that is not a monolithic macrovariable but a collage of different operational ideas that are activated in different contexts and issue areas.[70] Just as a person might identify themselves as gay, African American, conservative, Republican, and a biblical preacher, with different views and actions depending on what issue context is invoked, so too can nation-states have different programmatic attitudes depending on the issue area. If this is true, studying specific collective ideas about action will help to fill in the ambiguous answers we have thus far concerning continuity and change in the elements that we label, in aggregate, "identity." Continuity and transformation of identity constantly takes place (just as the structurationist imagery suggests), as specific beliefs about appropriate behavior in different issue areas are either reinforced or transformed in the interplay between expectations, behavior, and events.

There is one last broader implication of my argument that is illustrated but not demonstrated here. It is that international society—itself an emergent phenomenon—cannot be understood simply by the way that states interact and in doing so reconfigure their own roles or identities in a "self-other" dynamic. Instead the key link is the way that international interaction affects domestic struggles within states over definition of the collective interest. In the cases I present here, the interaction that is most salient is less one of self/other than it is one of effective ideas versus ineffective ideas. These seemingly "operational" concepts about how to achieve interests shaped both national interests and national identities. And when those change, so can international society.

Policy

Policymakers, like scholars, have heeded power and interest group arguments. Yet if my argument is right, effective policy action cannot be undertaken without attention to collective ideas—and the possibility that they will change. Understanding the past and better managing situations in the future requires that we pay more systematic attention to ideas—both in terms of the nature of the dominant orthodoxy and the replacement concepts that opponents offer. Perhaps policy analysis has ignored ideas with good reason. As one of my students noted, "It is a lot easier to measure guns and bombs than ideas." Not only are ideas difficult to assess but they are seemingly more flexible and subject to change than those factors, such as the number of missiles or influential interest groups, offered by realists or domestic politics scholars. "Talk is cheap" is a common judgment about the words of politicians. And perhaps most problematic for policymakers, my argument features the shaping power of collective ideas—constructs that seem beyond the pale of influence or too ephemeral for those who must focus on things they can affect in real time. None of these reasons, each with a kernel of truth, derails the relevance of what follows for policy analysis and action.

Assessing the existence and content of collective ideas is not simple, but it is also not impossible. By their very nature, foreign policy ideas will be in the public realm. They cannot be reproduced unless all have access to them. The symbols and "lessons" of national involvement in international relations, the debates and discourse of states, and the justifications leaders give for action are readily available. These can be studied and evaluated, a task that is possible for many aspects of "real time" diplomacy or civic action.[71]

We can also observe the expectations generated by ideas and government justifications, the consequences states experience, and the way that different actors attempt to interpret or "spin" results. "Ideapolitik," as I discuss further in the conclusion, means attending to ideational dynamics. Doing so does not provide all the answers, but it can provide a better sense of when actors both inside and outside a polity will be able to affect change— and when they cannot.

Finally, my argument demonstrates how ideas and events provide a structure within which individual and group decision making takes place. To highlight structure, however, is not to suggest that humans have no influence, that we are just flotsam and jetsam on a sea of larger unmovable discourses and symbols. It is to say, however, that our ability to influence the large groups of which we are a part—both national and international— depends on our ability to understand the way that broader collective ideas constrain and enable us. Effective leadership and social activism hinge on some understanding of what is more or less likely to happen.

What's Ahead

Arthur Stinchcombe once advised that when there are no theories to explain what we see, we must first invent them and only secondarily test them.[72] This book follows that priority with one notable advantage: I have benefited tremendously from scholarship scattered across various theoretical positions and fields within and outside of political science. Drawing on studies from these diverse traditions, in chapter 2 I develop a framework for explaining ideational change and continuity.

I then explore the usefulness and limits of this framework empirically by examining a number of cases that have been at the heart of historical and theoretical work on international relations. My aim in these chapters is not to provide in-depth analysis or to break new historical ground in terms of source material—that would require a book for each episode. What I hope to show is how much of the received historical consensus that does exist can be understood in a very different way when we look through an ideational lens. The plausibility of my argument across a breadth of countries, cultures, and geographical settings suggests not that it is "right"—the inquiry here is too limited to make such a case—but that it provides a set of useful concepts and causal mechanisms for further investigation.

Chapters 3 and 4 are structured around the default explanation for ideational change, that is, "shock," particularly the shock of war. Many of the fits and starts in the development of international relations in the twentieth century revolved around the world wars, and these offer a good opportunity for closer scrutiny. The experiences of two countries, the United States and Germany, are particularly useful. In chapter 3 I explore why the United States remained largely aloof from power politics after the First World War but then radically changed its orientation in the midst of the Second World War. In chapter 4 I examine Germany during the same period. Germany is an intriguing focus because of the anomalies raised by its defeat in World War I and subsequent return to the same basic ideas involved in that defeat. Also, in contrast to the United States, it is not simply an autonomous hegemon with societal dynamics relatively isolated from the efforts of outside parties. After both world wars, it was a penetrated country, one in which external actors figured importantly in internal ideational dynamics. This case, therefore, provides insight on the role of transnational forces in the formation of national ideas among weaker countries.

If the argument has some plausibility for this period in history, one might wonder how it holds up in other eras, especially when the "shocks" involved are less stark and more gradual. Chapter 5 addresses this question, covering two cases of dramatic ideational change: In the nineteenth century Japan changed its course in regard to self-seclusion. Near the end of the twentieth century the Soviet Union lurched dramatically closer to the West. Looking at these changes is useful because of their extreme nature, their contrast with longstanding continuity, and their historical timing.

Chapter 6, the conclusion, brings together the findings and discusses their potential relevance for international relations theory and especially the present day management of foreign policy. Toward that end the analysis returns to the question of possible shifts in the ideas that will guide China and the United States in the future. Social scientists typically aim to clarify causes; practitioners focus on the management of effects. This book is primarily about causes, but for practitioners it offers a framework that supplements the conventional analysis and conduct of statecraft. For those interested in the argument's relevance to issues other than foreign policy, appendix 1 briefly probes how it holds up against major studies of change and continuity in economic ideas.

[2]

Explaining Change and Continuity

Understanding why states sometimes fundamentally revise how they think about international politics requires some explanation of the way that collective ideas affect that process. This will be puzzling for those who only invoke ideas to explain social continuity, who believe that ideas as static institutional facts cannot, by definition, play a role in change. Others may find the whole enterprise objectionable, believing that ideas are merely the tools of politicians who are reacting to domestic or international pressures. Leaders *may* use ideas to rationalize their actions, but such ideas are hardly a constraint on their actions and certainly not a cause of them. Such arguments, however, are in important instances wrong: ideas *do* influence change and are not simply an inert product of change. Ideas are only part of the story, however. In this chapter I lay out a synthetic argument that specifies how ideas, in conjunction with other factors, invite change in some circumstances but not others. First, I develop a framework that attempts to account for both change and continuity in foreign policy ideas. I then turn to issues of method and measurement as well as alternative explanations. An appropriate starting point, however, is to address why we should focus on ideas at all.

WHY BOTHER WITH IDEAS?

In the traditional model of strategic (international) politics, actors (states) have preferences and some repertoire of strategies to achieve those preferences. They then behave instrumentally to get what they want. But how will they behave? In addition to preferences and strategies, actors must also have ideas or beliefs, that is, some notion about which strategy (of those available) is best suited to achieving the preferred outcome. For example, to know that states prefer security above all other goals tells us little about what behavior they believe will achieve it.[1]

Analysts commonly bridge this gap by relying implicitly on "rational beliefs" (aka Bayesian updating). That is, beliefs are acknowledged as important, but they are seen as largely following from evidence actors collect from the environment.[2] A prospective car buyer may want a smooth ride, but she may not know which car is best without test driving different models. By doing so, she will end up with a rational belief, reflecting the purposeful collection of information and the efficient use of it, about which car offers the smoothest ride.[3] No additional theory is needed beyond the information and experiences available to her to understand why the car buyer believed what she did.[4]

In important areas of international politics, however, there is a need to go beyond this thin theory to understand the exogenous sources of beliefs. This is so for two reasons: (1) international politics is characterized by complexity and uncertainty; and (2) states are corporate, not individual, actors.

Rational belief formation in international politics is often circumscribed by uncertainty, complexity, and unique situations. Probabilities of outcomes are difficult to assess because of the lack (or deluge) of information, limited possibilities for trial-and-error learning, unique circumstances, and the complexity of the issues and actors involved. The world of international relations is hard to fathom. Louis Halle once wrote that none of us has much absolute knowledge of the "vast external realm" that foreign policy must manage.[5] U.S. Secretary of Defense Donald Rumsfeld recognized this challenge in the "war on terrorism": "There are known unknowns. . . . There are some things we do not know. But there are also unknown unknowns—the ones we don't know we don't know."[6] Leaders understand the strict limits of their knowledge, but nonetheless they have to speak and act as if they do know, and the results often illustrate the gap. The British Viscount Cecil, one of the League's principal draftsmen, announced at the League of Nations Assembly in September 1931, "I know how rash it is to prophesy as to the future of international relations; but, nevertheless, I do not believe there is anyone in this room who will contradict me when I say that there has scarcely been a period in the world's history when war seemed less likely than it does at the present."[7] A week later, Japan invaded Manchuria.

Information feedback in international politics is often too limited and episodic to make it possible to correct suboptimal beliefs.[8] Dissimilar circumstances and rapidly changing conditions hinder states in learning from others' histories or even their own. Britain as a sea power could hardly copy Russia's grand strategy in the nineteenth century. Lessons from the last war learned in a single country rarely hold for the next war as seen in the rapid transition from the dominance of defense in World War I to offense in World War II—only a couple decades later.[9] Unlike shopping for a new car, states can only imperfectly test alternate ideas about means. Strategies are sustained by beliefs about other strategies that are never experienced (that is, counterfactual) or where learning takes place not on repeated tests involving frequent feedback but based on small and biased samples.[10] Sometimes it means copying others' efforts that appear effective, whether they are suited for one's own situation or not.[11]

Uncertainty is amplified by the inherent complexities of international politics.[12] If the simplest events can be infinitely described in terms of the "facts" associated with them, then understanding international relations magnifies this problem many times over. In practical and analytical terms, complexity makes ideas a more critical factor. As Douglass North explained, "If problem complexity is too great—possibly because of unreliable information on the state of the world—then substantive rationality results do not hold. One has to model the decision maker as holding a mental model."[13] The objective external world may speak for itself, but it does so in multiple languages all at the same time. Facing the simultaneous overload and scarcity of information, states, like humans, need theories to inform action and learning.[14] Indeed, nation-states need such ideas even more than individuals because of the role they play in group identity and in coordinating the behavior of many individuals.[15] In sum, given the complexity of international relations and the limited possibilities for trial-and-error learning, explaining where these ideas come from is a necessary challenge.

We also need to supplement standard rational models in understanding national beliefs in international politics because states are corporate actors that do not have minds, but are run by individuals who do. This fact has led some scholars to focus on human psychology as the locus of ideational phenomena.[16] While this scholarship has provided important insights, it has largely ignored a critical element. The formulation of national beliefs involves both some set of individual ideas and some conception of how individual ideas connect or aggregate to form the collective ideas that orient the group (states).

Individual cognition and decision making is an unavoidable component of the existence of collective ideas. But it is inadequate as an explanation for collective change. Change in individual ideas is neither a necessary nor sufficient condition for change in collective ideas. Even when the majority of individuals privately believe something different (suggesting the need for change), the collective orthodoxy may endure for a variety of reasons, including individual ignorance of others' own reassessment of what is proper and desirable, fear of social ostracism for challenging group beliefs, or a failure to agree on a new dominant orthodoxy.[17]

Individuals also may not act on their ideas to affect collective change because doing so involves effort or cost with no clear promise of any payoff—or worse, it may involve the possibility of harm. In April 1916 when the

United States was debating whether to become involved in World War I, Walter Lippmann tried to explain to a British friend why the magazine that Lippmann helped edit had offered ideas Lippmann did not even agree with: "My guess is that you have missed in the *New Republic* the emotional warmth toward the cause of the Allies our real feelings would justify. . . . We felt . . . that the traditional hostility to England in this country could not be overcome by a paper that didn't take what might be called a strongly American view of the situation. . . . But . . . our hearts have been with you every minute."[18] In the United States in the 1930s even President Roosevelt kept his internationalist views to himself; indeed, he voiced isolationist themes, because he believed the broader tide supporting aloofness was too strong and little could be gained from fighting it.[19]

Conversely, even when individual ideas remain constant, collective outcomes may change simply based on differing aggregation mechanisms or focal points. Similar to Kenneth Arrow's logic on preference formation, changing the order of idea articulation can change the collective outcome.[20] Most people have been in meetings that go in an unexpected direction simply because of a tangential point raised at the outset that takes on a life of its own.[21] In Hans Christian Andersen's story, *The Emperor's New Clothes*, the king dons an imaginary suit that all the citizens publicly acknowledge to be beautiful. This is a story about con men and self-censorship, but it also speaks to the issue of how timing affects social beliefs. Had the outspoken little boy (who finally declared the emperor had no clothes) been the first to see the "suit," the collective judgment about the attractiveness of the clothes (which most privately doubted) might never have formed—just as it was shattered when he finally shouted the truth.

The link between individual ideas and collective beliefs can also be complex because the same set of individual ideas can yield multiple collective ideas. Thomas Schelling illustrates this with the example of two people who have agreed to meet in New York City but then have to locate one another without communicating. Each party can think of many common and agreeable possibilities, but most important is that they meet. Schelling posits that they resolve the problem of many possible sites by each focusing on the most prominent known symbolic meeting place, the clock in Grand Central Station. This solution, however, is itself dependent on a preexisting collective orthodoxy about where one meets in New York in such circumstances. For example, Grand Central Station would not be the solution for two foreigners who are ignorant of the clock tradition.[22] The gap in our understanding (in the context of the Schelling problem) is why particular collective understandings become (or no longer are) dominant focal points.

In sum, two traits of international politics, uncertainty and the primacy of corporate actors, suggest that some models of belief formation (for example, Bayesian updating) can be problematic when applied to states as actors in the world arena. The point is not that a rationalist metatheory of state behavior is wrong; it is simply incomplete. We often require a theory of change (and continuity) in these national ideas to explain state action in the complex international arena.

AN EXPLANATION

In the early evening of October 17, 1989, the San Francisco Bay Area was rocked by an earthquake measuring 7.1 on the Richter scale whose epicenter was in Santa Cruz. The quake caused some six billion dollars' worth of damage; at the time it was the costliest natural disaster in the United States. The effects of the shock varied from neighborhood to neighborhood, however. Some areas, such as the Marina District in San Francisco, were badly damaged while others nearby were hardly touched. Some buildings remained solid while others pancaked. There were reasons for this apparent randomness, however. The first was geology. The Marina District rested on landfill that shifted easily under the shock, whereas the bedrock foundation of nearby neighborhoods remained steady. Building type also influenced damage. Unreinforced masonry buildings were more prone to collapse than were those with wood-frame construction. What is clear is that the quake's impact did not depend only on the quake itself but also on preexisting geology and building structures.

A similar dynamic ties political shocks such as wars, revolutions, and economic crises to collective ideas.[23] The point is not that shocks are irrelevant but that their effects depend on preexisting structures. Just as earthquakes of the same magnitude can have radically different implications based on the building construction or the geology of the areas affected, so too will societies affected by similar political shocks react differently based on conceptual construction (that is, collective ideas). The interaction between events and extant societal thinking matters; it may encourage reasoning agents to perceive the need or opportunity for change and, even more important, to coordinate with others to overcome extant constraints. My framework recognizes the recursive nature of these relationships; it gives codetermining weight to collective ideas, but it also allows for the influence of events and the instrumental efforts of calculating agents.

A necessary starting point is a reformulation of what change in collective ideas involves. Change, like the destruction and replacement of buildings in the aftermath of an earthquake, is not a single process. It can be thought of as having two analytically separate stages, both inviting collective ideation problems.

The first stage involves the *collapse* of the reigning orthodoxy, when it loses legitimacy and there is widespread agitation to replace it. This is no simple task because enduring ideas are likely to be institutionally embedded and have a cohort of hard-core supporters. Moreover, a large number

[28]

of individuals may be relatively disengaged, uninterested, or uninformed as to how others feel, or they may be generally unwilling to contribute to efforts for change. Those who would seek change may always be willing to think about and act for change, but they remain in the minority; and lacking support from partisans of the dominant orthodoxy or the disengaged middle, their efforts will be frustrated.

The second stage of ideational change requires the *consolidation* of a new orthodoxy, again inviting coordination and cooperation problems.[24] Actors may not be able to coordinate because of a lack of information on what outcome is acceptable to others and/or because they disagree on which set of beliefs is most desirable. Reform or revolutionary movements (both efforts to change ideas) that may bring together disparate factions in shared opposition to something frequently fall apart when that something disappears and a mutually agreeable replacement must be found.[25] Thus, even when ideational collapse occurs, failure to reach a consensus on a replacement could still produce continuity as society reflexively re-embraces the old orthodoxy.

What conditions then, favor collapse and consolidation?

Collapse

The collapse of an extant orthodoxy is driven by the interaction of (1) social expectations and (2) the experienced consequences of critical events. Collective ideas generate a set of prescriptions about how states should behave and what they might expect as a result. For example, the notion that free trade should be pursued because it improves overall economic well-being is a guiding principle of U.S. foreign policy. Leaders necessarily refer to and justify actions based on such notions, and these generate social expectations in societies that become an intersubjective baseline for evaluation. When what is expected to happen does not, there is pressure for collective reflection and reassessment.[26]

James Scott's study of peasant rebellions, for example, highlights the power of failed expectations. In explaining what is likely to generate an "explosive situation" among peasants—that is, incite them to collective action—Scott points to the violation of a set of social expectations: a "moral economy" about what is fair or, in other accounts, effective. The point is not that there is some set of objective economic needs that, if unsatisfied, will spark rebellion. Material conditions are certainly involved, but the critical element is how these are "culturally defined" or understood as being appropriate.[27] Barrington Moore's classic work *Origins of Democracy and Dictatorship* makes this point starkly: "What infuriates peasants (and not just peasants) is a new and sudden imposition or demand that strikes many people at once and that is a break with accepted rules and customs."[28]

One might expect cognitive biases (e.g., dissonance reduction, selective attention to evidence, attribution pathologies) of human psychology to mitigate the effects of such discrepant information.[29] These inertial human mental habits, however, are partly contained by the public nature of significant gaps between social expectations and results. Individuals can privately rationalize their own personal contradiction-prone excuses. This becomes more difficult to do for groups, especially when at least some individuals in those groups publicly voice differing (and critical) views. A gap between expectations and results gives those critics enhanced leverage in public debates.

A second critical factor in collapse is the different effect of desired outcomes (successes) versus undesired outcomes (failures). Extant collective ideas contain not only a notion of appropriate action but also a portrayal of what consequences constitute a success (or are socially desired) and what ones are a failure (or are socially stigmatized).[30] A range of studies indicates that failure (as opposed to success) is associated with a change in collective mind-set.[31] The standard proposition is that success contributes to policy continuity whereas failure leads to change.

This blanket thesis, however, needs to be modified because it neglects the key interaction with social expectations. When failure is accurately expected by prevailing notions it is unlikely to result in their transformation. Furthermore, there is a difference between unexpected failure and unexpected success. Both involve unfulfilled expectations, but in the former case cognitive reflection is more likely. People are more sensitive to losing something that they expect to have than they are to gaining something they did not expect to have.[32] Unexpected failure inspires more intense preferences than unexpected success, and it provokes more intense scrutiny.

This asymmetry in individual psychology is relevant to collective (not just individual) ideas because it has *social* implications. Indeed, taken at the individual level, we cannot be sure that key leaders would be prone to this sensitivity to loss, since in experiments, only three out of four people respond in the predicted way.[33] In terms of social consequences, however, this human tendency does affect individual incentives to shape group ideas. Individuals recognize that many others are likely to have similar inclinations in the same circumstances and they may be more willing to reveal and act on these inclinations. It is this effect that may spark (the often unexplained) "tipping" of opinion.[34] Undesirable consequences raise the salience of an event, encouraging individuals to rally around it as an issue deserving attention. These events allow individuals to confidently overcome "do you see what I see?" concerns resulting from the pressures of social conformity and the lack of information about collective preferences. Failure tends to foster a social urge to investigate and assign blame. People want to find out what went wrong and why. Events with desirable or unremarkable consequences tend to be ignored. As the 9/11 Commission recently concluded about U.S. inattention to taking action against Al-Qaeda before September 11, 2001, "It is hardest to mount a major action while a problem still seems minor. Once the danger has fully materialized, evident to all, mobilizing action is easier."[35] Unexpected successes do not draw critical social attention for reasons captured in the folk saying "If it ain't broke, don't fix it." Failures, in contrast, give critics of the dominant orthodoxy intersubjective, socially potent evidence to argue for the replacement of extant ideas.[36] In such circumstances, the social silencing of critics is inhibited and consensus on collapse is easier to achieve.

"Success" and "failure" can be highly subjective qualities and vary according to individual aims, views, and desires: one person's treasure is another person's trash. Yet just as with expectations, it is the intersubjective dimension of these traits that is central. That is, success and failure are relative to the social expectations attached to particular outcomes. These are necessarily decided not by the widely ranging criteria of individuals but with reference to prior collective benchmarks.[37] Individuals can willy-nilly believe what they want, but they cannot willy-nilly create collective ideas, norms, and other social institutions. Such intersubjective phenomena necessarily depend on others and their interactions. Of course, for any number of reasons events that appear to outsiders to be successes or failures can still be redefined by the societies involved as the opposite. The emphasis of many scholars on the inherently indeterminate nature of political processes and interpretation is well placed.[38]

Such indeterminacy, however, is shaped by particular ideational circumstances. For example, when the link between social expectations and consequences is weak or when the results of events are murky, then contestation over the meaning of events is more likely. "Spin" is not simply a phenomenon of contemporary politics and media. The ability to spin, however, is constrained by the reasons leaders give for their actions—that is, the ideas they claim they are implementing and the actual results that occur. Success and failure are social and political constructs, but public expectations and results set bounds on what can be constructed. This is especially true in free speech societies, but the premise is also relevant for closed, oppressive regimes where elites, the military, and other groups act as audiences who adjudicate results.[39]

My analysis here parallels Thomas Kuhn's in his seminal work *The Structure of Scientific Revolutions*.[40] Kuhn's analysis of paradigm change in science has stimulated several arguments on collective idea change, including in the study of politics.[41] Yet in Kuhn's account, and the applications to politics it has inspired, several aspects of change in policy ideas are neglected that I attempt to address in my framework. In his study of scientific ideas Kuhn pays little attention to the collective ideation problems—how it is that individuals publicly agree that contradictions exist and that the old idea is no longer sufficient (and likewise what the replacement will be), when there may be costs to doing so. In politics, such problems are more pronounced. Ideas are not as well developed, and objective evidence is even more elusive; the possibility for testing is limited, the number of actors is larger, and the individual payoffs for challenging orthodoxies are less pronounced. Standards of scientific evidence are not the criteria of judgment. The political and social elements of change are necessarily at the forefront, and it is these dimensions that receive special attention here.

A second weakness in Kuhnian arguments, at least in the realm of policy ideas, is a selection effect. In focusing on those anomalies that cause societies to question dominant orthodoxies, Kuhnians neglect anomalies that occur that societies ignore and do not cause change. This is the case when social expectations are not met (contradiction occurs) but the results are desirable. In such a situation (and contra Kuhnian logic), ideational transformation is unlikely because individuals have little incentive to act, or to believe that others will act, when results are acceptable. In the scientific realm, scholars would be interested in anomalies regardless of whether the outcomes are desirable or not.

The logic of interaction between expectations and events can be summarized, showing likely causal paths to collapse under different circumstances (table 2.1). The vertical axis refers to the social expectations resulting from collective ideas about what should be expected to occur and what is desirable. These form a baseline for distinguishing particular events as socially notable: what is a crisis depends on the lens through which it is viewed. Group (that is, state) behavior can either adhere to or violate ideational prescriptions. Ideational prescriptions are usually respected, but this need not always be the case: other factors besides ideas also can affect behavior and, for various advertent and inadvertent reasons, may do so in particular situations. Such prescriptions are not behavioral straitjackets, they are norms. States may deviate from them because of the actions of untamed bureaucracies, idiosyncratic leaders, or unusual circumstances. Whether states do or do not deviate from prescribed behavior has different implications for change. When adhering to ideational prescriptions, the collective expectation is that events will match, that prescribed action will bring desirable consequences. Proscribed action generates social expectations of undesirable consequences.

The horizontal axis reflects the actual outcomes societies experience vis-à-vis events. Events can have consequences that are either socially desirable (and considered a success) or undesirable (and seen as a failure). The interaction between expectations and consequences is central to whether ideational stasis or change results. The table suggests four ideal types, each with a logic of behavior for individuals, implications for whether political conflict is likely, and a specific logic of continuity or change in collective ideas.

Table 2.1 Collapse: Ideas and events

	Consequences	
Behavior	*Success*	*Failure*
Proscribed by ideas	A3. "If it ain't broke." *Continuity*	A2. "Told you so." *Continuity*
Prescribed by ideas	A1. "Old Faithful." *Continuity*	A4. "Do Something!" *Potential Change*

A1: "Old faithful" Continuity is likely when states adhere to ideational guidelines and the consequences are socially desirable. This would be a confirmation of extant beliefs and hence would help reinforce or reproduce them. The outcome would be fully in line with extant sensibilities and hence there would be nothing surprising about it. Societal actors would find little reason to reassess the prevailing orthodoxy and in any case would have few tools for convincing others that the orthodoxy should be changed.[42] Equally important, societies do not have an incentive to see whether their beliefs are objectively correct. After all, the desired outcome might occur for reasons unanticipated by ideational prescriptions. For example, a belief that a spirit looks after one's well-being may be bolstered by an absence of automobile accidents, but the actual causes may have more to do with driving lessons or minimal road traffic.[43]

A2: "Told you so" Continuity is likely in situations in which societies ignore ideational mandates in particular situations and the results are undesirable. Failures draw attention. In the usual effort to assign blame, the dominant orthodoxy's defenders are likely to reinforce their position by chastising the prior deviation from tradition. Critics, in contrast, are left with a difficult task if they try to effect widespread change. To the extent a potential replacement idea has some backing, its supporters will find it very difficult to convince fence-sitters, let alone partisans of the old orthodoxy, to commit to the new idea. This combination reinforces the old ideas.[44]

An illustration comes from German foreign policy in the post–cold war era. In December 1991 Germany unilaterally recognized Slovenia and Croatia and in doing so violated its postwar foreign policy tradition of multilateralism.[45] This decision, however, seemed to contribute to the spiral toward conflict in Yugoslavia and to the difficulties the European Community was having in formulating a common foreign and security policy. It sparked widespread international criticism and domestic debate. The result was "something of a trauma for German diplomacy. The principal conclusion drawn from the experience in Bonn was that henceforth Germany should

avoid such strong-arm tactics, and should keep in step with its major part-
ners."[46]

A3: "If it ain't broke" Continuity is probable even when ideational mandates (and societal expectations) are violated *but the results are desirable*. This
case challenges the legitimacy of the extant collective idea, but it does so
weakly. Because the consequences are favorable, a public debate on "what
went wrong" is less likely. People tend to pay attention to unanticipated
events when the consequences are disagreeable. When they are not, there is
no experience to motivate the uncertain costly effort to change existing policy or strategy. The continuity of this outcome with past ideationally
shaped behavior makes it far less salient than when expectations are violated with disagreeable results (as in A4 below). An incident becomes an
event or shock exactly because it disrupts the extant order, which in this
case does not happen. Individuals, therefore, are much less likely to challenge extant orthodoxies or believe others would be willing to do so.

Scott Sagan's study of U.S. nuclear weapons safety suggests that even
when behavior contradicts a collective idea, if the results are desirable, that
contradiction will be ignored and the idea will retain legitimacy. Sagan describes a military culture that strongly emphasized operational safety, but
at the same time prioritized military readiness (which might suffer from
too many safety restrictions) and encouraged the cutting of corners. A variety of military accidents occurred that contradicted the injunction on safety,
but because none of these resulted in actual nuclear disasters, little organizational change took place. What is interesting is how often the incidents
were suppressed or "operator error" (the fluke fault of an errant individual)—and not the underlying systematic problems—was held to blame.[47] In
the absence of concrete unwanted results, dominant ideas are unlikely to be
challenged effectively and change in entrenched practices is unlikely to
occur.

A4: "Do something!" Transformation is most likely when societies adhere
to ideational prescriptions but the actual outcome contradicts expectations
with stark failure. This combination challenges dominant beliefs. The extant
collective idea has led the society in a misguided direction—that is, prescribed behavior does not generate anticipated outcomes but instead highly
undesirable ones. This opens a window for a social self-critique—it gives opponents of the dominant orthodoxy leverage to make their case and to rally
support. For these opponents to successfully fight (or consider fighting) the
accepted collective wisdom, strong intersubjective evidence (to convince others) and motivation (to bear the costs) for doing so has to be present. Otherwise social sanctions and uncertainty as to whether others are of like mind or
will do their share can deter members from undertaking change.

This phenomenon is apparent in a range of similar situations where societal reactions differ in response to successes or failures. For example, few
demands are made for investigations of large unexpected gains in stock

market indices. Yet when a sharp drop occurs in the Dow Jones average, much attention is devoted to figuring out its causes.[48] Or consider the different reactions to the 1993 and 2001 terrorist attacks on the World Trade Center. In the first case, a more significant tragic result was averted by chance. The vulnerability to attack was clear at that time, but in the absence of significant negative results, little change occurred. On September 11, 2001, when the results were catastrophic, the U.S. approach to terrorism changed dramatically and rapidly.

In sum, the more significant the contradiction between expectations and consequences, the more severe the consequences, the more likely societies will face widespread discord, the more likely barriers to collective action will be overcome, and the more probable is collective reorientation. Whether such a reorientation occurs, however, depends on the second stage.

Consolidation

Not only must political actors undermine the old orthodoxy, they need to replace it with a new orthodoxy.[49] Consolidation is shaped in part by two types of factors: (1) the number of prominent ideas in a society that might serve as a replacement for the dominant orthodoxy, and (2) the perceived initial results of such new ideas.

When serious problems arise, policymakers go looking for new ideas but have to choose from the existing supply, those notions developed in the preceding period.[50] There could be as many ideas as there are people. Here, however, we are not talking about individually held ideas but instead those that have social salience, that is, those backed by important constituencies or activist subgroups and that have the ability to vie for new dominant orthodoxy. The distribution of such salient "replacement" ideas varies depending on the situation, and this has consequences: there might be no practical replacements (that is, the old ideas are hegemonic), one clear alternative, or more than one alternative. In each case motivated interest groups and activists attempt to build support for their favored orientation, either to maintain the extant orthodoxy or to replace it with their preferred alternative.[51]

The situations vary, however, in terms of the likelihood of consolidation. In cases where a single alternative idea exists, a more natural focal point of opposition is available and it is easier for those disenchanted with the old ideas to coordinate and effect change. In this case consolidation will be more likely. In the remaining two situations, however, consolidation faces greater hurdles. The larger the number of replacement plans and the greater the differences among them, the more difficult it will be to form a new orthodoxy. Each replacement camp will compete with others for back-ers and it will be harder to gather the necessary momentum to debunk the old one and avoid a divisive conflict over what will replace it. When a mode of thinking is so dominant that there are in effect no alternatives, the collapse of the old may simply lead to fumbling efforts to create new ideas, which struggle for support. In this instance change is not impossible, but it is less likely than when there is a clear alternative.

A second determinant of consolidation concerns the efficacy of replacement ideas. Replacement ideas tend to offer an explanation/solution for the results that caused the collapse of the preexisting orthodoxy. More important is that the new idea offers an effective plan for (future) action. Its advocates not only criticize old ideas but also provide a new operational map.[52] Any initial success, whether it is a product of the ideas or not, will help to solidify the new orthodoxy, encouraging efforts to institutionalize it.[53] Such results need not always be immediate, especially if the new orthodoxy has a logic of "pain then gain" (as do many economic austerity programs or long-term reconstruction plans). But such plans are unlikely to be institutionalized as a new orthodoxy until their supporters can claim that the expectations generated have been met. The more successful the results, the more likely the new thinking will become embedded in rules, procedures, symbols, and collective memory. Negative results can lead to a renewal of the consolidation struggle or even a default return to the old.

The crosscutting effects of the number and viability of alternative ideas can be visually illustrated (see table 2.2 for three consolidation scenarios).

B1: "Try harder!" The first type involves no or many alternatives to the dominant orthodoxy. In the absence of an alternative, a society is unlikely even to consider change, but will instead focus on perfecting the extant orthodoxy. Efforts to formulate ersatz ideas are likely to founder because of the lack of preexisting references, support, and organization. The Royal Navy in the first half of the twentieth century based its strategy on the supremacy of the battleship: victory would be won by a decisive clash of fleets. Even when the development of the submarine and airpower challenged this view in World War I, and Britain's strategic situation changed in

Table 2.2 Consolidation: Oppositional ideas and efficacy

Replacement ideas	Efficacy	
	Low	*High*
None, or many	B1. "Try Harder" *Continuity*	
Prominent alternative	B2. "Counterrevolution" *Continuity or volatility*	B3. "Long live change" *Change*

the interwar period (it needed to confront Japan, another island nation), Britain's naval strategy did not. The battleship culture was simply too strong institutionally; there were virtually no voices offering an alternative view, even among the British submariners.[54] Change was not an option.

A similar situation can result when there are several or many alternatives with different behavioral implications but no agreement on which one should be pursued. The resulting deadlock may allow supporters of the old orthodoxy and others to argue for a return of the old simply to allow coherent action. The French Revolution ended the old monarchic order but then collapsed during years of chaotic infighting over the nature of the new political regime. Napoleon's dictatorship resulted, and with his departure in 1815, the monarchy was reinstated in France.

B2: "Counterrevolution" In this scenario, an oppositional idea does exist, but results do little to sustain it. Here we would expect others to attempt to put forward alternatives (to the extent they exist), but because one effort at change has already failed the advocates of the old already gain a new lease on life. The old, after all, did "work" at some point, and its advocates will still be active (especially if collapse was not distinct). In response to the Great Depression, countries did try different ideas to replace the standard precrisis economic approaches, but in the early stages of the Depression these garnered no support and the result in a number of countries was a return to the precrisis economic ideas, even though they were not considered especially viable.[55]

Related to ideas about political order, Juan Linz argued over three decades ago that the consolidation of newly democratic regimes (i.e., the idea of democracy as desirable) depends on a demonstration of efficacy while avoiding failures. That is, in response to crises, solutions perceived as satisfactory by the populace are critical to the consolidation of a young regime's legitimacy. Moreover, what is perceived as satisfactory depends on expectations raised by initial (ideationally derived) proposals such as constitutions. Thus the fate of new regimes depends on their ability to fulfill expectations *relative to* the claims of opponents to be able to do so better.[56] Illustrating this idea, John Foran describes how in Nicaragua the Sandinista model and popularity thrived at first but then declined when the economy took a dive (as a result of the cut-off of American aid and the burdens of fighting the U.S.-funded contras).[57]

B3: "Long live change!" When there is a single prominent replacement idea (or new consensus among promoters of different alternatives), and it is linked to desirable results, it is likely to be adopted. Such a dynamic gives voice and power to previously marginalized concepts and their supporters. Studies of revolutions have shown that the formation of a viable replacement idea/regime depends on the availability of an alternative unifying scheme. Collective ideas—such as folk beliefs, historical memories, religious principles, or formally articulated ideologies—serve as a focal point that brings diverse actors together to form a new political order.[58]

Such a replacement idea, however, must show results: initial efforts with new ideas must be seen as efficacious. As Robert Jervis writes, "Success is apt to consolidate the power of those who advocated the policy, defeat to undermine it and strengthen the hand of those who had different views."[59] What is key, however, is not whether the new ideas actually caused the success but whether success seems to follow the adoption of new policies, which are perceived to be the source of the desirable outcomes. Stephan Haggard and Robert Kaufman document the supporting, albeit unsurprising, conclusion that in political transitions following economic crises, democratic consolidation is more likely when the government is able to generate economic successes.[60] Political supporters of the new position use such results as evidence of the efficacy of the ideas. Such support and widespread societal acceptance will encourage efforts to more deeply institutionalize the views in institutional rhetoric and rules, lessons of history, and cultural practices and symbols. In this way a new orthodoxy is born.

In the above I have treated collapse and consolidation as independent stages, but in fact the two may affect one another. We can posit that to the extent expectations are starkly articulated and the results especially negative (in collapse) the more likely some alternative (in consolidation) will appear feasible.[61] Individuals will be more motivated to find a replacement and accept the new rather than return to the old. Likewise, to the extent a possible replacement view has preexisting strong social support or corresponds to desirable outcomes, the less it will take to undermine the old orthodoxy. In such a case, a ready alternative with preexisting legitimacy reduces collective ideation barriers to discrediting a prior orthodoxy.

Some Possible Questions

My argument thus far leaves at least four issues that deserve further clarification. The first is the role of politics in the explanation: Does an emphasis on ideas mean politics is not relevant? The second involves the way that that rhetoric and justifications used by leaders—over which they have some choice—can shape outcomes. The third is whether change is simply a national affair or whether international influences matter too. The final matter involves theory synthesis: With an emphasis on ideas, how does the argument incorporate other types of factors?

The Politics of Ideas. With my focus on the holistic nature of ideas, some may wonder where the politics are in the explanation. For good reason, scholars often depict the formulation of a new orthodoxy as a highly contingent political battle.[62] The warp and woof of this battle, however, should not distract us from recognizing factors that narrow this indeterminacy and shed light on conditions that facilitate a new consensus. I shall resist the an-alytical temptation to plunge into the cases and trace the movement of ideas from their sources in a single human mind to the minds of others and the polity as a whole, amid the din and roar of the politics involved.[63] The problem with such a bottom-up view is it cannot explain why certain ideas (of the many possible) of certain people triumph. Analytically, it necessarily ignores the structuring effects that ideas (in combination with other factors) may have on the possibility of certain ideas succeeding and of others fail-ing. Change in collective ideas is inherently conflictual and political. But a focus on the contingent politics of the situation, by definition, will not tell us whether continuity is likely or not. Exploring the structural properties of ideas and events helps shed light on those politics that we would otherwise miss.

Justifications and Rhetoric. Although leaders must operate in situations shaped by ideas and their relationships to events, they also shape their own fortunes. The rhetoric leaders choose in justifying ideas and actions can be directly related to the expectations that are generated and the way societies will assess events. Politicians cannot say whatever they want, because some justifications will resonate more widely with existing ideas and hence be more persuasive. At the same time, it also seems likely that leaders have some choice in the degree to which they inflate or deflate expectations asso-ciated with different policies and, in some instances, the content of the ex-pectations. Hence authoritative political actors help set the "height of the bar" by shaping expectations of results that are likely from (1) implement-ing a dominant orthodoxy, (2) trying a new replacement idea, and (3) pur-suing a policy that contradicts a dominant idea in a particular circum-stance. In the cases I shall explore the degree to which leaders were able to choose the rhetoric and justifications for action (versus the degree to which they were constrained from doing so) and the impact such claims had on the actions and ideas that followed.

Transnational Influence. It might be inferred from this chapter that change is primarily a national phenomena—isolated in some regard from the influence of external actors. In some cases, especially when a powerful state, such as the United States, that is geographically isolated from other powerful states is involved, its molding of foreign policy ideas may be less prone to outside influence. In many circumstances, however, that will not be true. Foreign policy idea change is often an international or transna-tional phenomenon in that the actions of other governments and nonstate actors can influence collapse and consolidation. For example, states can use their resources (e.g., economic sanctions or military coercion) or their status (international legitimacy) to either enhance or challenge the standing of a dominant orthodoxy (and its supporters). Particular states, of course, differ in their vulnerability to external influence. Transnational influence on national ideas is greater in countries that are less powerful and/or more integrated in international society. We can posit, therefore, that the degree of transnational influence depends on the relative power and resources of the influence agent and on how such efforts play into collapse and consolidation dynamics in the target country.

Synthesis. In much of the above, I have featured the role of collective ideas because their role in foreign policy change has been murky. What should be clear, however, is that ideas are hardly the entire story of change and continuity. As indicated, the influence of ideas often depends on their interaction with other factors. My overall argument therefore is inherently synthetic.

Two types of factors, which I discuss in more depth below, regularly play a role in issues of change and continuity. The first is the relative power of the states involved. The fact that I am examining "great powers" presumes the relevance of power in the formation of international order. In terms of the framework outlined above, we can expect relative power to play a role in the causal mechanisms in several ways. For example, whether a state has success in matching the expectations of its dominant ideas—or pursues new ones—is likely to depend to some degree on the capabilities it has in hand. The United States successfully aspired to manifest destiny in parts of Mexico, but any such idea in Mexico of formally expanding into U.S. territory is unlikely to endure for long if the United States remains the dominating power. Relative power wielded from abroad can also shape the consolidation of replacement foreign policy beliefs—as seen vividly in Germany and Japan after World War II.

The second type of influence on the making of new ideas is what might broadly be called "domestic politics." While such politics are a constant factor in any policy decision, motivated interest groups and social movements play a particular role in ideational politics. Specifically, they are the means by which replacement ideas take shape and gain social salience. The consolidation of new ideas depends on the ability of social groups to mobilize a domestic populace prior to an actual occasion that has change potential. Such groups necessarily are the voice of criticism in bringing to the fore contradictions and shortcomings used to delegitimize old traditions in the collapse phase. Most important, such motivated groups are central in determining whether a leading replacement idea exists in the event of doubts about the old.

Overall, power and domestic interests can have an influence in a number of ways in the (un)making of national ideas. What is critical, however, is that such influence typically depends on interaction with prior ideas. Likewise, the reverse also holds. The role of ideas in change and continuity necessarily often hinges on reoccurring patterns of interaction with power and interests.

METHOD AND MEASUREMENT

This explanation of foreign policy ideas can be usefully evaluated in two ways. The first is by assessing it against evidence: Does the approach explain important particular historical episodes? The second way is to compare the argument with alternative explanations for those same cases. In this section I discuss the logic of both of these strategies along with measurement issues and case selection.

The Argument versus Evidence

Overall, if the argument is correct, we should expect situations involving the combination of unmet expectations and undesired consequences to be more likely to facilitate societal efforts for change than those where expectations are fulfilled or desired consequences occur. The more significant the contradiction between expectations and situations, the more likely it is that collapse will take place. To realize change, however, the consolidation of a new orthodoxy is also necessary. In situations where there are no alternatives, default to the old orthodoxy is more likely; where there are several alternatives with equal social salience, the outcome will be contingent on political struggles. When a prominent replacement idea exists and appears to demonstrate desirable outcomes, consolidation is more likely.

What should we look for that would cast doubt on the argument? If states overall do not adhere to any pattern or set of concepts about international relations, then studying episodic change in enduring collective ideas would be of doubtful value. If the mechanisms related to collapse and consolidation tend not to happen, we can suspect the argument is faulty. This would occur, for example, when

- dominant ideas lead to clear failed results and there is no pressure for change;
- dominant ideas change in the absence of any unexpected negative results;
- events contradict expectations while results are desirable, yet change still occurs;
- change occurs easily, even if there is no alternative or there are many alternative replacement ideas;
- new orthodoxies are institutionalized in the absence of results;
- leaders are able to manipulate foreign policy at will with no constraint from existing ideas;
- critics of government policies can easily organize to affect change regardless of how ideas and events interrelate.

[41]

These proposed benchmarks bring us back to the central methodological issue of how one measures such inherently elusive variables as dominant ideas, expectations, consequences, and replacement ideas. The major potential pitfall is a lapse into tautology by defining or measuring causes based on the outcome of the case. Hence, the meaning and measurement of dominant ideas, expectations, consequences, and replacement ideas deserves clarification.

As noted in chapter 1, dominant foreign policy ideas refer to notions about how to engage the international system that are collective and intersubjective, not simply those that are held by particular individuals. One might tend to identify dominant groups—be it elites, mass opinion, or certain social groups—and then look at their ideas in order to discover what is dominant. By doing so, however, one would ignore the social and structuring dimensions of the ideas themselves. Individuals and their interactions naturally influence collective ideas, but they also must confront them as "facts."[64] What I am attempting to do is to paint a picture of what these facts have looked like by drawing on indicators of intersubjective ideas and on the accounts of individuals about their social context. Dominant foreign policy ideas are typically embodied in national debates and speeches, decision-making discussions, symbols, encapsulated lessons of history, and organizational procedures. In the chapters that follow, my assessment of dominant ideas differs depending on the society, the indicators most appropriate, and my own language and area knowledge. I address the details of measurement of these ideas in more depth at the beginning of each case.

Expectations refer to what societies anticipate based on the dos and don'ts of the dominant idea and the justifications for the course of action chosen. For example, if the dominant idea prescribes a certain action and action is taken on that basis, societies will anticipate socially desirable results. If a proscribed action is undertaken, leaders will justify such deviance from the dominant idea by a particular set of outcomes that can be achieved by doing so. I measure these expectations according to the dominant ideas and discourse that precede the decisions taken. This is not a measure of the expectations of particular individuals or groups, but an attempt to identify the collective baseline for a society. These assessments can be separated from outcomes (change in collective beliefs) in chronological terms and in causal terms. My interpretation of particular societal expectations depends on evidence that generally precedes periods of change or continuity. Moreover, the coding is not tautological in a direct sense in that expectations alone do not automatically produce change: outcomes depend on consequences as well.

I assess consequences in terms of success or failure according to societal interpretations of events. Judging what is a negative or positive consequence for a particular society depends on the lens and aims of the society itself. One society's "loss" is another society's "victory." Such an approach raises concerns about whether "success" and "failure" are simply labels for other political processes, not objective causal conditions. Furthermore, one might worry that they are somehow defined by the analyst according to the outcomes being explained (i.e., we know a successful outcome based on whether change or continuity is observed), thus rendering the argument circular. There are two kinds of constraints that help to offset such concerns. First, using societal interpretations as to success and failure does not prevent us as outside observers from questioning such judgments based on the prevailing expectations and the outcomes that seemed to have occurred. Second, using societal judgments is chronologically and conceptually distinct from the outcomes to be explained (and hence not "true" merely by definition). The indicators of success and failure chronologically precede periods of change or continuity. And a societal assessment of failure does not automatically imply change (or success continuity), in that those outcomes depend on expectations as well.

Finally, I measure the number and social viability of replacement ideas based on the debates within specific nations over the particular issue—for example, international involvement and institutional commitments. These debates indicate what prominent alternative ideas, if any, exist in public discourse and exchanges. Prominence and social salience are linked to whether replacement ideas have high-level promoters and/or broad-based public backing before the significant events. Rough distinctions can be seen between situations where there is none, one, or more than one viable replacement for the dominant orthodoxy.

I weigh each of these factors based on the consensus in the massive historical literature that covers national discourse and debates, leadership rhetoric, elite and popular attitudes, media positions, and opinion surveys. In some cases I have utilized primary indicators of collective ideas. Given the geographical, cultural, and historical breadth of the cases, however, I have also relied extensively on secondary sources—especially those based on in-depth primary research conducted by area experts.[65] The most important check on my analysis is a "null" coding hypothesis: Is there an alternative assessment of these variables in these cases that is more plausible in light of the historical evidence? This constraint, along with the above efforts at independent coding, minimizes (but does not eliminate) the inherent danger of finding in the history what one wishes. As we will see in the cases, however, my argument does meet anomalies and inconsistencies that illustrate it does not work flawlessly in all situations.

The Argument versus Alternatives

Proving social science theories absolutely right or wrong may not be possible. The best we can hope for (à la Imre Lakatos) is finding arguments that are more persuasive than their competitors. If foreign policy ideas seem to show continuity and change in line with the timing and mechanisms of the best alternative arguments that exist rather than as described by my argument, then we have reason to place more faith and attention in those arguments than the one here. Therefore, a comparison of my argument with the logic of alternative ones helps to sharpen what is being said and not said and how accurate it is relative to prior accounts. Here I have chosen two major schools of thought in international relations today—one that emphasizes international imperatives and one that emphasizes domestic interests.

Strategic Adaptation.   The first alternative, one that features strategic circumstances, draws on the realist geopolitical tradition in international relations as well as international market adaptation approaches. The realist tradition envisions states as unitary actors, primarily concerned with physical survival in an anarchic world arena. Accordingly, states pay primary attention to the military and economic resources that might make them vulnerable, or that could provide future protection in a pinch.[66] A very close partner of this approach is an economic adaptation approach that expects states to incorporate whatever ideas are deemed as optimal by the extant international market structure.[67] States are assumed, given information, to understand conditions without difficulty. In both views, ideas play little role; they would simply be words actors use that either reflect or mask environmental imperatives.[68]

If this approach is correct, ideational continuity and change will vary with the international circumstances that states face, especially as they relate to security and wealth maximization. Thus states will maintain ideas that seem to work in terms of power and wealth given the information they have and the best practices they observe of others. We can expect to see changes in ideas when the balance of international power or threat indicates security and/or when wealth can be improved by doing so. States in the same structural position should respond to their circumstances in a similar way. Differences in ideas among similarly placed countries should wash out under the weight of the structural imperatives to think or act in a particular way.[69]

If the adaptation view is incorrect or incomplete, we will not see foreign policy ideas changing with strategic circumstances. States will not heed international threats in a timely fashion. They will not automatically copy effective and seemingly useful tools of power aggregation and management as displayed by other states. Furthermore, they may not seek out information that is readily available and central to security. States will respond to similar threats or circumstances in different ways, based not on geography or capabilities but on factors exogenous to the material and international determinants found in the strategic approach.

Parochial Domestic Interests. A second explanation of national conceptual development highlights domestic interests. It disaggregates the realist unitary state and highlights the strategic aims of individuals and interest groups attempting to use the state as a vehicle to fulfill more parochial interests. In this view foreign policy is not about the strategic interests of states, it is a product of attempts by internal groups—classes, sectors, coalitions, regions, elite cabals, special interests, political parties, bureaucracies, ethnic groups, social movements, or singularly powerful leaders—to hijack the state for their own purposes. Typically, these groups seek the accumulation of their own domestic power and resources rather than the maximization of national well-being.

There are a number of examples of this genre in the literature. Peter Gourevitch emphasizes interest groups in resolving exactly how it is that states respond to economic depressions. Ronald Rogowski and Jeffry Frieden both argue that the forces of the international economy matter to the degree that they influence relative interest group profit potential (and related political power). Jack Snyder depicts how interest groups are able to seize the state (and its ideational machinery) in ways that drive the foreign policy of states. Peter Trubowitz highlights the geographical and regional sources of national policy. An interest group logic is also reflected in accounts that focus on individual leaders. In effect, they are treated as powerful subnational entities that pursue agendas that are different (and hence distinguishable) from national interests.[70]

In this domestic interest view, collective ideas are simply those notions put forward by the most powerful groups or individuals. In the extreme case, ideas have no power to constrain groups, let alone constitute their interests. Instead, they serve as a vehicle for justifying particular actions. Thus, understanding changes in state orientation is a matter of understanding how the relative power and/or interests of smaller groups within the state shift (or endure), bringing new orthodoxies to the forefront of collective deliberation (or not). Ideas do not have a collective existence; rather, they are particular to subgroups formed by individuals who share ideas and interests. Ideas may be used instrumentally to legitimate more narrow interests, but they do not have any structuring effects. The ideas and preferences of societal groups are unaffected by national ideas.[71] If the domestic interest view is wrong, we will not see continuity or change in collective ideas in line with either the shifting interests of dominant groups or the relative power of competing groups and or individuals. As new leaders and new groups come and go ideas will endure. Likewise, the existence of a continuous elite will not prevent shifts in foreign policy ideas. If the ideational account is right we would expect shifts in dominant groups to be facilitated by the interaction of ideas and events, not the reverse. So instead of groups picking winning ideas, winning ideas (that is, new orthodoxies that emerge in the ways outlined above) give previously marginalized groups new prominence and rhetorical power.

These two alternatives, strategic adaptation and domestic politics, provide a good point of relative assessment, because of their breadth of explanation and prominence in the literature. One might still object that these two alternative arguments bias the analysis in favor of my argument, which incorporates elements of both, while the alternatives must stand on their own. That is true and indeed is exactly the point. A synthetic framework provides more and better specified explanatory power than any of these alternatives on their own, by capturing the way the different causal forces conjointly shape outcomes.

Case Selection

I explore the utility of the argument vis-à-vis alternatives through focused historical comparison. This method is well suited to the more contextual analysis required of an initial study of complex mechanisms related to the dynamic properties of ideas.[72] The comparisons involved are across time, across nations, and, in appendix 1, across issue areas. Do national foreign policy ideas vary most systematically with the factors I have identified or with the ones offered by the strategic adaptation and domestic politics approaches? Of course, I am not merely interested in "correlation," but also "causation": Do events unfold through mechanisms anticipated by my account or through those offered by alternative arguments?

The first part of the empirical analysis is a set of paired comparisons involving the United States and Germany after the external shock of two world wars. In the literature on learning in international relations, it is generally believed that defeat in wars leads to change in foreign policy ideas, whereas success reinforces the existing trajectory.[73] Although there is much to this view, these cases seem to suggest there are other dynamics involved. The United States triumphed in World War II but then dramatically altered its outlook on international relations. Germany, in contrast, lost the World War I but largely retained the same set of foreign policy ideas that existed prior to that conflict. Thus, these cases allow us to consider why major transformations occur, as well as why they do not (when by conventional wisdom they should). Understanding continuity is the necessary analytical twin to understanding change.

The cases also provide variations on the factors central to my argument, including extant dominant ideas, expectations, and perceived consequences. There is also variation in alternative explanations (e.g., leadership skill, interest group pressures, and systemic incentives) across this period. This variation is especially useful when set against the relative stability of other factors (political system, geography, type of shock). The cases also reflect variation in stronger (the United States) versus weaker (Germany) states, and therefore offer a window on the influence of asymmetrical transnational forces (or lack thereof) in collective conceptual change.

In the second part of the empirical work I examine two other countries and their foreign policy changes: Japan's turn away from isolationism during the Meiji Restoration and the Soviet Union's adoption of "new thinking" under Gorbachev. These episodes are useful for three reasons. First, they occurred in periods far removed from each other and the World War I and II era cases. Thus, they allow us to examine the historical range of the framework. Second, they offer extreme episodes of change *and* continuity (offering critical variation in what is being explained). Extreme cases are useful for observing the underlying causes and processes, because nothing is subtle. Finally, they offer episodes where there is no single big shock like the world wars; thus they provide insight to change that occurs over a somewhat longer time frame.

I will try to make my case by demonstrating (1) how continuity and transformation in dominant ideas were shaped by the logic above that determined collapse and consolidation; (2) that what leaders did and how they fared was affected by dominant ideas and their transformation; and (3) that existing explanations are insufficient or wrong unless they attend to the interaction of ideas and events. My analysis attempts to demonstrate that in these cases change and continuity varied more closely (both in terms of correlation and causation) with the mix of expectations, consequences, and alternative ideas than with the factors highlighted by the strategic adaptation and domestic interest politics approaches.

The social sciences have always been marked by strident debates between those who emphasize the uniqueness of history and those who wish to uncover and formulate broad generalizations that transcend particular circumstances. This study attempts to straddle that debate, sometimes uncomfortably. I posit some broad dynamics that I expect can be found in different geographical, historical, and cultural contexts. Yet these dynamics always depend on an interpreted content that is specific to particular countries and eras. The way that states believe their interests are best pursued can vary significantly, but the processes that govern when change or continuity occurs in those ideas seems to reveal many similarities.[74]

These similarities are not preordained or always present. The dynamics captured by my framework are based on a series of sui generis propositions. These propositions will not necessarily hold when all other things are not roughly equal, as is often the case. Moreover, the causal mechanisms posited are not always determining. They may in some instances be overwhelmed by unusual or contingent pressures. The approach therefore is probabilistic. I do hope to make an initial case that it is a generalizable phenomenon found across national situations in a variety of time periods. I also hope to illustrate that the same dynamics of collective ideas apply to issue areas other than broad foreign policy. For reasons of coherence, I save that dimension for appendix 1 where I explore shifts in collective ideas about economic policy. Some scholars suggest that any analysis invoking ideational causes is inherently nongeneralizable.[75] Not so. Similar processes, albeit involving unique substantive and historical trajectories, are clearly possible and, as we shall see, do seem to occur.

[3]

The Ebb and Flow of American
Internationalism

In the twentieth century, U.S. ideas about foreign policy were particularly important in molding world politics.[1] They were also puzzling—in some periods inclined toward integration with international society, in other periods not. Before 1939, the dominant U.S. conception of effective strategy was relative aloofness from Europe-centric international society. While welcoming economic and cultural integration, the United States abstained from political, and especially military, commitments to other major powers.[2] Nevertheless, during World War II, Americans accepted as their new orthodoxy the previously chastised "entanglement" in Europe's great power politics.

This shift is confusing, not because it occurred, but because it did not occur earlier, especially after World War I or during the Great Depression. The lag is important because it is widely believed that the U.S. refusal to provide international leadership in the 1920s and 1930s significantly worsened the Great Depression, helped produce conditions that fostered totalitarian and fascist regimes, encouraged Germany's and Japan's aggression, and allowed the scale and violence of World War II due to tardy U.S. involvement.[3] Why, in contrast to World War II, did the United States not embrace international security commitments vis-à-vis the European powers after World War I?

Standard answers to this question are wanting. Continuity after World War I was *not* a simple reflection of the power, threat, or technology conditions of the times, nor did it directly reflect the distribution of domestic interests or some overarching national identity. Change after World War II similarly defies such answers. The point is not that such factors were irrelevant—far from it—but that they had influence through their interaction with particular American ideas about how to engage the world. We must attend to the dynamic effect of these policy ideas and their relationship to events to understand the enigmatic evolution of U.S. foreign policy in the twentieth century.

U.S. ideational continuity after World War I resulted from both the renewal of traditional beliefs after that conflict and the inability of those seeking change to agree on a viable alternative. Collapse and consolidation are the two sides of the change coin. Efforts to undermine the pre–World War I "no entanglement" orthodoxy of aloofness ran aground on the rocks of what was described in the previous chapter as a type A2 "Told you so" situation. U.S. intervention in World War I violated the traditional wisdom against involvement in Europe's political and security affairs. Americans later viewed that involvement, despite being on the winning side, as a mistake. Defenders of tradition were quick to make political hay out of this feeling to straight-arm continental ties. Advocates of tradition also benefited from a standoff between proponents of change. Some of these "internationalists" wanted greater engagement on a unilateral basis, others favored more robust institutional commitments (i.e., the League of Nations), even involving the use of force. This standoff was not the main influence in this case, but it did reinforce a return to the old orthodoxy. Hence the United States did not address its international problems in the 1920s and 1930s by internationalist initiatives but by further withdrawal from such commitments.

The ideational dynamic in the run-up to the Second World War was almost exactly the opposite. The United States pursued its no-entanglement political-military strategy in the 1930s with unparalleled vigor. As the situation in Europe got worse, Americans renewed efforts, such as through the Neutrality Acts, to distance themselves from involvement. This rigid adherence to tradition, however, met increasingly disappointing results, setting up an A4 "Do something!" dynamic that undermined the no-entanglement position. This strong dynamic favored change, and the emergence of a new approach was facilitated by the existence of a clear alternative favoring U.S. engagement with Europe. It is noteworthy that this shift preceded—and hence was not caused by—the cold war. That the same orientation continued even as the cold war faded (see chapter 6) further reinforces its autonomy from the long bipolar U.S.-Soviet confrontation.

This explanation provides leverage in understanding foreign policy because it highlights the autonomous role of collective ideas in change; it is clearly distinguished from arguments for social beliefs as wind socks of international power distribution or as disposable political tools wielded by powerful domestic elites. Empirically, most of these latter arguments offer an indeterminate explanation for the rise of U.S. internationalism, because their logic suggests that change was equally likely after World War I or the onset of the Great Depression. Conceptually, they neglect an ideational effect: the necessary endogenous role of ideas in their own transformation.

Dominant ideas about appropriate foreign policy mediated which international conditions were most likely to produce change and which actors were able to push new ideas successfully while others failed. My argument helps explain a number of intriguing developments: why the United States would not commit itself to European stability despite successful intervention in World War I; why that occurred even though a majority of elites favored a greater international role; why President Wilson's popularity was not sustained in the League of Nations debate; why Roosevelt, the champion of World War II internationalism, advocated isolationist policies in the 1930s and why the shift to U.S. internationalism was enhanced by, but not rooted in, the cold war.

The chapter takes shape in three parts. First, I specify and measure continuity and change in U.S. foreign policy ideas. Second, I explain continuity and change. Third, I consider the utility and limitations of the argument vis-à-vis extant explanations.

IDEAS OF ACTING ABROAD, 1908–1950

The initial task is to document variation in the dominant American ideas about how to provide for U.S. security in the world arena. This first section, then, is not an explanation of ideas, nor an account of the politics of their making, but a description of the overall development of the ideas. The key dimension examined here is the degree to which the United States saw its interest served through internationalism, greater engagement with international society—especially political-military involvement with the European great powers that had created the international system of the twentieth century—versus the extent to which it favored separatism, an aloof, go-it-alone orientation that attempted to distance the United States from many of the institutions and norms of the dominant European international society.[4] This separatist impulse, one of the ideal categories described in chapter 1, is captured by such common descriptors as nonengagement, aloofness, and detached unilateralism. Americans viewed their national interests as best served by caution toward European political-military interactions, especially institutional security commitments to the other great powers to come to their aid with military forces.

U.S. separatism was a matter of degree. It was not the "isolationism" that revisionists and others have tilted against. The United States was actively engaged in economic and security matters. As some scholars have put it, the issue was not *whether* but *how* to engage the international order.[5] The additional calculation was *how much* to engage. In the interwar period, the "how" issue was decided in favor of minimal overt government involvement. The "how much" part excluded political-military precommitments to stability in Europe. This limit was especially striking given the immense capability of the United States after World War I to act otherwise. Yet even as its ability to shape the world outpaced that of all other countries, its urge to remake international society did not.

"Internationalism," in contrast, implied a basic integrationist orientation—a dominant belief that societal well-being was best served by committing national military power to relationships with the major powers in Europe and by supporting international institutions.[6] What is notable is that U.S. views did not vary all over the map in terms of separatism versus integrationism. Before World War II the dominant orthodoxy was one of no entanglement. During that conflict a major shift to an internationalist outlook is apparent. That transformation is represented in several measures.

First, the shift in American ideas during World War II but not after World War I is supported by an analysis of the vast secondary literature that characterizes dominant ideas by drawing on memoirs, personal papers, speeches, archival records, surveys of journals and newspapers, and public opinion data. Although there are some debates about the degree to which the United States was involved in economic affairs after World War I, or in imperial ventures in smaller countries even before that, there is virtual unanimity that the United States had an aversion to institutionalized involvement in great power affairs before World War II and yet embraced such commitments after World War II.

In this chapter, I supplement an interpretation of the secondary literature with a primary measure of ideas. One useful way to assess collective thought is through public symbols and discourse that reflect intersubjective beliefs. In the U.S. case one such indicator is a particular category of national statements on foreign policy. Each year, presidents give a ritualized State of the Union address to the country in which they discuss foreign policy.[7] These speeches tend to be highly symbolic and are rightly seen as efforts to capture the character, thought, and direction of the nation.[8] Presidents want to present their ideas in ways that sell, and they tend to rally support and legitimacy through appeal to societal traditions and norms. These speeches are much more than simply the views of the individual leaders that present them, given that personal opinions of presidents and their public discourse do sometimes diverge.[9] As an annual address, the State of the Union provides only a rough guide to the content and timing of change, but the uniform context and format makes it a useful point of comparison with previous State of the Union speeches.

The results of a content analysis of these speeches (see figure 3.1; see appendix 2 for a detailed description of the method) support the notion of continuity after World War I and change during and after World War II. The solid line on the chart displays the level of internationalism portrayed as desirable in the State of the Union address for that year. On the lower end, a "0" reflects the position that the United States should avoid getting institutionally involved in any major power international relations. From this perspective, the United States should live and let live, separate from Europe-centric international society. At the higher end, a "5" indicates a view that U.S. security is best served by being actively integrated in international political-military affairs, by joining international institutions, and by making precommitments of political and military support to other major powers.

To further probe whether the views expressed by the president represent collective or idiosyncratic sentiment, I have surveyed the editorial response of four newspapers (reflecting differing regions and partisan leanings), which are represented by different symbols in figure 3.1.[10] These are coded in terms of their support or criticism for the degree of unilateralism and internationalist themes in the State of the Union speeches. Symbols appear above the solid line (by ½ point) if the editorial for that paper in that year calls for more internationalism than in the State of the Union, on the line if about the same level, and below the line (by a ½ point) if the opinion favors non-entanglement. Collectively, these tell us whether the State of the Union is roughly reflective of broader sentiment. For example, if two or three papers disagree with the internationalist sentiment in a speech with no offsetting sentiment in the opposite direction, this would suggest the president's views do not resonate with those of broader society. While not a perfect gauge due to the limited nature of the editorial responses on foreign policy (sometimes a paper may not comment at all, in which case no symbol appears for it that year), the speeches, along with editorial reactions to them, offer a reasonable, easily reproducible representation of the dominant collective ideas on security policy before and after the world wars.[11]

The solid line representing presidential discourse indicates that World War I produced very little change in the commitment of the United States to political-military engagement, while World War II led to a sea change. Before and after World War I the debate stays in the range of more aloof ideas. During World War II, however, this measure takes a qualitative leap toward high levels of internationalism and then remains there after the war.

This pattern is somewhat different than an alternative view that sees the United States as being consistently ambivalent about international commitments throughout the century. That is, the United States has in all periods both supported and rejected international regimes and rules. It has vacillated between participation in world affairs and withdrawal.[12] This argument has merit in that it highlights that U.S. policy has never been totally coherent in terms of either accepting or rejecting international involvement. Factors other than dominant beliefs can, in particular instances, determine policy. But such a view also overlooks the variation in overall attitudes that characterized the different periods—an attitude pointed more toward non-entanglement before World War II and then toward a significant shift in the

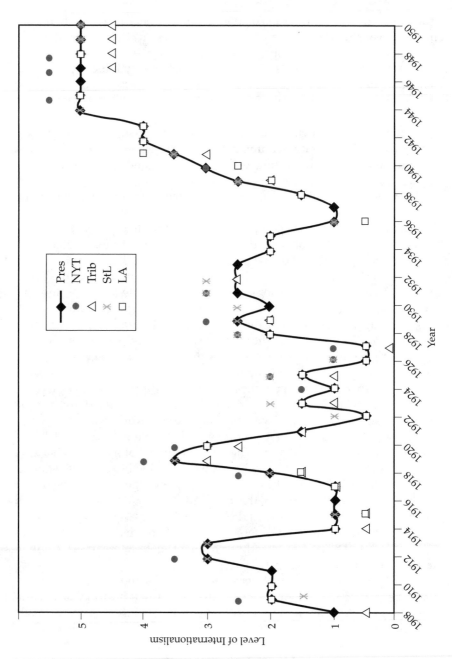

Fig. 3.1 American foreign policy ideas, 1908–1950

direction of internationalism during that conflict. In terms of overall policy, that swing seems to capture the overall thrust of the two periods better than the view that there was consistent ambivalence.

This presidential measure is confirmed by the editorial responses, which tend to agree with or collectively swarm around the State of the Union— that is, some agree, some disagree. In only one year did three or more editorials disagree with the State of the Union sentiment on internationalism.[13] In only five years were there two editorial responses disagreeing with the State of the Union without any others disagreeing in an opposite direction (the remainder either agreed with the speech or did not comment at all).[14] These results suggest the reliability of the State of the Union as an indicator of collective sentiment—presidents rarely voice a foreign policy position completely out of line with society, especially in the high-profile speeches surveyed.

Based on my reading of the State of the Union addresses, inaugural speeches, and the secondary literature, the following brief elaboration of the evolution of the collective American mind-set on security provides substantive depth.

The Legacy

The background to twentieth-century American thought can be traced to the country's founders. Contrary to the stereotype, they did not maroon themselves on the North American continent. Indeed, international commerce was seen as very desirable. What they stigmatized were political-military ties with major powers that would entrap the country in draining conflicts. Every year on his birthday, George Washington's 1796 Farewell Address to Congress is read aloud in Congress. In it he advises:

> The great rule of conduct for us in regard to foreign nations is, in extending our commercial relations to have with them as little political connection as possible. . . . Why by interweaving our destiny with that of any part of Europe, entangle our peace and prosperity in the toils of European ambition, rivalship, interest, humor, or caprice? It is our true policy to steer clear of permanent alliances with any portion of the foreign world.

Thomas Jefferson, in his first inaugural address on March 4, 1801, echoed the same theme, declaring his desire for "peace, commerce, and honest friendship with all nations, entangling alliances with none." Finally President James Monroe, the originator of the doctrine that declared the Americas a haven from European colonization, stated that "separated as we are from Europe . . . we can have no concern in the wars of the European Governments nor in the causes which produce them."[15]

More than tired phrases, the imprint of these ideas is evident even as the United States emerged as a great power at the end of the nineteenth century. The nation did become more active in the international arena, including forays into Asia, before the Civil War. Around the turn of the century it was involved in a war in Cuba and assumed an imperial presence in the Philippines.[16] But U.S. ideas remained largely constraining in terms of international commitments vis-à-vis the makers of international society, that is, the great powers of Europe.[17] Alliances and security agreements among the great powers were, of course, commonplace in Europe in the century before World War I, but the United States would have none of it. President Theodore Roosevelt was the most aggressive internationalist of his era, but his modest policy of state engagement with European major powers met relatively strong domestic resistance.[18] The United States had been attentive to the balance of power in Europe throughout its history, recognizing that a single dominant European power might indeed imperil its interests.[19] But such attention did not dictate *how* the United States should manage the threat (e.g., by not getting involved or by precommitting to the use of force), where it should defend itself (in the Americas or on distant shores), or when exactly intervention might be required.[20]

Continuity after World War I

In the pre–World War I period, the speeches of Presidents William Howard Taft and Woodrow Wilson show continuity across political parties. Both recognized that the place of the United States in the world was changing, but both strongly reflected traditional views. These leaders saw the need to interact with other nations, particularly major powers. But the main emphasis was on commercial activity—just as Washington had advocated. They continued to view Europe as a source of danger, the instigator of militarism (presidents decried the need for a standing U.S. army), and the cause of the much-despised imperialism. Thus, despite an increased willingness to engage commercially, Americans were hesitant to become involved in continental power politics. This became clear as World War I erupted and the United States tried to keep its distance. Wilson argued in 1915 that the United States meant "to live and let live." He chided those that would change "a nation that staked its very life to free itself from the very entanglement that had darkened the fortunes of older nations and set up a new standard here."[21]

Yet spurred by the German challenge to U.S. sovereignty and sea rights, the United States did intervene in the war. And when it occurred, Wilson began to prepare the country for a new peacetime direction. He argued in December 1919 that America's place in the world had fundamentally changed: "No policy of isolation will satisfy the growing needs and opportunities of America."[22] Yet what he was referring to specifically was not political and military affairs but commerce: America was no longer a debtor nation, but a creditor, and Wilson argued that it should engage the expanding world economic market even more. Judging by editorial reactions, these speeches were received with either approval or a somewhat mixed reaction (often reflecting partisan leanings). Nowhere in those State of the Union addresses did Wilson directly defend the controversial Article 10 of the Covenant of the League of Nations that would commit U.S. forces to preserving the peace in Europe. As discussed below, this was exactly what Congress (and the country) rejected.

In the wake of World War I and the defeat of the effort to join the League of Nations, Wilson's successors retreated to the safety of tradition. President Warren G. Harding declared in his inaugural address, "The recorded progress of our Republic, materially and spiritually, in itself proves the wisdom of the inherited policy of non-involvement in Old World affairs." The key, as Harding elaborated, was not noninvolvement per se but avoiding commitments that might impinge on the ability of the United States to decide its own course in each instance (hence precluding such commitments). "This is not aloofness," Harding succinctly declared, "it is security."[23] The United States would engage the world in finance and trade (through private parties), it would offer advice, and it would join in efforts to reduce armaments. But U.S. security was seen as best served by self-help, and Harding recommended the same to others.[24] President Calvin Coolidge largely echoed these themes, arguing for the avoidance of permanent alliances and Old World controversies; the efficacy of nonintervention; and the dangers of militarism, alliances, and balances of power.[25]

Interest groups certainly pushed and pulled on the extant ideational constraints, leading some to argue that U.S. policy was somewhat unstable and chaotic in the 1920s and 1930s.[26] But deviations in an integrationist direction during those years were bulges in, not the popping of, the separatist balloon. Such exceptions tended to be primarily in the economic realm—in specific sectors, limited in duration, and largely involving private parties (e.g., the Dawes and Young plans).[27] The United States selectively engaged in measures that fit its outlook, such as certain forms of economic exchange (which was always encouraged), economic influence for political ends, and disarmament (because arms and militarism were bad traits of the traditional powers), but it rejected other arrangements that precommitted U.S. forces or threatened U.S. neutrality.[28]

In sum, despite a militarily successful intervention in World War I and the president's own entrepreneurial efforts, the nation's aversion to commitments on security apparently changed little after the war was over.[29] The United States did continue its economic expansion—largely following the trend seen earlier under Taft's and Wilson's policies before the war.[30] But its basic hemisphere-focused, unilateral conception of strategy was mostly an extension, even a deepening, of the prewar orthodoxy. Even many so-called internationalists were opposed to strategic commitments. In 1921 a *Literary Digest* poll showed that American newspaper editors favored helping France if it were attacked, but opposed any formal guarantee. This survey captured the American belief that any precommitment of forces to Europe was harmful to U.S. security.[31]

Transformation in World War II

U.S. ideas about security in the early years of Franklin D. Roosevelt's presidency showed strong continuity with the ideas promoted by Wilson's Republican successors. As was true earlier, the United States was open to cooperating on reducing armaments, which were viewed as fostering militarism, threatening democracy, and encouraging war. Furthermore, the United States (although with less enthusiasm in the early stages of the Great Depression) had an interest in furthering international commerce. On issues of military-political commitments in major power politics, however, the traditional orthodoxy ruled.

The development of U.S. thinking on security from 1933, and especially *after* 1939, indicates the transition from the old to the new. There is a different balance of discourse between support for traditional and support for nontraditional ideas, which can be seen in three different phases. The first, from 1933 to 1938, reveals a one-sided balance in favor of U.S. political-military detachment from the European arena. For example, the internationalist-minded Roosevelt declared in 1934 that the "United States cannot take part in political arrangements in Europe," and that "self-help and self-control" were America's tradition. Despite the emerging tensions on the Continent, the United States could play only one role, a familiar one: stay out of it, defend the homeland, act as an example, and offer counsel.[32]

From 1938 to 1941 the balance became more equal. Roosevelt began to stress how other nations' acts affected the United States and the American way of life. On the one hand, FDR heeded tradition in warning against entangling alliances, on the other he derided those who "wishfully believe the United States can live in isolation" (while rejecting the idea that this meant the United States had to join the war).[33] By 1941–1942, the emphasis in discourse had shifted to the need to engage the turmoil in Europe—that the threat to the democratic way of life was immense and that the country's safety now depended on events abroad—especially the challenge of dictators controlling the resources of Eurasia. Roosevelt belittled isolationists as "selfish men who would clip the wings of the American people in order to feather their own nest."[34]

The third phase in American views on security began in 1942 and thereafter, when U.S. thinking clearly and consistently stressed one side of the ledger. The collective orthodoxy embraced the necessity of international co-

Table 3.1. American foreign policy ideas transformed

	Old	*New*
International involvement	"Our manifest destiny has been to stand apart studiously neutral." (Wilson, 1915)	"We cannot make America an island in either a military or economic sense." (Roosevelt, 1943)
Military engagement	"Our America can be no party to a permanent military alliance." (Harding, 1921)*	"Our national safety and the security of the world will require substantial armed services, particularly in overseas service." (Truman, 1946)
Relationship to major powers	"The United States cannot take part in political arrangements in Europe." (Roosevelt, 1934)	"Our own well-being is dependent on the well-being of other nations far away." (Roosevelt, 1945)*
International cooperation	"Ultimately, nations, like individuals, can not depend upon each other but must depend upon themselves." (Coolidge, 1924)	"Our guiding star is the principle of international cooperation. To this concept we have made a commitment as profound as anything in history." (Truman, 1949)

Sources: Fred L. Israel, ed., *The State of the Union Messages of the Presidents, 1790–1966* (New York, Chelsea House/Robert Hector, 1966); for quotes with asterisks, see *Inaugural Speeches of the American Presidents*, annotated by Davis Newton Lott (New York: Holt, Rinehart, 1961).

operation and multilateralism, of joining and even leading international society. The comparison of the old and new ways of thinking illustrates the distinct change (table 3.1). Compared with concepts before 1940, the collective American understanding of what provides security underwent a transformation. It was not that the United States foresaw and embraced an open-ended deployment of troops in Europe and elsewhere. In fact, U.S. presidents from Roosevelt to Eisenhower tried to avoid exactly such a possibility.[35] Nor was it the end of isolationist sentiment in the United States. The isolationism of Senator Robert Taft, a Republican who hoped to become the party's nominee in 1952, was part of Eisenhower's motivation to run for president—he wanted to prevent the renewed dominance of separatist thinking.[36] Taft's views no longer were the majority opinion, however: the dominant view denied that security was best served by standing apart as an unsullied example to, and/or good office for, others. Instead, it could be found through international engagement, cooperation, and most notably commitments of force to other major powers. The shift was in effect a move toward integration with the international society that the United States had previously held, in a political-military sense, at arm's length.

Table 3.2 United States international agreements

	1778–1899 (121 years)	1900–1914 (14 years)	1914–1939 (25 years)	1947–1960 (13 years)	1960–2001 (41 years)
Amity and commerce	272	71	192	3,008	8,007
Alliance	1	34	65	1,024	1,369
Multilateral	37	55	142	469	1,001
Totals	310	160	399	4,501	10,377
Per year average	2.6	11.4	16.0	346.2	253.1

Sources: James McCormack, *American Foreign Policy and Process*, p. 15; Igor I. Kavass and Mark A. Michael, eds. United States treaties and other international agreements cumulative index 1776–1949: cumulative index to United States treaties and other international agreements 1776–1949 as published in Statutes at large, Malloy, Miller, Bevans, and other relevant sources. (Buffalo, NY: W.S. Hein), 1975. Igor I. Kavass and Adolf Sprudzs, eds. UST cumulative index 1950–1970; cumulative index to United States treaties and other international agreements 1950–1970; 1 UST-21 UST, TIAS nos. 2010–7034. (Buffalo, NY: W.S. Hein), 1973. This table is based on treaties concluded. It excludes certain types of categories—e.g. those related to boundaries, consular activities, extradition treaties, etc. The data for the period of World War II are excluded in order to better contrast what came before and what came after.

The above discussion depicts the evolution of ideas, not behavior. Indeed, what I am trying to explain is change and continuity in ideas with the assumption that the ideas will roughly be related to patterns of behavior (although not every action or decision).[37] One rough measure of the correspondence between behavior and ideas (seen in table 3.2) is the degree of U.S. involvement as measured by treaty activity. The numbers show a significant difference before and after World War II.[38]

In what follows, I use the logic developed in chapter 2 to explain this evolution of U.S. foreign policy thinking. In the next section, I address ideational continuity through the interwar period, then transformation in World War II. In each case I first summarize my argument for that era, discuss the collapse phase in terms of expectations and consequences, and then address the consolidation phase in terms of replacement ideas and their efficacy.

WORLD WAR I AND CONTINUITY

Those who sought to overthrow the U.S. tradition of no entanglement and replace it with something new faced an uphill battle after World War I. American intervention defied the warnings of tradition against "entanglement," and the disappointing results did not match the expectations set by Wilson's justification for deviating from the orthodoxy. This interaction reinforced preexisting popular unilateralist ideas. Those who believed a change was still necessary, through either the League of Nations or a more unencumbered activism, could also not agree on a viable replacement idea to coordinate their different notions of internationalism. The result was a retreat to detachment from governmental involvement with Europe.

Disillusionment

Despite its tradition of aloofness from European conflicts, the United States intervened in World War I in the spring of 1917. Although Americans were generally averse to involvement, German submarine attacks on U.S. merchant shipping and civilian travelers, German hostility (as revealed by the Zimmermann telegram involving German-Mexican plans to invade the United States), and American hopes to shape the peace finally provoked action. The decision to intervene was exceptional because it involved a choice—no one declared war on the United States. Americans had been debating such a choice since the beginning of the war. After all, the United States could have followed the path that Franklin Roosevelt would later offer in 1936 when war again looked imminent, "through adequate defense to save ourselves from embroilment and attack."[39] Not doing so was an extraordinary step. When America declared war, the journalist Frank Cobb wrote, "The old isolationism is finished. We are no longer aloof from the world."[40] Those opposed to intervention—pacifists, pro-German groups, those focused on domestic reform, businesses with no economic interests in greater international involvement—consistently pointed out that it was contrary to American tradition and that there would be negative consequences. Senator George W. Norris (R-Nebraska), one of a handful in Congress who rejected Wilson's request to declare war, argued, "The working out of that problem is not an American burden. We ought to remember the advice of the Father of our Country and keep out of entangling alliances. Let Europe solve her problems as we have solved ours. Let Europe bear her burdens as we have borne ours."[41] Wilson worried both before and after intervening that doing so could have significant costs—that it could in fact change the unique nature of the United States, distinct from the European great powers, its potential as an example to other countries, and the fate of domestic reforms. The vocal minority consistently stressed this point and it was not easily forgotten.[42]

Most important in terms of setting the nation's expectations, Wilson justified U.S. intervention by appealing to an internationalist view of security. He argued that the world had to be made "safe for democracy." The secretive autocratic German government would be a continual threat to a durable peace of free nations.[43] Without U.S. intervention, democracy abroad might suffer further, and if democracy suffered the United States itself might be vulnerable. America's fate was now linked to those European countries. To be sure, there were those who wanted to intervene for geopolitical or status reasons, but these individuals—such as Senator Elihu Root, William Howard Taft, Abbot Lawrence Lowell, Henry Cabot Lodge—and groups—such as the League to Enforce Peace—had preferred involvement in earlier years as well. The key bloc that undergirded intervention—those who supported Wilson in the 1916 election—was a liberal one, especially the Progressives. Progressives favored domestic reform to control political corruption and corporate power and abuse. Progressives had previously opposed intervention because they feared it would sully American virtue and halt progressive domestic reforms. Wilson's argument that virtue and domestic reform would be furthered by international involvement persuaded them to think differently about the war. Wilson rallied his Progressive supporters to exactly this theme in the 1916 election.[44]

But the expectations generated by Wilson's justification for intervention in European affairs, and the standards it set for judging intervention, were not matched by the consequences of ensuing events.[45] Despite military victory, Americans found the fruits of World War I distasteful. Rather than victory euphoria, "disillusionment" is generally the phrase used to describe how Americans judged their intervention—a view that confirmed the wisdom of the no-entanglement logic and the authority of its supporters.[46] Discontent spread during the process of concluding and ratifying the peace treaty and the founding of the League of Nations. Wilson's promises of a democratic surge, which had helped inspire the intervention, went unfulfilled as many governments never made such a transition, and those that did struggled for survival. In addition, the Allies did not forsake imperialism but instead wanted to retain their colonies.[47] Americans were further repulsed by the revelations of "secret treaties" among the European powers to divvy up the spoils of the war.[48] Imperialism, secret treaties, and nondemocratic governments were key elements of what made European ties undesirable according to U.S. thinking, and exemplified what was wrong with the society of European great powers.[49] Negative sentiment toward Wilson's plans was further stoked by the difficulties in the U.S. domestic economy, which experienced rapid inflation in 1919 and a deep recession in 1920.[50]

Disillusionment was particularly prominent among those who formed the linchpin of Wilson's political support—the Progressives. They had been seduced by the promise of domestic reform and new wartime agencies and government powers such as the War Industries Board and the National War Labor Board. Despite such hopes, rather than seeing domestic reforms, involvement in Europe produced limitations on civil liberties (during the war) and a crackdown on the Left (after the war). Even in 1918, Wilson's support among Progressives splintered, and in the midterm congressional elections the Democrats lost the House and Senate. Wilson could not sustain the Progressive coalition that had given him a majority in 1916. The Espionage Act (1917) and Sedition Act (1918) muffled the Left, while the Right freely assailed Wilson as unpatriotic. Progressives also did not like the imperial aspects of the Treaty of Versailles and the Allied intervention in Russia. After the war, in addition to the seeming setbacks at Versailles, domestic reform was halted and reversed as wartime bureaucracies were disbanded and labor rights and civil liberties attacked.[51]

Overall, Robert Osgood captures the experience of the United States in World War I as one in which "disenchantment was heightened by the paucity of the crusade's material and spiritual rewards in proportion to the magnificence of the idealistic hopes it had raised and the seeming enormity of its sacrifices, both tangible and intangible."[52] This dynamic reinforced the no-entanglement orthodoxy. Meanwhile, the League of Nations and the alliance-type French security treaty rejected by the Senate, became "casualties of the general American reluctance to shoulder any further international commitments."[53]

Disagreement

The continuity in American separatism is ironic because there appears to have been support among important elites for something different than the prewar orthodoxy.[54] Discrediting the old ideas was not the only barrier to change after World War I. There was also disagreement as to what the new approach should be. At least two alternative frameworks to no-entanglement were prominent at the time: Theodore Roosevelt's balance of power approach and Wilson's nascent multilateralism. But consolidation of any new dominant idea proved difficult. Neither fared well vis-à-vis the World War I experience. U.S. leadership and unfettered internationalism (of either an institutionalist or geopolitical stripe) did not resolve what most viewed as the cause of the war and American troubles—the European buildup of men and arms that spiraled into conflict and America's failure to remain neutral.[55] In contrast to this validation of the old orthodoxy, the war and its aftermath offered little for the claims of those who would overthrow it. Deterring potential aggressors and managing the power void in Europe were not the major U.S. concern.

This standoff is epitomized in the fight over the Versailles treaty and the U.S. rejection of the League of Nations. The League seemingly had widespread support at the end of the war, but that quickly unraveled. The central symbolic issue in the struggle was Article 10 of the League's covenant, which obligated member states to protect one another from external aggression. Opponents of the League, led by Senator Henry Cabot Lodge (R-MA), wanted to alter this (and other) provisions of the treaty, in effect gutting any precommitment to use force. As almost all of these "conservative internationalists" (as Thomas Knock labeled them) were in the Republican

Party, partisan and international visions aligned to refute the deal Wilson had struck at Versailles. Proponents, especially President Wilson, opposed such reservations, believing they undermined the whole internationalist intent.[56]

Wilson's problems, however, were not just with conservatives and Republicans. Liberals and Progressives were also divided on the League, with some disenchanted by what had happened and some not eager to throw their support behind unfair peace terms that seemed to reaffirm the prewar situation. Especially given the results of intervention, internationalists were divided and had difficulty agreeing: "There was no clearly identifiable strategy for such men to follow in the foreign policy debates over the peace settlement and the League of Nations."[57] So while many favored change, the clashing visions of change impeded movement in any specific direction (movement that was already handicapped by the absence of collapse of the no-entanglement tradition). In a close fight, the treaty was rejected, and, as described above, the prewar aloof mind-set of the United States was affirmed.

This interpretation of World War I necessarily highlights the role of collective ideas as more important than the influence of political entrepreneurs—those who are not encumbered by tradition and rise above it to shape the ideas themselves, or those who make bad decisions and mold history in doing so. Some historians, for example, have underscored Wilson's role in America's ideational continuity in the interwar period. A president incapacitated by a stroke is commonly portrayed as having personally bungled the League of Nations issue, especially vis-à-vis the U.S. Senate, and, in doing so, launching the United States on a stay-at-home trajectory for the next two decades.[58] If Wilson had compromised and accepted reservations demanded by critics, it's likely that the Senate would have ratified U.S. membership in the League of Nations. Ratification on such terms, however, would likely have altered U.S. policies very little. As Wilson and others believed, doing so would have eviscerated the American commitment and role.[59] More important, if the United States had joined the League with reservations, it would have reflected rather than affected the U.S. attitudes that dominated the next two decades. The damage of the circumstances and debate after World War I had already occurred; even if the League of Nations had squeaked through the Senate, this alone would have been unlikely to stop the return to orthodoxy.[60] What seems more relevant in explaining Wilson's difficulties in persuading the public (since he was generally considered a skilled shaper of opinion) is the reinforced no-entanglement momentum that emerged from the war. Wilson's ability to persuade on this issue was confounded by the "basic intractability of the very public opinion that he claimed to read and shape into a common consciousness."[61]

In this instance, the combination of U.S. intervention in World War I, which deviated from the dominant no-entanglement idea, and the undesired results, which led to disillusionment, helped weaken any movement toward the collapse of the old way of thinking. Supporters of the old orthodoxy, in contrast, received political ammo with which to make their case that the founding fathers' view of the need to keep distance from Europe still held true. This combination of events also impeded the consolidation of a single viable replacement idea from the small but conflicted set of views that favored greater political-military international activism.[62] The result was that political-military detachment from European affairs and society emerged as an even more dominant guiding concept of interwar U.S. foreign policy.

WORLD WAR II AND TRANSFORMATION

In contrast to World War I, the events that led to and became known as World War II resulted in the transformation of the dominant American ideas about effective foreign policy. The interplay of ideas and events played a critical role in this transformation, as is anticipated by the type A4 "Do something!" scenario. As World War II took shape in the late 1930s, the United States clung rigidly to its aloof approach in the face of a series of events that strongly contradicted the notion that aloofness could sustain national security. This context enabled those groups and individuals who had been seeking change since World War I to coalesce effectively in something close to a B3 "Long live change!" scenario. The result was the transformation of American ideas about appropriate foreign policy during World War II.

Collapse of "No Entanglement"

In the early 1930s the United States was absorbed by the domestic economic difficulties of the Great Depression, not by matters abroad. But to the extent the country looked outward, the dominant idea about international relations was the separatist orthodoxy bequeathed by the World War I experience. As Charles Smith's study of public opinion asserted in the late 1930s, "As long as the memory of that war [World War I] remains, the people will insist that their government go to great lengths to avoid any future conflict."[63] While there were a variety of different emphases within this aloof sentiment, all agreed that involvement in the increasingly rough political waters of Europe was a bad idea. The expectation was that such involvement could do little good in Europe and only bring harm to the United States.[64] During the 1930s the United States clung tightly to beliefs that no-entanglement furthered security, that arms buildups fostered war, and that U.S. interests were best served by neutrality.

These beliefs generated the expectation that the United States could remain secure if it stayed out of European and world conflict. In 1937, Roosevelt was poorly received when he tried to ameliorate this sentiment by promoting U.S. internationalism.[65] FDR allegedly commented, "It's a terrible thing to look over your shoulder when you are trying to lead—and find no one there."[66] The newly developed opinion polling concluded in 1937 that 70 percent of the country believed it was a mistake for the United States to have entered World War I. Again in 1937, when asked whether the country would stay out of another world war, 56 percent replied in the affirmative.[67] America in those years distanced itself from Europe's brewing storm clouds and, when trouble did arise, tried to seal itself off by imposing strict neutrality laws.[68]

The events of the late 1930s eroded such thinking. In a relatively short time, a series of events—Italy's invasion of Ethiopia, the Spanish Civil War, Japanese expansion in China, Germany's absorption of Austria and the Sudetenland, Germany's invasion of Poland, and the fall of France—contradicted the notion of aloofness as security.[69] Not only was the world going to pieces around the United States—preceded by an economic depression fueled by a lack of international cooperation and engagement—but also eventually the United States itself was attacked at Pearl Harbor.

The shift in individual thinking as a result of these events, even as the no-entanglement orthodoxy endured, is apparent both in the opinion polls that began to be collected at the time and the accounts of elites. While Americans consistently rejected declaring war, their willingness to get involved changed dramatically from the desire for separation represented by the Neutrality Acts of 1935–1937.[70] This nascent shift is seen in opinion on a variety of proxy questions on international involvement. In 1936, 95 percent of those polled believed that, in the event of war, the United States should not get involved again. By the end of 1940, 60 percent favored helping England to win by supplying it with war matériel, even at the risk of war, rather than not getting involved.[71] Pollsters repeatedly asked the public whether they thought intervening in World War I was a mistake. As compared with 70 percent agreement and 30 percent disagreement in January 1937, by December of 1940, only 39 percent thought it a mistake, 42 percent disagreed, and 19 percent had no opinion. After Pearl Harbor the percentage of the population surveyed that saw intervention in World War I as a mistake fell below 20 percent.[72] In place of the anti-intervention, anti-entanglement sentiment, Americans (albeit never pro war) accepted the risk of getting involved, and increasingly favored no peace short of full surrender.

The views of many elites similarly shifted with these events. Roosevelt, whose public views often flowed with the tide of opinion, gained resolve from the 1938 Munich crisis to consistently advocate the importance of U.S. engagement in the mounting conflagration and of American internationalism in general.[73] The outbreak of the war in 1939 changed congressional sentiment toward the arms embargo on aid to France and Britain even in the face of energetic efforts by some to prevent such slippage.[74] Leading journals such as the *New Republic, Common Sense,* and the *Progressive* similarly shifted toward the need to engage the European crisis. The nation's leading columnist on foreign affairs, Walter Lippmann, joined the tide moving in favor of intervention after the fall of France, which was probably the preeminent event that undermined aloofness.[75] Many Americans saw that loss as a turning point, especially in terms of the likelihood that the United States would get involved in the war.[76] Finally, when Congress approved Lend-Lease aid in the spring of 1941, the internationalist *New York Times* declared it "the day when the United States ended the great retreat which began with the Senate rejection of the Treaty of Versailles and the League of Nations. . . . Isolation has failed."[77] For a decreasing minority, the German invasion of the Soviet Union and then Pearl Harbor resolved the issue. As Senator Arthur Vandenberg concluded, the Japanese attack "ended isolationism for any realist."[78] An ardent minority remained faithful to their belief in isolationism, but its run as a dominant orthodoxy had ended.

We might explain the change in American views by appeal to a single event: Pearl Harbor. Doing so would confirm the notion that some shocks speak for themselves. In particular, we might conclude (as conventional wisdom does) that this incident finally revealed the vulnerability of the United States to modern warfare. There is, of course, a point to this argument, but it is also possible to put too much emphasis on Pearl Harbor. This is clear when we consider similar events that did not cause change as well as shifts in U.S. thinking that existed prior to Pearl Harbor.

First, as explained in more depth below, the United States experienced events during World War I (submarine warfare, the Zimmermann telegram, the ability of the United States to project force to Europe) that indicated its vulnerability to modern warfare, but these did not change U.S. orthodoxy. The disconnect between technology and strategy is starkly seen in Charles Lindbergh, who by his own flight showed the ability of airpower to bridge the Atlantic. Yet he was an ardent isolationist.[79]

Second, the vast weight of individual opinion change had already moved toward internationalism *before* the Pearl Harbor attack. For example, elite opinion makers had largely shifted their views in response to such earlier events as the invasions of France and the Soviet Union. Likewise, polls had already shown a public shift to internationalism. The major swing in opinion on whether U.S. intervention in World War I was a mistake (68 percent agreement in October 1939 to 39 percent agreement in January 1941) had already taken place before the Pearl Harbor attack.[80]

Pearl Harbor, of course, with its alarming casualties and damage in a single day, did have an influence on public opinion, especially in the context of the preexisting expectation that the U.S. could ensure its security by staying out of the conflict. But Pearl Harbor was not the source of America's new way of thinking. On its own, a lone attack by Japan on the U.S. outpost, without the context of the war in Europe, would likely have produced an armed response against Japan, but not necessarily the broad shift toward internationalism. If we were able to wipe Pearl Harbor from the slate of history, to pretend the Pacific War never occurred, the United States would still have been involved in World War II (at least in Europe), and the major shift in U.S. attitudes underway before December 6 would have occurred anyway.[81] Pearl Harbor accelerated that shift, but did not cause it.

Roosevelt did not have to promise great results from intervention, as Wilson had done; instead, he simply made the case based on the threat that Axis control of other continents would pose to America in economic, political, and military terms.[82] The Japanese attack on Pearl Harbor and the German-Italian declaration of war did the rest of the work for him. As FDR, the frustrated internationalist, tried to hammer home to the nation in his fireside chat on December 9, 1941, "in these past few years—and, most violently, in the past three days—we have learned a terrible lesson." Isolationism, the president continued, had been a mistake.[83] The hard-core isolationists who had bitterly argued that the United States was not vulnerable and that its security was not at risk in the world crisis unconvincingly explained the Pearl Harbor attack as a plot Roosevelt had conjured up to draw America into the war.[84]

Consolidation of Internationalism

As much as the defenders of tradition tried, American engagement could not be dismissed by the notion that the United States had not been detached enough, because with each new challenge the country had tried harder and harder to distance itself. Nor could it be explained through an "arms equals war" thesis, popular in the interwar period, which held that arms producers, arms races, and arms buildups caused war and could be harmful to U.S. interests. By the onset of World War II, Americans had begun to understand that fascist aggression was *not* the product of an unintended arms spiral, but instead, that countries such as Germany and Japan had rapidly built up their arms explicitly for territorial expansion.[85]

In contrast to the gutting of the dominant orthodoxy, both of the main replacement ideas gained legitimacy. The first was the revival of Wilsonian internationalism. Bilateral and autarchic responses to the instability of the 1920s and 1930s seemed to contribute significantly to the economic distress that was a wellspring of the later aggression. Leaders also thought that the rise of autarchic policies might have been prevented or ameliorated by more effective international institutions and mechanisms. Not joining the League of Nations, many believed, was a mistake. Support for joining a postwar League of Nations shifted during the war, leaping from 37 percent in favor in May 1941 to 55 percent approval in November 1942 to 72 percent in favor in June 1944.[86] In the summer of 1943, 61 percent favored a "permanent military alliance" with Britain (25 percent were opposed)—a preference that contradicted the traditional warning against such relationships. In March 1945, 81 percent favored the United States joining a world organization that had the police power to maintain international peace.[87] International stability was now seen as depending on aid and open markets and American commitments, both economic and military. The United States adopted a new recipe for security: to actively engage major power political-military affairs, especially through multilateral agreements and institutions.[88]

The second influential development was the rise of "geopolitical theory," which saw Europe as the world's geographical pivot. This was fostered by a growing American consciousness of international interdependence—that the security of the United States was necessarily affected by conditions abroad. From this view, the United States had to be concerned with the distribution of power and with Europe's affairs. In the 1930s, amid the failure of the League of Nations to adjudicate aggression and the ascendancy of totalitarian governments, such a view of the world gained increasing credibility. Not to counter such buildups would allow totalitarian governments to expand and harness large amounts of power, which might threaten even a fortress America. If one of these totalitarian powers were to control Eurasia, even without a direct challenge to American territory, there was a fear that the United States would have to alter its way of life—that is, become a garrison state—to deal with the possible opponent.[89] This thinking had a clear link to the conservative internationalism of World War I, but it saw the need for sustained commitment in the key area of Europe as much more significant.

In the beginning phases of World War II, geopolitical thought and Wilsonian institutionalism fused in an ideational union to form a new dominant internationalist orthodoxy on how to manage great power relations. Those interested in maximizing power and those interested in promoting international peace agreed it made sense to engage in institutions and alliances, including both economic and military commitments.[90] This agreement (in contrast to the lack thereof after World War I) was paved by ideational dynamics that preceded (rather than followed) the cold war competition that would soon emerge. Activists, from international bankers to pacifists, worked through organizations such as the League of Nations Association, the Foreign Policy Association, the Council on Foreign Relations, the Carnegie Endowment for International Peace, the Century Group, and the Committee to Defend America by Aiding the Allies to encourage the United States to expand its international engagement and cooperation. This effort was in effect a social movement that helped develop and spread internationalism as a plausible policy idea.[91] The stark collapse of the old orthodoxy in the early 1940s further induced a meeting of the minds of those with opposing views of internationalism, in a way that the tradition-confirming experience of World War I did not. Those that remained committed to noninvolvement struggled to make their case but, given the evolution of collective ideas and events, they did not have the leverage to sway the broader society.[92]

This consolidation scenario largely follows the type B3 "Long live change!" scenario where a clear alternative and some demonstration of results leads to the dominance of a new orthodoxy. In this instance there was not one clear alternative, but both institutional and geopolitical internationalists agreed on the need for the United States to integrate in major power institutions and politics.[93] They offered a persuasive rationale for the failures of the interwar period as well as for the causes of the war (and how they might have been avoided). Internationalists also argued that they could deal better than isolationists with the emerging cold war in which the Soviet Union appeared as a Hitler-like threat.

This account suggests that U.S. foreign policy battles were simply a domestic debate that other countries did not influence. This is largely true, especially compared with Germany in the world wars, as explored in the next chapter. But it is not wholly accurate, because even large, geographically isolated powers are open to external influence in the making of national ideas. In the United States of the late 1930s and 1940s, the country most directly involved in such an effort was Great Britain. British officials, aware they would need the support of the United States in the coming war—and that such support would depend on Congress and the public, and not only on the president—initiated a public information campaign to generate support for Great Britain against Germany. The campaign tried to avoid a heavy hand (and to provoke isolationists) and offered a "strategy of truth," as seen from London, that attempted to build on pro-British currents in American public opinion. Although it is difficult to measure the success of this effort, it appears that it did help strengthen those who favored supporting Britain in a number of subtle ways. Most important, the campaign diminished the negative image of the British as elitist and self-centered and fostered an image of a democratic and brave-hearted country struggling against tyranny. This effort lent support to domestic American groups attempting to overturn neutrality laws and make the case for U.S. engagement.[94]

It would be tempting here to credit the shift to internationalism to Roosevelt's considerable political skill. In contrast to the image of the sick Wilson bungling the League of Nations, Franklin Roosevelt is depicted as a master politician who successfully used the levers of government and society to install internationalism as the new orthodoxy in foreign policy thinking.[95] This explanation has an element of truth, but it is an element different than conventional accounts. Wilson may have made mistakes, but those mistakes probably occurred more during the intervention itself. Specifically, Wilson may have had some flexibility in how U.S. intervention in world war was justified. For example, some critics of Wilson fault him for not explaining intervention as a needed response to Germany's threatening alteration of the European balance of power.[96] If it had been understood in this way there would have been no oversold expectations regarding democracy, imperialism, and the reconfiguration of international governance after the war. With realistically calibrated expectations, disillusionment would have been avoided and there would not have been the turtlelike withdrawal that occurred. Roosevelt, in contrast, was much more cautious in how the war was sold and justified.[97]

Leaders do have some flexibility in the way they justify policies (and hence mediate the gap between expectations and specific outcomes). The corollary, however, is that they do so within the constraints of the situation and sentiments they face. For example, Wilson could not have justified his policy on the need to manage the balance of power in Europe because this was exactly the type of posture eschewed by the old orthodoxy. It certainly would not have rallied the support of the pivotal Progressive bloc in the same way that Wilson's appeal to democratization did. Or consider Roosevelt's failure to formulate a proactive internationalist policy in response to the Depression and Hitler's aggression in the 1930s. When running for president in 1932, he was attacked as an internationalist, and he actually renounced his earlier support of the League of Nations, war debt leniency, and sweeping tariff reductions.[98] Indeed, at least in his first term, Roosevelt was an ardent nationalist, clearly giving priority to the recovery of the domestic economy at the expense of international efforts.[99] Regardless of Roosevelt's personal beliefs, his public positions largely varied with the dominant ideas he faced. His skillful efforts only emerged and succeeded in conjunction with the broad structural change in collective beliefs about security that took place in the 1940s.

Overall, the combination of the heightened adherence to noninvolvement, along with the shattering consequences that ensued, undermined the dominant consensus. The two main replacement ideas pushed the country in the same direction of engagement and active commitments to international institutions, even those involving military forces in Europe. Roosevelt and his advisers helped lead that shift and deserve credit for doing so. But the story of the revolution in American foreign policy thinking after World War II is not simply that of the wise leaders.[100] The success of their efforts depended on encouraging circumstances that were created by the interaction of preexisting ideas and the events that took place at the end of the 1930s and during the early 1940s.

ALTERNATIVE EXPLANATIONS AND SYNTHESIS

All of the above would be for naught if it could be shown that the ideas claimed to have causal influence were the result of other factors. Two prominent alternative arguments suggest U.S. foreign policy ideas were actually a product of either (1) strategic circumstances or (2) domestic interest group pressures. In addition, there are several arguments that emphasize national identity or other ideational influences different than the one I have highlighted. Although each offers important insights, none satisfactorily explains the variation. The point is not that strategic factors, or interest groups, or identity, are irrelevant but that collective ideas interact with power, interest groups, and identity and in some situations help to constitute them. Overall, then, the most persuasive account of U.S. ideas does not emphasize power, ideas, or special interests alone, but the regular ways they come together to shape change and continuity.

Strategic Adaptation

The most prominent explanation(s) of U.S. strategy feature strategic circumstances as the source of American ideas.[101] By this logic, the United States maintained its aloof stance after World War I because (1) the distribution of power, and/or (2) the perceived threats, and/or (3) the extant technology suggested detached unilateralism was an inexpensive and safe strategy. After World War II, the United States had more reason to build institutions and accept commitments because it faced a world where it was one of two great powers, because of the aggressive intent of the Soviet Union, and because military technology made it more vulnerable from afar (hence the need to defend at a distance). Although strategic circumstances were certainly crucial in understanding U.S. foreign policy, absent the way that such circumstances interacted with ideas we are left with an unsatisfying account. A closer look at key systemic factors—polarity, the balance of power/threat, and military technology—illustrates the gaps.

We might explain U.S. ideas, as John Mearsheimer (building on Kenneth Waltz's work) has attempted to do, by arguing that the world remained multipolar before and after World War I. Therefore, it made sense for the United States not to get involved but to let the European powers carry the burden in maintaining the balance on the Continent. The United States would "pass the buck" and let those countries do the heavy lifting. The United States would intervene only if a country—a "hegemon"—threatened to dominate the Continent and, by doing so, build a base of power that could challenge the United States in its own hemisphere.[102] Hence the United States intervened in World War I to stem the threat of a victorious Germany, but did not commit to European security after World War I because there was no country that could dominate the Continent. In contrast, after World War II, the intentions and power of the Soviet Union demanded U.S. engagement.[103]

This argument correlates well with American policies. It is vague, however, on when, how, and how much a state should be expected to do to stem the rise of a distant hegemon. American thinking, for example, did *not* seem to develop, as the theory suggests, in direct relationship with rising challenges from Europe. First, the main reason for intervening in World War I was not because a possible German victory imperiled U.S. security. Certainly Wilson did not explain U.S. intervention that way.[104] And even those who are thought of as "power" statesmen such as Theodore Roosevelt did not think of the United States as "a balancer of last resort in Europe." He advocated intervention in World War I based on German barbarism in Belgium.[105] A variety of authors since then, including George Kennan, Hans Morgenthau, and Henry Kissinger, have argued that the United States should have been motivated by power politics, but it was not. As Morgenthau expressed it, "Wilson pursued the right policy, but he pursued it for the wrong reasons."[106] The main incentives for U.S. intervention were its concern for its rights on the ocean as well as its moralistic impulse to redefine the world in its own image—especially when the war could be quickly ended by joining the Allies, and a more durable peace established thereafter.[107]

The second disjuncture between power circumstances and action occurs after 1933 when Hitler's rapid rearmament and radicalized nationalism suggested a qualitatively different situation. Yet as the geopolitical threat clearly emerged with Hitler's aggression in the 1930s the United States failed to respond—indeed, the country went in the opposite direction with the Neutrality Acts. One might argue this was simply a miscalculation, but if American ideas were driven by power and threat should there not have been some correspondence in the same direction—that is, some major move in U.S. conceptions toward engagement? Germany's aggressive intentions became apparent to observers in Germany and even to the highest offices of the U.S. government from as early as 1934.[108] Many Americans certainly hoped Britain and France would contain Germany. Yet, given the stakes, why didn't the United States government use readily available information to form a more accurate judgment of Germany's trajectory?[109] And when France fell and Britain abandoned the Continent and fled home from Dunkirk—when there was little left to stop German hegemony—the United States still did not join the fight.[110] It took the German declaration of war against the United States to induce direct American action. Clearly there were barriers to converting the change in U.S. presidential and even majority individual opinion in the late 1930s into guiding principles of American foreign policy.

The third disjuncture between a power view and U.S. thinking concerns the shift in American thinking to internationalism. The implication of the antihegemon argument is that the U.S. shift to internationalism was a product of the switch from a multipolar to a bipolar world with the advent of the cold war (and the accompanying threat of the Soviet Union dominating Eurasia). Again, however, there is a problem with timing. The fundamental shift in U.S. attitudes toward internationalism occurred *before* the cold war. During World War II—when the Soviet Union, a U.S. ally, was viewed *not* as a threat but as a future partner—the United States prepared to engage itself directly in exactly the type of long-term commitments, such as the United Nations and the Bretton Woods agreement, that it had shunned for most of its history.[111]

To be sure, the Soviet threat bolstered support for and led to a much more significant U.S. military presence in Europe than would have been the case otherwise. After World War II the United States demobilized its armed forces, including those in Europe, dropping from twelve million troops in 1945 to 1.5 million by June 1947. The cold war halted that decline as it did later efforts by President Eisenhower to reduce the presence of U.S. soldiers on the Continent.[112] We also cannot explain the scale of America's containment strategy—or perhaps that particular form of international commitment—without reference to the cold war. Nonetheless, the basic American conceptual shift that accepted the desirability of committing forces ahead of conflicts outside of the Western Hemisphere happened before the Soviet threat emerged.[113] Whether U.S. troops were or were not on the Continent in large numbers is a somewhat different issue than the fact of conceptual change. If we were to conjure a post–World War II situation where there was no cold war but there was turmoil and uncertainty that threatened international markets or the viability of European democracy, or that involved the emergence of an aggressive power in Europe (perhaps a rearmed Germany), it is also easy to imagine U.S. guarantees to prevent such a rise and the return or continuance of some U.S. troop presence on the Continent. This willingness to accept military precommitments, like the demand for a distant defense perimeter, was a crucial turn in U.S. thinking—a rejection of earlier thinking that would not allow such possibilities. This conceptual shift enticed the United States to become a full-fledged member, indeed leader, of the European-bred international society in a way that had been consistently rejected in the past.

A second form of strategic adaptation argument focuses specifically on the threats—not just objective power circumstances—that emanated from the Continent.[114] This was especially the case in the 1920s and early 1930s. Melvyn Leffler and John Braeman have delineated the way that its "overwhelming sense of security" was fundamental in shaping the attitude of the United States toward Europe and its aversion to getting pulled into squabbles that were simply a drain on national resources.[115] The United

States was not indifferent to instability in Europe in either its economic or political dimensions. Yet Americans believed that in the absence of a pressing challenge, economic means of influence were the most appropriate tool. Indeed, one could make the case that this basic attitude was justified until the late 1930s when Hitler's expansive plans were implemented and one could imagine that they might actually pose a threat to North America and not just to Europe. Before that time many saw the United States as secure. "Public opinion," Roosevelt noted, "is thanking God for the Atlantic Ocean (and the Pacific Ocean)."[116]

It is unquestionable that American policy in the interwar period was shaped by perceived threats. Yet "threat" cannot be considered apart from the dominant ideas about how to provide security. It was these ideas that offered guidance regarding when, how, and how much to get involved in European politics. Should the United States respond early to potential turbulence in Europe, perhaps preempting economic or strategic problems that might get worse later? Or should it conserve its resources, avoiding the costs of involvement in squabbles that are an ocean away? What is apparent is that Americans have thought differently about such questions in different periods.

After World War I, the United States saw its interests in Europe through the lens of economic relationships, goals, and tools. Peace resulted from economic well-being, which was a priority in an age of growing interdependence. U.S. leaders were generally averse to using power or political means to deal with stability and instability. They saw their desirable defensive perimeter as the borders of the United States or the western hemisphere. They could imagine political or military guarantees but distrusted such measures.[117]

The experience of World War I and the bitter fight over the League of Nations only enhanced this preference. Hence Wilson's Republican successors "decided to subordinate the questions of military guarantees and political entanglements, to accentuate the importance of economic and financial affairs."[118] From this perspective, one wholly in line with the tradition of aloofness, power balances and political stability were less central to American well-being than economic stability and prosperity. In contrast, after World War II the rise of geopolitics argued for a much more activist stance, an extended defensive perimeter that included Europe, early attention to disequilibria, and greater political-military commitments. In short, the notion developed that trouble on the Continent—even if were not an imminent military threat—could have profound implications for U.S. security. The point is not that either engagement or aloofness is necessarily best for all circumstances. U.S. presidents of the 1920s offered reasonable arguments against getting entangled. Different ideas offer different prescriptions. Change the dominant ideas and you get different U.S. policies on how to manage similar situations.

Consider for example the weighting of costs and benefits in judging what types of instability are a challenge to the United States. The no-entanglement orthodoxy in the 1920s saw little danger that necessitated anything beyond economic approaches (mostly by private parties) in the instability and power vacuum that characterized Europe in the interwar period. Yet from a geopolitical perspective, the broader question of whether U.S. commitments could prevent the rise of longer-term instability that could threaten the system and American interests worldwide should still have been an issue.

If potential threats were what drove the United States, World War I indicated a turning point demanding U.S. involvement, not withdrawal. World War I left a vacuum of power on the European continent. Germany was disarmed and France was critically weakened by the harsh conflict, much of it fought on French soil. Although a power vacuum is not an imminent threat, bad things can happen in vacuums and the logic of strategic adaptation is to take actions that prevent bad things from happening.[119] A country that quickly recovered, or some outside power, could dominate the Continent, an outcome considered anathema from a geopolitical view. Americans were well aware of the possibility of Germany reemerging as an aggressive power. During World War I President Wilson portrayed Germany, especially its militarized nature, as a threat to the world. After the war he wondered whether possible renewed German aggression had been given sufficient attention, and at another point he predicted that there would be another war within a generation if countries did not unite to do something to stop it from happening. Franklin Roosevelt similarly argued, as a vice-presidential candidate in 1920, that the main function of the League of Nations was to prevent another crisis—possibly ten years down the road from a revived Germany intent on revenge—from escalating into war.[120] More directly, the insecurity of France and the aspirations of Germany pointed to a highly volatile mix. Walter Lippmann wrote at the time, "We find ourselves in a world where four of the eight or nine centers of decisive authority have collapsed." He argued that the United States could not just return home "to gaze in rapt admiration at the Monroe Doctrine."[121] Many "Atlanticists" favored at least a commitment to France as a hedge against a resurgent Germany, but they were unable to make headway.[122]

In the past, Britain had always balanced against countries aspiring to dominate the Continent, but after World War I its capacity to do so was significantly diminished. Weakened by World War I and preoccupied with difficulties and challenges in its empire, Britain was not as able to deal with troubles on the Continent has it had been in the nineteenth century. In contrast, the United States had the economic power (producing more in the 1920s than the other six great powers combined) to take on that role; it just did not see its security in that way.[123] To be sure, the relative disparity in power and likely control the United States had over Europe after World

War I was not as great as after World War II, but it was dramatically different than the situation at the beginning of the century.[124] Yet there was no Anglo-American cooperation or nascent Atlantic pact to deal with the post–World War I power vacuum on the Continent, even though European countries invited the United States to do just that via alliance or military commitment.[125]

To appreciate how a shift in outlook—from the geopolitical aloofness of the interwar period to engagement after World War II—can shape how to deal with instability in times of peace with no direct challenge, we can usefully consider the post–cold war period. The dismantlement of the Soviet Union, juxtaposed against the consolidation of the European Union after 1989 and the relative stability of the 1990s, would seem to suggest that the United States might usefully withdraw. Yet what has occurred is that NATO has expanded with the support and commitment of the United States. The logic of this course is one that says early involvement in Europe's stability is a source of U.S. security. As John Mearsheimer puts it, "There is potential for dangerous security competition in Europe, and the United States is determined to keep the forces of trouble at bay."[126] Why the United States did not act more forcefully to keep trouble at bay in the 1920s and 1930s is a puzzle for the argument that a consistent geopolitical American mind-set has held sway in both periods.

Geopolitical thinking, however, was not the bread and butter of U.S. interwar foreign policy. It was only in the interwar period that it began to take root and grow as a political force in the United States.[127] U.S. concern with a country taking over Eurasia certainly was part of Wilson's case for the League of Nations. Yet the incorporation of geopolitics into the broad base of U.S. foreign policy thinking came through a different avenue, with the scholars who appeared on the scene—largely as refugees from Europe—in the late 1930s. The introduction of geopolitical ideas into the curriculum of American academic programs occurred in a preliminary way in the later 1920s and 1930s.[128] Geopolitical thinking became more widespread only after the shift in the U.S. orthodoxy in the early 1940s when some of the important works on geopolitics by Nicholas Spykman, Hans Weigert, and others were published.[129] In this sense, U.S. foreign policy thinking made geopolitical theory popular, rather than geopolitical theory being the driving force behind American foreign policy ideas.

A final strategic adaptation argument features the expanding reach of technology and America's corresponding vulnerability after World War II.[130] While the evidence in this area is mixed, it is as plausible to argue that the decisive change in technology vis-à-vis U.S. vulnerability occurred during the *First* World War. Several events in World War I shocked Americans and should have taught the lesson that the United States was no longer immune from enemies across the ocean.[131] German submarine attacks damaged the American sense of immunity. And more important, the Zimmermann telegram indicated the potential ability of European powers to directly threaten the *mainland* of U.S. territory, especially with the assistance of a country such as Mexico.[132]

Technology and capabilities at the time did allow the United States to project power to Europe *relatively* efficiently. U.S. intervention in World War I showed that transatlantic security-threatening force was more potent and successful than ever before in history. One proxy for this is maritime freight rates between Europe and America. Iron ships and steam propulsion had reduced the costs of shipping people and matériel across the Atlantic significantly (60%) in the two to three decades before World War I and a bit more in the late 1920s—a "revolution" in transport. After that, rates remained relatively stable until *after* 1950, when another decline began.[133] By this indicator, World War I, not World War II, more closely marked the most significant change in the costs of an invasion of the United States, inviting a similar shift in U.S. ideas about engagement in Europe. But that shift only came later, in a period of relatively stable maritime costs. As Henry Cabot Lodge argued, the ocean barrier that separated the United States and Europe in 1776 and 1812 no longer existed in 1914—steam and electricity had erased it.[134] This fact was made clear by the massive convoys and U.S. intervention that decided the outcome of the conflict: "The ability of the United States to use geographical distance as a means whereby national security could be protected had been seriously undermined."[135]

Some, apparently including FDR, were concerned in the interwar period that long-range bombers made the United States more vulnerable. But the exaggerated claims made in the late 1930s and early 1940s by Roosevelt and others were mainly aimed at jolting the United States out of its isolation. At that time they had little basis in reality.[136] And the Gallipoli failure during World War I did demonstrate that projecting force without a friendly port in an amphibious invasion against opposing forces was a difficult business.[137] Adding air defenses and strategic bombing against such a possibility (as after World War II) would make such a landing on the coast of the United States even more difficult. Nuclear weapons, of course, did not appear until after the shift to internationalism had already occurred. In sum, the objective reach and relative costs of technology, while certainly an influence, did not directly determine continuity and change in U.S. collective ideas on foreign policy.

The relevance of ideational dynamics to U.S. strategy in this period is apparent in a simple counterfactual: had Americans after World War I thought about their security in the same way as they did after World War II, they would have responded very differently to the power, threat, and technology conditions present at that time. Hence those conditions alone do not explain America's ideational stasis and change. After World War II the United States thought differently about how to deal with the continental balance of power and power vacuums there and elsewhere than it had after World

War I. Put another way, had the same conditions that existed after World War I repeated themselves after World War II, the United States would have accepted political-military commitments and other measures eschewed in the 1920s, even in the absence of a cold war and Soviet threat. We might attribute this to "learning." What a focus on ideas and events gives us is some understanding of why such learning did not occur in World War I and why it did after World War II.

To say that strategic adaptation arguments do not tell us all we want to know is far from saying that power, threat, and technology pressures played no role in the continuity and change apparent in U.S. foreign policy thinking. Even if the rise of U.S. power did not mandate an internationalist turn, without such power the United States could not have fulfilled such a role. The seeming absence of immediate threats in the 1920s certainly allowed U.S. aloofness in political-military affairs. German and Japanese threats in the late 1930s and early 1940s were critical in challenging the American notion that disengagement from the world could preserve U.S. security. There is no doubt as well that the increasing interconnectedness of the world, and the range and scale of military power, was a powerful factor in inducing the United States to forgo its aloofness, as was the increase in its relative power in global affairs. What is important, however, is that such changes were only understood through particular ideas about effective action. National ideas generally do not autonomously cause their own transformation, and they did not do so in this case. But neither do external pressures speak for themselves. Rather, what is important is the particular ways they interact—a dynamic that in this case produced continuity after World War I and change after World War II in ways that neither an autonomous ideational argument nor a strategic adaptation approach alone would anticipate.

Interest Groups

Another view of national conceptual development disaggregates the collective state to examine the interest groups within it. In this view, collective ideas are simply those notions put forward by the most powerful groups or some aggregation of many groups' views. The composition of interest groups behind U.S. foreign policy during this period has been described in a variety of ways including partisan (Republicans vs. Democrats), political ideology (Progressives vs. conservatives), socioeconomic sectors (those with overseas economic interests vs. those without), ethnic groups (pro-Germany vs. pro-British), and regional interests (isolationist Midwest vs. internationalist East and West coasts).[138] From this perspective, changes in state orientation are a matter of understanding how the relative power and/or interests of smaller groups within the state shift, allowing one or another to seize control of the national reins.

One form of this argument highlights how shifts in domestic interests and group power (due to their changing place in the international economy) determine policies and broader ideas such as internationalism.[139] For example, Jeffry Frieden has argued that the Great Depression fundamentally shifted interest group power in favor of internationalists, which led to economic internationalism. Yet the evidence seems mixed at best and the implications unclear. Arguably the Great Depression hurt internationalist interests because the collapse of the international economy should have strengthened those sectoral interests that benefited from the lack of competition—those Frieden calls isolationists.[140] If the internationalists did benefit more than the isolationists, such influence did not translate (consistent with some a priori explanation of shifts in either the power or interests of interest groups) into policy beyond some forays into economic (not security) policy thinking.[141] While there were some economic policy initiatives that favored internationalism in the 1930s (the 1934 Reciprocal Trade Agreements Act, the 1936 Tripartite Pact, debt forgiveness), there were also moves in the opposite direction (e.g., torpedoing the 1933 London Economic Conference, beggar-thy-neighbor devaluations, the Neutrality Acts).[142] Especially when we separate economic ideas from security ones (as the U.S. no-entanglement orthodoxy did) the Great Depression does not appear to break with the orthodoxy. U.S. ideas about security commitments did not change until a decade later—after the "Do something!" dynamics discussed above.

The causal effect that the interest group arguments rely on—that the strength of groups decides which ideas win—actually runs in the *opposite* direction in interwar America. The broader ideational shift toward internationalism allowed internationalist groups to be more persuasive and hence to gain strength. That is, U.S. economic internationalism took its most aggressive form after World War II because the shift in attitudes about political-military commitments helped reinforce integration in the international system in general. As Frieden concludes, "By the late 1930s, economic nationalists were isolated or ignored."[143] But this effect was not so much due to shifts in interest group power during the Great Depression as it was the result of ideational dynamics in the late 1930s that offered persuasive leverage to the groups critiquing the failing isolationism.

This is certainly not to say that shifts in economic interests due to the shifting places of sectors, regions, and the country in the world economy did not matter.[144] Such changes did contribute to the potency of pressures that favored a shift toward international engagement. The relevance of such pressures—and the movements and agents that do the heavy lifting of social action and persuasion—is clear. It is typically groups that are not dominant that work to make their views accessible and plausible to as many members of society as possible. Such activism is critical in establishing replacement ideas that can serve as a new orthodoxy if situations favorable to collapse and consolidation exist.

In the U.S. case, for example, nonstate actors aided by FDR's leadership succeeded in establishing a viable oppositional idea of internationalism that enabled the World War II transformation.[145] Absent that effort by a variety of groups, motivated by a variety of interests, from economic to philosophical, there may not have been a ready momentum to support the broad shift to internationalism that occurred. That such efforts failed after World War I speaks to the importance of conducive circumstances that allow groups to make their case at some times but not others, as well as to the difficulty of change when prominent groups push competing sets of ideas that produce stalemate.

National Identity, Generations, and Cycles

Some of the more prominent explanations for U.S. foreign policy, like the one here, also feature an ideational focus. One such account is not so much about specific policy views as it is an overarching orientation based on a sense of group self, or national identity, which is sometimes called "political culture." Keen observers of the United States have noted its enduring attitude of "exceptionalism" toward its place in the world. Self-image is a driving factor in behavior—the United States sees itself as a unique country that sets an example for other countries to follow—a "city on a hill."[146] This explanation offers much insight. The main problem is that such a continuous identity cannot explain variations over time (see figure 3.1). One might argue that such an identity does not uniquely determine dominant beliefs but instead provides the rhetorical symbols that can be employed for a variety of policies. For example, some scholars have identified elements of both withdrawal or "quietism" and "messianic" activism, of introversion and activism, of pacifism and bellicosity, of intervention and nonintervention in the personality profile of U.S. foreign policy. Different elements, these scholars posit, have dominated in different periods, shifting in a cyclical fashion.[147] There is much to these accounts, but we must still explain why some orientations dominated at one point and not another.[148]

One answer to this question comes from a focus on generational shifts in American attitudes. Michael Roskin, for example, argues that each generation prefers an orientation toward intervention or nonintervention based on the catastrophe experienced by the previous generation in overzealously pursuing the opposite orientation.[149] The post–World War II period to the late 1970s seems to fit this nicely with the United States becoming interventionist in response to the nonintervention period of the interwar era and then seemingly withdrawing somewhat in response to the Vietnam War.

The argument, however, encounters several difficulties. Most generally, it is not clear that attitudes break down along generational lines.[150] Shifts in ideas bridged generational divisions in both World War II and in the Vietnam War. Second, shifts do not always occur every generation. The attitudes about international commitments toward Europe show strong continuity through much of the first half of U.S. history. And with the historical record now longer than at the time Roskin wrote, any meaningful shift toward nonintervention (after Vietnam) seems shaky. What is more important is the way that events interact, not just with generational lessons, but with societal symbols about "right" behavior. The collective ideation problems discussed tell us much about why continuity is so potent in foreign policy orientations, why change does not happen every generation, but why it is more likely in response to some events rather than other events.[151]

Another argument related to identity highlights the "social purpose" of the American state. John G. Ruggie and Ann-Marie Burley contend that the shift in the U.S. government's role toward greater intervention domestically (i.e., the rise of the welfare/regulatory state during the Great Depression) also altered the views of policymakers in foreign policy toward greater engagement with or intervention in international society.[152] As the state became more interventionist domestically so too it became more active internationally as well. These explanations are revealing about the form that U.S. internationalism took when it occurred, but they are more ambiguous regarding the timing of the shift. If the change in the social purpose of the American state occurred during the Great Depression, why was there little difference in foreign policy thinking, especially about security, until the 1940s?

The causal influence between foreign policy thinking and the social purpose of the state appears to be at least a reciprocal one. Consider the First World War. During that conflict, Wilson associated support for a progressive interventionist program at home with intervention in the war and the postwar international order. Thus the Great Depression was not the first attempt to tie the government's domestic ethos and its external role. And the government's role did expand significantly in the First World War.[153] Yet, why in this instance, did the tie between interventionism at home and abroad not stick? One answer is that the inside-out arrow was reversed: external experience (the disillusionment from World War I) contributed to the end of domestic progressive social intervention.[154]

In this case, ideas related to foreign policy significantly influenced both domestic attitudes toward government and what might be considered overarching identity. The shift in ideas after World War II meant that the United States no longer saw itself as set apart from the rest of the world. To be sure, it still retained an image of itself as "exceptional" (not a unique view among national images), but there was a change. As opposed to John Winthrop's "city on the hill" where America would be a detached model for the amoral monarchies of Europe, the United States after World War II en-visioned itself as the "hill in the city": it embraced international society even as it saw itself as a superior form of political organization, not de-tached from, but within, that society. In so doing, the United States did not simply enact its identity (which rejected such a change) but instead its identity became what it believed—and had already accomplished—about how to deal with international society.

The transformation of America's beliefs during World War II, but *not* after World War I, suggests the relevance of paying attention to collective ideas about appropriate action even in explaining ideational transforma-tion. The point is not that collective ideas by themselves determine change and that power, threat, technology, interest groups, and identity are unim-portant. Rather, I have offered the more discrete argument that policy or-thodoxies interact with other factors in regular ways to shape subsequent dominant ideas.

As seen in both cases in this chapter, the relationship between social ideas and events played a key role. The United States entered World War I despite a general belief that entanglement in Europe was undesirable. In this case, an exception was justified, Wilson argued, because of the poten-tial to correct the malignancies that made entanglement harmful: the impe-rialism and nondemocratic nature of the major powers. But despite victory in that conflict, none of the rewards that Wilson claimed were inherent in jettisoning the old orthodoxy were apparent. In fact, the opposite was the case. This contradiction had much to do with the defeat of Wilson's interna-tionalist efforts after the war and America's limited commitments, despite its dominating power, in European politics in the interwar years.

In World War II the ideational dynamics were quite different than those in the earlier conflict. In the 1930s, the United States did not deviate from its no-entanglement orthodoxy but instead clung to it with autistic tenacity. The results, however, became increasingly onerous. This was potent mate-rial for internationalist critics of the old orthodoxy, and they capably seized on the opening to persuade the country to overthrow the old in favor of participation in, and the reinforcement of, international society.

The emergence of the United States in the twentieth century as the most powerful country in the world has meant that its ideas have shaped inter-national society. It would be a mistake, however, to attribute the decline and growth of international society simply to the ideas of one country. In-ternational relations by their very nature have to involve more than one na-tion. Leaders need followers, beggars need benefactors, imperialists need the colonized, and attackers need defenders. Understanding the broader rise of the post–World War II society among great powers demands that we look beyond simply the most powerful state to others as well, a task taken up in the next chapter.

[4]

Germany, from Outsider to Insider

War should be the ultimate arbiter of whether a foreign policy idea is feasible or not. Just as wars are seen as the road test for national power, so too should they help weed out faulty strategic concepts from effective ones. Amid the din and roar of international activity it can of course be difficult to judge whether faulty ideas were the cause of undesired results, or whether they were poorly implemented, or whether it was a fluke that better results were not realized. From this perspective, it may make sense to expect that states will develop simplified rules of thumb such as abandoning strategic notions that result in lost wars.[1]

Germany, however, did not do so. After suffering massive casualties and loss of matériel in the First World War, Germany then returned to roughly the same ideas that had fueled the conflict. German thinking about international involvement featured a set of beliefs favoring *armed expansion* that prioritized the utility of armed force and territorial acquisition in the heart of Europe. These ideas were a source of Germany's aggressive behavior that resulted in the Second World War. Germany favored a mode of international action that made it the black sheep of international society in the first half of the twentieth century. Yet after World War II Germany shifted from a resistant and revisionist approach to international society to becoming one of its leading citizens. Germany embraced a new set of ideas, one that argued for cooperative integration within the Atlantic-dominated system.

This history is familiar but on closer inspection yields anomalies for several well-known explanations. One straightforward account for the continuity in ideas after World War I is that Germany's geopolitical situation did not change and thus neither did its strategic ideas. The country still faced a multipolar world (in contrast to bipolarity after 1945), a circle of potential enemies, and the rising colossus in the east, the Soviet Union. The problem with this account is that none of these conditions in the interwar era (or in the Wilhelmian one) demanded a philosophy of armed expansion. German security could have been pursued through defensive alliances as ably as it was through offensive war.[2] Yet those ideas received little attention.

We also might be tempted to seize on relative "shock" as the answer to continuity and change: defeat in World War II induced change because it was more significant than in World War I. There is no doubt that this difference exists and that it mattered. Especially in the aftermath of the Second World War, Germany was virtually leveled: there was mass destruction and casualties, the nation was divided into two states, its territory was wholly occupied by the victorious powers, and what was left of its governing apparatus was disbanded. After World War I there was considerable continuity in the key institutions that formulated foreign policy.[3] This view captures some key aspects of change in World War II but it points to two puzzles.

First and most important is why World War I did not lead to change. After all, the scale of defeat in both instances by almost any ex ante measure should have been enough to provoke change. World War I may not have been as much of a shock as World War II, but at the time it was devastating. Out of a prewar population of sixty-seven million, two million soldiers were killed in combat, fourteen million died from illness, and five million were wounded. A multitude of German wives became widows. Depending on the year, civilian deaths in Germany increased from 30 to 60 percent during the war years (due to undernourishment and disease) and then fell sharply after. In the peace settlement, Germany lost all of its colonies, 13 percent of its territory, 50 percent of its iron production, and 16 percent of its coal production, along with a substantial part of its railway rolling stock and track.[4] Why was occupation (after World War II) and not just shattering defeat (as in World War I) linked to change? Second, if the material and administrative conditions after World War II were of such magnitude that they demanded a shift to the resulting ideas, why was there such a heated debate in Germany after that war, which suggests that other outcomes were possible?

Another time-tested explanation for German foreign policy is found in domestic politics—the struggle of particular groups and interests to control the state and its guiding principles. In one view, privileged elites associated with heavy industry and the large inherited agricultural estates in the eastern part of the country formed the coalition of "iron and rye" behind a policy of economic tariffs and military industrialization. By so doing they hoped to protect their wealth and position in society against the challenge from egalitarian-minded political parties such as the Social Democratic Party (SPD). In a second version, German political elites attempting to hold together a fractured political community, in order to protect their positions and their country, favored an expansive, nationalist foreign policy whose success would in turn foster unity and government legitimacy.[5]

[85]

These perspectives accurately capture the fact that German society was torn by class, religious, and geographical differences. Groups fought passionately over which ideas would guide the German state in all the periods examined. Yet the clash of such battles may distract as much as it illuminates. If there was so much pushing and pulling in domestic political battles, the considerable continuity in German foreign policy ideas from Wilhelm to Hitler is somewhat of an anomaly. This is especially true because the power and influence of the different groups waxed and waned over the period covered. Why then did certain ideas (or groups) triumph at particular times, while other ideas and groups did not?

We can make sense of these puzzles by paying attention to the interaction of ideas and events. The shock of war challenged preexisting ideas and supported alternative ideas in the two cases in different ways, facilitating continuity after World War I and change after World War II. The point is not that Germany's strategic circumstances or its domestic politics were irrelevant. Rather it is that their influence depended heavily on the historical trajectory of dominant ideas that prescribed Germany's optimal orientation to the world. How Germany understood its strategic circumstances—for example, its relative power position, its loss and destruction in war, and the response appropriate to them—was channeled in particular ways (and not others) by expectations based on dominant ideas and the critiques offered by those who would replace the dominant ideas with new ones. The typical domestic politics logic, in which powerful groups are able to select ideas of their choosing, appears again in this case in reverse: the rise of ideas fostered the power and legitimacy of some groups over others. That is, the interplay of ideas and events in Germany helped to determine which groups gained strength and influence and hence why they dominated.

Germany's defeat in World War I provided grounds for the overthrow of its prewar expansionist ideas. The problem for the new Weimar regime was what new ideas it would adopt. The Social Democrats in charge in the early days of the new republic cast their lot with integration. The Versailles treaty sharply and quickly undermined that fledgling position. The direct result was that the flickering coals of the old orthodoxy burst into flame, gaining critical leverage in German politics in the 1920s and then power under Hitler. In contrast, after World War II, both the extreme nature of the expectations and the extreme nature of the defeat caused the collapse of an armed expansion view that had dominated German foreign policy since at least Wilhelm II. This collapse did not automatically imply a particular new orthodoxy. Instead, Germans debated their new direction, with those favoring integration battling those supporting neutrality. The successes of the integration program of Konrad Adenauer, the first German leader after that war, helped cement the transformation of German ideas that have endured into the twenty-first century.

In this case we also clearly see that other countries, both in what they did and did not do, shaped the foreign policy ideas that triumphed in Germany. This effect stands out especially vis-à-vis the more autonomous development of ideas in the United States. Germany, however, was relatively weaker in the aftermath of both wars and therefore more susceptible to external influence. International actors distinctly influenced the collapse and consolidation phases of Germany's ideas after the world wars.

Although many of the major powers were involved, especially Britain and France, the underlying dynamic is most clearly seen in the role of the new dominant international power, the United States. After World War I, the minimalist role played by the United States in Europe helped to undermine those Germans who sought an alteration of Germany's traditional foreign policy concepts. The U.S. support that was offered after World War I was too little and of the wrong kind to help German proponents of internationalism. American aloofness did much to contribute to the German instinct to snub international society through a renewed emphasis on national autonomy and arms in dealing with the world in the 1920s and 1930s. Yet, after World War II, America's new internationalism played a critical role in the consolidation of German views around its now familiar integrationist orthodoxy. The story of Germany's integrationism, both in its decline and rise, has an unavoidable transnational component seen in the purposes and superior power of the United States.

In this chapter, I first document the evolution of German ideas about appropriate foreign policy for the first half of the twentieth century. The analysis then explains how it was that continuity occurred after World War I and transformation took place after World War II.

THE EVOLUTION OF *AUSSENPOLITIK* IDEAS

A necessary starting point is to characterize German foreign policy (*Aussenpolitik*) ideas and their development. The evolution of German strategic concepts shows rough continuity along a few central dimensions, from before the First World War through 1945. During that period, German leaders consistently expressed a belief that the expansion of German power on the Continent, which would ultimately require military means, was the best way to achieve security. The primary deviations from this pattern were when other approaches were considered during the 1918–1919 period and during Gustav Stresemann's tenure as foreign minister (1923–1929), when accommodation was adopted as a temporary expedient under the pressure of severe international restraints. Yet in key respects, the underlying ideas of interwar Germany displayed continuity with those of late Wilhelmian Germany. Hitler built on that legacy in an abhorrent form, especially in the genocide of the Jews and other minorities and the mass killing and enslavement of "subhuman" Slavs (and here there is a notable difference between

Wilhelmian and Nazi Germany), but the foundation of his expansionist ideas was aligned with the prior pattern.

After World War II, as West Germany reestablished itself as an independent political entity, a different orthodoxy toward foreign policy gained the dominant position. Rejecting the previous thinking, this view prioritized integration within Western European and transatlantic structures as the means to security. This was not simply a strategy to regain independent armed strength. Germany only reluctantly accepted remilitarization in the 1950s as a condition imposed by others for its integration in the existing international society.

This development raises several questions that merit attention before turning to the specifics of the ideas. First, were German ideas any different than those found in other states during the late nineteenth and early twentieth centuries? Many of the qualities traditionally attributed to Germany in this period—including nationalism, militarism, belief in the utility of force, and the glorification of war—were not unique to Germany. From the French garrison in Poland in 1919 (which, under the Treaty of Versailles, governed former Germany territory in what is now Lithuania), Charles de Gaulle wrote to his father: "Like most of my compatriots, I am ending this war overflowing with a general feeling of xenophobia and convinced that, in order to make ourselves respected, the reasoned use of our military force, the first in the world today, will be required."[6] Important leaders from other countries, France, in this example, shared traits that are often characterized as "typically German" but which were also found in other countries.

What is notable in Germany, however, is not the presence of militarism and a focus on state power but the intensity and widespread acceptance of such traits. Although most of the states of this period can be considered "nationalist," comparative studies typically highlight Germany as "the most activist, violent, and xenophobic species of the phenomenon."[7] For example, Alfred Vagt's well-known analysis notes, "The 'militarism of moods and opinions' has been more clearly in evidence in Germany than elsewhere. . . . Even in peace, the German seemed, until 1945, inclined to acknowledge the primacy of the military and accept its absolute good regardless of its use in war, its victories or defeats."[8] Paul Kennedy's comparative study of Britain and Germany before World War I finds that "Germany society was much more amenable" to the message of the chauvinists and arch nationalists found in both countries.[9] Although de Gaulle's comment above suggests little difference, it is worth noting that his views on modernization and offensive use of military force were not broadly accepted in his country in the interwar period, in part because they were deemed "inappropriate to the defensive pretension" of France.[10] Holger Herwig's work on the efforts of governments to "spin" their World War I experience also notes a difference: "While all states offered up their own versions of mythologized battle experience, the relative degree and virulence of mendacity manifested by

mythmakers in Berlin and Vienna stands in marked contrast to the more be-
nign efforts of Paris and London to fudge the historical record."[11] Germany's outlook on, and management of, foreign relations was both familiar
and different. Atypically, Germany consistently favored strategies more oriented toward the physical expansion of its territory and the political domination of Europe.[12]

The point of reference for what follows, however, is not so much how
Germany compared to other countries but how its own ideas compare over
time. How did Germany think about leaving or joining international society in different periods? This is no simple question. Clearly Germany was a
central fixture in the European core of international society as it took shape
in the nineteenth and twentieth centuries. War was not prohibited by the
rules of international society; it was part and parcel of it. Hedley Bull
pointed out that even as World War II unfolded, all the belligerents continued to respect particular rights and agreements that were part of that society. Bull also notes, however, that Germany's plans, if they had succeeded,
would have overturned the international system.[13]

This duality suggests that although Germany in the first half of the twentieth century was part of international society, it was a stigmatized member
of that society. The primary source of that stigma was its foreign policy
thinking, which contravened some of the basic rules of the community, including having the aim of overthrowing and dominating the system. As
Bull notes, one of the legitimate purposes of war in the system was to manage the balance of power.[14] Germany, however, believed that its security
would best be achieved not through balancing but through using force to
establish continental hegemony. Such a strategy, however, was not acceptable to other powers, even if other states, such as Russia and Italy, had their
own aspirations to improve their positions in the system. This "intrasoci-
ety" dispute among the stakeholders of international society threatened its
legitimacy in ways that other conflicts (except for Napoleon's campaigns)
had not.[15] This revisionism reached a pinnacle under Hitler: "It is not the
Treaty of Versailles we must destroy, but the Treaty of Westphalia."[16] From
this challenge to the existing order *before* 1945, Germany, in the aftermath of
World War II, became one of the staunchest defenders of international
order over the past sixty years.

My method of surveying dominant foreign policy ideas in Germany in
this chapter is different than in the last chapter. I rely much more on the secondary literature and less on a systematic analysis of primary documents.
Unfortunately, there is no comparable set of texts that reflect public discourse, such as the State of the Union speeches, through different periods.
Fortunately, the secondary literature is extensive and provides a view of the
collective aspect of German ideas in three ways. First, I assess how scholars
of Germany describe those views. Second, I assess the ideational constraints that key decision makers such as Stresemann and Hitler faced. As

with Wilson and FDR in the last chapter, by looking at the ways German leaders presented and explained policy, especially when compared with what was told to select domestic groups or with the policies actually chosen, we get a sense of the domestic biases and external pressures they faced. Finally, and to a lesser extent, the views of German historians in the different periods are examined. The way these historians presented Germany's situation and appropriate role in the world, given the important position of historians in Germany, offers some insight into the conceptual orthodoxies of the different eras. Together these three perspectives on Germany's collective ideas provide some sense of the major trends in continuity and change for the period covered.

Before 1914

German beliefs about foreign policy before World War I have their origins in Germany's founding national ideas. Napoleon's successful campaigns (and the liberal ideas his armies spread) acted as a powerful incentive to the Germanic regional powers and principalities to bond together to defend against a future invasion. A formal union, however, went unrealized until Bismarck's solution, which combined German nationalism and Prussian expansionism. Although many states have been importantly shaped by war or the threat of war, the making of Germany was part and parcel of military victories against Napoleon and a concentrated set of conflicts, the annexation of Schleswig-Holstein from Denmark in 1864, the Austro-Prussian War of 1866, and the Franco-Prussian War of 1870. This history, shaped by late development and geographical position, fostered a group-centric militarist orientation that crowded out Germany's liberal component (i.e., that which focuses on the importance of the individual within the nation).[17] Military values extended throughout society and the military itself was at the pinnacle of the status hierarchy. Every chancellor during the rule of the kaisers wore a uniform when attending the Reichstag. At royal banquets, high-level civilian officials were placed in lower positions of honor than military officials unless they had equivalent military ranks. Thus Theobold von Bethmann-Hollweg, as chancellor of the country (but only a major in the military), found himself displaced by generals and even colonels.[18]

This hierarchy encouraged Germany's embrace of the *Machtstaat* (power state)—a central authority that accumulated both material capabilities and administrative authority—as the solution to Germany's internal difficulties and external challenges. Territorial expansion for the purpose of national development became a central theme, even as Bismarck's skillful leadership bridled it after the wars of unification.[19] Bismarck was not as beholden to the new ideas as his successors, and he was better at not upsetting other nations' sense of acceptable behavior (e.g., the balance of power), but he too felt the pressure of the armed expansion idea as time went on.[20]

In the post-Bismarck Wilhelmian period, Germany's external orientation manifested itself in what Woodruff Smith has argued are two different international strategies. First was the notion of *"Weltpolitik,"* which had the dominant role in the prewar years. Weltpolitikers espoused an expanded global and imperial role for Germany, a country that had heretofore largely limited itself to continental politics. Because of its growing power and industrialization, Germany supposedly needed to gain territory to acquire the resources it needed to fuel its economic growth. Politically, a new group of leaders hoped to use this ideology to bridge fissures in German society. Specifically, they hoped to build a consensus among different groups that favored economic modernization but opposed political revolution. At the same time, popular pressures from below had resulted in a variety of nationalist pressure groups that also battled for control of the state. These groups, and the tensions among them, pushed in the direction of Weltpolitik.[21]

The second approach, *Mitteleuropa*, was often connected with the concept of lebensraum (living space). In this mind-set, German security deserved and needed an expanded and dominant presence on the European continent—indeed, economic and political hegemony. The social bases of this approach were those groups that saw themselves at the losing end of the rapid modernization or were proponents of German nationalism in the mid-nineteenth century. These included farmers who feared the end of protective agricultural tariffs, nationalists who believed seizing central Europe was necessary for German security and expansion, culturalists and racists who wanted to protect German "civilization," and businessmen who saw profits in a greater German territory. Mitteleuropa thinking aimed to preserve the interests (particularly agrarian interests) and culture of its supporters, without threatening the ongoing modernization.[22] Such groups built on the expansionary ethos that emerged from Germany's nation building earlier in the nineteenth century. In the pre–World War I era, Mitteleuropa was mainly an economic concept that involved German domination of a continental "free trade era."[23] In the Wilhelmian era such German political and economic expansion was considered necessary for the nation's "late" development and as a base for Weltpolitik.[24]

There are differences between these two strands, but there are also key similarities. Both Weltpolitik and Mitteleuropa shared a broader conception of how to provide for German well-being. They both saw geographical expansion as central to security, favored the aggregation of national power as an end in itself, and favored use of military means to achieve security.

Each strand also drew on the social Darwinist view of national evolution popular at the time that viewed national competition through the lens of the "survival of the fittest." In Germany, social Darwinism spread rapidly.[25] For a country on the rise in economic strength and political development, the "survival of the fittest" had broad appeal. Especially from the 1890s on, notions of conflict among nations weeding out the weak were widespread. Ideas about more land or space being central to the struggle for survival took root easily in Germany's emerging imperialist age, and these arguments were picked up by a variety of leaders including Chancellor Bernhard von Bülow, Kurt Riezler (private secretary for Chancellor Bethmann Hollweg), Admiral Alfred von Tirpitz, and Kaiser Wilhelm II.[26]

An important tension between Weltpolitik and Mitteleuropa was that Mitteleuropa favored continental expansion while Weltpolitik looked to an increased role for Germany in the world at large. Although Germany preferred continental expansion, its opportunity to pursue that option was arguably more limited. World War I itself was part of an effort to overcome those limits. From the beginning of the conflict, German war aims primarily concerned the Continent, not the colonies, in part because of the strategic circumstances Germany faced during the war. Blocked by British naval power, Germany turned to continental dominance as its best option.

The views of historians living in the Wilhelmian era speak to this mindset.[27] In Germany, the attitudes of historians, who have often served as the arbiters of cultural socialization, are revealing. Among these scholars (for example, Ernst Troeltsch, Friedrich Meinecke, and Friedrich Naumann), regardless of their political orientation, there was a dominant view of the role of the German state and its international purposes. They portrayed the development of state power and independence as desirable so that German society could develop according to its own innate tendencies, without interference.[28] This notion of a unique and besieged national trajectory encouraged a zero-sum realpolitik view that emphasized the importance of a powerful state to safeguard the nation's autonomy.[29] In later years this outlook would become especially radicalized such that the "national interest" demanded increasing German power as a priority over all other issues.[30] In the fall of 1914 Friedrich Thimme wrote in a letter, "We historians now wish to be the prophets of the new Germany. . . . If one cannot serve the fatherland with the sword, then at least it should be done with the pen."[31]

The dominance of armed expansion thinking should not suggest that it was the only foreign policy approach considered in Germany. Although meager compared to modern equivalents, there was a peace movement in Germany before World War I that rejected war and favored a liberal internationalist approach to security. This view, however, found little welcome among the larger public. In almost a mirror opposite to German student attitudes in the post–World War II period, when the British internationalist and pacifist scholar Norman Angell came to deliver a lecture at Göttingen University in 1913, students staged a mass protest *against* him. At his lecture in Berlin, a riot broke out.[32] To be sure there was no significant European integration movement in any country at the time. But the marginalization of internationalist views was more pronounced in Germany than in countries such as France, England, and the United States. This difference,

Roger Chickering argues, was rooted in a domestic political system resistant to reform and attached to the perception of conflict in international relations. Even German liberals and the German peace movement accepted the German state's dominant role and its quest for preeminence in Europe. At the onset of World War I the movement quickly endorsed Germany's policy.[33]

After 1918

The question of continuity—or change—in German foreign policy ideas after World War I has received extensive attention in the historical literature.[34] The heat of the exchange would suggest little consensus on the issue. Weimar political culture was described as fractured—a society of parochial interest groups battling like crows over a roadkill carcass.[35] A step back from the details of this debate, however, affords a glimpse of a dominant German approach to international society in this period—not necessarily one that all groups shared, but one they nonetheless had to confront. This is apparent both in historical analyses and in the way that different groups in the Weimar Republic believed they had to "sell" their policies to the German people.

In the early days after World War I, a shift in Germany's foreign policy concepts toward international society seemed possible. Some nascent forms of such thinking did exist in the Weimar era. The most important was the view offered by leaders of the new republic between November 1918 and the announcement of the treaty terms in May 1919. President Friedrich Ebert, Chancellor Phillip Scheidemann, and the foreign minister, Count Ulrich von Brockdorff-Rantzau, decried militarism and chauvinism and promised a new German role as a normal democratic nation in the community of nations.[36] A second grouping involved pacifists and liberal internationalists who favored a greater reliance on international institutions including the League of Nations.[37] Another approach that never gained widespread support was the "socialist internationalism" of the Communists and the left wing of the socialist movement, the Independent Social Democratic Party of Germany (USPD). This view favored a transnational class alliance to help reform and/or overthrow capitalism. Finally, there were those, including some industrialists and businessmen, who saw cooperation within Europe as desirable. This was especially true of sectors such as the chemical and electrical industries that were internationally competitive and favored exports.[38] In addition, there were some efforts to revive the relatively high level of economic collaboration among the German, French, and Belgian iron and steel companies before 1914. Some leaders in Germany did warn that unless the prewar international economy was renewed, Germany would in the long run be worse off.[39] Within two years of Germany's defeat and the signing of the armistice in 1918, however, the resurgence of an armed expansion approach in international relations had begun.

Germany's goals and its general approach to international relations were relatively consistent in the interwar period in key respects. Germany, Wolfram Wette suggests, had two paths available after World War I: it could pursue a policy of international understanding or it could attempt a policy of military strength.[40] Although tactics varied, the strategic path Germany favored after Versailles was the second one. As a goal, Germany envisioned a quick return to leading great power status, including hegemony in central Europe. The means of reaching that goal would ultimately rest on the renewal and use of military power in the service of territorial expansion.[41] When Germany pursued an integrationist path—for example, agreeing to the Pact of Locarno of 1925, which demilitarized the Rhineland and specified Germany's borders—such efforts were almost always seen as temporary expedients needed to gain room for international maneuvering. Leaders considered them necessary due to the tight (though relatively transitory) constraints imposed by other countries on Germany—constraints, which, when lifted, would allow Germany to renew its armed expansion approach.

Sharply divergent depictions of the nature of Germany's foreign policy during the Weimar period often center on one individual: Gustav Stresemann, the chancellor for a "hundred days" in the autumn of 1923 and then the foreign minister until his death in 1929. Some see Stresemann as a true forefather of European integration, a leader who understood that Germany's best hope lay in the peaceful acceptance of, and accommodation to, the contours of the interwar system in the 1920s, especially concerning cooperation with France. Others, however, consider him Hitler with a handshake—intent on restoring Germany's power position as a base for further power projection but, due to Germany's postwar weakness, doing it under the guise of reconciliation. Focusing only on Stresemann's individual inclinations, however, misses the broader picture. More important for understanding Germany in the 1920s is the milieu, both international and domestic, within which Stresemann operated.[42]

Internationally, Stresemann was forced to accept the material possibilities of Germany's weakened position after the war. Despite popular desires and demands, the Reich could not simply reassert its great power status and territorial desires. It had just lost a bloody conflict, was partially occupied, and did not have the resources to prevent the Allied powers from physically intervening. To make any progress on the international front, Germany had to accommodate the demands of the Allies for fulfillment of some aspects of Versailles.[43] Stresemann stood out as being more realistic than some of his compatriots.[44] He recognized that Germany had to rebuild itself economically before it renewed its military course.[45] As he would point out to his critics, "Our achievements in the field of politics, and especially in the sphere of foreign policy has hitherto fore been severely circum-scribed and is likely for some time to remain so. We are finding out how hard it is for a defenseless nation to carry on a foreign policy." It was not the case that he could not imagine using force or objected to it. It was that "forcible means must be excluded, as we have no means of putting them into practice."[46]

Politically, Stresemann was also constrained. He confronted an invisible fence in the domestic consensus that saw Germany's future role in interna-tional relations as different than that mandated by the Versailles treaty. Stre-semann is frequently described as pandering to the Right. That he did so may tell us more about Germany than about Stresemann. He was, after all, simply wielding one of the few successful tools he could use to maintain his domestic authority—the championing of a popular nationalism counter-poised against any form of international accommodation to the Versailles order.

Stresemann's integrationist efforts had to be sold at home in terms of the prevailing constraints of the revisionist orthodoxy that promoted restora-tion of the German military and the expansion of Germany's borders in the east.[47] When Stresemann explained the 1924 Dawes plan to provincial lead-ers he argued that once Germany had restored its economic power it could regain its political influence and "power of the sword," which he acknowl-edged was the decisive element in international relations. Stresemann may have used different words, but his ideas do not seem far removed from those attributed to Hans von Seeckt, the head of the German army limited by the Versailles treaty, "First we'll get strong, then we'll take back what we lost."[48] Regarding one of the keystones of Germany's interwar cooperation, the 1925 Pact of Locarno, Stresemann belittled its restraints on Germany (vis-à-vis Poland) in front of a domestic audience and suggested there would always be a way to start a war without appearing to be the initia-tor.[49] In a 1925 article Stresemann favored revision of the eastern border, re-capturing colonies, and German-Austrian unification (but doing so, he ar-gued, required cooperation with the other powers). Still the goal was to reacquire military power and territory. Stresemann knew about the secret rearmament of the Reichswehr that violated Versailles, but he did not, per-haps could not, oppose it.[50]

When Germany joined the League of Nations, its leaders, including Stre-semann, did not see such an action as a new approach to international af-fairs but simply as a means of achieving the revision of Versailles and the restoration of German power, even an Anschluss with Austria.[51] Strese-mann belittled many of his own integrationist diplomatic accomplishments such as Locarno and joining the League of Nations.[52] Yet whether or not Stresemann ultimately was a true advocate of international understanding should not distract us from the more important influence of his context. Ul-timately, his policies and their public justification had to conform to a set of ideas that represented more continuity than discontinuity with the armed expansion mind-set. Stresemann was fairly typical in his belief after World War I that Germany deserved a bigger and better place in international relations, that Germany did not cause World War I, that Germany was robbed at Versailles, that the treaty must be revised by any means possible, and that Germany should regain its greatness including adding territories in the east (e.g., Poland) and those with significant numbers of Germans (e.g., Czechoslovakia).[53]

After World War I, free traders, Europeanists, and multilateralists did exist in Germany. One might make the case that key leaders such as Stresemann—a "pragmatic republican" (*Vernunftrepublikaner*)—might have joined such a movement depending on circumstances. But the climate of opinion in interwar Germany quickly formed against such a development, even while German weakness and the uncompromising victors temporarily restrained the impulse toward militarism. Even the Social Democratic Party, historically a critic of the government, had been integrated into the mainstream polity during the war when it accepted a role in the government, and then peace without victory. In the interwar period it advocated peace ("socialism equals peace") but had relatively little influence on foreign policy, instead focusing on domestic and social policy. In general, those groups favoring integration and peaceful means of international interaction "had little influence on Reich policy, the republican parties, or the general public."[54] When the Great Depression hit, support for Weimar's parliamentary system waned, as did advocacy for "international understanding."[55] In such circumstances—where international constraints loosened and hard-line domestic demands increased—it is not difficult to imagine the pragmatic Stresemann, had he lived and remained in power, traveling the same path to Hitler that the Heinrich Brüning, Franz von Papen, and Kurt von Schleicher governments followed.

Once again, the views of historians writing during the Weimar period serve as a good bellwether of a broader dynamic. Scholars in the wake of World War I continued to propagate "national myths" such as the necessity of the power state, the primacy of foreign policy, and the notion of Mitteleuropa. There were those who highlighted power and national expansion—Georg von Below, Dietrich Schäfer, Ernst Marcks, and Max Lenz. Other scholars, such as Meinecke, Troeltsch, and Hans Delbrück, resisted some of the stronger themes of the ultranationalists during World War I and supported the Weimar Republic as a practical matter, but nonetheless they did not challenge the German foreign policy tradition. The rare scholars, such as Eckart Kehr, who defied the assumptions of most German historiography on the state and especially foreign policy were marginalized.[56] The deep-seated conceptions of foreign policy both shaped and reflected an enduring consensus that would play an important role in the Weimar Republic and its Nazi successor.

Before 1939 and After

Germany's notions about the appropriate way to approach foreign policy in the years before World War II are difficult to separate from the influence and leadership of Adolph Hitler. Hitler did not come to power based simply on his foreign policy—he was popular in the early 1930s because he promised some response (however ill-defined) to the harsh conditions of the Depression and a broader promise of national renewal (which was of course related to foreign affairs). His extreme foreign policy program was only possible, however, because of the nature of mainstream thinking.

Hitler spoke publicly before being elected about expanding the military and then leading those forces to expand Germany.[57] Immediately after forming his government in 1933 he met in secret with the Reichswehr's leadership and announced his plan for rearmament and the conquest of new living space in the east.[58] The starting point for Hitler's expansionist plans was the touchstone of the interwar German foreign policy mentality: the reversal of the Versailles treaty. To make his case, he emphasized Germany's "defeat by domestic opponents" in World War I and the injustice of the Versailles treaty.[59] More broadly he promoted what Gerhard Weinberg calls the doctrines of "race and space." In terms of race, Hitler viewed international relations as a struggle for survival and dominance among different racial groups in which civilizations with the purest races would dominate. Jews, in this view, were an inferior race and were largely to blame for Germany's defeat in World War I. Hitler also believed Slavs were inferior. His emphasis on space reflected the traditional orientation that favored territorial expansion: Germany needed land in order to feed its people in a perceived ongoing struggle for survival among nations and races.[60] This worldview allowed little room for anything more than temporary treaties and specifically eschewed multilateralism, which would limit the flexibility seen as needed to implement Germany's aggressive plans.[61]

Hitler's views, while in some respects extreme and idiosyncratic, also reflected a broader collectively shared notion of appropriate foreign policy.[62] Most Germans probably did not know Hitler's specific plans but "a majority of the population . . . was ripe for a degree of militarization of the social fabric . . . [including] eventual acceptance of the use of methods of force in foreign affairs."[63] Perhaps most Germans did not share his extreme anti-Semitism and racism, even if such prejudices were common, nor did they envision the scale of hegemony that Hitler sought. But a general belief in the desirability of German territorial expansion, of a dominant place in Europe, the need for military means, and the inevitability, if not desirability, of war did exist. As a recent massive volume on Germany's behavior leading to World War II concludes in its final sentence, "These policies were not only based on Hitler's *Lebensraum* ideology, but were also an expression of the claims to power and influence that groups of major importance in Germany had been advancing without interruption since the turn of the century."[64]

In the years after Hitler was appointed chancellor, a particular theme in Germany's outward approach to the world was the image of the Reich as a peaceful nation. Indeed peace—even if it contradicted the desire for international revision and German expansion—was a consistent element of Hitler's speeches.[65] Hitler mainly emphasized peace to avoid arousing a foreign reaction or preventive war before German had rearmed.[66] In effect, this tactic was a continuation of Stresemann's thinking, with a more specific and far-reaching plan for armed revision behind it. Hitler bluntly told some four hundred journalists and editors in the fall of 1938: "Circumstances caused me [up to now] to speak almost exclusively of peace. Only by constantly emphasizing the German Volk's desire for peace and peaceful intentions was I able to gain the German Volk's freedom step by step and thus to give it the armament necessary as a prerequisite for accomplishing the next step."[67]

Hitler's peace rhetoric was not taken at face value either domestically or abroad. Both Germans and foreign leaders distinguished between dominant ideas and cheap talk by comparing rhetoric to the overall discourse, mood, and actual policies. Within Germany, Hitler had made his plans for armed expansion clear to audiences across the country.[68] Once in power Hitler followed through with brutal efforts to consolidate power as well as to remilitarize. Likewise, other countries recognized the disjuncture between Hitler's peace themes and his revisionist military actions, which were rightly recognized as popular domestically. "The sight and sound of marching in Germany" caused the former Allies of World War I significant concern.[69] Neither foreigners nor many Germans appreciated just how aggressive Nazi foreign policy would be, and other countries (e.g., Britain and the United States) had sympathy with some German complaints about Versailles. What is clear, however, is that Hitler built on broad-based desires for "rearmament and revision of Versailles." Especially with the early successes of his bold foreign policy moves, many Germans saw how the threat or use of force would serve concrete interests in gaining territory and resources around German borders. Thus, while war may not have been popular, the dominance of armed expansion thinking made it relatively easy to revive as an option, especially given the military build up it nurtured.

This description of the German foreign policy orthodoxy before World War II provides a sharp contrast with what came later. To turn our attention to the postwar Federal Republic of Germany (hereafter FRG, "West Germany," or "Germany") is to cross not only six years but also a fundamental transition in global politics.[70] The new German foreign policy consensus took shape from 1945 to 1955, during the early years of the cold war. During that time, Germany's foreign policy was officially under the control of the

Allied High Command, and from 1945 to 1949 Germany did not have a government. From 1949 to 1955, the Allies oversaw Germany foreign policy. Still, the Allies could not directly control German thinking on foreign policy, only constrain its implementation. The record of the development of the FRG's foreign policy thinking reveals a stark shift from the ideas of even the interwar period.

German views changed in three fundamental respects.[71] First, they rejected great power status as an end in itself, and the Machtstaat concept lost appeal. Germans did still look to the state as the pinnacle of legitimate authority.[72] And Germans did want political recovery in the sense of not being a stigmatized or colonized political entity. But the notion that the power-seeking state served German well-being was no longer prominent. Konrad Adenauer, unlike Stresemann, did not seek a return to being an autonomous great power. The country turned its attention elsewhere. Germans sought success not in great power politics but in gross national product.[73]

Second, there was a major shift in the "master narrative" of German history based on nationalism. In particular, Germany no longer associated a sense of self with a tradition of "unifying" militarism.[74] The meaning of war and its import for Germany's view of itself had altered. The "fallen soldier" image, in which the sacrifice of German youth embodied the ultimate achievement and duty, was rejected as a symbol of national good. Nor did the military retain the high social status it had enjoyed earlier.[75] For a nation weaned on state-building by the sword, the low support for rearmament in the postwar era (despite the threat from the east) reflected the shift in ideas.[76]

The third major change, linked to the other two, was a belief that integration in a united Europe best served German security. Hence there was a basic reorganization from an image of national community to one of international community, specifically institutionalized internationalism in Europe and beyond.[77] Germany believed that cooperating with, rather than confronting, France and Britain served its security. This position was embedded in the country's basic text of postwar identity, the constitution. Article 24 of Germany's Basic Law of 1949 reads:

(1) The Federation may, by legislation, transfer sovereign powers to international institutions. (2) For the maintenance of peace, the Federation may join a system of mutual collective security; in doing so it will consent to such limitations upon its sovereign powers as will bring about and secure a peaceful and lasting order in Europe and among the nations of the world. (3) For the settlement of disputes between nations, the federation will accede to agreements concerning a general, comprehensive and obligatory system of international arbitration.[78]

This shift was not immediately apparent and was initially resisted by some groups on particular issues. For example, the Ruhr industrialists resisted restructuring plans related to coal and steel integration, and the opposition SPD leader, Kurt Schumacher, favored reuniting Germany before integration with Western Europe.[79] Historians, even those conservative ones who remained true to the national traditions in other respects—for example, Gerhard Ritter—moved from a German to a European perspective in their arguments. Yet in the decade after the war, as the Bundesrepublik took shape, integration became the dominant orthodoxy.

In the world of scholars, "the break with political and historiographical traditions was much deeper and more real after 1945 than it had been after 1918."[80] But this change took longer than suggested by the "Stunde Null" (zero hour) image of a country returned to its original state by defeat. Despite the shock of 1945 there was an enduring conservatism in Germany regarding historiography and especially the nationalist component of German history. Many scholars in positions of power and influence—such as Gerhard Ritter, Hans Rothfels, Hans Herzfeld, and Friedrich Meinecke—continued to defend the German national tradition and excuse Nazism as an anomaly. Their dominance of the field would not be broken until the late 1950s and the 1960s, when the new generation of historians began to have an influence—as became full blown in the Fischer controversy of the early 1960s when historian Fritz Fischer documented Germany's responsibility for World War I. That said, the early signs of such change were apparent in the first decade after the war. This included the emergence of scholars who explicitly criticized the nationalist tradition—for example, Ludwig Dehio, Karl Dietrich Bracher, Theodor Eschenburg, and Walter Hofer—and with the establishment of new revisionist historical institutes (e.g., the Institute of European History at the University of Mainz) and greater contact with other national viewpoints—especially that of American academics.[81]

Any detailed work on the response of individual Germans to the country's "zero hour" will reveal that there was no uniform reaction. Different individuals remember the wartime defeat differently. And initially there was no clear direction in the rubble of a devastated and divided country. Collective meaning, however, is different than the heterogeneous views of individuals or political parties. At that collective level, there was a fundamental uniform shift in terms of images of the state, the centrality of militarism to national identity, and the desirability of international integration versus autonomy. Despite different interpretations of its defeat, virtually all Germans after World War II rejected right-wing efforts at denial of German responsibility for the war.[82] The Federal Republic's integrationist orthodoxy was most fully realized in 1963 when the SPD, always in the non-Communist camp but more neutralist after the war, became the champion of NATO.[83]

How, then, in the face of significant military defeat in World War I, can the pattern of basic ideational continuity be explained? Likewise, how can we also account for conceptual transformation after World War II?

FIRE FROM THE EMBERS AFTER WORLD WAR I

The puzzle of German continuity in foreign policy ideas is usefully viewed in terms of collapse and consolidation. The interplay of ideas and events in World War I suggested a situation ripe for collapse: the loss contradicted expectations generated by armed expansion thinking. Yet ideational transformation also requires the consolidation of some new orthodoxy. In this case, consolidation around the new ideas offered by the young Weimar regime did not occur. The Versailles treaty and the lack of support from the Allies helped reverse a potential shift toward integrationist thinking in Germany. As captured in the B2 "Counterrevolution" scenario, this failure allowed supporters of a discredited orthodoxy to gain new life much as fire might reignite from dying embers. In this case the embers of the old view were still hot due to the particular circumstances of Germany's entry into the war and its subsequent defeat.

Defeat and Nominal Collapse

Germany's defeat in World War I was a disappointing loss that largely defied expectations about Germany's foreign policy. Clearly, the surrender and armistice in November 1918 was a sharp and unexpected rebuke to expectations of Germans regarding the fruits of the war. After all, as late as the spring of 1918, Germany had announced the beginning of its "final offensive." True, U.S. entry into the war in late 1917 was a worrying development in terms of German war prospects, and for most involved there were indicators that Germany was at the limits of both its military and societal ability to endure the burdens of the conflict.[84] But there were also encouraging signs. German troops in 1918 were fighting on foreign soil, they had defeated Russia, and there were few outward signs of imminent collapse. The events of fall 1918 were an unwelcome surprise.[85] Not only did the army suddenly succumb but the regime itself was capsized. Initiated by a naval revolt at Kiel (by sailors who did not want to pursue a doomed effort to take on the Royal Navy as the war ended), an insurrection spread throughout Germany, forcing the kaiser to abdicate. The Wilhelmian Reich was overthrown and the Weimar Republic began.

These circumstances favored a delegitimation of armed expansion thinking as predicted by the A4 "Do something!" scenario. Germany had pursued a set of ideas, and the result was defeat. This clear contradiction, however, was somewhat muddied by the massive effort Germany's leaders made at home and abroad during and after the war to depict the war as a "defensive" effort. Germany had not started the conflict, its leaders claimed, but was merely responding to the events unleashed by the assassination of the Archduke Franz Ferdinand and the Russian mobilization. In a series of brief speeches, the kaiser explained the meaning of the events to the riled German populace and legislators in the days following the assassination. Germany, he argued, had wanted peace but was being attacked by envious hostile forces that wanted to thwart its development. The kaiser denied offensive aims ("no lust of conquest drives us") and asserted that Germany had tried to avoid conflict but now had to face a "defensive" war: "They are forcing the sword into my hand."[86]

Although these claims were misleading (Germany played a major role in the spread of the conflict), few at the time were aware of this or willing to challenge such an assertion.[87] Instead, leaders from across the political spectrum rallied to the nationalist flag in what became a truce (*Burgfrieden*) among the previously feuding German political parties, all for the sake of national unity during the war.[88] Even the Social Democratic Party, previously the strongest opponent of German militarism and armed expansion, threw its support behind the war.[89] As the war continued, German war aims grew, but the initial defensive justification for the conflict (heavily propagandized by the government) was always maintained, and territorial expansion was justified the same way.[90]

Despite these efforts at spin, a collapse still occurred after World War I with the abdication and flight of Kaiser Wilhelm, the replacement of the Kaiserreich with the Weimar Republic, and the engagement of the new leaders of the republic with the Versailles project. But the puzzle is that potential new German thinking on foreign policy quickly gave way to old ideas. A variety of notions, including the "stab in the back" and "war guilt" myths, gained ascendancy, reviving German militarism and the privileged position of the armed expansion view of international relations. Why this occurred involved processes more closely linked with consolidation.

A Return to the Old

New ideas typically need some confirmation for their prospects if they are to be institutionalized as a dominant orthodoxy. This was especially true in the case of interwar Germany, where the collapse of the old ideas was muddied by German mythmaking. Those advocates of integration in 1918–1919 saw their short-lived aspirations undermined by a cutting rebuke to their whole program. They had promised that reconciliation via the peace treaty process would ensure Germany's welfare. Yet the terms of the Treaty of Versailles denied such hopes. The resulting frustration gave life to a series of myths that boosted the revival of the old thinking.

Any explanation of continuity in German foreign policy ideas into the Weimar period has to have at its core the conclusion of the Versailles treaty in 1919—what Hans-Joachim Koch called the "German Trauma."[91] The trauma resulted from the disjuncture between German expectations for the treaty and its actual provisions. Weimar's early foreign policy leaders, especially Count Brockdorff–Rantzau and President Friedrich Ebert, specifically articulated their understanding that the armistice (and hence the creation of the new republic) was directly related to the conditions embodied in Wilson's Fourteen Points. Wilson's program held out the possibility of an honorable peace—one in which Germany would retain its position as a great power by becoming a democracy. After Germany's adoption of the Weimar constitution, the actual terms of the peace treaty were announced, dashing such hopes. The new republic was saddled with an immense financial burden, blamed for a war that most Germans could not or would not begin to understand as their responsibility, subjected to a variety of annoying and intrusive demands, excluded from world trade, and not admitted into the League of Nations. The result was bitter disappointment.[92] Representatives from across Germany's political spectrum took part in the peace conference process and they all supported Brockdorff-Rantzau's frosty rejection of the terms of the Versailles treaty.[93]

In one fell swoop an otherwise divergent set of domestic interests became united around a single priority—revision of the Versailles treaty. The treaty became the "unifying bracket that clamped German politics together"[94]—particularly given the continuing nationalist and imperialist expectations many groups retained after 1918.[95] As Peter Gay notes, the reaction was a societal one, not just limited to particular interest groups: "Millions who had no stake in the lost colonies or the lost territories, who were untouched by the enforced disarmament, responded warmly to the demagogues who denounced Versailles."[96] Even the president of the German Peace Society, Ludwig Quidde, declared the treaty incompatible with the ideal for which he had worked.[97] The situation was a B2 "Counterrevolution" scenario as described in chapter 2 where a potential alternative orthodoxy floundered on its own unexpected failures, giving new life to traditional ideas.

The Versailles setback undermined the nascent integrationist sentiment. Those who supported an accommodation to the Wilsonian vision of the Fourteen Points were marginalized politically or changed their ideas.[98] President Ebert pointed to the classic "told you so" rhetoric of conservatives expected in such a situation when he commented that he "could not blame the Pan-Germans for the 'immodest haste with which they are digging up their former speeches and editorials in which the Social Democrats and other Liberals are ridiculed for their belief in President Wilson's program.' "[99] The more integrationist factions of the German political spectrum were put on the defensive by the weight of opinion that rejected the blow Versailles entailed for postwar hopes. The "direct result" was the Reichstag election of 1920 that significantly reduced the clout of both liberal democrats and the SPD.[100] This tidal shift gave leverage to the parties of the Right—that is, those most inclined toward militarist, expansive actions in the international arena—who became pivotal coalition makers.[101]

That Versailles was a key event in undermining the Weimar Republic and the reorientation of German foreign policy is an argument with a long line-age, most famously going back to Keynes's classic analysis. What has been less appreciated is the way that this worked, pitting the expectations set by early Weimar leaders against their domestic critics, who looked to renew the old. Germany's expansion-minded thinking did not simply reappear because Versailles proved that Germany was by its very geography sur-rounded by hostile powers. Had the early Weimar integrationist ideas tri-umphed, France would have been more secure and less aggressive in its own security efforts. Ironically, France's harsh demands at Versailles con-tributed to the German outlook the French least desired.

The strangling of a new German foreign policy outlook at Versailles links directly to the spread of two myths central to the revival of armed expan-sion thinking. The first was the "stab in the back" argument about the end of the war, the second the "war guilt" account of the conflict's origins. These myths, which sustained the old orthodoxy, did not thrive by coinci-dence. They flourished because Versailles discredited integrationist ideas. The stab-in-the-back account, for example, took wing among the broader populace in response to the "dishonorable conditions" of Versailles.[102] Each of these myths deserves brief discussion.

The stab-in-the-back myth arose out of the circumstances of Germany's military defeat. This legend held that Germany was in a position to win militarily but that it was undermined domestically by social (and other) democrats, Marxists, and Jews who wanted to strengthen their own domes-tic political position.[103] In reality, the German army was disintegrating in the field, with high desertion rates, a widespread refusal to fight, and plum-meting morale. It was the military's leaders, Paul von Hindenburg and Erich Ludendorff, not the politicians, who initially pushed for the arm-istice.[104]

The myth had some superficial plausibility for several reasons. First, some of the details of the surrender seemed to fit. Germany was never pushed on to its own territory, and its esteemed forces were still fighting.[105] Second, the military's desire for the armistice was purposely kept quiet so as not to harm Germany's prospects in negotiations. If the Allies knew the German military believed the situation was dire, then Germany's bargain-ing position would have been weakened. When Germany surrendered, mil-itary officials demurred from carrying out the task, because they did not want to saddle their postwar armed forces with responsibility for the de-feat. The government's civilian leaders signed the armistice, thus cement-ing their own tie to surrender, while distancing the military from its role.[106] Finally, when the soldiers returned to Germany they were welcomed as heroes "undefeated on the battlefield," even by leaders of the new republic, including (socialist) President Ebert.[107] No politician could afford to offend the soldiers—living symbols of German nationalism—in the newly competitive domestic political arena.

A specific example of interwar imagery linked to the revival of traditional ideas involves the "Langemarck" incident, which featured a battle in World War I where young German soldiers facing experienced troops supposedly fought bravely in a hopeless situation, even singing a nationalist anthem as they met their death. The story became a symbol of German pride and unity. As one author writes: "The Langemarck myth was the first significant example in this war of the successful attempt to reinterpret a *military defeat* as a *moral victory*."[108] Nationalist proponents celebrated Langemarck Day annually during the interwar period, and Langemarck became the embodiment of selfless patriotism that purportedly exemplified Germans. More broadly, it served to obfuscate the carnage of World War I by emphasizing the nobility of sacrifice—even in republican Weimar. In the interwar period, the official government guide to war memorials stated that the "fallen" German soldiers of World War I would return to spur the "living to resurrect the fatherland."[109]

The second myth involved German war guilt. Germans rejected responsibility for starting the war. Although this attitude might be attributed to a reaction to Allied charges of Germany's responsibility for the war (Article 231 of the Treaty of Versailles) there appears to have been a more direct source. Officials ran a cover-up from as early as 1914, with a more focused effort during 1918 and 1919, to manage documents and public relations so as to divert any blame from Germany. The German foreign ministry coordinated this campaign, but it reached into all segments of society, including schools, churches, and universities, and to writers and scholars. The most likely critics of the idea, the socialists, had supported the war effort—accepting the notion that they were protecting the nation against invaders—in the hope that proving their patriotism would lead to reforms after the conflict.[110] When the war did end, the SPD, specifically the new president, Friedrich Ebert, needed the military to maintain order.[111] To challenge the war guilt thesis would have threatened that alliance and perhaps any hope of a governing consensus. Instead of accepting German responsibility, the socialists favored a somewhat vague statement that capitalism and its protectors were to blame for the war.[112]

During the war such "patriotic self-censorship" of course involved elite manipulation, but it required a background of popular acceptance. The phenomenon was not just one of domestic propaganda (however important that was) but was also concerned with issues of instrumental external strategy and collective culpability.[113] Instrumentally, Germans had reasons to deny responsibility for the war, because such an admission might be linked to the size of the reparations payments. Weimar's first government also hoped for equal treatment as a democracy. The foreign office led by Count Brockdorff-Rantzau feared that admitting war guilt would jeopardize its standing vis-à-vis the Fourteen Points and expand the penalties of the peace settlement.[114]

Later officials were apparently also captured by the denial. One example comes from an effort by Weimar officials to bolster the appeal of the republic by developing and drawing on national symbols. Toward that end, a memorial service to honor Germans who died in war was held in 1924. At the service President Ebert voiced common sentiment, perhaps to spur domestic unity, by declaring that Germany had only gone to war in self-defense.[115] A second example involves Stresemann, who favored suppressing the truth in 1927 so as not to complicate his successful diplomacy after the Locarno treaty by the revelations.[116] In each case, short-term efforts to further political or national advantage led to the longer-term sustenance of an armed expansion approach. In some respects these actions were not just reacting to but helping to shape the international situation that Germany faced. For example, part of the hesitancy of the United States to assist Germany was a consequence of the German refusal to admit responsibility for the war.[117]

Every Weimar government blocked the disclosure of the empire's role in the outbreak of the war. Historians have extensively documented the widespread cover-up of the issue of guilt.[118] This scheme certainly testifies to the power of elite manipulation. But its success can be attributed as much to a receptive society as to the skill of the messengers. Few stepped forward to question the war myths—doing so would have had little effect under the circumstances.[119]

Together, the stab-in-the-back and war-guilt myths were important because they favored the continuity of armed expansion thinking. Their proponents claimed that Germany had not started the war and therefore its prevailing ideas could not be blamed for the results. Moreover, the disappointing outcome did not contain lessons because it resulted from a failure of implementation, not from the inadequacy of the substance of the ideas. These myths by no means erased the facts of defeat, but they provided a veneer of legitimacy for the old orthodoxy that otherwise would not have existed.

The Versailles treaty debacle was followed by a series of other incidents, almost all of which reinforced revanchism. For example, the monstrous inflation of 1923 and the economic turmoil of the postwar period in general were (misleadingly) linked by nationalists, and even some liberals, to the reparations payments of the treaty. The loss of Upper Silesia via League of Nations arbitration put adherents of the League in an awkward position and undermined the Joseph Wirth chancellorship. When the French occupied the Ruhr in January 1923, the "failure of the old liberal center" was complete.[120] And, of course, the Great Depression fostered the more extreme version of the German orthodoxy represented by Hitler.[121]

The struggle over new foreign policy ideas in Germany, unlike in the United States, was significantly shaped by other countries. Britain, France, and especially the United States played important roles. This is most evident in the fallout in Germany from America's disinclination to become "entangled" in Europe. That disinclination encouraged French insecurity and reinforced the voices of armed expansion in Germany. Peter Krüger argues that the initial American plan for a new international order and democratic reform in Germany was a threat to those who favored the traditional orthodoxy—especially conservatives. Thus the reaction from the Right was to make Wilson, not the old ideas, the scapegoat.[122] But the fate of such efforts depended in part on the policy of the Allies, including the United States. German postwar planning in 1918 was premised on an active U.S. role and the implementation of Wilsonian ideas.[123] When the peace terms appeared as a stark violation of that expectation, and when the United States withdrew from any brokering role (or security guarantee), Germany necessarily was cast back on its own devices in dealing with France's insistence on retribution, reparations, and security.[124]

When the United States did get involved, as it did primarily through private parties such as in the Dawes and Young financial plans, the results did affect domestic politics.[125] In most cases, however, America's actions were too little, too late. To affect the nascent German debate, the United States would have had to support the arguments of the integrationists by providing proof of the benefits of their approach from the outset. For example, had the United States been able to shape a more benevolent treaty in response to Germany's political reforms, had it more generously responded to Germany's economic difficulties, or had it calmed the French-German insecurity spiral through active involvement, the hand of Germany's integrationists would have been strengthened.

In the absence of such involvement, the underlying expansionist-nationalist sentiment limited the possibilities of the alternatives. It is no coincidence that both U.S. and German progressives were crushed in the 1920 elections—their fates, after all, were linked.[126] In Germany, opponents who might have voiced and led a new approach to foreign policy were effectively contained and/or co-opted by the armed expansion orthodoxy and its nationalist bedrock.[127]

The Great Depression had the effect of sharply enhancing preexisting biases. It dealt a decisive blow to the fragile Weimar democracy, discredited those liberal economic views that favored integration, and further enhanced the voices of those who argued the need for a self-sustaining German-dominated sphere in Europe.[128] The political-military orientation toward expansion already existed. When international markets closed down any offsetting economic integrative tendencies withered. Hitler's virulent form of expansion was the result.

Before World War II and Afterward

In the 1930s, German expectations that armed expansion would lead to security and prosperity swelled to a caricature in Nazi hands. This vision was violently punctured by the World War II experience. Given expectations, the extreme loss provided conditions suited to the collapse of the old orthodoxy. In contrast to World War I, the rationalizations for the war, and the results generated, left little rhetorical space for the myths that played a role in the continuity of ideas in the 1920s.

Although the circumstances favored a new approach, what that approach would be was a struggle to determine. There was no obvious alternative set of ideas in Germany at the time of its defeat. The Nazis had severely suppressed opposition movements favoring different foreign policy ideas, especially during the war.[129] Still, given the defeat and influence of the Allies, two positions vied for dominance. One was the pro-Western integration favored by Konrad Adenauer, head of the Christian Democratic Union Party and first Chancellor of the FRG (1949–1963). The second favored a neutral middle position between the Soviets and the West. Its leading proponent was Kurt Schumacher, who headed the Social Democratic Party. In the end, Adenauer's vision won out both because of Allied support, fortuitous early economic results, and Adenauer's successful effort to associate Schumacher with the discredited nationalism of Kaiser Wilhelm, Weimar, and Nazi Germany. Germany became a country that envisioned security as inherently tied to international rather than national community—what Peter Katzenstein has called a "semi-sovereign" state.[130] But that situation, certainly encouraged by the Allied occupation and the Soviet threat, was as much an acquired as an imposed preference.

Collapse of Armed Expansion

Given the dictatorial nature of Hitler's regime, it is difficult to separate the collapse of the foreign policy consensus from the collapse of Hitler's popularity, image, and regime. Hitler's main aims were largely connected to foreign policy.[131] In the years from 1937 to 1945, Hitler's fortunes rose and fell at the interface of social expectations and foreign policy results. These produced different combinations over time, but the ultimate destruction of Germany undermined the armed expansion view. Collapse was complete in this instance both because of the heightened expectations from Hitler's ambitions and because the foundational notions of expansive nationalism were unavoidably rebuffed.

Nazi foreign policy was based on the notion that external expansion and armed might were effective means of serving German security. Throughout the late 1930s, German propaganda consistently stressed the notion that

Germans wanted peace but that the country required certain changes in the existing international system. Restoring Germany's military power was a central focus. And, of course, once restored it would be a vehicle for further revisionism: to deal with "encirclement," Germany had to expand.[132] Hitler's apparent success in achieving results in the interwar period—the occupation of the Rhineland in 1936, the annexation of Austria in March 1938, the annexation of the Sudetenland in the Munich agreement of September 1938, and the occupation of the Czech rump and part of Lithuania in March 1939 were all bloodless (despite fears of war), all desired—reinforced his own version of armed expansion.[133]

Hitler actually worried that Germans were too tied to a desire for peace, especially when there was a negative popular reaction to his mobilization of troops related to the Anschluss.[134] Some in the leadership circle were wary of another imminent large-scale conflict—at least in 1938.[135] At that time, Hitler instructed four hundred journalists and media experts to prepare Germans for war and to highlight that force was needed to attain some objectives. In 1938 Hitler justified a series of expansionary efforts as being aimed at uniting German-speaking lands.

His success in using force, as much as any propaganda campaign, worked to stem criticism. For example, the September 1938 Munich agreement—which peacefully incorporated Czechoslovakia's German-populated Sudetenland—helped to undermine military officers who were considering a coup at the time. In a type A3 "If it ain't broke" situation, few Germans paid critical attention when Germany in March 1939 physically occupied the rest of Czechoslovakia, even though it no longer had German-speaking lands (and thus did not fit the previous justification of uniting the German people). As for domestic resistance to Hitler's thinking, "the Munich Conference and the abandonment of Czechoslovakia by the Western Powers administered to the anti-Hitler opposition a blow from which it could not recover."[136]

In the run-up to the German attack on Poland in 1939, Nazi propaganda stressed the need to be prepared militarily for an attack from the west. Moreover, Germany was pictured as facing encirclement. In a gloss from the more persuasive case made before World War I, the Third Reich supposedly wanted peace but had to expand in order to provide for its own security.[137] The quick victory over Poland further reinforced the dominance of Hitler's ideas. In a speech to two hundred senior officers in November 1939, the führer rubbed the noses of potential critics in his results in the Rhineland, German remilitarization, Austria, Czechoslovakia, and now Poland. Moreover, he used the occasion to build support for his next planned offensive in the west, arguing that he had been right before and that armed expansion would be right again.[138] And when France was later defeated there was even less room for opposition. Who could oppose a leader on such a roll? Observed Ian Kershaw, "Opponents of the regime themselves wrote later of the difficulties they faced in this climate of opinion and some even admitted that it was hard to remain aloof from the jubilant mood."[139]

Just as the early success helped to sustain the dominant orthodoxy, so too did the follow-on failures crack its foundations. The defeat of Germany in 1945, the so-called zero hour, signaled the collapse of lebensraum thinking, but Hitler's popularity and the approach to international relations he embodied came into question even before that time. The most critical event was the failure of the campaign against the Soviet Union. Unlike prior offensives, the German public was not prepared at all for Operation Barbarossa, the surprise attack on the Soviet Union in June 1941. Still the effort met early success and promised imminent victory.

That outlook quickly soured. The Soviet Red Army held and counterattacked at the gates of Moscow. Germans were highly dismayed when an emergency call for winter clothing went out in December 1941: they understood this meant the Reichswehr would spend the winter fighting on the eastern front.[140] Propaganda over the next year continued to preach imminent victory but ultimately raised false expectations.

No event was more critical in undermining the credibility of Hitler's strategy than the destruction of the German Sixth Army at Stalingrad and the surrender of ninety thousand German soldiers in the late fall of 1942, after a year and a half of hard fighting. As one analyst of public opinion notes, "Stalingrad was the greatest single blow of the war. Deep shock, dismay and depression were recorded everywhere."[141] The defeat led people to question whether Hitler's foreign policy program was really effective or whether earlier results were due to luck and/or incompetent diplomacy by Germany's opponents. Hans Woller notes that the defeat "opened the eyes of many who had been deceived by the ideology of national community" and by the "cumulative success of quick victories."[142] Stalingrad, on top of the German inability to stem Allied bombing, eroded support for Hitler and his foreign policy ethos.[143]

The way that unexpected and undesirable events feed an opposition is apparent even under Hitler's dictatorship. Stalingrad seems to have triggered a number of the most well-known resistance movements in Nazi Germany. For example, 1943 marked the public emergence of the first significant indicators of opposition to the regime since the earlier secret coup plans of 1938.[144] In Munich, the news of defeat at Stalingrad emboldened the White Rose student movement to its ill-fated public demonstrations.[145]

Why then did the government not use its monopoly on communications and force to suppress the inconvenient truth?[146] Nazi officials tried, but efforts to spin events had very different results than in the interwar period. Nazi propagandists attempted to salvage these defeats by explaining them through the lens of the "fallen soldier" image that was so popular in World

War I and the interwar period. Goebbels drew from the Langemarck myth playbook. His propaganda declared that shortly before the Stalingrad defeat, the German troops listened to one last address by the führer and then sang "the national anthem with raised arms together with us, perhaps for the last time in their lives, . . . what an attitude for German soldiers in this great time. . . . Stalingrad was and is Fate's great call of alarm to the German nation."[147]

Such themes and a variety of other tactics were used in an effort to downplay a significant defeat by emphasizing its heroic aspects through an appeal to nationalist sacrifice. But the gap between expectations and the magnitude of the loss was hard to bridge. Expectations of yet another victory had been repeatedly propagated before the battle, and the massive defeat had a stark effect on the viability of the dominant orthodoxy.[148] Before the end of the war and Germany's actual zero hour, "the majority of Germans had distanced themselves from the adventurism of the Third Reich."[149] Even in a hierarchical dictatorship, then, it is sometimes difficult to suppress an undesired disjuncture between expectations and results, even if it is possible to physically combat it (via the imprisonment and execution of those supporting opposing ideas).[150]

A key element of the collapse of foreign policy ideas in World War II was the physical condition of Germany and the scale of defeat as captured by the terms "zero hour," "super catastrophe," "end beyond all ends," "kaput" that Germans have used to describe it.[151] All the major German cities were smashed by Allied bombing. With Hitler dying in a Berlin bunker as the Red Army advanced from the east and the Allies from the west, the destruction of Germany was almost total. The country was completely occupied by the victorious armies.

As important as the material loss in World War II was the way the chain of events starkly discredited the symbols and prescriptions of the old foreign policy orthodoxy.[152] Although the sheer scale of defeat is a crucial part of the story, by itself it is unsatisfying because it relies on an undefined threshold effect of loss and destruction. Concretely specifying this level a priori, however, is an elusive task. The level of destruction, moreover, will have different effects depending on prior expectations shaped by ideas and related justifications of action. After World War II, there was less room for the type of mythmaking seen after World War I because of the way the extreme destruction contrasted with exaggerated expectations raised by Hitler's wielding of armed expansion thinking. U.S. soldiers painted Hitler's words—"Give me four more years time and you will not recognize Germany"—on the walls of towns they occupied.[153] Amid the devastation, the message was a poignant one. Notions such as expanding territory or the elevation of the military as the protector of the nation were shattered. Hitler's final message to the armed forces on April 29, 1945, from his besieged bunker in Berlin was a command "to win territory for the German people in the East."[154] The collapse of Germany's armed expansion thinking is captured in that utterly hopeless and illusionary appeal to the heart of the old orthodoxy.

Consolidation of Integrationism

Conditions favoring collapse of an existing collective idea does not mean that change has to occur. And if it does, we must still explain what type of change is likely. In the German case, however, the severe contradiction of expectations and results after World War II meant that some difference was likely, and the question soon became which of two forms it would take.[155]

The first was the pro-Western integration represented by Konrad Adenauer. This view asserted that Germany's well-being would be best served by integrating and sublimating German power within a broader Western entity. This approach rejected neutrality between the superpowers, placing integration ahead of reunification. Adenauer was willing to back rearmament (which was increasingly favored by the Western occupying powers to meet the Soviet threat) and the restructuring of the Ruhr industries, despite the unpopularity of those measures, in order to further integration. Such rearmament and restructuring would not be autonomous but within Western international institutions.[156]

Kurt Schumacher, head of the SPD, presented the second alternative view of Germany's foreign policy future. Schumacher too rejected the armed expansion legacy of Kaiser Wilhelm, Weimar Germany, and the Nazis. But he offered a conceptual orientation different from Adenauer's. Schumacher argued that Germany's security would be best served by neutrality between East and West and by an emphasis on reunification. This outlook rejected alignment with either side in the cold war, especially an embedded institutionalized form of cooperation.[157] This position tended to be supported by some proarmament nationalists, who were keen on reunification, and ironically by the peace movement, which opposed any rearmament.

What then decided the outcome of this struggle in favor of the Adenauer formulation? One might posit that it had nothing to do with foreign policy per se but hinged on domestic political positions and party dynamics. External policy, however, was directly related to internal policy and the two are not easily separated. Adenauer's program (and his power) was secured by the results encountered in the postwar era, themselves dependent on the influence of other countries, particularly the United States. Certainly the large postwar U.S. presence in Germany spurred greater involvement than would have been the case otherwise. And, likewise, the large Soviet presence next door gave West Germany incentives to turn westward, given its better treatment by the Western occupying countries. But the key point is that neither the Allied occupation nor the Soviet presence, as important as they were in what followed, determined outcomes. Rather, the result also depended on how ideas and events interacted as seen in the relative fate of the two orientations championed by Adenauer and Schumacher.

Adenauer gained leverage for the integrationist view by the way he positioned it vis-à-vis the lessons of World Wars I and II. Having seen the fate of Matthias Erzberger and Walter Rathenau (both Weimar officials associated with integrationism who were assassinated by nationalist political opponents) and the power of aggressive nationalism after World War I, Adenauer wanted to avoid appearing as simply a pawn of the West or its preferences, even while he favored integration. But he also rejected the nationalist mantle that had been so successful in dominating earlier German debates on foreign policy. The reason for this aversion was an acknowledgment that such a position had been effectively undermined by the Second World War and would also impede Western integration.[158]

Schumacher took a different lesson away from World War I. From his viewpoint, the failure of the Left, especially the SPD, after World War I was due to the fact that it had been overly integrationist, thus losing the support of nationalists. His reaction, therefore, was to champion the position, which favored unification and neutralism. He in no way wanted to revive the previous armed expansion mentality, but he also did not want to be portrayed as anti-German. Adenauer, believing that results of World War II had discredited the old Right and that opposing nationalism would gain him support from the Allied commissioners, was happy to push Schumacher in that direction.[159]

Adenauer's lead role in the postwar government, support from the occupying powers, and his tight control of foreign policy ensured that his preferred positions would at least be tried.[160] In the first couple of years after defeat Germany was not on its own feet, and foreign policy was not the central issue. In those years German suffering was acute and the country needed to recover from massive devastation. What led to the embrace and institutionalization of the integrationist position was its perceived success in relieving bad conditions. As Adenauer began to establish a distinct position on foreign policy, so too did Germany begin to recover. Most observers concur that the major cause of this outcome was the "German miracle"—the FRG's rapid achievement of economic stability and then recovery in the late 1940s and 1950s.[161] Unlike the Weimar Republic, the Federal Republic suffered no catastrophic inflation and recession as in 1923 or the Great Depression of 1929, both of which fed revanchist interests. As one author notes, had the FRG faced hard times or had its expectations been unrealistic (as in Weimar) the Adenauer government (and its foreign policy orientation) might have failed.[162] Foreign policy directly affected Germany's economic fortunes on such issues as reparations, industrial restructuring, foreign investment, and aid to Germany. Economic success, in turn, reflected the viability of its foreign policy ideas.

The German Democratic Republic (GDR or "East Germany") provided a stark comparison to the results in the West. In the East a more definite break with the capitalist, fascist past was made—under the thumb of the Soviet Union. The GDR regime based its legitimacy on a promise that hard work by Germans would eventually result in "living better." Some progress was made, but it was relatively bleak compared to that of the West. For those West Germans who looked East or thought Germany might do better somewhere in between, the East's dismal record helped legitimize the Adenauer vision. In East Germany, the Soviet model always had authority (thanks to the Soviet military presence), but after the 1950s it lacked legitimacy.[163]

This notion is underscored by the links between German foreign policy possibilities and U.S. foreign policy influence. As in the World War I case, Germany's debates did not take place in a domestic vacuum. Instead, external actors, especially the United States, played a critical role in the consolidation of the new German orientation in both an economic and military sense. U.S. leaders took to heart the lessons of the interwar period. The U.S. shift to committed engagement in European politics and its push for a European, not a national, solution "spilled over" transnationally to help move Germany in the same direction.[164]

The United States, unsurprisingly, supported Adenauer's integration leanings over Schumacher's neutrality. The Allies dismantled the Third Reich's foreign policy after the war, recalling all ambassadors and outlawing German autonomy in its external affairs until 1955.[165] The German military had almost completely fallen apart by war's end and was prohibited thereafter. The Occupation Statute signed in 1949 made any armed forces in Germany illegal. This represented an important organizational break with the past. But what made the integrationist view stick was broader foreign support in economic and political terms. In contrast to the abandonment of the Social Democrats at Versailles, the United States took the steps that helped Adenauer's policies produce results to match his promises. Draconian ideas such as the Morgenthau plan, which would have dismantled Germany as an economy and polity, were shelved. As the U.S. High Commissioner in Germany, John J. McCloy, wrote to Secretary of State Dean Acheson, "What German democracy needs and has never had is success in the eyes of the German people."[166] Such U.S. officials understood that any lasting legitimacy for their preferred view depended not just on imposing it but in making sure it produced the results promised by its German advocates.

In economic terms, U.S. aid in 1947–1948 (especially via the Marshall Plan) was a key turning point in the consolidation of integrationism because of the economic boost it created.[167] The United States also played a central role in helping to overcome opposition to integration—such as that of the Ruhr industrialists to the economic restructuring integral to the Schuman plan and the initiation of the European Steel and Coal Community.[168] Just as important was the West's political-military commitment to support Germany's security position. Allied willingness to commit its power and security to the FRG's outpost in Berlin during the 1948 airlift consolidated support around Adenauer's pro-Western orientation so that it became the dominant orthodoxy.[169] Germany's plan to rearm and join NATO in 1954–1955 met strong criticism from the SPD, but Adenauer had "relatively little trouble" in getting it approved in the Bundestag.[170]

In contrast, the events of the 1945–1955 period made the neutralist position much less credible. In the first place it pointed more in the direction of the type of interwar nationalism and diplomacy that was significantly undermined by World War II.[171] More significant, however, was the way that neutralism—that Germany could maintain an autonomous safe position between the superpowers—was fatally undermined by the Soviet example of its rule in the East (especially as compared with the prospects and results of the Western integration approach) and the threat Soviet expansion represented. This threat was not only in terms of political autonomy and freedom but also in terms of material welfare. By the late 1950s the institutional voice of the alternative view, the SPD, acknowledged the prevailing orthodoxy by accepting territorial defense and Western integration as its own position.[172]

POWER AND PAROCHIAL INTERESTS

This synthetic account illustrates how ideas interact with power circumstances and the efforts of parochial domestic interest groups. The insights of this synthesis, and the relevance of ideas, are further highlighted by examining the strengths and weaknesses of the two main alternative explanations for German foreign policy found in geopolitics and domestic politics.

Geopolitics

Much of Germany's approach to international relations in the twentieth century is seemingly captured by the strategic demands of its geography and power. As a postwar German language primer put it, "Germany has nine neighbors, and that is Germany's greatest problem."[173] When Germany was an autonomous power, surrounded and threatened by competitors, it maintained an expansionist approach toward international relations largely because it lacked security. Hence, after World War I Germany's vulnerable position in a multipolar world did not really change from what had preceded it, nor did its foreign policy thinking.[174] We might argue that this was induced by the nature of international anarchy—especially as a continental power surrounded by threats and perhaps facing an even more endangered position in the future as other powers gained in strength. With only temporary restraints on the expansion of Germany's territory, military, and industrial base, the leaders of Weimar accordingly adopted only superficial alterations in fundamental foreign policy ideas. However, when the international structure changed—as it did after World War II with the onset of the stable bipolar cold war and the division of Germany—so too did German views evolve.

Although there is much to this view, it overstates the degree to which the structure of power defines foreign policy thinking. Power alone does not lead directly to national ideas in most cases because such material facts do not necessarily reveal how one can best deal with any given situation. Germany gambled twice in the twentieth century that a policy of armed expansion would resolve its security concerns.[175] Yet both wars were huge risks, and it seems plausible, despite the near successes of those policies, that simply based on realpolitik other strategies would have worked better. In World War I, Paul Kennedy suggests that Germany's true realpolitik best option was undermined when Germany simultaneously challenged England while vying with France over Alsace-Lorraine, while unnerving Russia with possible expansion in the Balkans and the Middle East.[176] In the interwar period, was it more realistic to gain security by attempting to conquer all of Europe and antagonize France, the Soviet Union, Britain, and the United States, or was it more realistic to gain security via an alliance with, for example, France or Britain, to ease encirclement and to offset rising Soviet power and/or through some form of institutionalized European cooperation, such as the deepening of economic cooperation schemes?

Dale Copeland, for example, has cogently argued that rising Soviet power and its challenge to declining German power was the source of World War II.[177] But shifting power trajectories and a desire for security did not dictate to Germany which foreign policy was optimal. After all, if the Soviet Union was becoming such a threat to Germany, it should have also threatened France, and likewise Britain and the United States. Those countries would have had a huge stake in making sure the Soviet Union did not conquer Germany. This fact was recognized by American political geographer Isaiah Bowman, writing two months after World War II began: "In my view the strengthening of Russia may produce such disastrous effects upon Hitler's plans that it is neither idiotic nor fanciful to say that within ten years France and England may be fighting side by side with Germany in order to hold Russia in check."[178] Why did Germany not pursue a cooperative strategy with those countries so that if the Soviet Union attacked, Germany would have a massive industrialized presence on its side? There would have been risks in doing so, but surely fewer risks than were deemed acceptable under the armed expansion path.

After World War II, Germany might have as easily opted for neutrality, as Schumacher advocated, and perhaps have done just as well (e.g., the Austrian model). To be sure the United States would have been much less keen on such an outcome, but had Germans strongly favored it, it is possible that it might have accepted it. Finally, with the end of the cold war, although Germany did not undertake any major review of its multilateral-minded Western integrationism, a number of alternative strategies were possible.[179] In each historical period, then, the configuration of power is important but it does not specify the appropriate degree of rejection or integration with international society. Given this indeterminacy, we require, at a minimum, an additional logic to explain the evolution of the German foreign policy approach to the international system.

It would be equally misleading, of course, to suggest that ideas are some master factor that explain all, while power is irrelevant. This was hardly the case. If Germany's foreign policy were simply ideationally driven, there would be no reason that it would ever change: dominant ideas would be self-sustaining. In some instances it was the interaction of German ideas with countervailing power realities that undermined the concepts and opened the way for new ones. Likewise, there were clear instances where the balance of power explains why the ideas were not pursued more forcefully in day-to-day practice, including under Bismarck, Stresemann, and in the early Hitler period. Implementing the dominant ideas of armed expansion in periods when Germany was weak would have clearly led to very undesirable results, as was recognized by those leaders. Power or ideas in isolation will often be insufficient to explain events—instead, the particular interplay between the two gives us significantly more leverage on Germany's record.

Domestic Interest Groups

A second prevalent explanation of Germany's foreign policy beliefs highlights domestic interest groups and politics. Here we find the two classic "innenpolitik" explanations of the continuity of German foreign policy: (1) that it was based on the iron-and-rye coalition, or old guard elites, that favored militarism; (2) that the state pursued an expansionist foreign policy to increase the unity of the regime. Individuals and interest groups are always a part of any political decision or orientation and are usually the "active" motivators. Attention to the union of iron and rye and the foreign policy implications of narrow class and sectoral interests helps explain the origins of Germany's pre–World War I Weltpolitik, and one can see its applicability during the Nazi period.

Despite these strengths, however, this account has a number of explanatory gaps that highlight the importance of ideational arguments. These gaps all involve, in one form or another, the central weakness of interest group accounts—they cannot explain why certain outcomes emerge from the clash of many different and diverse interests. Logically the argument expects that outcomes should correlate with relative interest group strength: stronger groups should get their way in determining collective outcomes. In practice, however, such independent measures are difficult to come by, and the typical result is that interest group explanations rely on "influence" or "power" as indicated by who actually won. Since there will always be interest groups associated with any outcome the argument approaches tautology. We still know little about the causal influence of the interest groups themselves. What begs explanation is why some groups win out over others.

Group power and interests do not correlate with continuity and change in German ideas. First, ideas at particular times were not connected to easily identifiable strong interest groups such as the iron-and-rye coalition. For example, imperialist ideas seemed to take on a life of their own, becoming rooted in broader mass desires, often in ways that the elite groups that espoused them did not prefer.[180] Yet if interest groups are the cause of national ideas such an outcome is an anomaly. Our attention is instead directed not to narrow groups and their power and purpose but to why their ideas resonated with mass groups in the first place. Although still subject to debate, it appears that many of the nationalist groups of Wilhelmian Germany were themselves a product of popular pressures, and were not simply the product of elite manipulation or mass propaganda. As Michael Salewski's study of the year 1900 remarks on the popularity of Weltpolitik, "Wilhelm II, Bülow . . . and numerous representatives of the ruling class appeared less as leaders into as yet unfamiliar territory and more as promulgators of a widespread 'public opinion.'"[181] Iron and rye's support for such groups as the Navy League and the Agrarian League bolstered the effectiveness of their armed expansion views, but the resonance of the message also depended on whether it seemed plausible to the broader society. The notions the leagues offered fit with a preexisting strong nationalist orthodoxy biased toward militarist solutions. Collective ideas, not just parochial elite interests, seem to be central.

The shaping power of such dominant ideas is evident in Weimar even as the existing interest groups waned in strength or reorganized. Although there was some continuity from World War I to the interwar period in elite cadres such as bureaucrats, military officers, politicians, and industrial leaders, there were also changes.[182] Most important, a left-center coalition of parties led by the socialists—that is, those opposed to Wilhelmian iron and rye elites—controlled the government after the war.[183] The prewar nationalist organizations seemed to fade as many of their specific messages, such as support for colonization, were discredited by and/or seemed irrelevant in the new circumstances of defeat.[184] The union of iron and rye that seemed so influential was fragmented even before 1914, and in the war it was shaken and reorganized. The power of the Junkers was noticeably weak-ened.[185] Industry's influence continued, but this was as much a part of the national circumstances that demanded economic strategies (as opposed to political and military ones) as it was industry's inherent resources and pref-erences.[186] Industrialists were not especially impressed with their own in-fluence and often seemed to lose out when their preferences conflicted with political and governmental ones.[187] When the Right returned to dominance with the emergence of the Nazis and Hitler, industry was not a clear-cut supporter.[188] The führer's support came largely from the middle class, in addition to parts of most other subgroups in German society.[189]

Despite these changes in interest group positioning, however, the domi-nant mode of thinking about international affairs did not change. The im-plication here of course is that there was another cause separate from the in-fluence of the parochial domestic interest groups involved. Indeed, the glimmer of a quite different argument is apparent: the ideas themselves helped select which groups would rise to prominence by recognizing their appeal. This effect requires that we consider collective ideas as a force in themselves, needed by groups to gain approval and influence.[190] In this case interest group "power" originates in part in ideational dynamics: those groups that are able to influence policy do so because they successfully po-sition themselves to benefit from the cultural resonance of the dominant or-thodoxy. The preexisting strength of the armed expansion view helped make the alliance of iron and rye work; and the revival of this view in the interwar period after Versailles is what fostered the increase in power of the nationalist groups in that era as well. Rather than ideas arising from the parochial manipulations of powerful groups, it is more accurate to say that ideas empowered certain interest groups over others.

To suggest that a focus on interest groups does not tell us all we want to know is not to say such groups were unimportant or that a focus on ideas somehow subsumes such explanations. After all, a dominant orthodoxy does not determine the array of groups that are for or against its principles. If societal groups were simply a product of national ideas there would be no diversity—they would all be cultural clones with the same interests and worldviews. That groups have different interests suggests that they are constituted and shaped by forces outside of a societal-level orthodoxy. Thus, any complete explanation requires that we investigate how the inter-ests of different groups are constituted and what motivates and enables them to attract the support of other parts of society. In particular, a focus on such instrumental political movements tells us something about the re-placement ideas that might, under the right match of ideas and events, be-come a new orthodoxy.

Germany's attitudes underwent a curious evolution in the twentieth cen-tury, adapting to defeat in World War I by maintaining a traditional emphasis on militarist and expansionary ideas that challenged international society, and then, in response to World War II, embracing integration, multilateralism, and antimilitarism. Appeals that questioned international society won out after World War I, reinforcing the continuity of old ideas, but after the Second World War such appeals were on the losing side. There were skillful leaders, such as Stresemann and Adenauer, in both periods, yet fundamental change occurred only in the second. This variation was certainly influenced by the way the wars affected both the balance of power and interest group politics. But what is also apparent is that these factors are insufficient to account for continuity and change. We also need to heed the way ideas interacted with power and domestic interests.

The German case illustrates several noteworthy themes. The first is that change depends on *both* collapse and consolidation—and sometimes on the links between them. Germany had in fact helped initiate World War I and it had met a disastrous outcome, but change in foreign policy ideas did not occur. The lack of change does not fit with the "collapse logic" spelled out in chapter 2. Subjective German perceptions and political processes seemed to redefine a loss as merely a failed effort. Germans argued that the country had not been defeated and that its armed expansion orthodoxy was not defective, because domestic opponents had undercut the German "defensive" effort. Yet if Germany had in fact helped initiate the war and had in fact lost, why was there no collapse of the old orthodoxy? In fact, the old ideas were undermined by the results of the war, creating a revolution and the rise of an accommodationist SPD leadership in Weimar. Still, the answer to the question of continuity lies not in collapse dynamics alone, but elsewhere.

Change was impeded in this case primarily by the failure of consolidation epitomized by the Versailles fiasco. A German shift toward international society after World War I was fundamentally undermined because the fate of the emergent new ideas was pinned to the bitter disappointment at Versailles. How could the country place its hopes for security in international accommodation when that very accommodation—by way of the terms of the Treaty of Versailles—so profoundly contradicted the promises of its most ardent supporters? A flurry of otherwise unsustainable myths about what had occurred in World War I gained an energy they otherwise would have lacked.

The making of societal expectations and the judgment of events related to them is inherently a subjective social and political process that is in any particular instance unpredictable. Hence, how societies define outcomes is not always captured by "objective" circumstances. Germany's mythmaking was possible in this case because of unusual confluence of circumstances: the way the war was justified, the massive government cover-up of what really happened, and the specific circumstances of Germany's defeat. Yet while acknowledging the contingency of social interpretations and ideas it is also possible to recognize the way that ideas and results regularly shape mythmaking. After World War I, Versailles undermined a possible integrationist impulse and instead gave new life to the old thinking. In contrast, after World War II, the success of Adenauer's integrationism cemented its legitimacy in a way that to this day has yet to be tested. In both instances consolidation was as important as collapse in affecting continuity and change.

A second theme is the way that success can sometimes blur or at least overwhelm the implementation of ideas that might otherwise cause domestic criticism or resistance. As seen in the reaction to Hitler's risky expansionist scheme, when societies *perceived* the results as desirable, ideas are likely to endure—whether those ideas guided behavior or not. For example, when Hitler pushed his continental expansion beyond that entailed in his programmatic ideas focused on remilitarization and uniting the "German *Volk*," opposition to that disjuncture was silenced by the successful invasions of Czechoslovakia, Poland, and France. In general, the rise, fall, and rise of the opposition to Hitler in Germany closely tracked his fortunes in foreign policy. The hold of his broader armed expansion orthodoxy began to visibly unravel well before German territory was broached—with the startling setbacks of Stalingrad and the Allied bombing in 1943. Hence change in ideas is particularly likely when their prescriptions are pursued but the results are starkly undesirable.

A third theme involves transnational influence: the role that foreign countries—especially more powerful countries—play in domestic ideational battles. Both continuity and change within Germany were affected by what other countries did and did not do. After World War I, the United States, Britain, and France failed to take the actions that might have given life to German internationalism. Instead, the Allies pursued a harsh peace at Versailles that undermined the promises made by those who favored an integrationist course.[191] U.S. and British withdrawal and France's insecurity-based punitive measures strengthened traditionalists while undermining the integrationists. In contrast, after World War II, active Allied support and intervention did much to foster and legitimate those parties favoring integration in Western multilateral structures. This transnational effect—both on ideas and the actual results they have—may be a critical component of change in a variety of situations. It is worth noting that such a transnational effect often flows in the same direction as power: the influence of strong nations on weak nation ideas is greater than the reverse. The reason behind this general rule is straightforward: the strong are able to offer incentives to the weak to adhere to certain desired ideas, and penalize them for pursuing undesired concepts. Such influence can be important, but as discussed further in the next chapter, the shaping of ideas depends not just on power differentials but also on how the wielding of power relates to prior ideas and expectations.

[5]

Overhaul of Orthodoxy in Tokugawa Japan and the Soviet Union

Continuity and change in the way states conceptualize international relations is not unique to the era of world wars. Such dynamics are also intimately connected with other periods in modern history. The way that international pressures and domestic politics come together to affect national orientations toward international society have been especially apparent over the last two centuries, as travel and communication networks have connected all regions of the world. In this chapter I explore some of the historical range of foreign policy idea change and continuity by investigating two of the most stunning transformations in modern history: the "opening" of Japan in 1868 and Mikhail Gorbachev's "new thinking" in 1986. These two cases offer useful cross-sections of great power thinking across the nineteenth and twentieth centuries and some insight into changes that are more gradual and less the result of any one "big bang" such as major war.

In the middle of the nineteenth century Tokugawa Japan had, for the two hundred years between roughly 1640 and 1850, been largely voluntarily cut off from Europe and increasingly disengaged from Asia. The arrival of U.S. Navy Commodore Matthew Perry and his steam-powered ships in 1853, however, launched a fifteen-year struggle in Japan over foreign policy. In 1868, Japan abandoned its policy of seclusion, energetically integrating into the expanding European international society. In the twilight of the twentieth century is the more recent case of transformation, the Soviet Union's embrace of "new thinking" that favored cooperative, nonmilitary, and transparent ways of dealing with the world. Gorbachev's radical changes signaled his country's reentry into a capitalist, Atlantic-dominated system that the Soviet Union had rejected (to varying degrees) for seventy years. Focusing on such extreme cases of change would seem to be a source of bias by ignoring instances when change did not happen. These cases, however, are also intriguing for their continuity. Why did Japan and the Soviet Union maintain separatist international conceptions for so long? And why did such ideas finally give way?

Much of the extant historiography and political analysis views these variations as a product of either adaptation to international pressures or to domestic political struggles. Both of these dynamics are important, but neither adequately explains what occurred. In each case we need to incorporate the role of ideas to account for the stability of policy patterns and for their alteration. Ideas were not just a label for what power circumstances demanded or interest groups wanted; they had an independent causal influence irreducible to systemic pressures or to the manipulations of instrumental societal groups. Ideas set a baseline for the types of events that caused Japanese and Soviet elites to press for change and rally others to their cause. The existence and tenability of replacement ideas affected the speed and direction of change in each case.

International pressure, as with Germany after World War II, played a central role. Change in Japan in the mid-nineteenth century and the Soviet Union in the 1980s was not induced by any single event but by a series of internal challenges made starker by superior enemies and competitors. Internal challenges included economic difficulties and alterations in social structures. Externally, both countries attempted to remain detached from, and competitive with, countries that were superior economically, technologically, and/or militarily. In the face of the demands and superior resources of other countries, both Japan and the Soviet Union had difficulty remaining aloof. Increasingly, they experienced what Kenneth Waltz has called "socialization" and/or "selection" effects through international competition.[1] States tend to emulate the practices of those nations that are strongest or most capable. Pressures for states to adapt, lest they fall by the wayside or be taken over, played a direct role in the transformations in Japan and the USSR.

Such pressures, however, did not dictate if, when, and how the countries would adapt their long-term approaches to international relations. Japan, for example, did not walk in lockstep with external challenges in the way a strategic adaptation perspective would anticipate. Tokugawa leaders only casually pursued means to offset new foreign technologies that could threaten national survival. They wrapped themselves in an insular worldview that had economic and political effects that contributed to their vulnerability to foreign pressure. The Soviet Union, in contrast, was simply too strong militarily to have external forces dictate its course. No external power could force the USSR to do anything. Understanding the Soviet shift in foreign policy thinking requires that we look beyond, but not overlook, international power.

Explanations that emphasize domestic politics (and interest groups) are also prominent. In both cases, the existing regimes faced political challenges from internal opponents, especially during leadership transitions. Those attempting to seize and wield power at home used external policy to consolidate their position. But such parochial interest accounts are silent on why it was that certain new ideas on foreign policy either resonated with the broader society or were reviled at particular times. They cannot explain in general terms why critics were able to make hay out of existing foreign policy slogans in some circumstances but not others and why particular new orthodoxies won out.

These cases, like the others already explored, suggest an opposite causal relationship—that foreign policy ideas shaped interest groups and domestic politics. Groups often were able to seize power because they clung to ideas that had a collective resonance. By wielding dominant ideas—and by knowing when such ideas no longer held sway—groups persuaded fence-sitters and hence gained political strength.

National ideas about how to deal with the external world influenced the credibility and indeed the identity of the regimes themselves. The shifts from Tokugawa to Meiji Japan and from the Soviet Union to democratic Russia were initiated by debates over foreign policy. In Japan, the opening up of the country to "normal" international intercourse led to the end of the Tokugawa shogunate and the reassertion of a quasi monarchy (the "Meiji Restoration"). Over a century later, the Soviet leaders' embrace of "new thinking" contributed to the unraveling of seven decades of Communist Party monopoly on political power. The glue of the Soviet empire was dissolved and what remained was Russia as a normal state—according to standards set by the Atlantic definers of international society.

Transnational actors, including both purveyors of power and purveyors of ideas (with the two often joined at the hip), also played a role in ideational change—even though Japan and the Soviet Union had closed themselves off from many forms of international exchange. Japanese and Soviet citizens who traveled abroad brought back evidence that other societies had advantages and also ideas about how their countries should respond to such gaps. This information helped to establish and legitimize alternative approaches to the dominant orthodoxies. Sometimes, especially in Japan, outside influence was imposed, welcome or not, by the superior force of the Western powers. In the Soviet Union, transnational links help to account for why the Soviet Union adopted "new thinking" and not some other type of thinking. Western support of such groups—and Soviet contact with them over an extended period—fostered and gave legitimacy to the "new thinking" as the leading replacement for the old orthodoxy.[2]

The two cases also offer insights into the role of leadership. Each major transformation in the way a state approaches international relations seems inevitably linked to the leader in charge. Gorbachev, for example, is commonly portrayed as the key to the end of the cold war. Gorbachev did matter—some other leader might not have recognized that the circumstances were ripe for change or aggressively pursued the opportunity. Yet what we see in the Japanese case suggests caution in estimating individual influence: leaders rapidly came and went, yet the momentum toward change remained relatively constant. The ideas-events nexus in both instances affected incentives for leaders to attempt to alter national ideas and also their ability to actually do so.

The form of the analysis in the cases that follow is similar. I first discuss the puzzles of the case and present an overview of my answers to them. The next step is a brief description of how national ideas developed over time. My measurement of ideas in these cases is based primarily on how outside experts in the different periods and countries described them. This includes, however, evidence from the inside, as I also draw upon memoirs and decision-making records of the participants themselves that speak to the broader milieu in which they operated. I then examine how continuity and change can best be explained by comparing my argument with the alternatives.

JAPAN'S "EMBRACE" OF INTERNATIONAL SOCIETY

In the years around 1640 Japan reoriented its foreign policy by limiting its contact with Western powers and tightly regulating its relations with Asia. Despite a record of profitable trade, Japan threw out the Portuguese, excluded the English, and confined the Dutch to tiny Deshima Island in Nagasaki Harbor. In Asia, it attempted to set itself apart from the Chinese-dominated regional order, the "tribute system," which had taken shape well before Europe's expanding "family of nations." Japan's leaders halted the construction of all oceangoing ships. Japanese who attempted to leave the country or even return from abroad could be executed for doing so. Links with Asian countries were maintained, including at first a prosperous trade, but it was channeled through specific well-controlled relationships and ports. Japan had just come through an extended period of internal power struggles (and civil war), and the authority of the new Tokugawa leadership, as a recent battlefield victor, was tenuous. The seclusion policy was intended to bolster the legitimacy of the Japanese leaders and maintain "internal peace," that is, Tokugawa control, which was perceived as vulnerable to external influence.[3] This seclusion, which initially was more a policy of control (not closure) of external relations, endured and tightened over the next two hundred years. Japan resisted extensive relations with others, especially the increasing numbers of European, Russian, and U.S. callers from the late 18th century onward.

In the middle of the nineteenth century, however, Japan's thinking took a major shift toward integration within European international society. This process took some fifteen years, the Bakumatsu period between the Perry

Table 5.1 The development of Japan's foreign policy

Tokugawa era (1600s–1853)	Increasing seclusion
Bakumatsu era (1853–1868)	Struggle over foreign policy
Meiji era (1868–)	Integration into international society

visit of 1853 and the Meiji Restoration of 1868. This evolution can be broken into rough periods, as seen in table 5.1.

A shift toward international society in this case did not imply joining an array of formal institutions (which did not exist), but it did mean accepting the normal conventions of international engagement, which ranged from the establishment of embassies and trade to the practice of imperialism. More fundamentally, openness led to a restructuring of the Japanese polity in a manner its leaders believed best suited the country's adaptation to the "new" international environment. This history raises two key questions. Why did Japan maintain its separatist ideas for so long? And why did it shift toward integration?

Collective ideas in Japan, especially as they mediated external pressures and domestic political maneuvering, help us address these questions. Japan originally shifted to a policy of seclusion because its policy of openness was seen as ill suited to "Japan's interests," which were defined not from the perspective of some generic unitary actor but in terms of Tokugawa domestic political control and stability. This policy received affirmation (in the sense that the regime was able to make it stick with no adverse consequences) and, in a path-dependent manner, took on a life of its own. The dominant orthodoxy became "seclusion" in its full-blown sense a century after it was instituted. But it did so at a time when Japan would have been well served to be more attuned to developments in the West that would soon threaten its security and autonomy. Here we see ideas inhibiting adaptation to external pressures.

International pressure, nonetheless, played a large role in this history. Increasingly in the nineteenth century, technologically superior Western powers demanded that Japan open itself to trade and other forms of interaction, and they backed their requests with force. Japan's attempts to adhere to seclusion produced increasingly unsatisfactory results, leading to a type A4 "Do something!" scenario, and the virtual collapse of seclusion ensued.

Although they made some form of change likely, these external demands did not determine what new approach Japan would adopt, nor when it would change. For instance, strictly through the use of force, the Western powers might have been able to keep Japanese ports open, but doing so would have been very costly if Japan had adopted a guerrilla resistance approach in response. Japan, however, did not do so. Such a reaction was not ruled out by power circumstances, and it suggests we need to look to other factors to understand the specific ideas that were adopted. What was important about the power of the Western countries in Japan was the way it helped weaken the existing seclusion mind-set. Seclusion had been a key premise of Tokugawa order for the previous two hundred years. When the encroaching West undercut the viability of seclusion, Japan began to rethink not only its foreign policy but also the nature of its political structure.

Change in Japan, however, was not immediate, as witnessed by the fifteen-year Bakumatsu period of turmoil. Despite the clear direction of international pressures, the delay occurred because there was no developed alternative position to the hegemonic position of the seclusion or *sakoku* ("closed country") mind-set. The conditions for collapse were present (A4 "Do something!") but not those for consolidation (B1 "Try harder!"). Hence the seclusion orthodoxy retained its dominance even as Japan's leadership, due to external pressure, deviated from it in specific actions. Over the fifteen-year Bakumatsu period, however, a replacement policy of openness gained increasing salience, and the result of this consolidation was Japan's entrance into European international society immediately after the Meiji Restoration.[4]

In what follows I first chart the evolution of Japan's thinking on foreign policy. I then turn to explaining why it was so and not otherwise.

From Seclusion to International Society

Japan in the year 1600 (and through to the nineteenth century) was not a nation-state in modern terms but a bureaucratized semifeudal order with a governing class of some 260 hereditary lords (daimyo), each in control of his own domain. The loyalty of individual Japanese went first to the domain and only secondarily to the nation. This order was headed at the national level by the *bakufu*, which was in effect the most powerful daimyo or coalition of daimyo. Japan also had an emperor and imperial court, but these had only symbolic powers in the Tokugawa years. The bakufu was headed by a shogun but in reality it was often an oligarchy run by the executive council (Roju) made up of four to five daimyo.

Japan's view of the world, like that of other Asian countries, was heavily shaped by centuries of existence within the Chinese tribute system. This system placed China as the "elder" head of other nations in the region including Korea, Japan, Siam, and Burma. These junior members accepted China's leading role and paid "tribute" to China in a variety of rituals, including highly formalized visits and adherence to the Chinese calendar. In return, China gave certain trade advantages, outside legitimation, and aid in times of need.[5] In the pre-Tokugawa era Japan was relatively open to foreign interaction, most of it within the tribute system.

In the 150 years before 1600, Japan was racked by a violent civil war among the daimyo. An initial unity of the country was achieved in 1590 by Toyotomi Hideyoshi, who built on the efforts of his predecessor and mentor, Oda Nobunaga.[6] The succession crisis following Hideyoshi's death ended with a victory for Tokugawa Ieyasu at the battle of Sekigahara in 1600. Ieyasu initiated a fundamental reordering of the domestic order, based on two different lines of daimyo: those "inner" lords (*fudai daimyo*) who had sided with Tokugawa Ieyasu before the key battle of Sekigahara in 1600 and those "outer lords" (*tozama daimyo*) who did not accept Tokugawa rule until they were defeated. The resulting government structure featured a small central bureaucracy controlled by the fudai lords but an overall polity that allowed considerable autonomy to all of the daimyo who headed the different regions of the country. The tozama daimyo, who held some of the largest fiefs in Japan, were always considered a source of potential opposition to Tokugawa rule.[7]

Beginning in the early 1600s, Ieyasu began promulgating a series of changes that fundamentally altered Japan's external policy. Primarily this involved (1) the limitation of contact with Western powers; (2) the control of foreign trade and Japanese external contact; and (3) efforts to establish a Japan-centric (as opposed to Sinocentric) regional order. This policy placed greatest value on the domestic legitimacy of the Tokugawa regime, rather than on amassing power or accumulating wealth through trade. After such a long period of internal turmoil the Tokugawa shoguns saw external policy as a tool for political stability—the main threat to them was not foreign attack or domination but the perceived harm that foreign ideas could do to Japanese political and social order.[8] For the elites in charge, the danger was the loss of position and perks to an internal challenger.

The first way external policy was used to sustain internal stability was by limiting the Western, and especially Christian, presence. The spread of Christianity seemed to offer a direct threat when farmers inspired by the religion organized large protests against the Tokugawa regime.[9] Contact with Westerners was virtually eliminated except for the tightly controlled "non-Christian" Dutch presence on tiny Deshima Island off Nagasaki.

Japan's thinking on foreign policy was not one of strict "isolationism" in the seventeenth and early eighteenth centuries.[10] Japan was integrated in a regional Asian order that was based on separation and autonomy (China and especially Korea were relatively sequestered as well). Moreover, the bakufu allowed interaction and trade with other countries through specifically designated relationships. For example, Japan traded with China through regulated ports near Nagasaki and on the Ryukyu Islands, with Korea through the Tsushima Islands, and with the Ainu people on the islands to the north through the Matsumae domain.[11]

Despite this range of contacts, Japan did distance itself from the emergent international system that took shape as Western powers pushed into

Fig. 5.1 Map of Japan about 1850

the Pacific from 1600 to 1850. Moreover, Japanese leaders attempted to re-place the Sinocentric world with one where Japan was at the receiving end of infrequent (and over time, increasingly rare) tributary missions from Korea, Holland, and the Ryuku Islands.[12] The Asian regional system was a formal one that strictly controlled interaction. Under the Tokugawa foreign policy regime, this interaction became even more restricted.

Even if it was not the original intent of the Tokugawa founders, Japan be-came more isolated in the eighteenth and early nineteenth centuries. Trade and other contacts with Asian powers declined in the eighteenth century because Japan's silver, a primary export, was being depleted, and because isolation was self-reinforcing. Lack of contact came to be seen as natural and even as a criterion of bakufu competence: being closed was a good thing that a good government should ensure.[13]

Increasing numbers of Western ships made contact with Japan in the late eighteenth century and first half of the nineteenth, but all were turned away. Russian, Dutch, British, U.S., and French attempts to establish trade relations with Japan were uniformly rejected. The bakufu response to these attempted incursions, moreover, was to tighten the sakoku rules even further. Japan made plans to strengthen coastal defenses and in 1825 instituted a policy to drive away any approaching foreign ships. Authorities were instructed to arrest or kill promptly—"without thinking twice"—any foreigners who reached Japanese soil.[14]

The famous 1853 visit of Matthew Perry to Japan, which in popular lore "opened" Japan, was only the beginning of a struggle over what Japan would do. There is no easy and reliable way of determining what was in the minds of individual members of the Japanese elite at the time, but some evidence about the distribution of opinion has survived. In response to Perry's visit, the head of the bakufu senior council tried to establish a consensus by circulating Perry's demands to at least some of the other daimyo. Their responses suggest that the elite, probably primarily the fudai daimyo, was fairly divided over how to respond to the pressure to open (see figure 5.2).[15] Over the next fifteen years, a battle over the future of Japan's foreign policy would be waged, one that would involve external pressure, internal political struggle, and ideational influence.

In 1868, with the onset of the Meiji Restoration, Japan replaced closed-country thinking with an open-country orthodoxy. This new openness em-

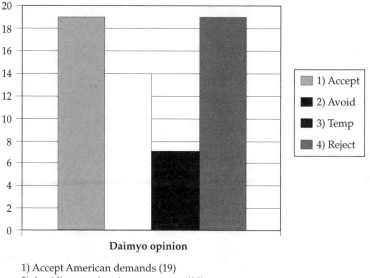

Daimyo opinion

1) Accept American demands (19)
2) Avoiding war is primary concern (14)
3) Allow some American trade temporarily until Japan
   is strong enough to go to war (7)
4) Reject demands outright (19)

Fig. 5.2 Daimyo opinion on seclusion versus openness, 1853

braced most of the prevailing ways of Western international society, including international trade, a significant foreign presence in Japan, diplomatic recognition and reciprocity, and a variety of forms of emulation of formerly banished countries such as Britain, France, Russia, and the United States. For most Japanese, however, openness was not a welcome embrace of global society but a shift necessitated by external danger. Japan, the openness supporters argued, could no longer defend itself without Western weapons and doctrine. Therefore it must do all it could to avoid war and engage in trade that would allow it to acquire knowledge and technology.[16] Nonetheless, Japan's approach to international relations in 1870 would have appeared heretical to most of Japan's leaders of 1850.

What Japan embraced in this shift was a commitment to becoming a normal power at the turn of the twentieth century according to the standards set by the West. The repertoire of such states included practices seen as distasteful by today's standards of internationalism—for example, formal imperialism. Japan was also brought in on a distinctly unequal basis because the provisions of the treaties favored the West. Japan was intent on revising them. And as can be seen in the events that played out over the seventy-five years after 1868, for Japan an embrace of international society *did not* produce a more peaceful or more harmonious policy. It did represent a radical shift in how the Japanese thought about managing their external relations.

Continuity and Collapse of Sakoku

The evolution of Japanese foreign policy can be usefully examined in terms of the loss of legitimacy of closed-country thinking and the emergence of open-country thinking as the new foreign policy touchstone. Three questions appear central: Why did the seclusion mentality endure for so long? Why was Perry's visit significant for change? And why did the period of transformation stretch out over fifteen years?

Despite increasing foreign intrusions and worrisome signs for the future, sakoku thinking endured for several reasons. First, seclusion suffered no glaring setbacks. While foreign ships did show up, they were effectively turned away. Japan suffered no major problems during the eighteenth and nineteenth centuries. Sakoku became increasingly dysfunctional over time from a strategic perspective, yet there was no obvious setback that could spark the social processes necessary for change. For most of the two hundred years Japan was in an A1 "Old faithful" scenario in which the old thinking was viable.

A second reason has to do with inertia and domestic political legitimacy. The seclusion policy during this period developed very deep roots, with a two-hundred-year pedigree and a standing that tied it closely to the entire Tokugawa political and social order. Indeed, the founding and consolidation of that order was based in part on the success of the policy. All sides in Japan agreed that seclusion was desirable. No one living in 1850—or their parents, grandparents, and great-grandparents—had experienced another way of dealing with foreign powers. Two centuries of seclusion had established the policy as a strong social norm.

The arrival of Matthew Perry's fleet in Ugake Harbor in 1853 was a turning point in Japan's seclusion policy. Many foreigners already saw the appearance of steam-powered ocean navigation as a powerful bridge for international interaction and cooperation. The Dutch King William II sent a proposal to Japan in 1844 asking for expanded trade: "This process is irresistible, and it draws all people together. Distance is being overcome by the invention of the steamship."[17] Townsend Harris, who would later be the proconsul for the United States in Japan, echoed these ideas: "The steamship will make the whole world like "one family."[18] But the increasing presence of foreigners in Japan was not only a product of the steamship—foreigners had appeared in greater numbers in Japan for decades.[19]

Perry, unlike others before him, however, would not leave in the face of Japanese resistance to outsiders. The United States was intent on acquiring ports in Japan to refuel and purchase supplies for its China trade and for whaling. In his initial visit in July 1853, Perry had only two frigates and two sailing ships, but his forces were still capable of repelling any effort to force him to leave. He made clear to the Japanese that there would be consequences should the U.S. requests be denied. Although his main aims were doubtlessly national advantage for the United States, what Perry declared as his goal was not only a few privileges but firm assurances that Japan would do nothing less than accept integration into the Western-dominated international society.[20]

In his first visit, Perry succeeded in delivering his message from President Millard Fillmore to the shogun—thus symbolically breaching a key divide between official Japan and the foreign "barbarians." Perry did not want to press his luck with limited forces, and he left for China to resupply. He returned in February 1854 with more ships and this time was able to conclude a treaty that allowed for limited port visits by U.S. ships for resupply as well as expanded trading privileges.

The Japanese accepted these terms but not only because of Perry's boldness and his superior naval forces. The issue of a Western threat to Japan had been a pressing one at least since 1842 when word was received of Britain's victory over China in the first Opium War. Given China's dominant historical role in the region, this loss made a significant impression. Japanese leaders worried that unless they opened, they would be the next victims of the expansion of international society.[21] This same effect was apparent when Townsend Harris, the American official who represented the United States in the wake of Perry's initial agreements, was able to achieve more extensive opening after news of the British and French victory over China in the Second Opium War (or "Arrow War") of 1858 reached Japan.[22]

Japan's seclusion had been under increasing pressure from at least the turn of the century. Perry's ultimatum contradicted the assumption that Japan could effectively manage the foreign presence through seclusion.[23] His visit turned a high-level, behind-the-scenes debate on seclusion into a pressing public discussion among a broader elite. Yet, despite the crisis caused by Perry's visit, there was no rapid cascade towards new ideas in Japan—not for fifteen years. Why?

Certainly part of the answer, as noted above, is that seclusion thinking had deep roots, which not even Perry's rupture could immediately sever. After all, the Perry visit did not cause widespread death or economic disruption—the type of concrete undesired effects that are more likely to provoke a domino effect of opinion in favor of change. The depth and longevity of the seclusion mind-set was also important for a reason directly connected to the argument here—it inhibited the development of a replacement orthodoxy. The alternative position of openness (*kaikoku*) was barely developed when Perry arrived. The primary source of support for such thinking was the small community of Japanese Western experts, known as "Dutch scholars" because they studied and learned about the world through the contained Dutch trading presence on Deshima Island. This community had a relatively important impact because of its knowledge of the foreign, which was passed on to Japan's leaders. Yet closely monitored by the regime, few in numbers, and lacking in status, the Dutch scholars did not represent the kind of broad social force that could effect change.[24] Overall the Tokugawa system and the seclusion policy "wrapped society in an ideological orthodoxy so powerful that it prevented individuals and groups from acting with true creativity or independence, and for all but a small number of eccentrics on the margins of normal life, they made alternative ways of thinking unimaginable."[25]

A second equally important reason for the fifteen-year period of turmoil over change involves domestic politics. Nineteenth-century Japan experienced a weakening of its political structure due to long-term economic difficulties, famines, governmental ineffectiveness, and social change.[26] Some Japanese—including powerful figures among the politically marginalized tozama daimyo—favored restoring imperial rule (which had only been symbolic under the Tokugawa Bakufu). An increasingly vocal and active opposition formed around the emperor and his court. This movement, known by its rallying cry "Sonnō!" ("Revere the Emperor!"), aimed to replace the Tokugawa political structure with an emperor-centric regime. In this political contest, keeping the country closed became a political tool because of its accepted appropriateness. A broader anti-foreign symbolic sentiment that had developed over the centuries of isolation fueled a second type of activism known by the rallying cry, "Jōi!" ("Expel the Barbarian!").[27] Sonnō became linked to Jōi in a reactionary movement to preserve Japanese tradition and unity.

Supporters of this movement were inspired by class, geography, and ideology. Samurai who gradually lost position and perks to economic modernization and social change believed that a return to traditionalism, would revive their fortunes. Daimyo and regions that were not in the ruling system but were part of the "outer lords"—such as the rulers of Chōshū and Satsuma—saw a chance to gain political power, or at least to not lose their independence. And some favored Sonnō Jōi as part of an ideological movement related to nascent Japanese nationalism and xenophobia not only vis-à-vis the West but also Chinese culture. This group used bakufu concessions toward openness in foreign policy as evidence of weakness, a violation of valued tradition, and a rallying point for different types of grievances against the government.[28]

Some of the first Japanese leaders to recognize the need to change the seclusion orthodoxy were those in the bakufu who in their interaction with foreigners came face-to-face with the difficulty of continued exclusion. But even if inclined to shift to openness, many in the bakufu did not publicly support it because they feared the loss of political support to the Sonnō Jōi opposition. The Jōi supporters, likewise, did not necessarily believe in a return to the exclusion of the past two centuries, but they rejected any immediate concessions to foreigners in favor of resistance. Even if Japan met defeat, armed resistance would unite the samurai and make any occupation violent and costly—or so some thought.[29] In Japan circa 1853 and for fifteen years afterward "closed country" remained the dominant orthodoxy. Although the old approach to seclusion had been undermined, there was no clear replacement that had a broader social basis. Yet Perry's threat and the promise of more of its kind demanded a response.

The bakufu was torn by two pressing demands, both familiar to students of globalization: external pressure to open up and internal pressure to resist.[30] With no clear new course, the default position was inertia: maintain the old orthodoxy unless absolutely pressed by superior force to yield in particular cases. Dominant ideas in Japan had not changed, but because of external pressure, Japan was forced to deviate from preferred beliefs by taking steps toward openness. By doing so, Japan was in a situation between type A3 "If it ain't broke" and A2 "Told you so" scenarios in which at least some of its policies deviated from orthodoxy and partisans argued over the results. In an effort to square the circle the bakufu tried to appease foreign demands in a way that would limit foreign penetration of Japan as much as possible. Thus Japan restricted access to particular ports and was more inclined to allow Japanese to go abroad than to let foreigners in.[31]

The domestic political debate as to what to do in foreign policy became at least three-sided. On one side were those who wanted to continue to exclude foreigners physically by improving defenses. A second group saw the need to open to the West to enhance Japanese capabilities by acquiring knowledge from abroad. They recognized that in the short run resistance would lead to a conflict that could not be won.[32] Still a third group favored an in between "grudging accommodation" approach that would be conciliatory but still limit foreign influence in Japan. The debate, then, was not about what was ultimately desired (the exclusion of foreign influence), but about how that task could best be managed.[33]

In the first part of the Bakumatsu period, these alternatives were still taking shape and blocked one another. Hence, the seclusion orthodoxy retained its dominant hold. But in later years, efforts to adhere to sakoku were undermined by the mismatch between expectations generated from doing so versus the results. Neither the armed opposition nor grudging accommodation supporters saw their positions confirmed by events. The prescriptions offered by the armed opposition proponents were undermined because Japan was not able physically to resist foreign power. The Western powers had developed superior weapons during Japan's seclusion and were able to overwhelm Japan's limited conventional defense efforts. Furthermore, the grudging accommodation approach seemed unable to defend Japan's purity, as the foreign presence spread with each new bakufu concession. Meanwhile, increasing contacts with and information from the West bolstered the openness position.

The bakufu, caught between foreign demands and domestic political pressures, agreed to the openness as demanded by Harris and at the same time pledged itself to ejecting the foreigners. In 1863–1864, two important fiefs, Satsuma and Chōshū, attempted to pursue the implementation of seclusion on their own and engaged in tests of armed strength with the encroaching foreign powers. The French and British handily rebuffed them, and Japan was subsequently saddled with huge indemnities for its resistance, which violated prior treaties. These payments were especially difficult given an ongoing currency crisis. To continue to keep Japan foreigner-free cost the country dearly in money spent on physical defenses and in substantial indemnities paid to foreigners.[34] Although Japan worked harder to sustain sakoku, it did so with diminishing results: "More and more foreign troops were being stationed in Japan. More and more foreign activities were taking place on Japanese soil: trade, tourism, teaching, religious proselytizing, and arms selling."[35]

The events of 1863–1864 transformed the attitudes of leaders, especially in the stronghold of Jōi thinking, Chōshū.[36] Even the core expulsion proponents of the rebellious provinces reconfigured their outlook after the futility of resistance became apparent and better relations with foreign powers evolved.[37] Okubo Toshimichi, an anti-bakufu leader from Satsuma, wrote in September 1865, "The eyes of the so-called irresponsible-extremist group have for the most part been opened and their views changed, so that they recognize the impossibility of expulsion and recommend extensive opening of the country."[38]

These same leaders, however, kept such a change in attitude to themselves. They found that maintaining a public stance of resistance to foreign intrusion was useful for rallying key groups in the domestic insurgency against the bakufu.[39] As Saigo Takamori, a leader from Satsuma, noted, " 'Revere the Emperor, Expel the Barbarians' is simply an excuse to overthrow the Bakufu. We would claim 'jōi' to motivate our people."[40] Sakoku ideas in this instance were weapons to be used for a variety of ends. Even if war was undesirable and some accommodation with the foreigners was necessary some believed it was important for domestic unity to raise the threat of war.

Despite Tokugawa Japan's relative seclusion, transnational influence contributed to the shift to openness. The cutting off of conduits to Europe did impede the transformation of national ideas about foreign policy. When Japan's contact with the outside increased so did the strength of the open-country kaikoku forces. More Japanese were sent abroad in the years after Perry's visit. These envoys brought back plentiful information that helped to strengthen the case for reform—engagement with the West was necessary, and, for many, even desirable. One example involves two young samurai from Chōshū who went to London in 1863 to learn about the foreigners. What they saw of Western capabilities was so alarming that they hurried back to warn the authorities in Chōshū not to attack the Western forces.[41]

One indicator of a robust dominant collective idea is when even opponents accept its legitimacy. This was exactly the dynamic in the Meiji Restoration. The dominance of open-country thinking emerged only after its opponents gained domestic political control. Ironically, they would be the new orthodoxy's defenders, even though one of their complaints against the old regime was exactly its willingness to abandon sakoku.[42] In 1867, the two rebellious provinces, Chōshū and Satsuma, joined in a campaign with other tozama fiefs that led to the fall of the Tokugawa shogunate in the autumn of 1868.

The new Meiji regime embraced openness to the Western world. Those leaders who overthrew the bakufu had realized in a variety of other interactions with the foreigners, especially in the events of 1863–1864, that sakoku was no longer a viable strategy. In 1868, Japan officially declared itself an open country. The "Charter Oath," which the young emperor announced as the regime's founding principles, stated Japan's intention to abandon the "evil customs of the past" in favor of principles of international justice and to seek "knowledge . . . throughout the world."[43] Symbolically, the new emperor soon appeared in Western clothes.[44] The Meiji foreign policy orientation was "not a change of heart, but an avowal of ideas that had already taken place."[45]

This account in some respects challenges the notion that ideas matter. How was the Meiji regime able to abandon an idea, Jōi, that seemed to have mass appeal? Dominant social ideas should have encouraged political support for those who defend them. After all, if the Meiji forces gained political support by championing Jōi, they also should have been somewhat constrained by its mass appeal once in power. The unifying theme of the rebels, "Revere the Emperor, Expel the Barbarians!," would seemingly have foreshadowed a return to sakoku. But instead the new rulers abandoned seclusion.

Three considerations help explain how the sakoku orthodoxy could rally important groups to unseat the Tokugawa regime yet not constrain the policy that followed. First, the clash between expectations and results during the fifteen-year Bakumatsu period encouraged "openness" partisans and increased their numbers. Likewise, it did much to deflate seclusion enthusiasts. Thus, especially among the daimyo, few true sakoku supporters were left after the Meiji came to power. Second, the Meiji Restoration was not merely about foreign policy—therefore the Meiji rulers could deviate from Jōi while retaining legitimacy in other areas. The new emperor's legitimacy was not tied to the same standards that had characterized the Tokugawa leadership. Third, the Meiji regime did pay a cost for abandoning Jōi—it had to confront residual antiforeign sentiment among those (such as the lower samurai) who were devoted to sakoku and who took part in armed rebellions.[46] The Meiji leaders quickly set up governing structures that disenfranchised such groups.[47] And the Meiji reorientation proved effective in improving Japanese industrial and military power and national autonomy. This demonstrated efficacy did much to diminish dissent and institutionalize the openness paradigm. The Meiji government discouraged attacks against foreigners as violations of international law. They argued that only by accepting such law could Japan establish its prestige internationally. Indeed, Japan's new goal was to be a "normal" power, especially in ending the unequal status the West had imposed. After consolidating power at home, the Meiji regime adopted the norms set by European international society and embarked on its own imperialist expeditions that resulted in the Sino-Japanese War of 1894–1895 and the Russo-Japanese War of 1904–1905.[48]

Power, Politics, and Ideas

In Japan's shift from closed country to open country we see the influence of power, domestic politics, and dominant ideas. The best explanation, however, is not found in any of these as a monocausal explanation but instead through an account that encompasses the specific ways they interacted.

Consider for example a pure form of the strategic adaptation argument that emphasizes that Japan had to change in accord with international threats or it would be defeated and dominated. This realist account of foreign policy suggests that the specific interests and ideas of states are shaped by international pressures to survive. Hence, faced with an inability to compete with the more militarily powerful West, Japan shifted ideas in order to improve its relative position and security.

This explanation captures a good deal of what happened. Foreign power was directly behind events that caused contradictions for the prevailing closed-country view. The external challenge from the more militarily advanced West fueled a series of incidents that undercut the bakufu in both foreign policy effectiveness and economically, due to the resources Japan needed for defense and the turmoil the treaties caused in Japanese markets. Sakoku promised security and well-being through exclusion, yet the threat and exercise of foreign power proved that such a policy was unsustainable. As direct foreign military pressure increased, more Japanese came to embrace the need to open up. Those who did not, such as some of the lower samurai, were disenfranchised in the early reforms of the Meiji regime. For Japan in the nineteenth century, the asymmetry in power between Japan and the powers that wanted to open it virtually guaranteed that Japan would have to adopt a different approach to foreign policy.

As important as the adaptation perspective is, however, it is also insufficient in two respects. First, it cannot explain why Japan for so long refused options, such as copying foreign military capabilities, that would improve its relative power position and its ability to protect its autonomy. After all, one of the reasons Japan was subject to external coercion in the mid-nineteenth century was because it had ignored the external arena for so long. Japan outlawed firearms and did not keep up with military technologies being developed abroad that might impinge on its seclusion. Moreover, its relative detachment in terms of trade meant that there was no transfer of key technologies critical to security.[49] Had Japan been more open there would have been greater European presence from an earlier time, and more Japanese would have traveled abroad and learned about the West. Such interactions would have allowed more effective transmission of information that would have helped Japan cope with the increasing European and U.S. challenge.

A realist perspective expects states to devote considerable attention to gathering information about what might affect their national security. Japan did allow a few links to remain open to the West and other parts of Asia for the purpose of gathering information from abroad. As the foreign presence grew in the late eighteenth and early nineteenth centuries, Japan also expanded its effort to collect information in order to deal with the challenge. It opened a dedicated translation office in 1811, enlarged its translator corps, and opened the Institute for Western Learning. Between 1853 and 1868, some three hundred Japanese went abroad.[50]

Yet, given what was at stake, Japan's information gathering and competitive efforts were late, limited, and not suited to the obvious threats faced, despite warnings from some within Japan.[51] As one Japanese scholar of Western learning wrote in 1840, the Japanese "hear the thunder and block their ears" and, lacking knowledge, evaluate their security with all the "contentment of a frog in a pond."[52] The modest Japanese expansion in effort was not particularly effective at yielding good information. For example, Japan's leaders thought Holland was a major power in Europe and in 1808 believed the United States was still a colony. Even when Japan expanded its information gathering on foreigners, it also instituted new limits and obstructions.[53] Those who tried to defy such limitations by writing about external challenges to Japan or the need for reforms to meet them were sanctioned—for example, the "purge of the barbarian scholars" in 1839.[54] For Japanese, resisting the dominant orthodoxy had stark costs including arrest, torture, and execution—simply for gaining foreign knowledge or criticizing sakoku. Many of those silenced offered good arguments based on solid evidence about the threats to Japan. But the sakoku maxims privileged insularity and domestic political control over realistic adaptation to external challenges.[55]

The desire for such information and the ability to do anything with it was blocked by an orthodoxy that both served the privileges of existing elites and shaped their worldview, as well as that of the broader polity. Prioritizing domestic political dominance or cultural tradition at the cost of security makes no sense from a perspective that expects states to adapt strategically and rationally. Hence realism captures something very important about change in this case but less about the continuity that preceded it. Japan pursued options in international relations with seeming casual regard (from a realist perspective) for the security or economic implications of doing so.[56]

We might attempt to salvage the strategic adaptation case here by noting that Japan, after all, was fairly secure from foreign powers for a long time and that it did eventually pay a big price for its neglect. There is a certain truth in both these points but also an important flaw. Japan may have been secure, but at some point it was not—realism cannot address why Japan should have left itself so vulnerable given available information and why it did not do more to seek out better information. Realism deployed as a theory of ideational continuity and change for individual states cannot explain why Japan ever got itself into such a pickle.

The second gap in the realist argument is that it cannot tell us why Japan responded in the way it did. Of the options Japan considered, all of them aimed to improve Japan's relative security, ranging from armed resistance to complete openness. For example, a Shinto priest and scholar, Hayashi

Ōen, argued that Japan, despite its weakness, should resist all efforts at intrusion by foreigners. Although initial defeats were likely, he believed that this approach would unite all samurai in a resolute resistance that would make occupation of Japan too painful to maintain by countries from so far away.[57] Certainly the defeat of the Satsuma and Chōshū efforts to resist by conventional means suggested such a strategy was ill fated. But the all-out guerrilla resistance suggested by Ōen was never attempted; it is difficult to experiment with a strategy that requires an all-out commitment. Doing so would have been a gamble, but no more of a gamble than the decisions North Vietnam made in strategy against the United States, or than Japan itself made in attacking Pearl Harbor in 1941. Realism provides an opaque picture of why the alternative of an open country was chosen.

Japan's change might also be explained as simply a product of the struggle of different interest groups for political power. From this perspective, collective ideas result from shifts in internal groups and the political battles they produce. In Japan in the mid-1800s there was a significant, complex, and interesting struggle for political power and control. Much ink has been spilled in attempting to describe that struggle, but such attention does not necessarily get us closer to an explanation of why certain foreign policy ideas triumphed. Arrayed against the bakufu was a shifting coalition, including leading daimyo and their fiefs, members of the imperial court, and the ranks of samurai mobilized by the conflict. These groups were not natural allies, but had they united before 1868 they would have been powerful enough to overthrow the bakufu as seen in the later Meiji Restoration. But none of the groups acting alone, or the bakufu, could impose a solution for most of the Bakumatsu period. Efforts to produce collaboration among the daimyo failed.[58] The foreign crisis and debates over the proper reaction served as the glue for the opposition; the interaction of ideas and events gave them influence in rallying other groups. Ideas were certainly used as weapons by domestic partisan interests, and the ideas were influenced by which particular groups had political power. This seemed to be the case, for example, when the leaders of the Sonnō Jōi movement championed one set of ideas (closed country) to oust the Tokugawa Bakufu but then adopted another (open country) when they gained power in the new Meiji regime.

Another link between domestic politics and international affairs is through the leaders that shape their times. We often see great changes in history as the product of skillful leadership—of someone with wisdom and foresight that stands above, and guides, the crowd. What is apparent in this case, however, is the limited role of any particular personality. Individual Japanese leaders of varying personal persuasions were deposed, assassinated, and overthrown, but the evolution of policy nonetheless moved in favor of openness. Indeed, the rebels who eventually upset the bakufu cart and put in place the Meiji Restoration took up openness exactly where their predecessors left off and pushed it a step further.

Foreign policy ideas cannot be reduced to domestic politics, because ideas shaped those politics as much as they were shaped by them. The tozama daimyo in Chōshū and Satsuma did not simply seize the state and shift ideas because they grew strong; rather, they grew strong in part because the bakufu was no longer able to fulfill the sakoku ideas central to its legitimacy. The collapse of sakoku preceded and encouraged the Meiji Restoration. As Marius Jansen asserts, "The old order was unsustainable when confronted by the crises of foreign affairs."[59]

The sakoku orthodoxy about foreign policy was both a constraint on Japanese actions and a tool that could be wielded in domestic political battles. Many, for example, took up the banner of Jōi even as they understood that Japan must open itself. They did so as a means of rallying support against the bakufu. This was especially the case for the leaders of Satsuma and Chōshū after 1865. They were able to do so because the sakoku mindset was firmly entrenched in the broader polity, most importantly in the lower classes of samurai.[60] The sakoku orthodoxy lost its constraining effect to kaikoku when the forces that led the opposition gained political power. Confronted by a pressing external challenge, the new Meiji leaders opted for change in foreign policy thinking under the banner of traditionalism, of the restored emperor.

Just as power and domestic politics do not suffice as monocausal explanations, neither do ideas convince on their own. After all, if dominant ideas were the sole cause, there would be no reason to expect that Japan, whether under Tokugawa or Meiji rule, would have ever changed its seclusion policy. Ideas did matter but only through their interaction with external pressures and the maneuvers of domestic actors in search of political power. It was specifically the contradiction of the unwanted Western intrusion for the Tokugawa seclusion policy that undermined it and it was the absence of a replacement (under the influence of the heavy sakoku orthodoxy) that helps explain the fifteen-year lag in change in ideas. The ultimate triumph of open country was in part a dialectical response to the old sakoku orthodoxy, but it was an outcome also shaped significantly by external pressures and domestic politics.

The interrelationship between external events, domestic politics, and ideas is seen in the making of national identity in Japan. Many in the Tokugawa era thought of themselves primarily as members of their fief or domain more than as members of some unified body, "Japan." One of the main vehicles of collective Japanese consciousness was the wall established between Japan and the foreigner. This was a founding principle of the Tokugawa order, and it was to some degree dependent on the fulfillment of seclusion.[61] Challenges to seclusion affected how the Japanese thought of themselves and their prevailing leaders. The undermining of the closed-country orthodoxy helped produce a very different national consciousness among Japanese and a new, desired role in the world—as a "normal" great power.[62] Here, as in other cases, we see that ideas in a specific policy area—foreign affairs—did not necessarily derive from some preexisting macro-identity because, as seen in the Meiji Restoration, they helped to make that identity as well.

Perry's arrival was not only about a specific set of demands on trade or the care of shipwrecked sailors. His aim was certainly to further U.S. interests in the Pacific, but he also issued a hand-delivered invitation from international society—join the group (as an unequal member) or suffer the consequences. This implied a shift to greater integration in the existing order and acceptance of the predominant, Western-generated rules. If isolation and domestic tranquility were the objectives, the bakufu's fears about opening were well founded, as the Bakumatsu period and Meiji Restoration later proved. External pressure, refracted through dominant ideas about foreign policy, encouraged the internal domestic shifts that resulted in both integration in international society and the Meiji Restoration.

THE SOVIET FOREIGN POLICY IMPLOSION

One of the most stunning—and studied—events in recent international relations is the transformation the Soviet Union led by Mikhail Gorbachev. As part of that change, Gorbachev dramatically implemented new thinking in foreign policy that represented a radical break in the way the Soviet government conceptualized how it would engage the world.

Similar to Japan in the 1640s, Russia in the wake of its 1917 revolution sought separation from the society of Western powers. Leon Trotsky, as the new head of foreign affairs, exclaimed, "What diplomatic work are we apt to have? I will issue a few revolutionary proclamations to the peoples of the world, and then shut up shop."[63] Perhaps Trotsky knowingly exaggerated—after all, the Soviet Union did soon accommodate many aspects of normal diplomatic engagement as Lenin realized world revolution would not take place and the Soviet Union needed to integrate into the existing system to survive. Joseph Stalin's "socialism in one country" accepted, indeed welcomed, a system of sovereign nation-states in which overt attempts by one country to change another's domestic order were prohibited. During World War II, Stalin's Soviet Union teamed with the Western capitalist countries to defeat Nazi Germany just as any other big power might be expected to do in the face of a dire common threat. After Stalin's death, Nikita Khrushchev initiated a wave a major reforms, including in foreign policy, where he rejected the traditional Soviet position that war between Communist and capitalist countries was inevitable in favor of "peaceful coexistence." Indeed, the Soviet Union's involvement in the international system was different from that of Tokugawa Japan. Even before Gorbachev the USSR took part in a number of the organizations and arrangements of the international system especially as they existed after the 1950s.[64]

To say that the Soviet Union was more integrated in international society in 1980 than it was after its revolution—or than Japan was in 1850—is not to say it was a "normal" power by the standards of the Atlantic-dominated international society. Even after Khrushchev, the Soviet Union adhered to a belief in the inevitable competition between the capitalist and socialist blocs, that the correlation of forces would favor socialism, leading to its eventual victory and the formation of a new international system. The Soviet Union also significantly limited the ability of its citizens to take part in the existing system. This detachment seemed to intensify in the early 1980s when the Soviet Union, under a variety of global pressures to open up, moved in the opposite direction. For example, the Soviet Union shut down its direct-dial foreign telephone circuits, penalized its citizens who had foreigners in their homes without permission or who passed on "professional secrets," put up barbed wire around foreigner compounds, and increased the surveillance and intimidation of foreigners.[65] The Soviet intention to stand apart from and eventually overturn the capitalist West made it an outlier in international society for much of its existence before Gorbachev.

The foreign policy revolution Gorbachev led fundamentally redirected Russia's external and internal trajectory. It was not the case that he brought the Soviet Union from revolutionary to loyal citizen in international society but rather that he moved the country's thinking further in line with dominant principles—including capitalism, democracy, and free trade—of the international society of the late twentieth century. Although some elements of the new thinking have not survived the Soviet Union's decomposition, Russia has shortened its prior distance from the Atlantic-centric international system and is now much more integrated with, and accepting of, prevailing norms and institutions.

Scholars have already generated a considerable list of causes for this transformation. Most prevalent are relative decline in the USSR's international power and domestic socioeconomic problems; but the list also includes a generational change among Soviet leaders, Gorbachev as a charismatic and visionary leader, the erosion of Communist ideology, and the influence of transnational actors.[66] Where many of these variants fall short is that they assume the conditions the Soviet Union faced, whether internal or external, speak for themselves, that social ideas are all product and not at all productive. This, however, was not the case, as this history viewed comparatively helps to illustrate.

To highlight ideas in explaining Soviet new thinking is to join a crowded field.[67] In this chapter I build on this prior work in two ways. The first is through attention to collective, and not simply individual, ideas. Some ideas—such as the old thinking—are best seen as collectively held and therefore prone to different dynamics than individual ideas. When we begin to think of ideas as being collective an unavoidable social element is evoked, one that cannot be reduced to the psychology of one actor, or to individual attitudes "added up." In this case, as in others, social ideas are embedded in institutions and perhaps popular thinking, even though in practice the most active agents in regard to foreign policy are elites that appeal to broader constituencies for support. As Gorbachev has pointed out, the changes in the Soviet Union were (and had to be) driven from the top down, but their implementation relied on broader constituencies, especially elites, as well as popular sentiment.[68]

The second contribution is to delineate the way that ideas influence their own transformation. Several of the analyses of change in the Soviet case offer a rich account of the particularities of the new thinking, but they do not speak to the general causal properties of such a shift. I take the opposite approach by probing the new thinking through the general framework of the preceding chapters.

Two comparisons offer insights about the relative magnitude of causes and the timing of changes. The first is a somewhat simple contrast with the absence of change in the Soviet Union during earlier periods of political opening and economic crisis—specifically, the early 1960s. If economic conditions or strategic insufficiency were central, change in this earlier period would have also seemed likely, yet it did not occur. Second, the other cases in the book, especially that of Meiji Japan, provide points of comparison that allow us to better specify the unique versus the general aspects of the Soviet foreign policy revolution.

What this analysis indicates is that Soviet foreign policy underwent radical change because of the significant mismatch between Soviet expectations and consequences experienced in the late 1970s and early 1980s. This disconnect was different from earlier periods in Soviet history because of the significant gap between well-specified and ambitious expectations and the especially disappointing results fueled by an economic crisis and disruption in the Soviet resource lifeline (oil). The old foreign policy thinking was clearly under assault by 1985, but the unresolved question was what the new thinking would be. Gorbachev's "mutual security" ideas emerged as the frontrunner because of the preexisting social consensus behind that position (largely among the intelligentsia) and because of the role of transnational forces in strengthening that view.

The rest of the chapter addresses why that change occurred. I first describe the change of ideas from old to new. I then account for this change with a focus on ideational influence vis-à-vis existing power and interest group arguments.

From Old to New Thinking

The shift of ideas is sharp and clear in the Soviet case. The differences between the old and new Soviet thinking can be briefly described. From the revolution onward, Soviet leaders tended to view international relations through a Marxist-Leninist prism. From this "old thinking" perspective, the world was split into two irreconcilable camps, socialist and capitalist. Capitalism was deemed inherently violent and imperialist, prone to seeking domination over other countries, especially socialist ones.[69] The Soviet Union had its own form of internationalism, "socialist internationalism," which held that socialist parties and countries would align and support one another. This vision was opposed to the Western conception of political liberalism and capitalism.[70]

Soviet security doctrine took concrete shape in its "correlation of forces" thesis. Soviet leaders posited that the best way to ensure the well-being of the country in light of the capitalist threat was by amassing power, above all military power. This accumulation and display of power would lead others to join, not counter, the Soviet bloc and would produce better relations with the West. Indeed, Leonid Brezhnev, the leader of the Soviet Union from 1964 to 1982, held that it was primarily the expansion of Soviet power that explained détente with the West.[71]

The old thinking orthodoxy was not simply boilerplate for those who directed the Soviet Union's interaction with the world. Instead, it was a basic lens through which Soviet leaders understood international relations and by which they planned foreign policy. This was true for both the defenders of Soviet ideology and the pragmatic liberals. As Anatoli Chernyaev, one of Gorbachev's central new thinking advisers, writes, "Even the most 'progressive' of us had been trapped by the old ideological system of values and ideas about the future."[72] Georgi Arbatov, advisor to old and new thinkers, points out that foreign policy dogma was not simply "fed the masses while the 'high priests' ate completely different food, and coldly and rationally calculated policy on the basis of some higher interests visible only to them. Maybe Stalin was like that. But not those leaders I knew."[73] Georgi Shaknazarov, an international affairs advisor in the Central Committee and under Gorbachev, called the Soviet regime "a total ideocracy."[74]

Gorbachev became general secretary of the Soviet Communist Party in March 1985 and was somewhat conservative at first. He did offer a fresh style of diplomacy with rhetoric largely free of the turgid weight of Marxist-Leninist discourse. He also initiated a reform of the foreign policy and diplomatic apparatus. But Gorbachev realized during his first year that he had to do something more to change the direction of the immense inertial Soviet state. He wanted to provide a programmatic basis for reorganizing the Soviet system (perestroika) because he recognized that "unprecedented measures in defiance of longstanding orthodoxy needed an ideological cover—including Lenin's name—for better acceptance by the people."[75] Here then were the roots of new thinking as a doctrine. Orthodoxies must not only be debunked, they must be replaced with something else.

The heart of the new thinking was an end to efforts to revise the international system or separate from the West as a means to security. Whereas previous Soviet economic and military strategy set itself apart from the West, Gorbachev after 1986 began to break down the Stalinist maxims that promoted confrontation with the West. He argued that capitalism was no longer expected to expire anytime soon, that the Soviet Union did not have a monopoly on the truth, and that it could learn from others. Some of these themes had been foreshadowed by prior leaders, for example, by Khrushchev's rejection of the inevitability of war or by Brezhnev when he stated that the two systems were economically interdependent.[76] The new thinkers in the Soviet Union, however, saw themselves as doing something radically different. In Alexander Yakovlev's words, they "threw out the [Stalinist] psychology of a besieged fortress" and according to Gorbachev embraced "the fact that we live in an interdependent, contradictory, but ultimately integral world." Concluded Gorbachev, "The new thinking wasn't just some policy shift, it required a major conceptual breakthrough."[77]

Gorbachev's mutual security approach posited that class struggle and conflict between the two systems was not the driving factor in international relations. The new thinking emphasized universal interests over class interests. Thus, general problems such as weapons proliferation or pollution of the environment could be given priority over the spread of socialism. War in the nuclear age, Gorbachev emphasized repeatedly to domestic and international audiences, was mutual suicide. And any security had to be mutual security. In part Gorbachev's approach was intended as a political one-upsmanship of the United States in defining international society.[78] Yet in stark contrast to the correlation-of-forces model, Gorbachev rejected military means as the main tool of security.[79] The change was especially dramatic because it happened in a relatively brief time frame, primarily in the years from 1986 through 1989.

Although some of the more liberal "mutual security" rhetoric that Gorbachev employed did not survive him, key elements of new thinking did. Most significant, Russia continued to embrace integration into international society in the decade after the end of the cold war. That was a significant change in the way the country approached foreign policy as compared with its "old thinking" past.[80]

Why did this transformation occur, and why did it occur in the 1980s? Answering this question requires attention to why the old thinking fell apart when it did and why the new was seized on.

Old Thinking Undermined

The sources of the erosion of old thinking in Soviet foreign policy are found in the relationship between the expectations generated by the old orthodoxy and the events and consequences the Soviet Union encountered in trying to implement it. If the extension and projection of Soviet military power was to be the main way to achieve security for the Soviet Union, the late 1970s and early 1980s brought sharply diverging results in several areas.

One such area was in Soviet-American relations. Brezhnev's "offensive détente" was met by an equally hard line from the United States, first under President Jimmy Carter and then President Ronald Reagan.[81] This reaction from the United States was at odds with the central proposition of the correlation-of-forces mind-set, that Soviet power would be met by U.S. co-operation. Instead, the United States promised to take the arms race to a whole new level, one where the economically burdened and technologically challenged Soviet Union might not be able to compete.[82] The result threatened a crucial source of the Soviet Union's legitimacy—coequal superpower status.[83] Previously, no matter how the Soviet economy struggled, the Soviet Union could still claim to be a superpower. Boris Ponomarev, the head of the Central Committee's International Department, defended the old thinking against the reformers, arguing, "What's wrong with our foreign policy? Didn't we open up outer space? Create international ballistic missiles? Are you against the use of force, the only language that the imperialists understand?"[84] A high-tech arms race would undermine the status of those achievements and make apparent to all the shortcomings of a key pillar of legitimacy in the Brezhnev years. Soviet political officials "fixated" on U.S. military space research programs such as "Star Wars," but the Soviet military was primarily concerned with technology leaps in conventional warfare.[85]

Another area of contradiction was Soviet policy toward Europe. Soviet leaders had always hoped to release Europe from its political orbit around the United States. With this goal in mind, the Soviet deployment of SS20 medium-range nuclear missiles targeted at Western Europe in the 1970s was an extension of correlation-of-forces thinking. The deployment was intended both to provide defense and bring home to Europe that it would be at risk of nuclear attack from the SS-20s while the United States, which was out of their range, would not, perhaps driving a wedge in the Atlantic alliance. The result, however, was increased U.S.-European solidarity and the matching deployment of U.S. Pershing and ground-launched cruise missiles that could hit more quickly and accurately, putting Moscow at greater risk.

Third, the notion that increasing Soviet power would bring allies into the socialist camp was discredited by a number of developments. Perhaps most important was the widening of the Sino-Soviet split, highlighted by Chinese domestic reforms and the normalization of relations between China and the United States at the end of the 1970s. This was accompanied by a loosening Soviet hold on Eastern Europe. The Polish crisis of 1980, for example, was a major challenge to the notion of harmony in intrasocialist relations.[86] Finally, Soviet efforts in the third world seemed to take a turn for the worse. This was most apparent in the Soviet occupation of Afghanistan, which Gorbachev called "a bleeding wound."[87]

Overall, then, the Soviet expectation that its military strength, especially its nuclear parity with the United States, would ensure détente and increase its number of allies or decrease those of its opponents went unfulfilled. Instead, Europe, the United States, and China moved together in a tighter balancing coalition against the Soviet Union. And brethren socialist countries such as Poland, Afghanistan, and China drifted away despite the flexing of Soviet muscle.[88] Scholars of Soviet foreign policy have noted the discrepancy between expectations and events in the USSR during this period. Craig Nation writes, "Assumptions of competitive coexistence . . . were not being borne out by the facts. . . . The foreign policy dogmas of the Brezhnev leadership did not correspond to realities."[89] Allen Lynch concludes that the "accumulation of trends and events . . . led to a serious discrediting of the traditional ideological school of 'scientific communism.'"[90] William Wohlforth notes, "The deterioration of the Soviet Union's position after 1980 represented a greater challenge to the old thinking than any earlier setback had done."[91] And George Breslauer writes, "Elite audiences . . . realized to their chagrin that the arms buildup under Brezhnev had not, after all, shifted the correlation of forces to the advantage of socialism."[92]

The danger of such conclusions is being able to see perfectly after the fact the "sources" of the new thinking by simply describing the events that preceded it as causes. We know the match of expectations and events was "critical" in 1985 because change in fact occurred. So why were the defied expectations of the early 1980s so important? After all, certain Soviet foreign policy expectations had fallen short in earlier years, indeed even in times when there were domestic economic problems, leadership change, and apparent windows of opportunity for policy innovation.[93] So what was different in the 1980s?

The period of the early 1960s provides a useful brief comparison in answering this question. In the first years of that decade many of the same conditions seen in the 1980s existed, yet a fundamental reform of foreign policy (and other areas) did not occur. Khrushchev had emerged as the dominant leader in the post-Stalin succession of the 1950s. He promised that the Soviet Union would catch up and overtake the capitalist world and would "bury" the United States. But in the years that followed, his foreign policy suffered setbacks in the second Berlin ultimatum and in the brinkmanship with the United States in Cuba.[94] Moreover, the economy also showed trouble signs. The shortcomings of the Soviet extensive growth model probably became apparent in the early 1960s. This emerging weakness was part of the inspiration for the reforms instituted by Alexsey Kosygin, who succeeded Khrushchev as premier of the Soviet Union in 1964. The reforms attempted to shift the economy from heavy industry and military spending to light industry and consumer goods.[95] Finally, the 1960s also saw the first significant schism in Sino-Soviet relations. So why did these setbacks, themselves challenges to extant expectations, not spur reforms similar to those introduced by Gorbachev?

Three dynamics emphasizing collective expectations versus results and the distribution of replacement ideas help to explain this difference. The first is that the Brezhnev regime significantly inflated expectations regarding results from the old thinking mind-set. Unlike Khrushchev's grandiose boasts, which were more rhetorical than operational and more systematically disseminated in the West than internally, Brezhnev's themes were a central part of propaganda at all levels of foreign policy. As William Wohlforth points out, ideologists and writers during the Brezhnev era established an enormous corpus of writings and thinking on how the correlation of forces was shifting in favor of socialism and how this was a force for détente and peace with the capitalist West. This edifice of expectations made the shortfalls of the 1980s even more significant and apparent.[96]

The second reason relates to a difference in the economic situation as seen through existing Soviet models. Clearly there were indications building over time that all was not well in the Soviet economy. Gorbachev tells an anecdote that reflects this belief:

> A certain lecturer, speaking about future communist society, concluded with the following remarks, "The breaking day of communism is already visible, gleaming just over the horizon." At this point an old peasant who had been sitting in the front row stood up and asked, "Comrade Lecturer, what is a horizon?" The lecturer explained that it is a line where the earth and sky seem to meet, having the unique characteristic that the more you move toward it, the more it moves away. The old peasant responded: "Thank you, Comrade Lecturer. Now everything is quite clear."[97]

Increasing numbers of Soviets became aware of the relative performance of the Soviet economy through their travels to the West: "They wander through the streets for hours looking at the incredible variety and abundance of things exhibited in the shop windows (most noticeably things to eat) not believing their eyes."[98] From the 1960s onward Soviet officials experienced this phenomena firsthand. For example, Gorbachev's visits to Europe in the 1970s left a deep impression: "The question haunted me: why was the standard of living in our country lower than in developed countries?"[99]

The Soviet economic situation worsened considerably in the late 1970s and early 1980s.[100] Economists began to adopt new measures of economic effectiveness, which painted a darker, more accurate picture.[101] The economy was an important topic for foreign policy discussions because it sustained the Soviet side of the correlation of forces. The accumulated record of continuing relative decline played a role in adding to the internal tension in the 1980s. The 1960s was not preceded by a period of accumulated failure. In the 1950s, Soviet economic growth was above the world average. One study estimates that the economic problems of Khrushchev's era were probably not apparent before 1960.[102] The situation was, of course, the reverse in the period leading up to Gorbachev's reforms.

The significance of the USSR's problems was brought into sharp focus by the plummeting price of oil in the 1980s. In the 1970s, the oil market contributed to a Soviet mind-set that fits the A3 "If it ain't broke (don't fix it)" category described in chapter 2. Oil and gas revenues made the USSR's economic and geopolitical position seem more viable than would otherwise have been the case. With capitalist economies shaken by the oil shocks, the Soviet Union looked relatively strong, with a promising future. This outlook, however, did not reflect the viability of Soviet economic or geopolitical thought but rather the size of the USSR's huge oil reserves. The Soviet Union's oil discoveries of the 1960s came on line just as the 1973 OPEC oil crisis hit, swelling Soviet coffers with windfall gains.

The Soviet situation, therefore, appeared strong, but not because the USSR's foreign policy was strategically sound. Between 1973 and 1985, 80

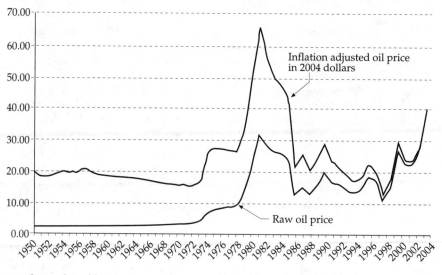

Source: http://www.economagic.com and http://www.imperialoil.com

Fig. 5.3 Crude oil prices, 1949–2004

percent of Soviet hard currency earnings came from energy exports.[103] As Arbatov notes, "Oil riches only made us poorer—we just bought things instead of reorganizing to make them."[104] Another Soviet analyst writes that the "billions of oil dollars poured into the decaying Soviet industries as a result of the energy crisis of 1973 were used as a drug providing for temporary relief and creating the illusion of a magic solution."[105] The newfound wealth relieved pressures to reform standard ways of thinking. When oil prices flattened and then plummeted in the 1980s, the enormous fissure in the USSR's economic possibilities and geostrategic reasoning came into full view.[106]

A third reason for the shift in the 1980s concerns international ideological positioning and primacy. While the USSR competed with the United States on material and ideological grounds, it also competed with its socialist brethren—especially China—for leadership of the socialist countries. This competition induced the USSR to move in different directions at different times. In the 1960s, China's attack on the Soviet Union from the ideological left helped shut down any reform there. Soviet leaders were concerned that they were being outdone in Marxist-Leninist thought and became more orthodox. Yet in the late 1970s, China, struggling with its own economic and strategic problems, implemented reforms that worked well. This both pressured (due to Chinese success) and allowed (China no longer challenged ideologically from the left) the USSR to move in the same direction as China to deal with its own economic problems.[107]

For these reasons it became easier for different interests to recognize the need for change in the 1980s and to accept the risks of doing so. More and more critics joined the chorus denouncing the old ways. As William Wohlforth writes, "Most noteworthy is the apparent agreement among representatives of so many of these tendencies, whether reformist or conservative in outlook, that new initiatives were needed."[108] George Breslauer echoes this thesis, noting the gap between expectations and results under the correlation of forces orthodoxy made leaders "susceptible to an alternative way of thinking about global politics."[109] By the end of Brezhnev's leadership in 1982, conditions were ripe for change; by the time Gorbachev's predecessor, Konstantin Chernenko, died, the incentives were that much greater.

The argument is often heard that another leader might have done something totally different than Gorbachev did—and that is no doubt true. The leadership of Yuri Andropov, who was general secretary from 1982 to 1984, and especially Chernenko proved that the old system was hard to change. But the inaction of each of these leaders put increasing strain on the system. Andropov, a longtime insider and KGB chief, initiated some limited reforms but then fell ill and died. His successor, Chernenko, was physically incapacitated from virtually the beginning.[110] Any other leader would also have faced significant pressures to change. As Gorbachev allegedly declared to his wife on the night before becoming general secretary, "We cannot go on living this way."[111] Gorbachev was elected in the Politburo with strong support, even from conservatives who would later split with him, because it was expected he would make changes.[112]

The Revolution

The remaining critical piece of the puzzle involved consolidation: What new set of foreign policy ideas would the Soviet Union adopt? This was no easy matter, as seen in the faltering leadership choices in the wake of Brezhnev's death. Gorbachev came to power with the expectation that he would make changes, but even he did not have a clear idea of what he would do in foreign policy.[113]

In theory, there were several approaches around which a new consensus seemed feasible. The Soviet Union could have simply continued its old ways with some degree of intensified "status quo plus" strategy. In a minor fashion, this was the dominant reaction between 1982 and 1985, when there was both continuing support for the old thinking and groups who preferred change but could not agree on what the new ideas would be. An effort to push for more efficiency from the existing system was Gorbachev's initial reaction as well, one largely within the prevailing mindset.[114] A second possibility was "geostrategic retrenchment" involving market reforms within an authoritarian system that remained competitive with the West. By following this alternative, as with the first, the cold war would not have ended, and it is not clear that there would have been a major reorientation in the Soviet approach to international society (although positions toward certain countries, such as Japan, might have changed). The third possibility was to adopt some radically different program such as the new thinking.[115]

George Breslauer identifies four broad groups that contended over these alternatives. The Brezhnev old guard, people like Viktor Grishin and Grigory Romanov (party secretaries in Moscow and Leningrad, respectively), were the "standpatters" who favored maintaining most of what existed. The "puritans" were those like Yegor Ligachev who simply wanted to root out the corruption of the old order. The "technocrats"—people such as Nikolai Ryzhkov (who became premier of the Soviet Union under Gorbachev)—aimed to apply new methods to correct administrative and production biases. The final group contained the political reformers, those who became associated with the reforms that did take place. Gorbachev over time took up themes favored by each of these groups (as later did Russian president Boris Yeltsin) but ended up favoring reformers.[116] The different positions were hardly equal competitors in 1985, however; new thinking had a social salience that placed it in a privileged position vis-à-vis alternatives.

Four factors shaped the momentum around new thinking and the marginalization of other possibilities. First, the alternatives to new thinking largely implied a continuation of the threat environment that characterized the cold war—they offered changes in, not of, Soviet foreign policy thinking. Some version of their principles had been tried over the past twenty years—for example, limited reforms and détentes—with little success.[117] The power of the new thinking position was its break, both rhetorically and substantively, with the discredited prior orthodoxy.

Second, social support for integration into international society as a replacement for existing Soviet foreign policy had already taken shape by the time Gorbachev had reached power—what Robert English has chronicled as the "coalescing . . . [of] a powerful alternative world view."[118] The origins of this outlook are found in the post-Stalin thaw and especially in Khrushchev's denunciation of Stalin at the Twentieth Party Congress in 1956. Memoirs of new thinkers consistently reference the thaw as the beginning of recognition of the need to engage the world and that capitalism need not be inherently hostile to Socialist countries.[119] By 1985 this "thaw generation" began to take over the controlling positions of power. Moreover, by that time the Soviet Union contained a much larger and better-educated citizenry. In 1959, 36 percent of the adult population had received secondary education; by 1986, that figure had doubled, to over 70 percent. Likewise, the country had urbanized: from being a largely rural population before World War II, the USSR in the 1980s was as urban as Italy.[120] These social and intellectual trends, along with the increasing numbers involved, made Russia much more receptive to Western ideas and to new thinking in foreign policy. An active intellectual community—although only a small part of the population, it was well placed in leadership and policy positions—increasingly saw Russia's future as one of integration with the liberal West. This was the primary replacement idea that took shape and made change in the later 1980s easier. By definition the "new thinking" stood in opposition to the "old thinking," even if Gorbachev portrayed the West as having old thinking as well.

Those who supported the status quo or opposed structural reforms fought back in the early 1980s with more success than they would find later. For example, in 1982, conservatives attempted to limit the spread of the new foreign policy ideas being generated at Moscow's Institute of World Economy and International Relations (IMEMO).[121] In 1983–1984, Soviet agencies (on Andropov's directive) identified a heightened threat of war from a hard-line United States led by Ronald Reagan, and the result was a more intense cold war environment that favored old thinkers.[122]

Later reactionary efforts by status quo conservatives, when Gorbachev launched his second phase of reforms in 1987, were less successful. In 1988 fissures over the radical direction of perestroika appeared in the leadership itself and in the pages of leading newspapers such as *Sovetskaya Rossiya*.[123]

By this point, however, the old orthodoxy was largely beyond recovery. The match of expectations to consequences had generated significant contradictions that were magnified by glasnost (Gorbachev's policy of truth and uncensored information)—for example, the various structural problems in the economy. Gorbachev's initial half measure of "intensification" did little to change the situation and instead fed a momentum for more far-reaching reforms. Conservatives had little to draw on regarding the interaction of ideas and events that would make their case for a return to the old thinking. Moreover, they could not agree on what new direction to pursue and spent valuable time arguing among themselves.[124] Meanwhile, Gorbachev repeatedly called attention rhetorically to the necessity of the radical changes he was encouraging by responding to his critics, "There is no alternative."[125]

A third reason why the conservatives failed, and Gorbachev's ideas served as the new focal point for reform, involves transnational politics. The United States and Western European governments and nongovernmental organizations threw their status-granting support and resources behind new thinking and Gorbachev. During the long period of old thinking dominance, foreign nongovernmental actors helped to develop and nurture new thinking as a plausible replacement paradigm, which at least had strong support among the elites and the intelligentsia. Groups such as International Physicians for the Prevention of Nuclear War, the Dartmouth Conference, and the Pugwash movement had made contacts and exchanged ideas with Soviet intellectuals, members of think tanks, and policy officials for years. Some of these ideas and information, otherwise suppressed in the USSR, helped to sustain and strengthen the reform forces at critical junctures. Most important, they were readily available when Gorbachev found that he needed a new formulation to guide state policy. The prestige of being associated with prominent foreigners, and more broadly with international opinion, granted further legitimacy to reform efforts in the early stages of Gorbachev's efforts.[126]

Although transnational ideas did matter, there is no simple link between the amount of transnational contact and the success of new ideas. Soviet foreign policy thinking did not vary directly with the level of transnational contact. Khrushchev's thaw and innovations in foreign policy thinking took place in the virtual absence of transnational contact,[127] but later, under Yeltsin, there was some retrenchment in the new thinking despite the unprecedented level of transnational links. What must also be considered is the background of ideas and events onto which such ideas are projected.

Finally, the new thinking's emergence also involves some degree of individual influence and sheer contingency. The extent of change that the new thinking embraced and the way it unfolded certainly was due in some measure to Gorbachev's personal political ability and charisma. He pushed events in a particular direction and was particularly skilled at not letting groups that might oppose the transformation—the standpatters, puritans, and technocrats—coalesce and block reforms.[128] But we should be careful not to place too much emphasis on Gorbachev "the man" to explain what happened and too little on the interaction of ideas and events. Many highlight Gorbachev as being the key element in the success of new thinking, that he made different decisions than either Andropov or Ligachev or Grishin would have made.[129] There is a truth in this but it is also one that is limited in two ways.

Any other leader, especially a reform leader, chosen in 1985 would have eventually had to make roughly the same decisions that Gorbachev made. They would have had to pursue a strategy of external accommodation in order to solve both external and internal problems. That does not mean they would have called it "new thinking" or that it would have been as ambitious as Gorbachev in terms of radical restructuring, but eventually major changes would have been needed. In previous chapters we have seen countries that went in different directions in response to such internal and external problems. Nazi Germany chose to defy the international system while Meiji Japan opted for integration. But unlike Germany, where new foreign policy thinking was undermined by the Versailles treaty, the potential new way was not discredited and the USSR's old ways were not easily recoverable. The USSR also faced a different constraint than had Germany. It could not imagine a path where the use of force, in an age of mutual assured destruction, would resolve its problems. Interwar Germany was obviously different in this regard.

There is another pitfall in putting too much weight on Gorbachev's leadership as the central factor in the new thinking: Gorbachev did not create the new thinking in his head but was dependent on others and their ideas. Gorbachev relied on a coterie of people in a number of Soviet research institutes and party departments for a diagnosis of the ills of the USSR and its future direction.[130] He did not seem to know at the beginning of his leadership what he would do in international affairs. Ligachev, for example, describes the situation as a "fight for Gorbachev's mind."[131]

It seems as likely that Gorbachev, characterized by Janice Gross Stein as an "uncommitted thinker," was affected by collective ideas as it is that the new thinking was the product of his own internal mental processes.[132] Gorbachev's selection as general secretary was hardly predetermined. Still, there was a consensus, especially by the time of Chernenko's death—seen even in the support of the generally conservative regional Communist Party bosses for change—for someone who would undertake reforms.[133] That those ideas outlived Gorbachev suggests the broader resonance they held for society.[134] Gorbachev and his advisers were prone to being influenced by the alternative to the "old thinking" that was most cohesive among the Soviet elite, the new thinking that counseled radical change by accommodating international society.

The interaction of ideas and events offered strong incentives for change at some point in the years after 1980. Expectations fostered in the late 1970s and into the 1980s helped fuel dissatisfaction with the results, which did not match the expectations. That the replacement adopted would most likely be some kind of engagement with the West was also likely, because it was the most developed alternative. Accounting for the specific elements and timing of the new thinking and the way it played out demands a much more detailed and contingent analysis, including the role of Gorbachev.

The analysis in this case largely ends with the transformation of the remnants of the Soviet Union into Russia and the independence of the other constituent republics of the USSR in 1991. A final puzzle remains, however, and that is why the new thinking has endured since then. Consolidation depends on an alternative and results. These conditions largely held during the 1986–1990 period when the Soviet shift brought accolades, new international economic possibilities, and considerable positive domestic feedback from liberalization. Unlike Meiji Japan, however, there has yet to be a significant improvement in Russia's development and international standing. This absence has of course provided rich material for critics and leaves the basic continuity of Russia's integration somewhat anomalous for the main argument. We might argue that this continuity is a fragile one and that Russia is vulnerable to revanchist pressures. The fact that it has not occurred yet, however, may be best explained by other considerations, such as Russia's weak international position, or the control of the state by special interests, or the fundamental institutional change in that country that would not allow a similar policy to the old thinking. Each of these responses is plausible, but none fits the logic of chapter 2.

Alternative Arguments

More broadly, much academic and policy wisdom questions whether ideas were simply the product of other factors in this case. Most important, scholars have argued that the international distribution of power—specifically relative Soviet decline—was the wellspring of the shift.[135] If that were true, ideas would seem to be the product, not the producer, of the new thinking revolution. This realist argument sheds light on important and central elements of what occurred. Consider the counterfactual: What if the Soviet Union in the 1980s were doing better than the United States economically and was leading the microelectronic revolution? Obviously, regardless of transnational ties or the intellectual appeal of "common security" there would have been drastically reduced pressure to adapt. Brooks and Wohlforth, in particular, have made a strong case that Soviet economic decline predisposed the Soviet Union toward different foreign policy ideas in the 1980s.[136]

Where this approach is less persuasive is on the timing of change, and especially the new orthodoxy chosen. A strict focus on decline in this case cannot account for why some results and situations were seen as so perilous while other ones were not. Soviet decline, after all, had been apparent since the beginning of the 1960s. To be sure, it was worse in the 1980s, but that tells us nothing about what threshold of decline is likely to trigger change. In effect, how countries assess material conditions depends on the preexisting ideas and the horizon of expectations they generate: some combinations of expectations and results are more likely to induce change than others. From this view, ideas and material conditions conjointly cause outcomes.[137] It wasn't simply that results were dramatically different in the 1980s than in the 1960s; expectations were much more sharply defined in the later period, so that the contradiction between the two augured well for some sort of change.[138]

Another problem for the strategic adaptation explanation in this case is why it was that the Soviet Union turned to new thinking as the solution. Even more than was the case in Meiji Japan, the USSR had flexibility in responding to pressures because outside powers could not force a change. There were several possible options for the Soviet Union other than the new thinking. Some alteration was likely, given the material and ideational conditions of the 1980s, but this did not mean the Soviet Union would consolidate around new thinking and reengagement with international society as an alternative. As noted above, the country could have embraced a strategic withdrawal without ending the cold war. New thinking had a preexisting social momentum, in part due to doubts about the effectiveness of the alternatives, that made it a distinct rallying theme for change.

Similarly, arguments that focus on coalitional dynamics or domestic politics have difficulty explaining why, once in control, a coalition would ever change its ideas. Jack Snyder, for example, has emphasized how ideas tend to become institutionalized and through their "blowback" capture elites and publics, especially in countries that are not democracies. Yet as we have seen in both Japan and the Soviet Union, even nondemocratic regimes can overcome blowback and change. (And the history of the United States, especially in the interwar period, illustrates that blowback exists in democracies as well.) Certain combinations and events are much more likely to induce change than others, even while controlling for regime type. Snyder correctly posits that democracies are more likely than authoritarian oligarchies to adapt to strategic pressures. The Soviet Union, however, is a case of authoritarian adaptive transformation short of military defeat.[139] We might blame the slow adaptation of the Soviet Union on its political structure, but if it had been a democracy with the same oil wealth in the 1970s, it too might have been slow to change. Indeed, it may have been because the USSR was authoritarian that the transnational ideas of mutual security were enacted so quickly.[140] Thus authoritarian regime type can sometimes facilitate change, just as it can inhibit it in other ways, as seen in this and the Japanese and German cases.

The domestic interest and domestic structure approaches also have a hard time explaining why one outcome, rather than another, occurs in the tangle and tussle of political competition. This issue also confronts realist and ideational arguments that look only at evidence relating to individual views. Individual views, however, will be insufficient for explaining national change, because of collective ideation problems.[141] Individuals in particular circumstances will be inhibited from articulating, and especially from acting on, their views. In this case, most old guard thinkers probably understated or did not act on their preferences in the critical 1986 to 1990 period because of a social momentum against such thinking. Gorbachev certainly played a role in that momentum, but it would be more accurate to say he rode it well rather than that he caused it. The interaction of ideas and events provides insight into the circumstances likely to favor collapse, while the number of prominent alternatives and their relative efficacy shapes the likely focal point of new orthodoxies.

Both Tokugawa Japan and the Soviet Union imagined that the appropriate way to engage the world was through separation from, rather than further integration with, international society. Yet over time each became subject to international and domestic pressures, which caused a radical shift in foreign policy ideas toward an embrace, not a rejection, of international society.

To point to globalization or modernization pressures, however, should not imply that they are the sole agents of change, nor is such change always in the direction of integration. We cannot rely on vague global pressures to explain change in Japan and the Soviet Union, because doing so cannot tell us why change occurred when it did. Pressures for integration existed in both Japan and Russia for long periods before change took place. Likewise, as we have already seen in previous chapters, globalization pressures do not always induce notions of integration. If that were true, Tokugawa Japan would never have withdrawn from the international arena in the 1600s and the Soviet Union after 1917 would have never proclaimed its status as a socialist island governed by principles different from those of other countries.

The reactions of specific nations over time can only be understood if we also look at the particular ideas they hold, the way such concepts relate to events, and the status of possible replacement notions. Both Japan and the Soviet Union held expectations based on long-held social ideas that were sharply contradicted by events, in the 1850s and 1980s respectively. These contradictions opened up fierce domestic arguments over what each country should do. Further feedback indicating the problems of the old approach strengthened critics and gave them grounds on which to argue for a change.

This dynamic was, of course, different in the two cases as well. Japan faced more severe international constraints and had a much weaker opposition in favor of integration. Stronger countries, through military force, certainly played a central role in Japan's reorientation, but the development and social bases of those favoring opening was relatively limited initially. This produced a longer transition period for Japan than otherwise would have been the case, as it experimented with different possibilities for a new foreign policy orientation. In the Soviet Union, international pressures were somewhat less, but the opposition view was better developed. Thus, when the correlation of forces thinking was under siege in the early 1980s, the country had a new thinking replacement idea and constituency to turn to. Indeed, other conceptual alternatives were hardly considered. The outcome was not predetermined—if it had been, Andropov and Chernenko would have governed differently. The likelihood, however, of both a shift and the direction of that shift was considerable at some point after Brezhnev, given the background of ideas and events.

These two cases also indicate the thick connection between international and domestic politics. Not only did their foreign policy ideas change but both states changed the very nature of their political structures and identities. This might suggest that foreign policy ideas were just an outgrowth of more fundamental domestic political and identity changes. In fact, the influence went as much in the opposite direction. The viability of foreign policy ideas in both Tokugawa Japan and the Soviet Union was directly related to the viability and legitimacy of the regime itself. The failure of "closed-country" and "correlation-of-forces" ideas to fulfill the expectations they generated did much to undermine the existing regimes. A difference between the two is that Meiji Japan helped legitimate open-country thinking through its subsequent political, economic, and international accomplishments. The absence of a similar trajectory in Russia suggests that integration thinking in that country is fragile or that other factors outside my argument better account for continuity.

In each case, transnational agents helped to spread ideas that helped strengthen the case for change. In Tokugawa Japan these forces were almost nonexistent, but in the period between Perry's arrival and the Meiji Restoration, Japanese people traveling abroad and the foreign presence in Japan brought new knowledge that bolstered openness advocates. In the Soviet Union, the impact of contact with foreigners and foreign societies in the development of Russian new thinking is well documented. These agents succeeded, however, only when there was an accommodating structural dynamic—that is, one where the interaction of preexisting ideas and events allowed for consideration of some alternative idea.

Finally, the cases suggest something about the role of leaders in major foreign policy change. There would seem to be a difference in the two cases. In Japan, a string of short-term leaders were seemingly swept along by history, making only tactical changes that were quickly overtaken by the broader stream of events. In the Soviet Union, Gorbachev stands out as the quintessential "Great Man," leading his country in directions previously unimagined. This has led many to posit that understanding the sources of Soviet new thinking means focusing on Gorbachev's personality. In at least one respect this may be true. The external constraints on the Soviet Union in the 1980s were less than they were on Japan in the mid-nineteenth century. There were no outside powers that could physically coerce the Soviet Union to do what it did. Thus internal factors, including leadership personality, may have figured more centrally. Still the fact that the outcome in both cases was similar while leadership varied (strong in the USSR, weak in Japan) raises questions about the centrality of personality. In both cases, however, the ideational circumstances were similar and in both cases they shaped the personal ideas and actions of the leaders in power. The art of leadership, evident in Gorbachev and the Meiji restorers, seemed to be the ability to recognize the ideational circumstances that allow for transformation and to act accordingly.

[6]

The Next Century

As major powers orient their foreign policies, so too do they help constitute international politics. Occasionally, states dramatically revise the way they think about the international arena, at times stepping away from the prevailing order, at others, seeking integration. Here I have attempted to understand why these shifts sometimes occur—*and* why they often do not. This chapter briefly summarizes the findings. My main emphasis, however, is on the implications of the argument for the future, especially for the foreign policy thinking in two countries central to global politics in the twenty-first century, the United States and China.

FINDINGS

To understand big changes (and their absence) in the ways states think about the world, we have to pay attention to the nature and influence of the ideas themselves. Doing so does not ignore other factors: the overall argument is a synthetic account that shows how ideas combine with power and domestic interest pressures in regular ways—even across time, geography, and cultures—to shape the way states arrive at ideas about the international system. I have focused on ideas because their effect on change—especially on their own transformation—has not been extensively explored or well understood. Ideas play a central role by helping to shape the expectations of societal actors that motivate them to question traditional behavior in some situations but not in others. Likewise, the supply and efficacy of new ideas affects whether people go beyond questioning the national approach to international relations to successfully transform it. Ideas have a distinct influence that cannot be reduced to strategic circumstances or instrumental domestic politics. A full explanation of foreign policy change, however, cannot ignore strategic incentives and parochial domestic interests, but must show how enterprising agents, environmental feedback, and collective ideas come together to maintain societies on their prior foreign policy tracks or switch them to new ones.

Change Reconceived

The analysis reinforces the importance of disaggregating the concept of ideational change itself. Rather than a single entity, such change is better understood as consisting of two stages: collapse and consolidation. First, societal actors must somehow concur, explicitly or tacitly, that the old ideational structure is inadequate, thus causing its collapse. Second, actors must consolidate a new replacement idea, lest they return to the old orthodoxy simply as a default mechanism. In many ways these stages are ideal and often not easily distinguishable. Still, in some instances they are distinct—we can observe the delegitimation of the old orthodoxy, yet, due to the absence of any new paradigm, the old endures. This effect was apparent in foreign policy in Germany following the First World War and in Japan during the Bakumatsu period. That collapse does *not* always lead to consolidation suggests that the two phases have different determinants. To understand these we have to first recognize that we are explaining two phenomena, not one.

Equally important is recognition that individuals face collective ideation hurdles (in affecting both collapse and consolidation) that make coordination difficult and/or create incentives to shirk efforts to challenge dominant beliefs. Such ideas are often embedded in institutions—including bureaucracies, constitutions, and educational requirements—that are hard to manipulate.[1] The massive effort needed to rearrange foreign policy ideas was evident in the Federal Republic of Germany after World War II, when reforms included a new constitution, new educational procedures, and a completely revamped system of military socialization. Individuals rightly recognize the significant costs involved in attempting to effect change. Daring to challenge dominant ideas or to think differently about foreign affairs can bring social and political stigmatization as well. The "Dutch scholars" of Tokugawa Japan were seen as a strange breed, set apart from mainstream society. In the early 1930s President Franklin D. Roosevelt hid his internationalist views in the face of the "no entanglement" hegemony. "New thinkers" in the Soviet Union who worked within the system for decades adjusted their public views in the years and decades before 1985, depending on prevailing moods.

When Old Ideas Crumble

What it is that motivates actors to overcome these barriers depends in part on the somewhat different sources of collapse and consolidation. In the collapse stage, outcomes appear driven by the interaction of expectations and results. Whether or not an event facilitates change depends on its relationship to preexisting ideas and the consequences of experienced events. In most situations expectations are either not violated or the consequences experienced are desirable (or unremarkable). Thus change agents typically found it difficult to overcome the weight of tradition.

These dynamics are affected by a number of factors. One is the social embeddedness of the old orthodoxy. The longer it has existed, and the more institutionally ingrained it is, the longer change will take and the greater will be the negative consequences needed to achieve social momentum for change. In Tokugawa Japan, the two-hundred-year-old orthodoxy was under direct assault and revision for some fifteen years before change occurred. Likewise the gap (and intersubjective contradiction) between expectations and results is shaped not only by the degree of negative consequences (as seen in Germany's "zero hour" after World War II) but also by the horizon of expectations established. The more exaggerated the expectations generated, the more likely a contradiction will be evident. Brezhnev's specific and heightened claims for the "correlation of forces" doctrine made it particularly brittle in the early 1980s when negative results began to accrue. Wilson's ambitious aspirations regarding the benefits of intervention in the First World War helped to set the stage for the disillusionment that followed. In these cases, other factors also affected such fortunes—for example, "consequences" were often influenced by the balance of power, which allowed some ideas to succeed and others to fail. The key point is that collapse was not only a product of consequences but of how those consequences related to prior ideas.

When New Ideas Take Hold

Consolidation, like collapse, is a challenge for those seeking change. Even when activists agreed that the old view had to go, they sometimes were not able to agree or coordinate on a replacement. Two factors enhanced the ability of agents to form a new orthodoxy: (1) the existence of a prominent replacement idea and (2) some initial positive results. Where those conditions existed—as they did in Meiji Japan, in post–World War II United States, in post-World War II West Germany, and in Gorbachev's Soviet Union, change (given collapse conditions) was more likely to occur and endure. Proponents of change found it easier to coordinate as well as to convince others to go along. Where the conditions did not exist, efforts at transformation flagged as seen in Bakumatsu Japan, in Germany and the United States after World War I, and to a certain extent in the USSR in the early 1960s. In each of these cases, the presence (or absence) of motivated interest groups and social movements played a central role in whether a socially viable replacement idea was (or was not) available.

Viewing collapse and consolidation as separate analytical stages should not mean that we overlook the interaction that occurs between the two. This relationship is witnessed in two ways. First, the absence of consolidation can affect collapse. This dynamic is evident in the fate of internationalist ideas in Germany after World War I. Germany's failed armed-expansion approach regained legitimacy when nascent German integrationist ideas were squashed by the Versailles setback. The second link between the two stages is apparent in the impact of collapse on consolidation. When collapse is sharp, consolidation is easier because there is little legitimacy left in the old. This was the case in Germany after World War II, when the issue was not whether a new view of international relations would take hold but which one would do so.

Transnational Influence on National Ideas

Ideational battles over foreign policy ideas were not only internal domestic matters. Foreigners and their governments were interested in these outcomes and often became involved. This transnational effect, however, seems to vary depending on relative power and geographic remoteness. Transnational influence was greater in weaker countries than in stronger countries, and in those countries easily accessible through transportation versus those that were more remote geographically. The combination of these two traits (power and proximity) in relation to the United States in the interwar period made it least vulnerable to transnational efforts. Still, even in this case there is evidence of foreign (i.e., British) influence on U.S. decisions in the late interwar period.

Transnational influence can affect both the collapse and consolidation phases. In terms of collapse, foreign countries played a significant role in the fate of ideas in other countries in a very material way. This was particularly true in the contradictions the actions of more powerful countries caused for prevailing expectations in weaker countries. For Tokugawa Japan, the aggressive expansion of European powers in Asia challenged notions that the "closed country" orthodoxy was even possible let alone able to provide security. Likewise, U.S. policies under Carter and Reagan helped to undermine Soviet correlation-of-forces thinking, which expected an enhancement of détente and Soviet security. Certainly the powerful Allied response to Hitler during World War II was a source of "consequences" that literally demolished his version of Mitteleuropa. In some circumstances, however, the weak also appear able to influence the strong, as seen in Britain's lobbying in the United States for support in the 1930s. This persuasive effort helped contribute to the view that the United States could not maintain its security by remaining aloof from the snowballing European conflict.

Transnational effects are equally apparent in the consolidation stage. In several cases, nonstate actors helped to establish the plausibility of replacement orthodoxy. This was apparent in the Soviet Union where, in the decades before 1985, a variety of contacts between East and West systematically developed the plausibility and spread of the "mutual security" approach, which Gorbachev seized as his own. A similar influence is apparent in the lessons learned from the Japanese missions abroad in the Bakumatsu period. Another dimension of consolidation influence is the role foreign countries can play in making new orthodoxies succeed. The U.S. impact on the different outcomes in Germany after World War I (weak Allied support of internationalists and no change) versus World War II (massive support of internationalists and a shift to integration) exemplifies this effect.

Anomalies

The chapters above also indicate tensions and seeming anomalies for the central argument. One anomaly involves Germany's reaction to World War I when the mix of ideas and events suggested collapse was likely. Instead, the old orthodoxy took on a new life in the years that followed. That outcome clearly contradicted the conditions expected for collapse. However, as noted, change is a product of collapse and consolidation, and in the German case the Versailles debacle thwarted consolidation and helped renew the old as seen in the B1 "Try harder!" scenario. A second anomaly involved Germany's use of peace rhetoric in the 1930s, shaping a set of expectations about the immediate prospects for peace that were then systematically violated with little penalty in terms of domestic opposition.[2] A third and similar tension occurred when the champions of the Meiji Restoration used the closed-country rhetoric but subsequently rejected the very ideas that gained them popularity. These last two examples both contradict the theoretical proposition in chapter 2 that leaders should not be able to manipulate foreign policy ideas at will unconstrained by existing ideas. Parts of each situation fits my account, but others remain points of friction. A final tension involves the basic continuity of integrationist thinking in Russia, in the absence of significant positive results through the 1990s. Such a situation would suggest the likelihood of more significant change or backsliding due to weak consolidation of the new thinking. This may yet occur, but that it has not may signal the importance of other factors outside of the argument.

GREAT POWERS AND THE FUTURE OF INTERNATIONAL ORDER

These findings, anomalies not withstanding, suggest the usefulness of heeding ideas and their transformation for understanding great power politics. In the first chapter I proposed that important debates over the future of international relations hinge on the trajectories of national ideas about foreign policy. This section uses the argument to explore those trajectories. No two countries are as important in this regard as the United States and China. The United States stands as the most powerful country in the world in the first decade of the twenty-first century—and perhaps the most powerful in any international system since the Roman Empire. China, on the other hand, is a massive country of growing wealth and importance, and possibly the next heavyweight in the international system. The trajectory of these countries is a large reason why they are so central to future international relations and why they receive so much attention. Yet to understand what these goliaths will do we need to know not only their power trajectory but how they will think about international affairs as well.

The Future of the Bush Revolution

There is a widespread perception that the United States since the September 11, 2001, terrorist attacks has been in the midst of a "revolution" overturning its dominant (what I will call "Atlantic Pact") foreign policy ideas that have been in place since World War II.[3] Table 6.1 captures some of the spirit of this commentary. These views imply that U.S. ideas showed basic continuity with the post–World War II orthodoxy, at least until the first year of the administration of George Walker Bush ("Bush 43") in 2001. They also suggest that the changes that loom in U.S. foreign policy are fundamentally about the nature of international society itself.[4]

Two questions follow: First, why is this potential change appearing now and not after the end of the cold war? Second, how likely is it that the United States will abandon its Atlantic Pact integrationist outlook to embrace what I shall label the "American Supremacy" view of the Bush revolution over a longer period? After both the cold war and the 9/11 attacks, scholars and policymakers have offered different visions of what "grand strategy" the United States *should* pursue. Such discussions have largely ignored, however, what strategy the country was *likely* to pursue. Focusing on ideas and events helps to identify scenarios in which U.S. foreign policy ideas are likely to change and the direction they may go.

The end of the cold war (sometimes compared to the ends of major military wars, including World War I and World War II) seemed to provide an a priori occasion for rethinking U.S. foreign policy.[5] It was a bracing and unanticipated shock that reordered the existing power structure of the international system. Yet U.S. ideas displayed basic continuity in the 1990s,

[166]

Table 6.1 A foreign policy revolution?

"What made Bush's proposed foreign policy different—and potentially even radical—were not its goals but its logic about how America should act in the world. It rejected many of the assumptions that had guided Washington's approach to foreign affairs for more than half a century."
Ivo Daalder and James Lindsay, 2003
"The Bush administration has helped spur a worldwide debate not only about the purposes of American power, but about the objectives of the international system as a whole."
Phillip Zelikow, 2003
Tensions in transatlantic relations are over . . . "what kind of world order we want."
Joschka Fischer, just before the United States invaded Iraq, 2003

Sources: Ivo Daalder and James Lindsay, *America Unbound: The Bush Revolution in Foreign Policy* (Washington DC: Brookings Institution Press 2003), 40; Philip Zelikow, "The Transformation of National Security," *The National Interest* (Spring 2003), 17–28; Joschka quote from *Der Speigel* 13/2003 (March 24, 2003). See http://www.spiegel.de/spiegel/english/0,1518,242042,00.html.

even as U.S. power, both due to the collapse of the USSR and the dynamic U.S. economy, gained new preeminence in the international arena. Given this shift, those who focus on the balance of power predicted a major change in the dominant ways of thinking about foreign policy in the United States and other countries. Scholars such as Kenneth Waltz and John Mearsheimer offered specific and bold predictions about what would happen, including the forecast that NATO would collapse.[6] Their analyses were models of intellectual honesty and rigorous adherence to a coherent power-based view. Yet, for at least a decade, those views did not receive robust confirmation.[7]

This continuity is due to the relationship between ideas and events—specifically a type A1 "Old faithful" scenario in which the collapse of the Soviet Union reinforced the U.S. view that its integrationist perspective was correct, hence making efforts to change that orthodoxy difficult. Leaders in the United States believed that U.S. commitments abroad, both in terms of sustaining a united international community via economic integration and in containing Soviet expansion, were by and large a success.[8] George H. W. Bush (41) purposefully resisted crowing over the victory, but most recognized that the long-term strategy worked well.[9] Here we see a classic A2 "Told you so" scenario, where adherence to the dominant orthodoxy brings desired results and reinforces that point of view. A favorite debating topic among U.S. security experts after the end of the cold war was what new grand strategy the country should adopt in light of its altered circumstances. Yet these advocates found it difficult to get agreement or traction in the policy world. The "I told you so" dynamic in that situation explains why so little actual effort was mobilized to change the institutions and symbols of the long-held view.[10]

The September 11, 2001, attack on New York City and Washington, D.C., was likewise a political earthquake that had a significant national impact.[11] Since that day, American foreign policy is rarely discussed without some reference to "9/11." It is an event that is most often compared to Pearl Harbor, the symbolic shifting point in the United States from aloofness to international commitment.[12] In the wake of the terrorist attacks, the Bush administration has led a debate and policy that represents what the historian John Lewis Gaddis called *potentially* "the most sweeping shift in U.S. grand strategy since the beginning of the Cold War."[13]

This new "American Supremacy" view is distinct from the post–World War II Atlantic Pact orthodoxy in its three-part structure emphasizing unilateral action (as a rule, not as an exception), the preventive use of force (vs. reactive containment), and in the geographical reach of its efforts to intervene overtly (not covertly) in the domestic affairs of other countries including forcible democratization.[14] None of the legs of this stool are new; it is their combination, intensity, and the ways in which they are presented that creates a qualitative difference. In the first case, the new thinking minimizes the multilateralism ethic that has been a foundation of the postwar order. The United States has of course always acted unilaterally at times; the difference is that it was justified as an exception, not as a norm.[15] The United States now identifies great power cooperation as one of the pillars of its national security strategy. Yet this view of cooperation is not one of institutionalized multilateralism but of "coalitions of the willing," where states are brought together to deal with issues of the moment—usually in cases where the United States cannot do it alone and/or multilateralism is easy.[16] In the second case the United States has declared that containment, and the general proposition that force only be used in reaction to others' aggression, is obsolete. Security from this view depends on when a danger looks imminent enough to justify the preventive use of force. Finally, the approach advocates the need to intervene to democratize the regimes of potential enemies and countries of interest. The United States, of course, has previously intervened with large-scale, overt use of force in the domestic regimes of other countries (the covert use of force continues to acknowledge post–World War II sovereignty norms); but the states affected were usually in the Western Hemisphere (e.g., Cuba, Grenada, Nicaragua, Panama). What the Bush (43) administration did in its first term was to extend its view of what was appropriate intervention to include countries outside of this hemisphere with the express purpose of changing their regimes.[17]

It is not surprising that other states (e.g., France, Germany, China, and Russia) would resist this shift, because it represents an alteration of the norms as they existed up until 2000.[18] The post–World War II international society, based on multilateral, reactive (not preventive) force, largely sovereignty-respecting rules, would be shifted in a direction perhaps preferred by the United States but not by many other countries.[19] Since 9/11 the United States has turned toward this foreign policy that is noticeably more muscular, more unilateral, and more expansive in its aims of reengineering the international system than arguably any since the end of World War II. In terms of the integrationist-separatist-revisionist ideal types, current U.S. policy seems to represent a notable shift from integration toward revision.

Will this potential shift endure? After all, the ideas to date are largely the product of one administration, even if they have sub rosa precedents in the Clinton administration.[20] Three different outcomes seem possible. The first is that the American Supremacy view will become embedded as a new dominant U.S. orthodoxy, replacing Atlantic Pact thinking. The second is that the apparent changes will be reversed and the United States will reembrace ideas it now seems to be leaving behind. The third is that it will turn to something substantially different than either Atlantic Pact or American Supremacy thinking. An examination of collapse and consolidation dynamics—and the interaction between ideas, expectations, and results—sheds light on the conditions and likelihood of these three different possibilities.

Scenario #1: Triumph of American Supremacy. The first possibility—the consolidation of an enduring American Supremacy orthodoxy—faces several challenges. The first is that its supporters are trying to replace a view that was not obviously discredited by 9/11. There was no obvious connection between the general Atlantic Pact orthodoxy and the 9/11 attacks or the challenge of terrorism. Indeed, many of the initial U.S. reactions were that the United States needed to adhere more closely to its tradition. For example, as George H. W. Bush (41) put it, "Just as Pearl Harbor awakened this country from the notion that we could somehow avoid the call to duty and defend freedom in Europe and Asia in World War II, so, too, should this most recent surprise attack erase the concept in some quarters that America can somehow go it alone in the fight against terrorism or in anything else for that matter."[21]

The implications of the attacks for foreign policy thinking, therefore, were ambiguous. What was clear is that 9/11 transformed the Bush (43) presidency begun in January 2001. Seemingly revisiting the "oceans equals safety" thesis that FDR attempted to refute before World War II, President Bush reflected, "The strategic vision of our country shifted dramatically, because we now recognize that oceans no longer protect us, that we're vulnerable to attack."[22] National security became paramount and terrorism the defining issue of his first term. The sense of outrage, that something had to be done, left the U.S. administration with an opportunity to pursue more ambitiously expansive ideas—ones that may have been percolating among some groups for some time but which could not be implemented in the 1990s.[23] However, 9/11 permitted certain notions to flourish, such as the need to use force more aggressively (and unilaterally) and to spread U.S. values in order to achieve a "balance of power that favors human freedom" wherever possible.[24]

A notable feature of the roll out of the American Supremacy view is that it has occurred without the collapse of the Atlantic Pact orthodoxy. September 11 did not directly undermine the view that engagement with existing international society added to security. The Bush administration did challenge the credibility of deterrence in an effort to build support for its preventive force doctrine. And important officials in the administration have questioned the efficacy of international institutions and traditional alliances, for example, those with "old Europe."[25] The problem of course is that this is a view that has not received systematic articulation and is not widely accepted. In the run-up to the invasion of Iraq there was a contentious debate, including within the Republican Party, about the desirability of preventive war versus containment.[26] September 11 therefore did not delegitimize the old ideas, but it did allow an opportunity for a worldview different from cold war internationalism to get an airing.

U.S. history offers precedents for President Bush's attempt to consolidate a new orientation to the world in the absence of the delegitimation of the old. Consider Teddy Roosevelt's advocacy of greater American involvement in major power politics, Wilson's push for intervention in World War I and support of the League of Nations, and FDR's attempt to turn the country in an internationalist direction before 1940. In these cases, the degree of collapse affected the prospects for consolidation.[27] The absence or shallowness of collapse since 9/11 puts a heavier burden on consolidation, especially in terms of its advocates demonstrating the efficacy of American Supremacy thinking. Hence if the American Supremacy view is to endure it will depend on the expectations it raises and the results that such a view appears to cause.

The justifications and rhetoric of the U.S. government related to American Supremacy ideas—and the specific actions they lead to—will importantly affect consolidation. Military victory will not do the task alone. The United States also "won" the First World War, but ended up seeing that effort as a defeat. Woodrow Wilson had promised that the U.S. intervention would make the world safe for democracy, put an end to imperialism, and reshape the nature of great power relations. It did none of those things, and he was held to task for it. The Bush administration has justified its foreign policy deviations from the Atlantic Pact view on two grounds: (1) that it will increase the security of the United States; (2) that it will provide a feasible model of world leadership and systemic governance.[28]

The steps that would lead to the first, and by far more important goal, is the preventive use of force against terrorists, those who support terrorism, and countries that have weapons of mass destruction that might be transferred to terrorists. Equally important, democratization of "rogue states" would further serve national security by removing the sources of grievances that encourage people (mainly young men) to turn to violence when they are frustrated by the lack of voice and opportunity at home. Regarding the second rationale, the United States has gambled that other major powers, despite reservations, would realize the benefits of forceful U.S. leadership and would ultimately support it. Hence a new era of great power cooperation could bloom.[29]

How successful the United States is in meeting these expectations will be critical to whether the Bush revolution becomes a turning point in U.S. foreign policy or whether it fades into history as a notable deviation in the post–World War II Atlantic Pact orthodoxy.[30] Especially given the absence of clear collapse, the American Supremacy view needs to claim notable results if it is to replace Atlantic Pact thinking.

Scenario #2: Atlantic Pact Renewed. The second possible outcome of the current debates over foreign policy is that the Atlantic Pact view will be reaffirmed, in much the same way (although more desirable than) U.S. aloofness was reenergized by the First World War or Germany's armed expansion view was renewed by the defeat at Versailles. Less need be said here because the conditions producing this result are largely the opposite of those in scenario 1. To the extent the American Supremacy view is discredited by the events that lie ahead, the Atlantic Pact (which continues to have significant supporters that span the partisan divide) could gain new vibrancy.[31] Cooperation, Atlantic Pact defenders argue, is the key to the battle against terrorism: declining multilateralism will defeat the goal. These defenders of the post–World War II orthodoxy are clearly the most prominent group responding to the challenge from American Supremacy thinking, and it is the most likely position to emerge dominant in the event of continuing difficulties (e.g., such as those in Iraq beginning in the spring of 2004). The Atlantic Pact view has the weight of tradition on its side.

Scenario #3: The Tight Perimeter. There is, however, another possible outcome that could emerge out of the current play of ideas and events in U.S. foreign policy. What seems at stake in the first two possibilities is a choice between two different forms of U.S. internationalism recalling the divide between conservative and liberal internationalists after World War I.[32] The American Supremacy advocates would be heirs of the conservative tradition and the Atlantic Pact defenders would present the liberal internationalist case. The overall debate may signify an unraveling of the cooperation between these two views formed during World War II.

This third scenario would result from a chain of events that might undermine any form of internationalism. This could occur if another significant terrorist attack against U.S. citizens takes place—especially one on U.S. soil. If after all the effort expended abroad in Afganistan and Iraq, the United

States still cannot prevent such attacks, any form of distant defense and diplomacy will face a difficult test of validity vis-à-vis the onslaught of critics. This is especially true if it is accompanied by international criticism of the United States: the difficult prospects facing, and lack of enthusiasm for, Atlantic Pact multilateralism (fed by anti-Americanism and U.S. reaction to it) could help to delegitimate any form of internationalism. After all, if U.S. efforts to help itself and the world are only met with the hostility of friends and enemies alike, Americans will wonder, What is the purpose of the whole effort?[33]

In such circumstances it is not unthinkable that the relatively marginalized anti-internationalist groups in the United States would gain new momentum. Pat Buchanan and his fellow travelers would look prescient.[34] "Off-shore balancing"—code words for a significant political-military retreat—would look more inviting. The challenge of terrorism would no longer be confronted abroad but instead be met with ever more vigorous "homeland defense" efforts, especially those focusing on immigration, imports, and antimissile measures.

The obvious barrier to such a strategy is the continuing economic internationalism of the United States. How could the United States rein in its perimeter with so many interests abroad? Such a potential shift would not involve, at least at first, the economic internationalism that has characterized U.S. foreign policy in both the Atlantic Pact and American Supremacy views. Yet the question correctly presumes a link between economic and political-military stability, and it is not clear to what degree this interdependence is appreciated either by American elites or the public. There are certainly sectors of the American public that favor a renewed economic nationalism and who would take advantage of the same conditions to "defend American jobs."

Overall, the potential American Supremacy revolution is one that attempts to reorient U.S. foreign policy before the earlier Atlantic Pact orthodoxy has collapsed. The closest historical analogy to such an effort is Wilson's attempt to move the country toward an institutional internationalism after the First World War. Yet aloofness found new momentum instead. By that standard, American Supremacy will need an unusual string of successes to remove the doubts of the critics who wield considerable tools—including historical symbols and popular opinion—in sustaining their preferences. The likely outcome of the revolution, then, is a tack back to more mainstream Atlantic Pact views.[35] There, is however, the additional possibility that another dramatic attack—especially coupled with unfavorable international opinion and diplomacy toward the United States—could provide the circumstance for a radical shift to a more separatist orientation that would invoke memories of America's pre–World War I no-entanglement orthodoxy.

Ideas and the Rise of China

Just as the twenty-first century is being shaped by the United States as the dominant power in the system, so too will China, an emerging potential giant, influence it. The future of China in world politics is almost always discussed in terms of its rapidly increasing might. Yet if both power and ideas shape national policy (and ideas are not simply the slave of power shifts) then we need to explain the sources of ideas as well. Let us for a moment accept the premise that China will continue to "rise" in relative power. In what follows I briefly summarize the content of Chinese foreign policy ideas. I then speculate on the future trajectory of Chinese ideas about international order and the circumstances under which they might remain as they are or alter dramatically.

At least since the time of Deng Xiaoping's leadership, the prevailing trend in China's orientation toward the existing rules, institutions, and norms of the international system has been toward integration.[36] China has not sought separation from the international system, nor has it aspired to overturn it. Instead it has increasingly favored involvement, and this has manifested itself in significant increases in institutional membership as well as more informal cooperative behavior with the existing powers.

This integrative orientation was cautious in the early Deng period, but in the past fifteen years has picked up considerable momentum. There is room to debate the depth of Chinese integration—whether it is shallow or enmeshed—but the trend is clear.[37] China has left behind that "world revolution" and "three worlds theory" rhetoric of revisionism and gives less emphasis to its former primary role as "leader of the Third World."[38] At the Sixteenth National Congress of the Chinese Communist Party in November 2002 there was virtually no mention of this traditional theme. China today shows most of the characteristics of a "normal" great power, accepting the basic principles of the existing international order and taking part in its institutions. Hence, China joined the World Trade Organization (WTO), has aligned with the United States since the 9/11 attack, and participated in the spring 2003 G-8 meeting and the October 2004 G-7 talks. The promotion of "the Five Principles of Peaceful Coexistence"[39] or the call for a "new political and economic order that is fair and rational" seem vague enough to suggest no real commitment to major revision of international society except when that society precludes Chinese influence.[40]

To suggest that China accepts the basic principles of the contemporary international order is not to say that it prefers no change in world politics. Certainly China is dissatisfied with some aspects. Two important ones are U.S. power and the status of Taiwan. China favors "multipolarization," which means that all states (or at least great powers) would have a more equal say and the United States would have less influence—especially in using force to achieve its goals or to intervene in the domestic politics of other countries (i.e., China).[41] That sentiment, however, is hardly unusual and might be shared by many if not all the major powers. China has a special sensitivity in such matters due to the symbolic importance of its legacy as a colonial subject for the legitimacy of the Communist regime (which restored China's autonomy). The second, and related, issue is Taiwan, where China favors unification and rejects any move that enhances Taiwanese independence. On this issue (as with Tibet or other disputed territories), China portrays itself as the defender of the extant rules. Unification with Taiwan in China's view is a "domestic issue" over which a sovereign state must make its own internal decisions.

Even as China seeks integration, Chinese leaders pay close attention to power and geopolitics. Indeed, to the extent China is interested in joining international society, it should by the very principles of the system have an interest in balance of power politics. And China is certainly focused on increasing its own power and balancing U.S. power in Asia.[42] Yet attention to power is hardly the sign of a revisionist country. Indeed, one might argue that the *neglect* of power realities is the hallmark of revisionist states—for example, Nazi Germany's utopian goals of world conquest, Japan's gamble at Pearl Harbor, and Brezhnev's expansionism in the face of decline.

Finally, China may have most of the attributes of a normal emerging major power in the international system, but it is distinct from other contemporary great powers in one important way: it is the only one that is not a democracy. This trait suggests tensions and disagreements with what some consider to be emergent norms of international society on human and political rights.[43] Despite this standing, it is notable that China is not advocating that states adopt a similar political system to its own, or that human rights norms are illegitimate. Instead, Chinese emphasize that principles such as "sovereignty," "stability," and "territorial integrity" should trump such considerations. China does not rule out democracy in its future, it just insists that it will follow its own path, style of democracy, and timing. Right now China's notion of democracy is "the democracy of dictatorship" and "democratic centralism" where power resides in the hands of the Communist Party and all other Chinese political groups must take direction from it or pay a price. Chinese citizens, however, attest that their political situation today is vastly more liberal and open than it was in the pre-reform period and becoming more so.[44] That is still a long way from the notion of democracy in the West, however.

The debate over China, of course, is not about what China wants today but about what it may want tomorrow. The "rise" of China could lead to a fundamental reorientation of Chinese desires. Important literatures focusing on power and power transitions point out that rising powers are typically identified with dissatisfaction with the existing order and that the result is usually conflict.[45] But this need not be the case, as national orientations do not march in lockstep with either power or threat. During the First World War, the United States emerged as the dominant power in international relations, but its involvement and goals *did not* expand—they contracted—in the interwar period. State ideas do not walk in lockstep with strategic challenges. China in the Qing era *did not* alter its isolationist ideas to deal with the encroaching and threatening European powers, even though the security situation certainly suggested the danger of maintaining those ideas. And in terms of power trajectories, Britain and the United States *did not* go to war at the turn of the twentieth century, even as the United States surpassed Britain as the dominant international power. Most power transitions have occurred without conflict.[46] National responses to systemic incentives can rarely be understood by reference to external conditions alone.[47]

The alternative to this view, indeed one that is a response to the concerns it provokes, is China's argument that its future will be a "peaceful rise." Building on arguments offered by scholars, China's new leaders General Secretary Hu Jintao and Premier Wen Jiabao have argued that China's modernization depends on peace and that China's "rise" would not lead to policies that pose threats or come at the expense of other countries. China would remain faithful to an integrationist foreign policy.[48] Yet such statements are at a certain level just words, absent some recognition that change does sometimes occur even if it is not foreseen. China in the past has declared itself committed to foreign policy principles that were subsequently altered.

Thinking about likely scenarios in the contemporary Chinese case, especially regarding the future, demands some general notion of what shapes continuity and change in attitudes toward international society. If the argument here is useful, it suggests that the onset of change will depend on the interaction of at least two factors: (1) expectations generated by existing ideas about appropriate behavior, and (2) the results experienced. Situations involving the combination of unmet expectations and undesired consequences are likely to facilitate change. Situations in which expectations are fulfilled and/or desired consequences occur favor ideational continuity. As in the past, the future of China's contemporary integrationist orthodoxy depends on the expectations it generates and the results that are experienced.[49] How then is the current orientation to international society justified? In what terms does the Chinese leadership promote integration as desirable or effective? Two central themes of Chinese ideas provide the basis of expectations.

The first is that integration will enhance sovereignty. That is, integration must prevent the type of colonial subordination of the past and the infringement of China's territory by outside powers.[50] Integration facilitates such a goal by providing access to institutional forums where global politics are decided that might affect China's autonomy. Such integration also confers the imprint of major power status, which confirms that the country is no longer an object manipulated by more powerful Western countries but an important actor itself. The most concrete marker of sovereignty, independence, and territorial integrity for China is Taiwan. China expects that its participation in the extant institutions and conventions of world politics will help it to fulfill a desire (seemingly widespread across the political spectrum) to unite the mainland and Taiwan.

The second, and arguably most important, criterion of current policy is that integration within the existing international order provides the best means for national economic development.[51] China remains a government run by a communist party, but the legitimacy and popular support of the government does not rest on socialist ideology; it is based on economic performance. "Well-off Society" not "Workers Unite" is the national mantra. President Jiang Zemin's 2002 address to the Sixteenth National Congress of the Communist Party of China put this claim starkly:

> It is essential for the Party to give top priority to development in governing and rejuvenating the country and open up new prospects for the modernization drive. . . . The progressiveness of the Party is concrete and historical, and it must be judged by whether the Party promotes the development of the advanced productive forces.[52]

The dominance of the integration orientation in contemporary Chinese foreign policy is largely based on economic considerations. Integration serves China's rapid development. These two themes, economic modernization and sovereignty, can of course contradict one another, a fact that does much to explain the complexity of contemporary Chinese policies.[53] Integration can lead to limitations on sovereignty. For example, membership in the World Trade Organization brings with it significant implications for the Chinese social and political order, not the least of which is major turmoil in the Chinese agricultural sector as well as another surge in wealth inequality among Chinese.[54]

The durability of China's integrationist foreign policy will depend on how results match expectations related to sovereignty and economic growth. Events related to China's integration that represent significant setbacks for expectations on either of those issues would be occasions in which China would be likely to rethink integration. First, events supported by the international community that are perceived as neocolonial or that move Taiwan toward independence could help to undermine China's current integration orthodoxy.[55] Much will depend on the particular circumstances and whether they make the mainland government seem somehow responsible for such a setback. Taiwanese efforts to establish formal independence cause deep concern in China—indeed, of the type that can set the stage for China to take actions unexpected by those who do not appreciate the degree to which reunification is supported by even "reformist" governments.

A second situation where the integrationist orthodoxy might come under attack in China involves significant setbacks to its economic modernization. From this viewpoint (and in contrast to the rise of China debate) the most likely scenario in which China would be likely to alter its integrationist mind-set is *not* with the growth of Chinese power but with ruptures in that trajectory. It may be more likely that China's growth levels off than that it achieves world economic dominance in twenty years' time.[56] Vis-à-vis expectations developed by both Chinese and foreigners, this could be a deeply disillusioning experience. The motivating source in such a scenario would be the juxtaposition of undesired results against overly optimistic expectations generated by leaders who feel compelled to invoke them for legitimacy. Should economic growth decline, those opposed to reform and opening would mobilize groups with grievances. China's rapid integration and modernization has led to daunting gaps between rich and poor. Involvement in the WTO is putting significant pressures on poor farmers and peasants who cannot compete. As long as the economy is booming some of these people can transfer to other types of jobs or the government can provide transfer payments. But if growth levels off or declines, this system could become brittle. Critics of the current orthodoxy would attempt to use such conditions to rally political authority around a new dominant approach to the international system.

What exactly a new approach would look like depends both on the situation and on a key factor that is especially elusive in the Chinese case: the nature and distribution of replacement ideas about international society among influential domestic groups.[57] Jiang Zemin cautioned against "Right tendencies" and especially "Left tendencies" within China.[58] The danger from the Right is pursuing liberalization at the expense of the party and social stability. The danger from the Left is critiquing reform and opening as a step toward capitalism and promoting class struggle. In foreign policy such tendencies would translate into factions that prefer even more aggressive Chinese participation in the world economy versus those who believe China's involvement in the current order should be halted and/or reversed. A third group might favor less involvement in the Western order, perhaps in favor of Asian regional ties, and a more assertive posture vis-à-vis other major powers.[59] In the event of future crises that challenge integration, those who emphasize withdrawal would likely occupy the rhetorical high ground because they offer a clear alternative to dominant ideas (as opposed to even more ardent prointegration reformers) and might more effectively draw from the language of nationalism to make their case.[60] To the extent that a portrait of factions in China is overdrawn (e.g., because the decision-making dynamic is one of consensus, not groups fighting over control) then any change in foreign policy thinking will demand especially negative results and could take time, just as it did in Tokugawa Japan. If the main factions in China agree that "isolation is the major factor explaining China's decline" then a significant shift away from an integrationist orientation will be difficult.[61]

This argument offers a different course than either of the two alternatives—engagement and containment—championed in current debates as the best way to manage relations with China. It suggests that which one is appropriate depends on the nature of extant debates and expectations in China. If the goal is to incorporate China into the international system in a way that makes the system operate in a fashion acceptable to all, doing so means helping to make sure those who have staked their legitimacy on the positive aspects of integration have something to show for it. To the extent nonintegrationist sentiments dominate Chinese policy, containment would be more appropriate. Moreover, it is important that efforts be made to strengthen those groups and factions that would support, in the event of significant setbacks to reform and opening, alternatives that are more desirable than an aggressive revisionist nationalism. In either case, it is clear that the future of Sino-American relations will depend on both power and ideas.

It is ironic that as China increasingly moves to embrace international society, the United States is showing signs of changing the rules of that order.[62] In the cold war era and its immediate aftermath in the 1990s, the importance of countries being democratic was never as important as it is in contemporary international society. Likewise, intervention in the domestic affairs of other countries always occurred, but it has become increasingly prominent in recent years. China is ready to embrace a Western international society governed by cold war norms of sovereignty, a society marked by great power collaboration and multilateralism but one that respects different internal preferences. China wants a modern Concert of Europe: countries may be dictatorships or democracies, but they can still cooperate in creating and maintaining international order. This looked like a bargain the United States would accept in the immediate aftermath of 9/11 and the onset of the "war on terror." Yet if American policy embraces unilateral armed intervention and aggressive democratization, it is a bargain that could be increasingly brittle in Asia.

THE STUDY OF INTERNATIONAL POLITICS

In the first chapter I foreshadowed the implications of the argument for the scholarly literature. Here I want to briefly highlight three broad guideposts for the study of international relations as well as some gaps that need further attention. The first guidepost involves the role of ideas in change.

The second speaks to the usefulness and pitfalls of multicausal explanations. And the third returns to a central relationship that has gained new importance: the link between globalization and domestic politics. Finally, I discuss the limits of the argument and the research possibilities it suggests as well.

Ideas and Change

Collective ideas are a key source of state action in the global arena. Scholars who have done much to demonstrate that "ideas matter" will find this statement banal. What I have tried to do, however, is to illustrate the irreducibility of ideas in an area—that of change—where ideas have been most ignored or questioned. It may be straightforward to admit that collective ideas promote continuity in group behavior. Yet proponents of such a view still could (and usually do) claim that national ideas themselves are driven by extra-ideational phenomena, such as the distribution of international power, the parochial aims of domestic interest groups, the whims of state leaders, or unexplained "shocks." The results here, depicting the recurring way ideas play a role in their own transformation, suggest a more significant influence—one not reducible to international pressures or domestic interests. Indeed, what we often see is ideas shaping the forces—such as interest groups or reactions to threat and power—that critics claim give rise to ideas. The implication is that the role of ideas in the study of change in social phenomena deserves broader application. In appendix 1, I briefly explore that potential in the realm of economic policy.

Synthetic Explanation and the International
Relations Theory Canon

A second implication for the study of international relations is to qualify the argument just made. An ideational approach may in fact be necessary, but it is unlikely to be sufficient for explaining the complex phenomena of international relations that are most puzzling. Paradigmatic debates that pit fundamental forces in world politics (e.g., power, national ideas, interest group pressures) against one another can only take us so far, because complicated phenomena are most likely to be multicausal. To capture the most basic components of many international episodes requires leverage from more than one paradigm—at least as paradigms are constituted in the contemporary literature.[63]

This is a position that most scholars already intuitively accept. Yet to invoke multicausality as a solution should rightly raise a warning flag—too often it simply implies a weak reliance on an incoherent gaggle of causal factors whose specific means of influence are not examined but are merely noted like items on a grocery list or partitioned in a large-n regression.

What is needed is an overarching framework that can be used to integrate different factors in a coherent explanation.

My approach has been to construct an explanatory framework that shows how various types of causal factors—power, interest, and ideas—from different schools *interact* in particular ways, through specific mechanisms, to produce different outcomes.[64] Ideas about appropriate behavior regularly result from prior ideas (as ideational theory claims) mediated through constraints often imposed by the international distribution of power (as realism emphasizes). Interest groups and individuals (emphasized by liberal theory) in turn supply new ideas and use the interaction of expectations and results to make their case. As seen from Meiji Japan to the Bush revolution, the regular ways these factors interact enables and constrains political dynamics, usually maintaining dominant foreign policy ideas but in some scenarios allowing dramatic revisions. This is admittedly a rough synthesis, but it suggests a direction for future work that might prove useful.

Globalization and Domestic Politics

In an era of increasing interdependence and shrinking distance among national communities, it may be tempting to assume that traditional debates about levels of analysis can be subsumed by one overarching globalization narrative. Citizens and states are no longer independent entities but subject to the same global forces. Debates over levels of analysis are increasingly challenged by real world national boundaries that have become more porous. This line of reasoning has an undeniable truth to it, but it is also one that can be overstated. The analysis above indicates that it must be heavily qualified substantively and heuristically.

In terms of substance, history from Tokugawa Japan to 9/11 suggests that global forces have always affected reticent nations that have attempted to isolate themselves in one way or another. Globalization is not new. As impressive as contemporary breakthroughs in communication and travel technologies are, they will some day look quaint, just as the international telegraph and steamship travel today appear old-fashioned. Technological pressures for globalization have been steadily increasing over time but the harmony and scope of international society has waxed and waned. Clearly something else is going on besides a "shrinking world" that shapes such variation. National ideas should not be overlooked in that dynamic. Although we see more cohesion in international society today than in the 1930s, that need not be permanent. National attitudes could change again, just as they did when the long peace of the nineteenth century gave way to the world wars of the twentieth century. And today the rise of transnational ideas—radical Islam's terrorism, for example—that bring together groups across national lines represent a new challenge.

My focus on national ideas would seem to stake out a clear position on the classic levels-of-analysis question: Should we focus on the traits of individuals, or on nation-states, or on the international system to explain international relations? Indeed, especially if the most immediate concern is foreign policy, attention to notions embedded in national communities may well be justified. After all, the largest—and sometimes the most passionate—affiliation of most individual and collective identities is that of the nation. Yet there is more going on too. What I have tried to show is how national ideas about international society are shaped in regular ways by both domestic and international factors. It is right to argue that there is no reality that matches divides between "levels-of-analysis." Transcending such divides, however, does not mean churning them in a food blender. Instead, the challenge is to demonstrate how national and international factors work together. Conceiving of collective ideas as a pivot for both nations and organized transnational movements provides one possible approach.

Limitations and Future Research

My argument also has notable limitations, some of which suggest areas that deserve further study. Four issues stand out. First, the argument may be limited in terms of the types of change and types of ideas that it explains. It will not encompass every case of change in ideas, because many varieties of such alterations exist. I have focused on a particular type of change, relatively rapid discontinuous ideational transformation. Shifts in collective ideas can also take place in a much slower series of steps over time.[65] So too can alterations emerge within the general logic of a dominant idea. And of course, the changes that do happen need not be triumphs of the new with the complete dismissal of the old: a type of layering-on can and often does occur.[66]

Second, the importance of different domestic political institutions, largely neglected here, also influences the collective ideation hurdles faced in challenging dominant ideas. In general, my ideational model says more about why societies might demand change than whether they will be able to realize change. Political settings vary tremendously in terms of the institutional ability of authorities to control information, social aggregation, and perhaps even individual calculations. Such an influence was evident in the "revolutions" of Eastern Europe at the end of the cold war. A key factor was not just that their citizens saw the ideas undergirding those regimes as no longer legitimate but that political authorities, especially Soviet General Secretary Gorbachev, signaled that dissent would no longer be met with physical repression.[67] The cases examined above include both democratic and authoritarian regimes, and in both types collective ideas played a role. One might think that authoritarian regimes are less prone than democracies to the change dynamics posited because they can more effectively inhibit collective action. That is true. But it is also true that autocracies can affect change more rapidly once a consensus is reached—as we saw in Gorbachev's new thinking.[68] Still, the influence of institutions is notable and deserves further investigation.

Third, the argument also tells us little about the sources of the replacement ideas that are so central to consolidation. The number of, and social support for, replacement ideas is largely inexplicable by the factors I highlight. That is a part of the story that takes place offstage and it certainly deserves more attention. The social movement literature in international relations and other fields has usefully highlighted factors that make some ideas take root and spread in a society, attracting a devout following that serves as a beachhead for subsequent influence. Why some ideas take hold as possible replacement ideas—and others do not—is a rich area for study.[69]

Finally, one dynamic that has appeared repeatedly in the cases above is the way that the justifications leaders offer for their policies serve as an enhancer or deflator of expectations. While dominant ideas create a general field of expectations, the particular ways that leaders justify policies can provide important specifics. This is especially true in high-profile instances where states deviate from prescriptions offered by dominant ideas. Thus Woodrow Wilson's explanation for getting enmeshed in the First World War—despite a U.S. tradition against "entanglement"—served as an important baseline for postwar evaluations. Similarly, justifications by George W. Bush as to what could be expected from the U.S. invasion of Iraq has figured importantly in debates over the desirable direction of future U.S. foreign policy. Even when states are simply implementing dominant ideas, leadership justifications can play a role in the continuing legitimacy of those ideas. For example, Leonid Brezhnev's exaggerated claims for the benefits of correlation-of-forces thinking helped make that approach appear especially weak when undesirable results did occur. What is arguable in each of these cases is the degree to which leaders had to use the particular justifications they did or whether they had room to maneuver. Understanding better how rhetoric and justifications play a role in international relations, as well as how much latitude leaders have in offering them, is an important task.

IDEAPOLITIK IN PRACTICE

If this case for a reorientation in the way we think about international relations has any merit, practical implications for policymakers and social activists also follow. My argument has drawn on the work of both those working in a strategic actor framework and those favoring a more sociological approach. The latter category, often termed "constructivist" in the international relations literature, has particularly been viewed as insightful in terms of scholarship, but irrelevant in terms of policy prescriptions.

Part of the reason for this asymmetry is the misguided notion that rational and cultural analysis are necessarily opposites and mutually exclusive.[70] Because policymakers operate in real time, they necessarily tend to operate via a strategic actor model—both in terms of their own planning and in terms of the inferences they draw about the sometimes opaque decision making and nature of other countries.

To focus on collective ideas, however, is not to deny strategy. Typically, states will instrumentally pursue their interests and in a reasoned way connect means to goals. The manner in which countries conceptualize reaching their goals, however, is not a straightforward matter. The international arena is endlessly complex, and variance in state notions of how to achieve goals may be as important in shaping outcomes as the actual goals themselves or the strategic calculations vis-à-vis others. It therefore makes sense in the conduct of foreign policy to (1) pay attention to the ideas of nations and transnational groups, (2) anticipate change in those ideas, and (3) help shape such notions when possible.

Analyzing Collective Ideas

States often rely on the guiding influence of dominant ideas in managing their affairs, and it is worthwhile to understand them. This is not a simple task, but it is also not impossible. Such ideas are typically not in a manual or on a website, and deciphering them is aided by cultural expertise. Yet unlike the mental ideas of individuals, which often are difficult to access, foreign policy ideas are necessarily embedded in public discourse—in symbols, speeches by officials, and even in institutional rules and procedures.[71] These ideas play coordinating and legitimizing functions and are difficult to manipulate for short-term strategic purposes. Collective ideas, therefore, offer clues to the likely behavioral patterns of a state.

They do not, however, tell us everything about behavior. For a variety of reasons, states do sometimes act contrary to tradition in particular circumstances. Dominant ideas are not straitjackets, and attention to the potential that states will ignore or misrepresent them is important. In entering the First World War, the Wilson administration thumbed its nose at warnings that doing so was unnecessary entanglement in Europe's affairs. A gap between observable ideas and behavior can also occur when states purposely attempt to mislead external observers, as was the case with Hitler's peace offensive. This is difficult to do (given that other states and internal critics can always match words to behavior) and also comes with consequences. Hitler worried in the 1930s that the mood of the German masses might not be up to an immediate war, and he was fortunate that his early campaigns were overwhelmingly successful. Nonetheless, the possibility of purpose-ful manipulation means that analysts cannot rely only on public rhetoric, especially in governments that control public rhetoric. Instead, what is needed is multisource analysis in rhetoric, past pronouncements, institu-tional procedures, private discussions, and actual behavior as a check against strategic disinformation.[72]

Anticipating Change and Continuity

Recognizing the ripeness of circumstances for change is a difficult task. It appears, however, that ideational transformations are more likely in some situations than in others. When events seem to sharply contradict existing social ideas *and* when the consequences are undesirable, dominant ideas are vulnerable. This is especially the case when social dynamics—the trans-parency of information and attitudes, the confidence individuals have that others like them are experiencing the same things they are and are also mo-tivated to act—are strong. For example, the more people are negatively af-fected by a single event, the greater the probability of change. A single plane crash with a hundred deaths is more likely to evoke a response than a hundred fatal car crashes, even if the latter is much more likely to hap-pen.[73] This effect helps to explain why such widespread national events as war, economic depression, and revolution are so often associated with soci-etal change.

The structure of collective ideas can also give clues as to the likely direc-tion of change. Public discussions of dominant ideas will inevitably include criticisms by those attempting to alter the prevailing orthodoxy. Often this criticism tends to coagulate around one replacement idea, but sometimes several exist. The more robust and singular that thinking about a replace-ment is, the more likely that particular view will represent a strong influ-ence on the direction of future change should the opportunity arise.

Ultimately, whether the supporters of a new orthodoxy are able to imple-ment their idea—and embed it in collective calculations and routines as well—depends on results. A new collective idea is more likely to be institu-tionalized to the extent it can gain legitimacy through at least a correlation with desired results. Consolidating a new orthodoxy requires both rhetori-cal and material support that contributes to the fulfillment of the expecta-tions it generates.

Effecting Change/Sustaining Continuity

As illustrated in the preceding chapters, political agents do affect battles over ideas. The power of orthodoxy does not render such efforts meaning-less, but it may take long, hard work to succeed. Some of the most effective political actors in the histories reviewed here were those groups that went to great effort to establish the credibility of a replacement idea—the Bolsheviks in Russia before World War I, internationalists in the 1920s and 1930s in the United States and Weimar Germany, the opposition movements to Hitler, the new-thinking dissidents in the Soviet Union, and those advocating opening in Tokugawa and Bakumatsu Japan. And of course political leaders such as FDR and Gorbachev, who recognized that bold actions were possible under some conditions but not others, certainly had an influence.

What the findings further suggest is that societal actors—both those in the government and those outside of it—can mold national ideas at home and abroad. This effect was most evident in the influence of the United States on West Germany after World War II, tilting the balance in favor of integration. The impact was twofold. It had helped discredit the prior armed expansion approach by contributing to the military defeat of Nazi Germany. And in the postwar era it ensured that the emerging integration mind-set promoted by Adenauer got the support that led to its consolidation in the society as a whole. Neglect can have an effect as well, as seen in the deleterious impact of the United States and the Allies on the post–World War I collapse of internationalism and democratic stability in the Weimar Republic. These situations also suggest that the ideas of the strong will often have more influence because of the resources they have to project their ideas.

Ideational influence, however, is not limited to the strong molding the weak. Nonstate actors in the United States did much to influence new thinking in the comparably powerful Soviet Union during the cold war. In the early stages of World War II, a weaker Britain had more influence on the United States than vice versa. Moreover, a variety of recent research suggests that "weak" agents of civil societies can be influential both within and across borders.[74] The effects of international terrorism demonstrate this in a particularly heinous fashion. In the history I examined, activists both in and outside government are critical in a specific way: they help to establish the social saliency of replacement ideas. Often out of the spotlight, and sometimes leading to naught, such efforts remain a necessary element of ideational transformation. In the absence of such alternatives, continuity may prevail simply because of the lack of a new orthodoxy to guide action.

Similar great powers in similar situations have thought about their foreign relations in very different ways. Those differences have shaped not only each country's foreign policy, they have also helped constitute international order for over two centuries. The expanding reach of technology in the late nineteenth century seemed to suggest that international understanding had arrived—either by steamship or by telegraph. The embrace by countries such as Japan of Western norms of diplomacy helped confirm that view. World War I was an abrupt wake-up call. When the United States balked at taking a leadership role commensurate with its power in the interwar period, the way was cleared for a revisionist power to topple any further development of international order. When Germany renewed its armed expansion views and joined with Japan, World War II was ignited. Yet during that conflict, the sea change in U.S. views toward internationalism signaled the birth of the latest version of Atlantic international society. An embrace of the principles of that order by other major powers such as Japan, the United States, and Germany helped to solidify it.

Not all countries, of course, accepted the new order. The Soviet Union and its brethren Marxist-Leninist regimes maintained their distance from, and even sought the transformation of, the Atlantic Pact order. The reforms in China that began in the late 1970s and the new thinking revolution in the Soviet Union in the 1980s mean that no major powers are currently outside the bounds of contemporary international society—assuming the United States maintains its own Atlantic Pact ideas. This situation has led some to posit an end point in history—a final agreement on how societies, national and international, should conduct themselves.[75] Others see a whole new type of international integration based on the decline in communication and travel costs.[76] Not coincidentally, the "English School" (primarily British scholars responsible for the initial formulation of the concept of international society or interested in its development) has decided in these early years of the twenty-first century to reconvene after two decades of dormancy.[77]

History, however, suggests that we should be skeptical of any permanent fixtures or irreversible directions. Even as countries have become increasingly close, and relations among their peoples denser, the solidarity of international society has waxed and waned. Globalization appears less like a train racing in one direction in the twenty-first century than as a series of tides that will come and go. The end of the cold war has meant the end of one version of ideological schism in international relations. It has not meant the end of ideas—as the spread of radical Islamic terrorism makes disturbingly clear. Nor has it meant the end of contestation over the shape and content of international order, which will depend, for the foreseeable future, on the attitudes of major groups in the international arena, most importantly, nation-states.

It is therefore important to consider the possibility of ideational collapse and consolidation in ongoing cases of potential national transformation—especially involving major powers. As we have seen, the interplay of ideas in the United States and China could begin to constitute a new international society in the early hours of the twenty-first century. The ability of individuals who seek to overturn enduring approaches to international politics—and they exist in each country—will depend not just on their skills or the groups to which they belong or even the strategic situation their country faces, but also on each nation's collective expectations and experienced events. International politics in the future, as in the past, requires not only an understanding of the power and parochial interests of nations but also of their ideas—and the possibility that they will change.

Appendix 1

The Transformation of Economic Ideas

In this appendix I explore the argument in an issue area other than foreign policy: national economic policy, including macro, monetary, and trade issues. A considerable literature, which aims to incorporate the influence of economic ideas on policies, has bloomed in recent years.[1] I reexamine this literature through the lens of the argument in chapter 2. Because these works were written without knowledge of my argument; to the extent they reflect similar causes and mechanisms, the more likely it is that the argument is useful and applicable to other policy issues as well.

Several broad themes are apparent in this literature. First, countries often react differently to the same crisis or shock—that is, we cannot simply appeal to the nature of the shock to understand why countries pick the economic ideas they do.[2] They do so at least in part because they encounter their circumstances with a different set of expectations based on differing prior ideas. Thus, the events entail different meanings. States act according to their own experiences, using criteria that may or may not be optimal given the circumstances they face.

Second, change in dominant economic concepts suggests they follow a pattern similar to the two-stage collapse and consolidation process. Some type of initial shock, brought on by a clash of events and expectations, produces a challenge to the dominant orthodoxy. This in turn leads to a period of political skirmishing and de facto experimentation, culminating in either consolidation around a new orthodoxy or a return to the old. Which particular outcome occurs depends on the interaction of expectations and results and the distribution and viability of replacement ideas.

Finally, states will often adopt policies that correlate with desired results even when there is no clear evidence that those policies caused those results. In these cases no one—or at least not the majority—can be bothered to verify actual causes; they settle simply for results. This might make sense for an individual who needs to conserve on search costs. Yet, given what is at stake for societies, most people appear almost uninterested, gadflies aside. When the outcomes are positive, few ask questions—and those that do are ignored by society. Change in such a situation is unlikely.

To highlight an ideational dynamic is not to overlook the emphasis the different studies put on factors such as skilled leadership, institutional structures, interest group politics, coalition dynamics, or environmental (e.g., market) pressures.[3] Rather the point is to show how important parts of these independent analyses can be captured by the argument of this book, including not only similar causes and effects but the particular causal paths described in the scenarios in chapter 2. This is evident in work addressing ideas in such diverse areas as state control of the economy, macroeconomic policies, industrial strategy, trade, and monetary policy. Studies on these topics can be divided into two broad historical groupings: (1) the era of the Great Depression and World War II, and (2) other eras.

THE GREAT DEPRESSION AND WORLD WAR II

Undoubtedly the most concentrated work done on the transformation of economic ideas is that which looks at the changes wrought by the Great Depression and World War II. Here we see two major shocks that are generally thought to have reconfigured the economic world. On closer inspection, however, these shocks led to change in ideas in some countries, but not others, and to different outcomes in different countries.[4] Why? Studies that have looked at Keynesianism, industrial strategy and macroeconomic policy, trade, and economic development shed some light on the ideational aspects of these variations that help answer this question.

Keynesianism

A number of scholars have examined why Keynesian ideas emerged in the 1930s and 1940s and why the reception of those ideas varied so much across even industrialized countries.[5] Overall, the similarity of change in many countries—the broad turn to state intervention and management of the economy—seems to have occurred as a result of the Great Depression and World War II. The Depression helped to discredit the expectations generated by the prevailing view that the economy was a self-regulating entity that did not need state intervention. In particular countries, Keynes's thinking on state intervention, however, only came to have an influence after World War II.

Some countries embraced Keynesian ideas while others distanced themselves. Britain and the United States, for example, favored a more free market, less interventionist approach to managing the economy before World War II, and especially before the Great Depression. After World War II, however, these countries incorporated Keynesian state management of the economy. In contrast, Germany moved away from direct government management of demand and employment after the war. Keynesianism was not as welcome. Instead, the dominant economic orthodoxy became the "social market economy" model, under which the state makes the rules and provides a social safety net for a self-regulating private sector that features cooperation among firms and between trade unions and employers.

These different outcomes appear to have similar sources in the intersection of undesired consequences and different prior orthodoxies. In Britain and the United States a prewar liberal view was rejected after World War II because of its failure to meet expectations and its (seeming) disastrous results in the interwar years. In Germany, however, demand management and price controls, ideas closer to Keynesianism, were discredited. This occurred because Keynes's ideas were linked to state-directed economies, which was too close for comfort to the disasters of Nazi central control as well as the meager returns of the Allied Control Authority's continuance of price controls after the war.[6]

The fate of new ideas offered in response to these crises varied significantly with the seeming results they produced. In the absence of some reinforcing outcomes for replacement ideas, there was often a return to the prior orthodoxy. In the United States during the 1930s, for example, plans that foreshadowed Keynes's ideas—such as the first New Deal's emphasis on public spending (albeit without Keynesian deficit spending)—initially met with poor results. The downturn of 1937 threw the New Deal into "an acute crisis."[7] In Britain and the United States the war provided a new lease on life for Keynesian ideas. The success they had then helped to solidify their standing in the years that followed. Likewise the consolidation in Germany of "social market" thinking after World War II can be traced to the "German miracle" of economic growth in the 1950s.[8] It is not clear that the new ideas were the source of that success, but they were embraced and institutionalized as if they had been.[9]

Industrial Strategy vs. Macroeconomic Policy

Different countries' notions about macroeconomic policy and industrial strategy were also put to the test during the Great Depression. A comparison of the two raises an intriguing puzzle.[10] Macroeconomic policy across Britain, France, and the United States looked very similar after the crisis. But in contrast to this shared response, the three nations pursued different industrial policies. Why?

Two factors appear central: the nature of the dominant beliefs that characterized the two issue areas before the Depression, and the consequences experienced in using those policies in response to the downturn. Going into the Depression, the "industrial culture" of the countries differed. Each nation had a different pattern of institutionalized beliefs about how to structure industries and economies. For example, the United States had a market-centric orthodoxy involving policy beliefs focused on antitrust and the restriction of the government financing industry. Britain's firm-centric industrial culture was matched by policy concepts that supported small firms. Finally, France had a state-centric view where the government was very active in directing economic development including control or ownership of important industries.[11]

The disastrous and unexpected economic consequences of the Great Depression, however, cast doubt on these policies. The dominant orthodoxy in each country was discredited, producing a surge of interest in alternative policies, specifically, in the *opposite* ideas to the preexisting orthodoxy. Thus, France moved to laissez-faire, the United States turned to state-led cartelization, and Britain experimented with encouraging monopolies. But these policies never stuck, because at the time they were initiated they seemed to garner no positive results.

In contrast, in macroeconomic policies, all countries rejected the same basic approach—adhering to the gold standard and cutting spending in hard times—and adopted the exact opposite strategy of devaluing the currency and increasing government spending. This change, however, stuck because it appeared to coincide with "success"—that is, an upturn in economic fortunes. According to Frank Dobbin, nations came to believe in policies that preceded economic growth, even though (as economists later argued) they did not cause that growth.[12] Thus poorly understood fluctuations in economic fortunes played a central role in affecting which policies were seen as effective and thus adopted.[13]

Trade Policy

Still another economic issue area where an ideational logic seems to hold involves U.S. trade policy. America's shift from protectionism to a more free market approach has been a defining factor in the making of the international economy in the twentieth century. U.S. trade policy after World War I—for example, the Fordney-McCumber and Smoot-Hawley tariffs—was an extension of long-standing dominant ideas about appropriate commercial exchange. These tariffs were not appropriate for either the U.S. position in the global economy or the economic efficiency of U.S. producers, which suggested that a more open economy better served American interests. Nonetheless, the protectionist orthodoxy, embedded in institutions, held that the United States could expand exports without opening its own markets. This orthodoxy prevailed even while most economists believed that liberalization was needed. The hegemony of protectionist ideas was potent.[14]

What changed this orthodoxy? Judith Goldstein's analysis of United States trade policy argues that the Great Depression acted as a shock that broke the ideational and institutional logjam favoring protectionism. Why it was the Great Depression that had this effect demonstrates the causal mechanisms discussed above: the consequences of protectionism were ruinous and dramatically contradicted the expectations of ideationally driven behavior, while a single replacement view (liberalization) seemed to promise better results. The contrast between expectations and negative results allowed opponents of protectionism to challenge the orthodoxy with an alternative. When desirable results correlated with those efforts, a major transformation was socially embedded.

This shift does not appear to be simply an adaptation to circumstances or "an enlightenment triumph."[15] Correct long-term policies can be rejected simply because they do not appear to produce results, whereas less efficient options can gain ascendancy because they appear to correlate with satisfactory effects. Societies as a whole do not question the causal logic of their ideas when the results are desirable. Individual critics and gadflies who try to point out any contradictions will make little headway. Yet when starkly negative results are encountered, societies are much more likely to behave like scientific realists and question, however superficially and reactively, the causal mechanisms posited by their beliefs.

This conclusion is clear when we consider what appears to be something close to a type A3 "If it ain't broke" don't fix it logic behind early twentieth-century U.S. trade policy. In 1913 the United States deviated from its tradition of protectionist trade legislation by passing the rate-reducing Underwood tariff. This move toward openness might be explained as reflecting the changing nature of domestic interest groups at the time, as well as the growing power of the United States in the world. Moreover, the results that followed were relatively solid, although they were somewhat overshadowed by the onset of World War I in 1914. Still, the absence of immediate negative feedback made this departure from tradition less likely to appear on the public screen as an issue worthy of debate. Only when the economy went downhill after World War I and imports surged was there an A2 "Told you so" reaction. Harding led the return to "normalcy" and a renewal of protectionist tradition in 1920–21.[16]

Economic Development

A final example from the world wars era involves the transformation of ideas on economic development in South America. Specifically, Argentina and Brazil went in a direction different than the international liberalization seen in the Western countries discussed above. This variation is largely due to the different starting point of the countries in South America. Before the Great Depression, these countries considered their economic development as best served by a liberal model of integration in world markets and growth through exports. Yet the Depression and World War II cut off those markets (and imports) and undermined the strategy. Argentina and Brazil no longer wanted to be vulnerable to the type of dependence that had caused such hardship in the 1930s and 1940s. They experimented with more nationalist import-substitution strategies that met with some success, leading to their continuation after the war.[17] This occurred even though the international arena in the 1950s and 1960s became more conducive to the success of a liberal program. The United States moved toward lower tariffs, international institutions facilitated exchange, and international capital was more readily available. In South America, however, integrationist thinking had been discredited, creating the new aloofness from the international economy. Brazil and Argentina thus adhered to an import-substitution orthodoxy, even as increasing opportunities for the success of a liberal policy became available.[18]

OTHER ERAS

The dynamics seen in events surrounding the Great Depression and Second World War are also found in other eras, although the role of ideas is sometimes not so explicitly acknowledged. Still, studies on economic policy and trade in the nineteenth century, as well as those on monetarism and monetary integration in the 1970s and 1980s, speak to the role of ideas in change.

The Rise of Free Trade

This effect is seen in the rise of free trade thinking as a new "economic culture" in Britain in the nineteenth century. Although there was no "great depression," a series of economic setbacks—hunger, industrial distress, and bank failures—provoked a rethinking and quest for alternatives. The Manchester movement promoted free trade as the most effective policy and had established itself as a challenger to the dominant mercantilist orthodoxy. But this movement only succeeded under the conditions described by the A4 "Do something!" to B3 "Long live change!" sequence in chapter 2. Prompted by an economic downturn, the country lurched to the free trade alternative in the early 1840s. The partial repeal of tariffs in 1842 seemed to generate positive results, reinforcing the turn away from protectionism. The new orthodoxy was then more broadly implemented with the repeal of the Corn Laws in 1846 and a number of related measures.[19]

The 1873 Depression and Economic Policy

Peter Gourevitch's landmark study of the effects of the two "great depressions" (1873 and 1929) on national economic policies speaks to some of the same sources of change as I have advanced.[20] Gourevitch offers a rich synthetic historical explanation for the different responses of countries to depressions. Generally, however, he accords "economic ideology" (perceptions, models, values, traditions) a secondary role—one important in shaping the alternatives available to societies or in helping to form social coalitions. He rightly critiques extant economic ideology explanations as being able to explain continuity but, because they stress constants, unable to account for change.[21] Yet this reasoning presumes that because ideas do not explain all of change, they play *no* role in change. Specifically, it overlooks the impact of ideationally driven expectations and their particular interaction with events.

For example, in analyzing the 1873 depression, Gourevitch posits that this event represented the same shock for the different countries, which all shared a basic free trade, classic liberalism orientation.[22] But this was not so. These countries differed in their commitment to free trade. As Gourevitch notes, Britain had a much more liberal free trade ideology than Germany, which leaned toward interventionism.[23] It is not surprising then that their ideas took different forms over time, as they responded to different sets of expectations and different types of replacement ideas. Here we see that "policy legacies" (collective ideas) can influence how actors in the same position respond differently to similar circumstances.[24]

Gourevitch provides a penetrating analysis of the coalitional and leadership factors at work. His general argument, however, does not account for why one group or set of ideas wins out over another.[25] His conclusion, that ideology helps social coalitions form, explicitly recognizes the way ideational factors have an influence. But it begs the questions of why and when this is likely to occur. My framework suggests when crises are likely to provide an opportunity for change and, depending on the nature of the replacement ideas, what new directions are likely, if any.

The Shift to Monetarism and Monetary Integration in the 1970s and 1980s

A final case involving change in economic ideas takes us to the 1970s and 1980s. In Britain (and the United States) during the 1970s the previously dominant Keynesian ideas—with their origins in World War II—came under heavy assault. They appeared insufficient to explain the problems brought on by the 1974 economic crisis induced by the Arab oil embargo and consequent global oil shortage.[26] The key reason for this challenge was that the expectations generated by Keynesianism were contradicted by the negative results. The Keynesian model could not anticipate or solve the problem of stagflation—unemployment and inflation rising together. Yet societies did not immediately embrace a new orthodoxy. Why?

A negative anomaly was not enough to provoke change: there had to be an alternative. In the British case, no widely accepted replacement model existed, and the government subsequently fumbled its way through several years of problematic incomes policy and concessions to labor unions.[27] In the meantime, monetarism took shape as a viable alternative. In 1979 it achieved dominance when its political supporters, the Conservative Party led by Margaret Thatcher, came to power. The change to monetarism might appear as simply a result of a switch in political parties that also brought a different policy agenda. The interaction of ideas and events, however, produced Thatcher's victory as much as it can be said that Thatcher's victory "caused" the change in British economic thought.[28] Thatcher came to power in the wake of failures that seemed to result from the continued adherence to Keynesian ideas.

Kathleen McNamara builds on this analysis to explain variations in European monetary integration. European governments attempted to institute a monetary collaboration plan (the "snake") in 1972, but as a collective venture it collapsed within a year. In contrast, the European Monetary System (EMS) initiated in 1979 worked well until 1992 and was the foundation for more ambitious follow-on efforts.

The difference in these outcomes, according to McNamara, can be accounted for by the shift in the willingness of states to forgo the autonomous conduct of monetary policy because of a change in ideas about what policies work. In many countries, a Keynesian consensus favored domestic policy autonomy as a means to growth and employment (implying intervention) over international monetary cooperation (which required nonintervention). The oil crises of 1974 and 1979, however, delegitimized the Keynesian consensus. These crises allowed discursive space for critics of the old orthodoxy to challenge the dominant notions. Yet change required a replacement concept, a new compass for economic policy. This appeared in the form of the monetarist "neoliberal" paradigm, which seemed to explain such puzzles as the simultaneously increasing rate of inflation and unemployment. Most important, countries watched Germany successfully experiment with the idea. The result was a widespread turn to monetarism, a shift that also fostered successful international monetary cooperation in the EMS.[29]

This brief analysis suggests that the same dynamics found in foreign policy ideas also apply to the realm of economic ideas. The works I have looked at are limited and necessarily biased (they all focus on ideas to some degree). Nonetheless, they were not informed by the logic of my argument. That so many illustrate the same mechanisms of continuity and change suggests the potential to apply the argument more broadly in other issue areas.

Appendix 2

Analysis of Presidential Discourse

Figure 3.1 is based on a content analysis of all the State of the Union addresses between 1908 and 1950. I assessed the passages relating to foreign policy in terms of positive and negative statements about different types of actions for enhancing U.S. security and welfare. I assigned numerical scores for the text in terms of its language and causal arguments relating to foreign policy on a six point continuum (0–5) that measures no-entanglement versus internationalist sentiment (in half point increments):[1]

0 The United States should avoid getting involved in international relations with major powers. To the extent possible the United States should live and let live. The country can best lead by example. (This end of the spectrum is stronger to the degree rhetoric also denigrates the opposite end.)

1 The United States should necessarily engage the world, but it should do so without binding itself in institutional arrangements.

2 The United States should play a larger role in world affairs. This might involve some limited institutional commitments such as arms control and the mutual lowering of tariffs. But traditional political-military alliances or general commitments to collective security institutions should be proscribed, especially with Europe.

3 The United States should play a large role in the world, especially in economic affairs. There is a positive attitude toward the benefits of international institutions, but not toward those involving military precommitments.

4 The security of the United States would be best served by more substantial international commitments and agreements, even those that involve military precommitments.

5 The security of the United States depends on actively constructing international institutions and relationships that tie it to other major powers, and to which it gives political-military backing. (This end of the spectrum is stronger to the degree rhetoric also denigrates the opposite end.)

The line in figure 3.1 reflects my coding. A second coder (blind to the purposes and content of the study and my coding) also assessed the passages according to the above 12 possibilities. We assigned the same value in 39 percent of the 41 observations. In 37 percent we differed by ½ point, in 15 percent by 1 point, in 10 percent by 1½ points, and in one observation by 2 points.

I also surveyed the editorial response to the State of the Union addresses of four newspapers (reflecting different regions and partisan leanings): the *New York Times,* the *Chicago Tribune,* the *St. Louis Post-Dispatch,* and the *Los Angeles Times.* Sometimes they offer only passing comments on foreign affairs, sometimes they only address the domestic portions of the speeches. Those editorials that make no mention of foreign affairs or do not contain enough to code are not included—hence each paper may not have a symbol for every year. I have coded these (and placed them on figure 3.1) in terms of their response to the State of Union depending on whether they call for more internationalism, less internationalism, or about the same level of internationalism as the president's speech for that year:

1. If the editorial calls for more internationalism than is proposed in the State of the Union address, then the symbol for that year is placed a half point above the line.
2. If the editorial suggests that there is about the right level of internationalism in the address, the symbol is placed on the line.
3. If the editorial calls for less internationalism than is proposed in the State of the Union address, the symbol is placed a half point below the line.

The content of "less" and "more" is defined by the 6-point scale above. Again, a second coder assessed the editorials. In 71 percent of the editorials (n=92) we assigned the same rank. In 25 percent we differed by 1 rank. And in 4 percent we had opposite rankings.

Notes

Chapter 1. Great Power Ideas and Change

1. For works that demonstrate the influence of national policy ideas, see, for example, John Odell, *U.S. International Monetary Policy: Markets, Power, and Ideas as Sources of Change* (Princeton: Princeton University Press, 1982); Emanuel Adler, *The Power of Ideology: The Quest for Technological Autonomy in Argentina and Brazil* (Berkeley: University of California Press, 1987); Paul Egon Rohrlich, "Economic Culture and Foreign Policy," *International Organization* 41 (1987); Kathryn Sikkink, *Ideas and Institutions: Developmentalism in Brazil and Argentina* (Ithaca: Cornell University Press, 1991); Peter Hall, "Policy Paradigms, Social Learning, and the State," *Comparative Politics* 25, no. 3 (1993); Judith Goldstein, *Ideas, Interests, and American Trade Policy* (Ithaca: Cornell University Press, 1993); Judith Goldstein and Robert O. Keohane, *Ideas and Foreign Policy: Beliefs, Institutions, and Political Change* (Ithaca: Cornell University Press, 1993); Charles A. Kupchan, *The Vulnerability of Empire* (Ithaca: Cornell University Press, 1994); Alastair Iain Johnston, *Cultural Realism: Strategic Culture and Grand Strategy in Chinese History* (Princeton: Princeton University Press, 1995); Jeffrey W. Legro, *Cooperation under Fire* (Ithaca: Cornell University Press, 1995); Peter Katzenstein, *The Culture of National Security: Norms, Identity, and World Politics* (New York: Columbia University Press, 1996), and *Cultural Norms and National Security: Police and Military in Postwar Japan* (Ithaca: Cornell University Press, 1996); Dan Reiter, *Crucible of Beliefs* (Ithaca: Cornell University Press, 1996); Elizabeth Kier, *Imagining War: French and British Military Doctrine between the Wars* (Princeton: Princeton University Press, 1997); Thomas U. Berger, *Cultures of Antimilitarism: National Security in Germany and Japan* (New York: Columbia University Press, 1998); Sheri Berman, *The Social Democratic Moment: Ideas and Politics in the Making of Interwar Europe* (Cambridge: Harvard University Press, 1998); Kathleen R. McNamara, *The Currency of Ideas: Monetary Politics in the European Union* (Ithaca: Cornell University Press, 1998); James J. Walsh, "When Do Ideas Matter? Explaining the Successes and Failures of Thatcherite Ideas," *Comparative Political Studies* 33, no. 4 (2000); Mark Blyth, *Great Transformations: Economic Ideas and Institutional Change in the Twentieth Century* (New York: Cambridge University Press, 2002).

2. Hedley Bull, *The Anarchical Society: A Study of Order in World Politics*, 2nd ed. (New York: Columbia University Press, 1995), 13.

3. This is true whether structure is defined in terms of power (see John G. Ruggie, "Continuity and Transformation in the World Polity: Toward a Neorealist Synthesis," in *Neorealism and Its Critics*, ed. Robert O. Keohane [New York: Columbia University Press, 1986]) or norms

(see Paul Kowert and Jeffrey Legro, "Norms, Identity, and Their Limits: A Theoretical Reprise," in *The Culture of National Security,* ed. Peter Katzenstein [New York: Columbia University Press, 1996]).

4. Hidemi Suganami, "The International Society Perspective on World Politics Reconsidered," *International Relations of the Asia-Pacific* 2, no. 1 (2002); Timothy Dunne, "The Social Construction of International Society," *European Journal of International Relations* 1, no. 3 (1995), 347.

5. Exemplars of interest approaches include Helen V. Milner, *Resisting Protectionism: Global Industries and the Politics of International Trade* (Princeton: Princeton University Press, 1988); Jack Snyder, *Myths of Empire* (Ithaca: Cornell University Press, 1991); Andrew Moravcsik, *The Choice for Europe: Social Progress and State Power from Messina to Maastricht* (Ithaca: Cornell University Press, 1988); power approaches include Kenneth Waltz, *Theory of International Politics* (Baltimore: Addison-Wesley, 1979); Joanne S. Gowa, *Allies, Adversaries, and International Trade* (Princeton: Princeton University Press, 1994); John J. Mearsheimer, *The Tragedy of Great Power Politics* (New York: Norton, 2001); and institutional approaches include Robert O. Keohane, *After Hegemony: Cooperation and Discord in the World Political Economy* (Princeton: Princeton University Press, 1984); Lisa L. Martin, *Coercive Cooperation: Explaining Multilateral Economic Sanctions* (Princeton: Princeton University Press, 1992); G. John Ikenberry, *After Victory* (Princeton: Princeton University Press, 2001).

6. See, e.g., note 1 and the large literatures on identity and norms, key works of which are reviewed in Emanuel Adler, "Constructivism and International Relations," in *Handbook of International Relations,* ed. Walter Carlsnaes, Thomas Risse, and Beth Simmons (London: Sage, 2002).

7. See Jeffrey W. Legro, "The Transformation of Policy Ideas," *American Journal of Political Science* 44, no. 3 (2000). Some approaches in economics reflect this same bias; see Chris Mantzavinos, Douglass C. North, and Syed Shariq, "Learning, Institutions, and Economic Performance," *Perspectives on Politics* 2, no. 1 (2004): 75–84. A second issue in the psychology literature is the deluge of hypotheses on individual mental activity, many of which indicate tendencies that appear mutually contradictory. For example, cognitive dissonance theory versus learning theory (e.g., Hovland attitude approach). See Robert Jervis, *Perception and Misperception in International Politics* (Princeton: Princeton University Press, 1976); Deborah Larson, *Origins of Containment* (Princeton: Princeton University Press, 1985).

8. Work in comparative politics—often produced under the label "historical institutionalism"—displays similar strengths and weaknesses on the problem of change as the international relations literature. See, e.g., Sheri Berman, "Ideas, Norms, and Culture in Political Analysis," *Comparative Politics* 33 (2001); Mark Blyth, "Structures Do Not Come with an Instruction Sheet: Interests, Ideas, and Progress in Political Science," *Perspectives on Politics* 1 (2003).

9. E.g., Michael Brown, ed., *The Rise of China* (Cambridge: MIT Press, 2000).

10. Denny Roy, "Hegemon on the Horizon? China's Threat to East Asian Security," *International Security* 19, no. 1 (1994); Richard Bernstein and Ross Munroe, *The Coming Conflict with China* (New York: Alfred A. Knopf, 1997); Mearsheimer, *Tragedy of Great Power Politics,* 396–402. Thomas Christensen, "Posing Problems without Catching Up: China's Rise and Challenges for U.S. Security Policy," *International Security* 25, no. 4 (2001), offers a nuanced account that the problem is not overall power but specific capabilities in specific scenarios.

11. Exceptions include Weixing Hu, Gerald Chan, and Daojiong Zha, *China's International Relations in the 21st Century: Dynamics of Paradigm Shifts* (Lanham, Md.: University Press of America, 2000); Alastair Iain Johnston, "Treating International Institutions as Social Environments," *International Studies Quarterly* 45, no. 4 (2001).

12. When I refer to "power" I mean the capabilities and resources of states rather than their "influence."

13. The vast majority of power transitions take place without conflict. See Indra De Soysa, John R. Oneal, Yong-Hee Park, "Testing Power-Transition Theory Using Alternative Measures of National Capabilities," *Journal of Conflict Resolution* 41, no. 4 (1997).

14. E.g., Ivo Daalder and James Lindsay, *America Unbound: The Bush Revolution in Foreign Policy* (Washington, D.C.: Brookings Institution Press, 2003).

15. For more on the difference between collective and individual ideas see Alexander Wendt, *Social Theory of International Politics* (Cambridge: Cambridge University Press, 1999), esp. 150–64; Legro, "Transformation of Policy Ideas."

16. See, e.g., Jervis, *Perception and Misperception;* Robert Jervis, Richard N. Lebow, and Janice Stein, eds., *Psychology and Deterrence* (Baltimore: Johns Hopkins University Press, 1985). Note that Jervis often gives examples that refer to the ideas of groups, but for him the salience of this distinction is less important.

17. Therefore, collective ideas are distinct from "public opinion," in which some majority of individual views is assumed to constitute a dominant view. Charles Taylor, "Interpretation and the Sciences of Man," *Review of Metaphysics* 25 (1971), makes the classic distinction between collective opinion and aggregate individual opinion.

18. Jervis, *Perception and Misperception,* 238. Jervis goes on to note the institutionalization of ideas and their collective effects.

19. Emile Durkheim, *The Rules of Sociological Method* (New York: Free Press, 1966); Max Weber, *The Protestant Ethic and the Spirit of Capitalism* (New York: Scribner, 1976).

20. Taylor, "Interpretation and the Sciences of Man"; Margaret Gilbert, "Modeling Collective Beliefs," *Synthese* 73 (1987). John R. Searle, *The Construction of Social Reality* (New York: Free Press, 1995), esp. 24–26, refers to this as "collective intentionality." Collective intentionality plus status produces "institutional facts," which roughly correspond to the dominant collective ideas studied here. "The remarkable feature of institutional structures is that people continue to acknowledge and cooperate in many of them even when it is by no means to their advantage to do so" (Searle, 92).

21. Durkheim, *Rules of Sociological Method,* 70.

22. Jerome H. Barkow, Leda Cosmides, and John Tooby, eds., *The Adapted Mind: Evolutionary Psychology and the Generation of Culture* (New York: Oxford University Press, 1992).

23. Brad Shore, *Culture in Mind: Cognition, Culture, and the Problem of Meaning* (New York: Oxford University Press, 1996): 3–4.

24. E.g., Paul DiMaggio, "Culture and Cognition," *Annual Review of Sociology* 23 (1997); Richard Nisbett, *The Geography of Thought: Why We Think the Way We Do* (New York: Free Press, 2003).

25. Joanne Martin, *Culture in Organizations: Three Perspectives* (New York: Oxford University Press, 1992). See also Phillip Selznick, *Leadership in Administration: A Sociological Interpretation* (New York: Harper and Row, 1957), 14–16, 38–42; and James Q. Wilson, *Bureaucracy: What Government Agencies Do and Why They Do It* (New York: Basic Books, 1989).

26. See e.g., Sonja A. Sackmann, "Culture and Subcultures: An Analysis of Organizational Knowledge," *Administrative Science Quarterly* 37, no. 1 (1992).

27. David M. Kreps, "Corporate Cultures and Economic Theory," in *Perspectives on Positive Political Economy,* ed. James E. Alt and Kenneth A. Schepsle (New York: Cambridge University Press, 1990).

28. See Benedict Anderson, *Imagined Communities: Reflections upon the Origin and Spread of Nationalism,* 2nd ed. (London: Verso, 1983); Maurice Halbwachs, *On Collective Memory,* trans. L. A. Coser (Chicago: University of Chicago Press, 1992); David Kertzer, *Ritual, Politics, and Power* (New Haven: Yale University Press, 1988).

29. Karl Marx, "The Eighteenth Brumaire of Louis Bonaparte," in *The Marx-Engels Reader,* 2nd ed., ed. Robert Tucker (New York: W. W. Norton, 1978), 595.

30. For different answers to this question in international relations scholarship, see Legro, "Transformation of Policy Ideas."

31. Robert A. Divine, *Second Chance: The Triumph of Internationalism in America during World War II* (New York: Atheneum, 1967).

32. Margaret Weir and Theda Skocpol, "State Structures and the Possibilities for Keynesian Responses to the Great Depression in Sweden, Britain, and the United States," in *Bringing the State Back In,* ed. Peter B. Evans, Dietrich Rueschemeyer, and Theda Skocpol (Cambridge: Cambridge University Press, 1985); Peter Hall, "Policy Paradigms, Social Learning, and the State," 279; Stephen Ellingson, "Understanding the Dialectic of Discourse and Collective Action: Public Debate and Rioting in Antebellum Cincinnati," *American Journal of Sociology* 101, no. 1

(1995): 107; Frank Dobbin, *Forging Industrial Policy: The United States, Britain, and France in the Railway Age* (Cambridge: Cambridge University Press, 1994), 5; Berman, *Social Democratic Moment*, 21.

33. In broad terms such ideas are generally "more fluid, pragmatic, amenable to the proof of success or failure, and leave a certain latitude to language, experience, and even the critical faculties of individuals." These can be contrasted with a second category that "are generally more homogeneous, affective, impermeable to experience or contradiction, and leave little scope for individual variations," such as many religious beliefs. Serge Moscovici, "The History and Actuality of Social Representations," in *The Psychology of the Social*, ed. Uwe Flick (Cambridge: Cambridge University Press, 1998), 226–27.

34. Goldstein and Keohane, *Ideas and Foreign Policy*, 18. I do not see these ideas as technical or changeable as do Goldstein and Keohane.

35. Barry Posen, *The Sources of Military Doctrine: France, Britain, and Germany between the World Wars* (Ithaca: Cornell University Press, 1984). The ideas I examine, however, are not always so self-conscious and purposely formed as seems to be the case in Posen's conceptualization, which invokes images of wise leaders cloistered in a map room charting a nation's overall plans.

36. See http://www.state.gov/m/rm/rls/dosstrat/2004/23503.htm. On the general dynamic see Robert K. Merton, "Bureaucratic Structure and Personality," *Social Forces* 17 (1940): 560–68; Phillip Selznick, *TVA and the Grass Roots: A Study of Politics and Organization* (Berkeley: University of California Press, 1949), 69–70, 250–59; Selznick, *Leadership in Administration*, 16; Jervis, *Perception and Misperception*, 418–23; Ann Swidler, "Culture in Action: Symbols and Strategies," *American Sociological Review* 51, no. 2 (1986): 276–77; Wilson, *Bureaucracy*, 32–33.

37. Ernest R. May, "The Nature of Foreign Policy: The Calculated versus the Axiomatic," *Daedalus* 91, no. 4 (1962).

38. Ibid., 667.

39. Johnston, *Cultural Realism*; Kupchan, *Vulnerability of Empire*; Goldstein, *Ideas, Interests, and American Trade Policy*; Legro, *Cooperation under Fire*.

40. See, for example, Posen, *Sources of Military Doctrine*; Paul Kennedy, *The Rise and Fall of Great Powers* (New York: Random House, 1987).

41. Paul Kennedy, ed., *Grand Strategies in War and Peace* (New Haven: Yale University Press, 1991); Arthur Stein and Richard Rosecrance, eds., *The Domestic Bases of Grand Strategy* (Ithaca: Cornell University Press, 1993).

42. See John Lewis Gaddis, *Strategies of Containment: A Critical Appraisal of Postwar American National Security Policy* (New York: Oxford University Press, 1982).

43. On different forms of international society, see Hedley Bull and Adam Watson, eds., *The Expansion of International Society* (Oxford: Oxford University Press, 1984); Christian Reus-Smit, *The Moral Purpose of the State: Culture, Social Identity, and Institutional Rationality in International Relations* (Princeton: Princeton University Press, 1999); Gerrit Gong, *The Standard of Civilization in International Society* (Oxford: Oxford University Press, 1984), 14–21, lists the standards as they evolved by the early twentieth century.

44. Hence internationalism here does not imply peace or harmony. Cf. Kjell Goldmann, *The Logic of Internationalism: Coercion and Accommodation* (London: Routledge, 1994), 2.

45. In Jon Elster's formulation, interests plus beliefs produce action. See his introduction to *Rational Choice*, ed. Jon Elster (New York: New York University Press, 1986). On the broader rationalist "state actor" framework of the different schools, see Andrew Moravcsik, "Taking Preferences Seriously: A Liberal Theory of International Politics," *International Organization* 51, no. 4 (1997), and Jeffrey W. Legro and Andrew Moravcsik, "Is Anybody Still a Realist?" *International Security* 24, no. 2 (1999).

46. On the inability of rationalist approaches to account persuasively for such ideas within their own logic in the uncertain realm of international politics, see Albert S. Yee, "Thick Rationality and the Missing 'Brute' Fact: The Limits of Rationalist Incorporation of Norms and Ideas," *Journal of Politics* 59, no. 4 (1997).

47. In trying to understand such lags, Stephen Krasner notes that "some catalytic external event seems necessary to move states to dramatic policy initiatives in line with state interests"

("State Power and the Structure of International Trade," *World Politics* 28, no. 3 [1976]: 341). A number of sociologists have focused on the distinction between "settled" and "unsettled" periods, believing that the likelihood of change is much greater in the latter. See especially Swidler, "Culture in Action," and Harry Eckstein, "A Culturalist Theory of Political Change," *American Political Science Review* 82, no. 3 (1988). In *After Victory,* John Ikenberry studies "rare moments" of institutional change at the international level following wars. For other examples or reliance on "shock," see Mancur Olson, *The Rise and Decline of Nations* (New Haven: Yale University Press, 1982); Robert Higgs, *Crisis and Leviathan: Critical Episodes in the Growth of American Government* (New York: Oxford University Press, 1987); Jack A. Goldstone, *Revolution and Rebellion in the Early Modern World* (Berkeley: University of California Press, 1991); Yuen Foong Khong, *Analogies at War: Korea, Munich, Dien Bien Phu, and the Vietnam Decisions of 1965* (Princeton: Princeton University Press, 1992), 35; Berger, *Cultures of Antimilitarism,* 12–15, 207.

48. Indeed some research indicates that actors confronting a crisis tend to avoid innovation and instead retreat to even greater reliance on preexisting patterns. Barry Staw, Lance Sandelands, and Jane Dutton, "Threat Rigidity Effects in Organizational Behavior," *Administrative Science Quarterly* 26 (1981).

49. E.g., William Appleman Williams, *The Tragedy of American Diplomacy* (Cleveland: World Publishing, 1959); Emily S. Rosenberg, *Spreading the American Dream: American Economic and Cultural Expansion, 1890–1945* (New York: Hill and Wang, 1982); Frank Costigliola, *Awkward Dominion: American Political, Economic, and Ideational Relations with Europe, 1919–1933* (Ithaca: Cornell University Press, 1984).

50. Even when the strong are involved with the weak, explaining international outcomes demands looking at both sides. See, e.g., John Gallagher and Ronald Robinson, "The Imperialism of Free Trade," *Economic History Review,* 2nd ser., 6 (1953).

51. Robert C. Lieberman, "Ideas, Institutions, and Political Order: Explaining Political Change," *American Political Science Review* 96, no 4 (2002), suggests that change can emerge endogenously from friction among clashing ideational patterns. To show this, however, would require explaining why friction is caused in some circumstances and not others and this means invoking exogenous forces. See too Mlada Bukovansky, *Legitimacy and Power Politics: The American and French Revolutions in International Political Culture* (Princeton: Princeton University Press, 2002).

52. Students of revolutions have long noted these separate dynamics in efforts to overthrow regimes, but similar ones are found in the transformation of more specific policy ideas. See, e.g., Jack A. Goldstone, "Ideology, Cultural Frameworks, the Process of Revolution," *Theory and Society* 20, no. 4 (1991).

53. On the consolidation stage in the literature on revolutions, see Goldstone, "Ideology, Cultural Frameworks"; Charles Tilly, *The Formation of National States in Western Europe* (Princeton: Princeton University Press, 1975); John Foran, "Discourses and Social Forces:The Role of Culture and Cultural Studies in Understanding Revolutions," in *Theorizing Revolutions,* ed. John Foran (New York: Routledge, 1997).

54. See Otto Hintze, *The Historical Essays of Otto Hintze* (New York: Oxford University Press, 1975); Alexander Gerschenkron, *Economic Backwardness in Historical Perspective* (Cambridge: Harvard University Press, 1962); Hans J. Morgenthau, *Politics among Nations: The Struggle for Power and Peace* (New York: Alfred A. Knopf, 1973); Theda Skocpol, *States and Social Revolutions* (New York: Cambridge University Press, 1979); Waltz, *Theory of International Politics;* John W. Meyer, John Boli, George M. Thomas, and Francisco Ramirez, "World Society and the Nation-State," *American Journal of Sociology* 103, no. 1 (1997).

55. For a review and critique of this literature, see Stein and Rosecrance, *Domestic Bases of Grand Strategy.*

56. This is at the heart of the "failure of leadership" that has motivated a range of studies of interwar U.S. foreign policy. See chapter 3 of this book and, e.g., Charles Kindleberger, *The World in Depression* (Berkeley: University of California Press, 1973).

57. For other examples, see Kennedy, *Rise and Fall of Great Powers;* Snyder, *Myths of Empire;* Stein and Rosecrance, *Domestic Bases of Grand Strategy;* Kupchan, *Vulnerability of Empire;* Stephen Walt, *The Origins of Alliance* (Ithaca: Cornell University Press, 1987).

58. For recent examples, see Jeffry Frieden, "Sectoral Conflict and U.S. Foreign Economic Policy, 1914–1940," *International Organization* 42, no. 1 (1988); Ronald Rogowski, *Commerce and Coalitions* (Princeton: Princeton University Press, 1989); Snyder, *Myths of Empire;* Moravcsik, "Taking Preferences Seriously"; Peter Trubowitz, *Defining the National Interest: Conflict and Change in American Foreign Policy* (Chicago: University of Chicago Press, 1998).

59. E.g., Fred I. Greenstein, *Personality and Politics: Problems of Evidence, Inference, and Conceptualization* (New York: W. W. Norton, 1975); Larson, *Origins of Containment;* Daniel L. Byman and Kenneth M. Pollack, "Let Us Now Praise Great Men: Bringing the Statesman Back In," *International Security* 25, no. 4 (2001).

60. See, e.g., Friedrich V. Kratochwil, *Rules, Norms, Decisions: On the Conditions of Practical and Legal Reasoning in International Relations and Domestic Affairs* (Cambridge: Cambridge University Press, 1989); Nicholas Greenwood Onuf, *World of Our Making: Rules and Rule in Social Theory and International Relations* (Columbia: University of South Carolina Press, 1989); Wendt, *Social Theory of International Politics;* John G. Ruggie, *Constructing the World Polity: Essays on International Institutionalization* (New York: Routledge, 1998). Such works in international politics have had similar counterparts in other subfields and disciplines, especially American political development and comparative political economy.

61. Kowert and Legro, "Norms, Identity, and Their Limits"; Legro, "Transformation of Policy Ideas"; Blyth, "Structures Do Not Come with an Instruction Sheet." Note there are exceptions to this generalization, e.g., Hall, "Policy Paradigms, Social Learning, and the State."

62. Adler, "Constructivism and International Relations," 102.

63. Anthony Giddens, *Central Problems in Social Theory: Action, Structure, and Contradiction in Social Analysis* (Berkeley: University of California Press, 1979); Alexander Wendt, "The Agent-Structure Problem in International Relations Theory," *International Organization* 41, no. 3 (1987), and *Social Theory of International Politics;* David Dessler, "What's at Stake in the Agent-Structure Debate?" *International Organization* 43, no. 3 (1989). Different scholars tend to black-box different aspects of this process. For example, Wendt treats states as unitary actors. See, e.g., Jeffrey T. Checkel, "The Constructivist Turn in International Relations Theory," *World Politics* 50, no. 2 (1998): 326.

64. Margaret Archer, *Culture and Agency: The Place of Culture in Social Theory* (New York: Cambridge University Press, 1996), xxv. Wendt, *Social Theory,* 313–69, sketches a general logic of change but not one that answers Archer's critique.

65. See Peter M. Haas, "Introduction: Epistemic Communities and International Policy Coordination," *International Organization* 46 (1992); Martha Finnemore, *National Interests in International Society* (Ithaca: Cornell University Press, 1996); Richard Price, "Transnational Civil Society Targets Land Mines," *International Organization* 52, no. 3 (1998); Margaret Keck and Kathryn Sikkink, *Activists beyond Borders* (Ithaca: Cornell University Press, 1998); Thomas Risse, "Let's Argue!: Communicative Action in World Politics," *International Organization* 54, no. 1 (2000); Frank Schimmelfening, "The Community Trap: Liberal Norms, Rhetorical Action, and the Eastern Enlargement of the European Union," *International Organization* 55, no. 1 (2001); Jeffrey T. Checkel, "Social Learning and European Identity Change," *International Organization* 55, no. 3 (2001); Rodger Payne, "Persuasion, Frames, and Norm Construction," *European Journal of International Relations* 7, no. 1 (2001); Neta Crawford, *Argument and Change in World Politics: Ethics, Decolonization, and Humanitarian Intervention* (Cambridge: Cambridge University Press, 2002).

66. This is evident also in the social movement literature that highlights the influence of cultural frames. See Doug McAdam, John McCarthy, and Meyer Zald, eds., *Comparative Perspectives on Social Movements: Political Opportunities, Mobilizing Structures, and Cultural Framings* (Cambridge: Cambridge University Press, 1996).

67. Johnston, "Treating International Institutions," examines how individual belief change occurs within institutions, but he "black-boxes" the link from individuals to collective change. See Finnemore, *National Interests in International Society,* for another argument on how international institutions shape individuals and national ideas.

68. E.g., see Alexander Wendt, "Collective Identity Formation and the International State," *American Political Science Review* 88 (1994): 385; Mlada Bukovansky, "American Identity and

Neutral Rights from Independence to the War of 1812," *International Organization* 51, no. 2 (1997): 209. See too Henry Nau, *At Home Abroad: Identity and Power in American Foreign Policy* (Ithaca: Cornell University Press, 2002), 34; Wendt, *Social Theory of International Politics*, 231: "Interests presuppose identities because an actor cannot know what it wants until it knows who it is."

69. Wendt, *Social Theory of International Politics*, 342, echoes a key insight from organization theory: "We are—or become—what we do."

70. Ibid., 230–31, embraces a similar philosophy. Wendt also refers to "concentric circles of identification" where identity might vary from case to case based on tensions between different elements of identity (338).

71. Leaders do need to worry about the misleading rhetoric of other states, as Nazi Germany's record shows (Hitler was for "peace" in the early 1930s), but such rhetoric also contains a web of expectations that can entrap its weavers. The violation of "peace" rhetoric in 1938 was the beginning of destabilization in Hitler's Germany and a clear signal to others that real trouble was afoot. See Mark Haas, *Ideology and Great Power Politics, 1789–1989* (Ithaca: Cornell University Press, 2005).

72. Arthur Stinchcomb, *Constructing Social Theories* (New York: Harcourt, Brace, 1968), 3.

Chapter 2. Explaining Change and Continuity

1. Robert Jervis, "Realism in the Study of World Politics," *International Organization* 52, no. 4 (1998): 982–83; David Lake and Robert Powell, eds., *Strategic Choice and International Relations* (Princeton: Princeton University Press, 1999).

2. Some scholars have turned to collective ideas both to explain how societies make decisions under uncertainty and to resolve multiple equilibria problems, e.g., Thomas C. Schelling, *The Strategy of Conflict* (Cambridge: Harvard University Press, 1960); David M. Kreps, "Corporate Cultures and Economic Theory," in *Perspectives on Positive Political Economy*, ed. James E. Alt and Kenneth A. Schepsle (New York: Cambridge University Press, 1990); Geoffrey Garrett and Barry Weingast, "Ideas, Interests, and Institutions," in *Ideas and Foreign Policy*, ed. Judith Goldstein and Robert Keohane (Ithaca: Cornell University Press, 1993). Typically ideas are invoked, not explained, in these, analyses.

3. Jon Elster, ed., introduction to *Rational Choice* (New York: New York University Press, 1986), 12–14, argues that beliefs are rational when they (1) have inductive plausibility given the evidence, (2) are caused by the evidence (3), are caused in the right way (not be mistaken inference), and (4) are internally consistent.

4. For other distinctions between the argument that follows and "Bayesian" rational learning accounts see Jeffrey W. Legro, "The Transformation of Policy Ideas," *American Journal of Political Science* 44, no. 3 (2000): 430.

5. "Foreign policy addresses itself, then, to the external world as a legend, to the external world that men create in their own minds": Louis J. Halle, *Dreams and Reality: Aspects of American Foreign Policy* (New York: Harper and Brothers, 1959), 317–18.

6. Department of Defense News Briefing—Secretary Rumsfeld and Gen. Myers, February 12, 2002, http://www.defenselink.mil/transcripts/2002/feb2002.html (1/14/05).

7. As cited in Christopher Thorne, *The Limits of Foreign Policy: The West, the League, and the Far Eastern Crisis of 1931–1933* (London: Hamish Hamilton, 1972), 4.

8. In "Shared Mental Models: Ideologies and Institutions" (*Kyklos* 47, no. 1 [1994]), Arthur Denzau and Douglass North argue that in politics (as opposed to competitive economic markets) the competition that generates accurate beliefs is underdeveloped. For a good discussion of "Knightian" uncertainty that features uniqueness, not complexity, see Mark Blyth, *Great Transformations: Economic Ideas and Institutional Change in the Twentieth Century* (New York: Cambridge University Press, 2002), 9–10, 30–34.

9. Thomas Christensen and Jack Snyder, "Chain Gangs and Passed Bucks: Predicting Alliance Patterns in Multipolarity," *International Organization* 44, no. 2 (1990).

10. Robert Jervis, *Perception and Misperception in International Politics* (Princeton: Princeton University Press, 1976), 235; Philip E. Tetlock, "Social Psychology and World Politics," in *The Handbook of Social Psychology* (4th ed.), ed. D. T. Gilbert, S. T. Fiske, and G. Lindsey (New York: McGraw-Hill, 1998), 870–72.

11. Often the reasons for particular choices may have more to do with nonefficiency grounds—see, for example, Dana P. Eyre and Mark C. Suchman, "Status, Norms, and the Proliferation of Conventional Weapons: An Institutional Theory Approach," in *The Culture of National Security: Norms, Identity, and World Politics,* ed. Peter J. Katzenstein (New York: Columbia University Press, 1996), 79–113.

12. Kenneth F. Boulding, "The Learning and Reality-Testing Process in the International System," in *Image and Reality in World Politics,* ed. John C. Farrell and Asa P. Smith (New York: Columbia University Press, 1968), 2–3, 9, argues that these complex conditions inhibit even folk learning based on simple feedback. Images of the world, he argues, tend to be more literary than based in reality testing.

13. See Denzau and North, "Shared Mental Models"; Douglass North, "Economic Performance through Time," in *The New Institutionalism in Sociology,* ed. Mary C. Brinton and Victor Nee (New York: Russell Sage, 1998), 248–50.

14. Denzau and North, "Shared Mental Models," 14–17; Alice E. Eagly and Shelly Chaiken, *The Psychology of Attitudes* (Fort Worth, Texas: Harcourt Brace Jovanovich College Publishers, 1993), 628–32.

15. See, for example, Edward Schein, *Organizational Culture and Leadership* (San Francisco: Jossey-Bass, 1985); James Q. Wilson, *Bureaucracy: What Government Agencies Do and Why They Do It* (New York: Basic Books, 1989); Kreps, "Corporate Cultures and Economic Theory"; Samuel P. Huntington, *The Clash of Civilizations and the Remaking of World Order* (New York: Simon and Schuster, 1996), 29–31.

16. Jervis, *Perception and Misperception in International Politics;* Janice Gross Stein, "Political Learning by Doing: Gorbachev as an Uncommitted Thinker and Motivated Learner," *International Organization* 48, no. 2 (1994): 155–83; Yuen Foong Khong, *Analogies at War: Korea, Munich, Dien Bien Phu, and the Vietnam Decisions of 1965* (Princeton University Press, 1992); Deborah Larson, *Origins of Containment* (Princeton University Press, 1985); Jonathan Mercer, *Reputation and International Politics* (Ithaca: Cornell University Press, 1996); Tetlock, "Social Psychology and World Politics."

17. For examples and more on the distinction between collective ideas and individual or even aggregate individual ideas, see Emile Durkheim, *The Rules of Sociological Method* (New York: Free Press, 1966); Charles Taylor, "Interpretation and the Sciences of Man," *Review of Metaphysics* 25 (1971): 3–51; Margaret Gilbert, "Modeling Collective Beliefs," *Synthese* 73 (1987): 185–204; Alexander Wendt, *Social Theory of International Politics* (Cambridge: Cambridge University Press, 1999); Legro, "Transformation of Policy Ideas."

18. John A. Thompson, "The Exaggeration of American Vulnerability: The Anatomy of a Tradition," *Diplomatic History* 16, no. 1 (1992): 37.

19. See chapter 3.

20. Kenneth Arrow, *Social Choice and Individual Values* (New Haven: Yale University Press, 1951).

21. Gilbert, "Modeling Collective Beliefs."

22. As in this example, collective ideas often appear as a solution to collective action problems. See Schelling, *Strategy of Conflict;* Barry Weingast, "A Rational Choice Perspective on the Role of Ideas," *Politics and Society* 23, no. 4 (1996): 449–64; Kreps, "Corporate Cultures and Economic Theory."

23. This analogy is suggested by Marshall Sahlins, "The Return of the Event, Again," in *Clio in Oceana: Toward a Historical Anthropology,* ed. Aletta Biersack (Washington, D.C.: Smithsonian Institution Press, 1991), 43–44.

24. Arthur Stein, *Why Nations Cooperate: Circumstance and Choice in International Relations* (Ithaca: Cornell University Press, 1990), 25–54, discusses these problems with respect to states agreeing on international regimes.

25. Gene Burns, "Ideology, Culture, and Ambiguity: The Revolutionary Process in Iran," *Theory and Society* 25 (1996): 350–51.

26. Robert W. Kates and William C. Clark, "Environmental Surprise: Expecting the Unexpected," *Environment* 38, no. 2 (1996): 8; Jack S. Levy, "Learning and Foreign Policy: Sweeping a Conceptual Minefield," *International Organization* 48, no. 2 (1994): 305.

27. James Scott, *The Moral Economy of the Peasant: Rebellion and Subsistence in Southeast Asia* (New Haven: Yale University Press, 1976), 10. He writes that resistance occurs "not only because needs were unmet, but because rights were violated." (Scott, 6)

28. Barrington Moore, *Social Origins of Dictatorship and Democracy* (Boston: Beacon Press, 1966), 474; Barrington Moore, *Injustice: The Social Bases of Obedience and Revolt* (White Plains, N.Y.: M. E. Sharpe, 1978), 4–5, 321, 457, elaborates the argument. His thesis is that rebellion is more likely in cases where actors perceive some sort of injustice based on expectations related to social rules and their violation. This perception of injustice, however, may not be apparent to objective observers, so that it is necessary to see how people themselves judge their situation. Normally, mass political action is spurred by some precipitating event.

29. Jervis, *Perception and Misperception*, 143–45, 288–315; Eagly and Chaiken, *Psychology of Attitudes*, 559–625; Philip E. Tetlock, "Close-Call Counterfactuals and Belief-System Defenses: I Was Not Almost Wrong But I Was Almost Right," *Journal of Personality and Social Psychology* 75, no. 3 (1998).

30. For example, military victory might objectively be coded as success, but whether a society sees it as such depends on the ideational framework through which it is understood—e.g., U.S. disillusionment after World War I.

31. Charles Perrow, *Normal Accidents* (New York: Basic Books, 1984); John Odell, *U.S. International Monetary Policy: Markets, Power, and Ideas as Sources of Change* (Princeton: Princeton University Press, 1982), 371; Douglas Arnold, *The Logic of Congressional Action* (New Haven: Yale University Press, 1990), 32–33, 51; Peter Hall, "Policy Paradigms, Social Learning, and the State," *Comparative Politics* 25, no. 3 (1993): 275–95, 280; Frank Dobbin, *Forging Industrial Policy: The United States, Britain, and France in the Railway Age* (Cambridge: Cambridge University Press, 1994).

32. Daniel Kahneman and Amos Tversky, "Prospect Theory: An Analysis of Decision under Risk," *Econometrica* 47, no. 2 (1979).

33. These are rough numbers based on Daniel Kahneman and Amos Tversky, "The Framing of Decision and the Psychology of Choice," *Science* 211 (1998): 453–58. One might argue that leaders are more likely to be risk takers and less prone to conservative framing effects.

34. Timur Kuran, "Now Out of Never: The Element of Surprise in the East European Revolution 1989," *World Politics* 44, no. 1 (1991); Timur Kuran, *Private Truths, Public Lies: The Social Consequences of Preference Falsification* (Cambridge: Harvard University Press, 1995); Mark Granovetter, "Threshold Models of Collective Behavior," *American Journal of Sociology* 83 (1978): 1420–43; Sushil Bikchandani, David Hirshleifer, and Ivo Welsh, "A Theory of Fads, Fashion, Custom, and Cultural Change as Informational Cascades," *Journal of Political Economy* 100 (1992); Malcom Gladwell, *The Tipping Point: How Little Things Can Make a Big Difference* (Boston: Little Brown, 2000).

35. *9/11 Commission Report: Final Report of the National Commission on Terrorist Attacks upon the United States* (Washington, D.C.: GPO, 2004), 350.

36. Sometimes such demands will be thwarted by the claim that a given idea did not receive a fair test. Jervis, *Perception and Misperception*, 275, argues this is likely when the original values are deeply rooted, when a policy is implemented half-heartedly, or when there are unique circumstances in the original case that would not affect future cases.

37. This is the thrust of the social memory literature. See Maurice Halbwachs, *On Collective Memory*, ed., trans., and intro. by Lewis A. Coser (Chicago: University of Chicago Press, 1992); Paul Connerton, *How Societies Remember* (New York: Cambridge University Press, 1989).

38. Deborah Stone, "Causal Stories and the Formation of Policy Agendas," *Political Science Quarterly* 104, no. 2 (1989); Colin Hay, "Narrating Crisis: The Discursive Construction of the 'Winter of Discontent'," *Sociology* 30, no. 2 (1996).

39. Bruce Bueno de Mesquita, Alastair Smith, Randolph M. Siverson, and James D. Morrow, *The Logic of Political Survival* (Cambridge: MIT Press, 2003); Gerard Alexander, "Institutionalized Uncertainty, the Rule of Law, and the Sources of Democratic Stability," *Comparative Political Studies* 35, no. 10 (2002): 1153–57.

40. Thomas S. Kuhn, *The Structure of Scientific Revolutions,* 2nd ed. (Chicago: University of Chicago Press, 1970). For critiques, see Imre Lakatos, "Falsification and the Methodology of Scientific Research Programmes," in *Criticism and the Growth of Knowledge,* ed. Imre Lakatos and Alan Musgrave (Cambridge: Cambridge University Press, 1970), 91–196; Gary Gutting, ed., *Paradigms and Revolutions: Appraisals and Applications of Thomas Kuhn's Philosophy of Science* (Notre Dame, Ind.: University of Notre Dame Press, 1980).

41. A good example is Hall, "Policy Paradigms, Social Learning, and the State."

42. When an approach produces a desirable outcome people "satisfice" and ignore the possibility of even better alternatives. Herbert Simon, *Models of Man* (New York: Wiley, 1957).

43. A similar example of the dynamic of type A1 is evident in general deterrence theory. A societal belief that the general threat to impose costs on a potential attacker prevents aggression would be supported by an absence of attacks. Hence the normal absence of attacks upholds that belief and few policymakers question the validity of deterrence. The problem, of course, is that the absence of attack may have little to do with the casual mechanisms (the threat to impose costs that changes the intentions of the would-be aggressor) asserted by the theory. See Richard Ned Lebow and Janice Gross Stein, "Rational Deterrence Theory: I Think, Therefore I Deter," *World Politics* 41 (1998).

44. Of course, opponents to the dominant orthodoxy who warn of its defects can also use the same rhetoric when disasters happen. See, for example, Michael Roskin, "From Pearl Harbor to Vietnam: Shifting Generational Paradigms and Foreign Policy," *Political Science Quarterly* 89, no. 3 (1974): 302, on how U.S. internationalists used Pearl Harbor to challenge the country's interwar "isolationism."

45. Wolfgang Krieger, "Toward a Gaullist Germany? Some Lessons from the Yugoslav Crisis," *World Policy Journal* 11, no. 1 (1994): 26–39; Hanns W. Maull, "Germany in the Yugoslav Crisis," *Survival* 37 (1995–96): 99–130, 102–5; Beverly Crawford, "Explaining Defection from International Cooperation: Germany's Unilateral Recognition of Croatia," *World Politics* 48, no. 4 (1996): 482–521. Arguing against this common interpretation is an official who was responsible for policy; see Michael Libal, *Limits of Persuasion: Germany and the Yugoslav Crisis, 1991–1992* (Westport, Conn.: Praeger, 1997), 148–56.

46. Maull, "Germany in the Yugoslav Crisis," 105.

47. Scott Sagan, *The Limits of Safety: Organizations, Accidents, and Nuclear Weapons* (Princeton: Princeton University Press, 1993), 284.

48. Jeffrey Fuhrer, *Beyond Shocks* (Boston: Federal Reserve Bank of Boston, 1998).

49. Peter Berger and Thomas Luckmann, *The Social Construction of Reality* (New York: Anchor Books, 1966), 157–58, emphasize the importance of an alternative. Change need not always entail the complete disappearance of the old: a type of layering-on of the new over the old can also occur. See, e.g, Judith Goldstein, *Ideas, Interests, and American Trade Policy* (Ithaca: Cornell University Press, 1993), 1–2.

50. Martha Derthick and Paul Quirk, *The Politics of Deregulation* (Washington, D.C.: Brookings Institution, 1985), 57.

51. These are the types of efforts that are covered in depth in the literature on social movements. See Doug McAdam, John McCarthy, and Mayer Zald, eds., *Comparative Perspectives on Social Movements: Political Opportunities, Mobilizing Structures, and Cultural Framings* (Cambridge: Cambridge University Press, 1996); Margaret Keck and Kathryn Sikkink, *Activists beyond Borders* (Ithaca: Cornell University Press, 1998); Birkland, *After Disaster,* usefully discusses the role of advocacy groups in change. On the importance of some existing social support for a particular idea, see Daniel C. Thomas, *The Helsinki Effect: International Norms, Human Rights, and the Demise of Communism* (Princeton: Princeton University Press, 2001), 22.

52. This Kuhnian dynamic of an alternative approach having an answer for a problem is found in Hall, "Policy Paradigms, Social Learning, and the State," and Kathleen R. McNamara,

The Currency of Ideas: Monetary Politics in the European Union (Ithaca: Cornell University Press, 1998), 6, 145.

53. Among others making this point, see Jervis, *Perception and Misperception*, 238; Derthick and Quirk, *Politics of Deregulation*, 55; Goldstein, *Ideas, Interests, and American Trade Policy*, 16.

54. See Jeffrey W. Legro, *Cooperation under Fire* (Ithaca: Cornell University Press, 1995), 62–80.

55. See, for example, Frank Dobbin, "The Social Construction of the Great Depression: Industrial Policy during the 1930s in the United States, Britain, and France," *Theory and Society* 22 (1993), on industrial strategy in several countries, and Margaret Weir and Theda Skocpol, "State Structures and the Possibilities for Keynesian Responses to the Great Depression in Sweden, Britain, and the United States," in *Bringing the State Back In*, ed. Peter B. Evans, Dietrich Rueschemeyer, and Theda Skocpol (Cambridge: Cambridge University Press, 1985), 139, on the fate of Keynesian ideas in the United States in the 1930s.

56. Juan Linz, *The Breakdown of Democratic Regimes: Crisis, Breakdown, and Reequilibration* (Baltimore: Johns Hopkins University Press, 1978), 20–22, 40, 50.

57. John Foran, "Discourses and Social Forces:The Role of Culture and Cultural Studies in Understanding Revolutions," in *Theorizing Revolutions*, ed. John Foran (New York: Routledge, 1997), 216–18.

58. As Goldstone argues, "[Elites] taking the various particular complaints and the various elite and folk ideologies (and forging from these elements an ideology with broad appeal) is critical to the construction of a dominant coalition." Jack A. Goldstone, "Ideology, Cultural Frameworks, the Process of Revolution," *Theory and Society* 20 (1991): 412; Jack A. Goldstone, *Revolution and Rebellion in the Early Modern World* (Berkeley: University of California Press, 1991), chap. 5; Foran, "Discourses and Social Forces," 208–9. This is a prominent theme in Judith Goldstein and Robert O. Keohane, eds., *Ideas and Foreign Policy: Beliefs, Institutions, and Political Change* (Ithaca: Cornell University Press, 1993), 17–20.

59. Jervis, *Perception and Misperception*, 238.

60. Stephan Haggard and Robert R. Kaufman, *The Political Economy of Democratic Transitions* (Princeton: Princeton University Press, 1995), 8.

61. Change is more likely the starker the expectations are and the more consequential the negative results.

62. See, e.g., Peter Gourevitch, *Politics in Hard Times* (Ithaca: Cornell University Press, 1986); Peter Hall, ed., *The Political Power of Economic Ideas* (Princeton: Princeton University Press, 1989); Peter Katzenstein, *Cultural Norms and National Security: Police and Military in Postwar Japan* (Ithaca: Cornell University Press, 1996). There are huge literatures—e.g., writings on social movements, political entrepreneurs, interest groups, historical studies on particular struggles over specific ideas—that address the political contestation issue.

63. For such an account based on individual ideas and political contingency, see Craig Parsons, "Showing Ideas as Causes: The Origins of the European Union," *International Organization* 56, no. 1 (1992).

64. See Durkheim, *Rules of Sociological Method*; John R. Searle, *The Construction of Social Reality* (New York: Free Press, 1995), 23–26; Wendt, *Social Theory of International Politics*.

65. These sources are typically based on analysis of some combination of memoirs, personal papers, speeches, archival records, surveys of journals/newspapers/broadcasts, literature, national holidays, national monuments, and public opinion data.

66. Here I try to amalgamate various versions of realism—offensive, defensive, classical, neoclassical. Authors from different realist schools who offer analyses that more or less reflect the view of ideas I describe here include Kenneth N. Waltz, *Theory of International Politics* (Baltimore: Addison-Wesley, 1979); Stephen Walt, *The Origins of Alliance* (Ithaca: Cornell University Press, 1987); Joseph Grieco, *Cooperation among Nations: Europe, America, and Non-Tariff Barriers to Trade* (Ithaca: Cornell University Press, 1990); Michael C. Desch, *Civilian Control of the Military: The Changing Security Environment* (Baltimore: Johns Hopkins University Press, 1999); Dale Copeland, *Origins of Major War* (Ithaca: Cornell University Press, 2000); John J. Mearsheimer, *The Tragedy of Great Power Politics* (New York: W. W. Norton, 2001).

67. Alexander Gerschenkron, *Economic Backwardness in Historical Perspective* (Cambridge: Harvard University Press, 1962); Immanuel Wallerstein, "Three Paths of Development in 16th Century Europe," *Studies in Comparative International Development* 7, no. 2 (1972): 95–101; Richard Rosecrance, *The Rise of the Virtual State: Wealth and Power in the Coming Century* (New York: Basic Books, 1992).

68. Waltz, *Theory of International Politics*, expects states to adopt strategically effective ideas over time either because they emulate "winner" states or because those with losing ideas are "selected out" by competition in the international arena. This approach, however, offers few clues as to when particular states are likely to adhere to their dominant ideas or change them.

69. Of course, they may not do so, and if they do not they may be vulnerable to defeat and political extinction in the competitive international arena. But such a case would be an anomaly for a realist logic that attempts to account for variation in national policies. See Colin Elman, "Horses for Courses: Why Not a Neorealist Theory of Foreign Policy," *Security Studies* 6, no. 1 (1996).

70. For example, Gourevitch, *Politics in Hard Times*; Jeffry Frieden, "Sectoral Conflict and U.S. Foreign Economic Policy, 1914–1940," *International Organization* 42, no. 1 (1988); Ronald Rogowski, *Commerce and Coalitions* (Princeton: Princeton University Press, 1989); Jack Snyder, *Myths of Empire* (Ithaca: Cornell University Press, 1991); Andrew Moravcsik, "Taking Preferences Seriously: A Liberal Theory of International Politics," *International Organization* 51, no. 4 (1997); Peter Trubowitz, *Defining the National Interest: Conflict and Change in American Foreign Policy* (Chicago: University of Chicago Press, 1998). On "great man" arguments see Daniel L. Byman and Kenneth M. Pollack, "Let Us Now Praise Great Men: Bringing the Statesman Back In," *International Security* 25, no. 4 (2001). The latter type of argument would generally treat actors' goals and ideas as a product of psychological as well as rational imperatives. See Larson, *Origins of Containment*; Gross Stein, "Political Learning by Doing."

71. Hence Snyder's *Myths of Empire* argument on "blowback" is not captured by a pure interest group explanation because domestic groups become the target of ideas rather than the producer of them in line with their interests.

72. The main limitation is the reliability of the findings given the small number of case studies.

73. Jervis, *Perception and Misperception*; Dan Reiter, *Crucible of Beliefs* (Ithaca: Cornell University Press, 1996).

74. See Ruth Berins Collier and David Collier, *Shaping the Political Arena: Critical Junctures, the Labor Movement, and Regime Dynamics in Latin America* (Princeton: Princeton University Press, 1991), 35–36.

75. Clifford Geertz, *The Interpretation of Cultures: Selected Essays* (New York: Basic Books, 1977), 26.

Chapter 3. *The Ebb and Flow of American Internationalism*

1. Charles Kindleberger, *The World in Depression* (Berkeley: University of California Press, 1973); Stephen D. Krasner, "State Power and the Structure of International Trade," *World Politics* 28, no. 3 (1976); John G. Ruggie, "International Regimes, Transactions, and Change: Embedded Liberalism in the Postwar Economic Order," *International Organization* 36, no. 2 (1982).

2. Americans saw themselves as part of the cultural and legal aspects of European society but "excluded from the European balance of power system and strategic aspects of the system, and the system excluded from them." Hedley Bull and Adam Watson, eds., *The Expansion of International Society* (Oxford: Oxford University Press, 1984), 138–39. As many historians have documented, in any absolute sense, the United States was always involved in major power politics. Revisionists led by William Appleman Williams, *The Tragedy of American Diplomacy* (Cleveland: World Publishing, 1959), have accurately argued that the United States was not isolationist. Revisionists focus on American business activity in the international economy, which often was facilitated by the U.S. government. For a critique of the revisionist argument see Warren F. Kuehl and Lynne K. Dunn, *Keeping the Covenant: American Internationalists and the League of Nations* (Kent, Ohio: Kent State University Press, 1997).

3. The list here includes scholars such as Frank Costigliola, *Awkward Dominion: American Political, Economic, and Ideational Relations with Europe, 1919–1933* (Ithaca: Cornell University Press, 1984); Kindleberger, *World in Depression*; and John Lewis Gaddis, *The United States and the Origins of the Cold War* (New York: Columbia University Press, 1972), 2, 18–20, 23–24. It also includes policy officials such as Henry Stimson, Franklin D. Roosevelt, Dean Acheson, Walt Rostow, and Lyndon Johnson; see Bruce Kuklick, "History as a Way of Learning," *American Quarterly* 22 (1970): 614–15.

4. This continuum is slightly different than the useful two-fold dimension—internationalist-isolationist and non-military (or cooperative)–militant—of foreign policy identified by some scholars. See, for example, John Milton Cooper, *The Vanity of Power: American Isolationism and the First World War, 1914–1917* (Westport, Conn.: Greenwood, 1969); Eugene R. Wittkopf, *Faces of Internationalism: Public Opinion and American Foreign Policy* (Durham: Duke University Press, 1990).

5. See Melvyn Leffler, "Political Isolationism, Economic Expansionism, or Diplomatic Realism: American Policy toward Western Europe, 1921–1933," in *Perspectives in American History*, vol. 8, ed. Donald Fleming and Bernard Bailyn (Cambridge: Charles Warren Center for Studies in American History, Harvard University, 1974); John Braeman, "Power and Diplomacy: The 1920s Reappraised," *Review of Politics* 44, no. 3 (1982).

6. Some favored international activism without commitments. I distinguish these views below.

7. For the full texts of these speeches see Fred L. Israel, ed., *The State of the Union Messages of the Presidents, 1790–1966* (New York: Chelsea House/Robert Hector, 1966).

8. Frank Klingberg, "The Historical Alternation of Moods in American Foreign Policy," *World Politics* 4, no. 2 (1952), also examines these speeches for how positively they view action abroad and the space devoted to international relations. He documents "extrovert" and "introvert" periods that differ from the focus here on separatism and internationalism. For a historian's analysis of these speeches, see Ernest R. May, "National Security in American History," in *Rethinking America's Security: Beyond the Cold War to New World Order*, ed. Graham Allison and Gregory F. Treverton (New York: Norton, 1992).

9. See, for example, the "internationalist" Franklin Roosevelt's favorable pronouncements on isolationism in the 1930s.

10. The papers are the *New York Times*, the *Chicago Tribune*, the *St. Louis Post-Dispatch*, and the *Los Angeles Times*.

11. Public opinion polls are not as useful a measure both because they did not exist until the 1930s and because they reflect individual, not necessarily collective, views. There is not a symbol for each paper in every year because sometimes the editorials did not address the foreign policy aspects of the speeches. This absence might fairly be taken as a sign of isolationism. Thus, if anything, my measure of international affairs in this period underestimates the degree of U.S. nonengagement.

12. See Louis J. Halle, *Dreams and Reality: Aspects of American Foreign Policy* (New York: Harper and Brothers, 1958): 1–7; Edward Luck, *Mixed Messages: American Politics and International Organization, 1919–1999* (Washington, D.C: Brookings Institution Press, 1999), 2–4. Walter Russell Mead, *Special Providence: American Foreign Policy and How It Changed the World* (New York: Knopf, 2001), argues that the United States has four different policy traditions that have all been present throughout history and which offer different prescriptions for U.S. international behavior. Mead offers no theory of why a particular orientation dominates at any one time.

13. In 1915 three editorials favored less internationalism, while one agreed with the sentiment of the State of the Union.

14. In 1926 and 1928 two favored more internationalism, while a third agreed with the president. In 1931 two favored more internationalism. In 1939 and 1940 two favored less internationalism, while a third agreed with the president.

15. *Inaugural Addresses of the American Presidents*, annotated by Davis Newton Lott (New York: Holt, Rinehart, 1961).

16. Mead, *Special Providence*, 12–29, summarizes the considerable U.S. activity in the international arena in the nineteenth century.

17. The United States was, of course, involved in other areas such as Latin America and the Philippines. For an account of U.S. activity at the end of the nineteenth century see Fareed Zakaria, *From Wealth to Power: The Unusual Origins of America's World Role* (Princeton: Princeton University Press, 1998).

18. Raymond Esthus, *Theodore Roosevelt and the International Rivalries* (Waltham, Mass.: Ginn-Blaisdell, 1970), 2–3, 70–72, 83–84, 149–50; Frank Ninkovich, *Modernity and Power: A History of the Domino Theory in the Twentieth Century* (Chicago: University of Chicago Press, 1994), 14–15; William C. Widenor, *Henry Cabot Lodge and the Search for an American Foreign Policy* (Berkeley: University of California Press, 1980), 159, 194.

19. Hans J. Morgenthau, "The Mainsprings of American Foreign Policy: The National Interest vs. Moral Abstractions," *American Political Science Review* 44, no. 4 (1950): 834–35.

20. Frank Ninkovich, *The Wilsonian Century* (Chicago: University of Chicago Press, 1999), esp. 60, 64–68, 125–28. pursues a similar theme.

21. 1915 State of the Union address, in Israel, ed., *State of the Union Messages.*

22. 1919 State of the Union address, in Israel, ed., *State of the Union Messages.*

23. 1921 Inaugural Address.

24. 1921 and 1922 State of the Union addresses, in Israel, ed., *State of the Union Messages.*

25. 1923 State of the Union address, in Israel, ed., *State of the Union Messages*; 1925 Inaugural Address. Coolidge's "internationalist" causes were advocated within the traditional consensus. For example, he argued that U.S. involvement with the World Court was strictly voluntary (1924 State of the Union address, in Israel, ed., *State of the Union Messages*) and that the Kellogg-Briand Pact, which renounced the use of war as an instrument of national policy, did not limit unilateral action in any way (1928 State of the Union address, in Israel, ed., *State of the Union Messages*).

26. Joan Hoff Wilson, *American Business and Foreign Policy, 1920–1933* (Boston: Beacon Press, 1972), x; Jeffry Frieden, "Sectoral Conflict and U.S. Foreign Economic Policy, 1914–1940," *International Organization* 42, no. 1 (1988): 59–90, 60.

27. Melvyn P. Leffler, *Elusive Quest: America's Pursuit of European Stability and French Security* (Chapel Hill: University of North Carolina, 1979); Priscilla Roberts, "The Anglo-American Theme: American Visions of an Atlantic Alliance, 1914–1933," *Diplomatic History* 21, no. 3 (1997): 360; Frieden, "Sectoral Conflict," 75, argues that in the 1920s "the internationalists were almost always defeated, forced to compromise or forced to adopt some form of semi-official arrangement that kept the process out of the public eye."

28. Zara Steiner, "The War, the Peace, and the International State System," in *The Great War and the Twentieth Century*, ed. Jay Winter, Geoffrey Parker, and Mary R. Habeck (New Haven: Yale University Press, 2000), 289–91.

29. Wayne S. Cole, *Roosevelt and the Isolationists* (Lincoln: University of Nebraska Press, 1983), 6–7; T. H. Buckley and E. B. Strong, *American Foreign and National Security Policies, 1914–1945* (Knoxville: University of Tennessee Press, 1987), 90; Thomas N. Guinsberg, "The Triumph of Isolationism," in *American Foreign Relations Reconsidered, 1890–1993*, ed. Gordon Martel (New York: Routledge, 1994), 90; Alexander DeConde, ed., *Isolation and Security* (Durham: Duke University Press, 1957), 23 and 25.

30. See Costigliola, *Awkward Dominion*, 22, 69; Carl Parrini, *Heir to Empire: United States Economic Diplomacy, 1916–1923* (Pittsburgh: University of Pittsburgh Press, 1969), viii, 14; Leffler, *Elusive Quest*, x, 39.

31. Charles DeBendetti, "Alternative Strategies in the American Peace Movement in the 1920s," *American Studies* 8, no. 1 (1972): 69–79; "What We Will Do if France Is Attacked Again," *Literary Digest*, December 31, 1921, 5.

32. 1934 State of the Union address, in Israel, ed., *State of the Union Messages.*

33. 1940 State of the Union address, in Israel, ed., *State of the Union Messages.*

34. 1941 State of the Union address, in Israel, ed., *State of the Union Messages.*

35. James McAllister, *No Exit: America and the German Problem, 1943–1954* (Ithaca: Cornell University Press, 2001).

36. Richard Melanson, "The Foundations of Eisenhower's Foreign Policy: Continuity,

Community, and Consensus," in *Reevaluating Melanson and Eisenhower: American Foreign Policy in the 1950s*, ed. Richard Melanson and David Mayer (Urban: University of Illinois Press, 1987), 43–44.

37. This is what the bulk of research on ideas in politics has demonstrated—that "ideas matter" for behavior. See citations in chapter 1, n. 1.

38. There were of course vastly more opportunities for international treaty making after World War II—in part due to the shift in U.S. ideas.

39. 1936 State of the Union address, in Israel, ed., *State of the Union Messages*, 2822.

40. As quoted in Arthur S. Link, *Wilson: Campaigns for Progressivism and Peace* (Princeton: Princeton University, 1965), 430–31.

41. Speech in the U.S. Senate, April 4, 1917. Reprinted in William Didley, ed., *Opposing Viewpoints in American History* (San Diego: Greenhaven Press, 1996), 149–52.

42. See Link, *Wilson*, 264–69; Cooper, *Vanity of Power*, 167–73; Stuart Rochester, *American Liberal Disillusionment in the Wake of World War I* (University Park: Pennsylvania State University Press, 1977), 35, 44–45.

43. Speech to Congress, April 2, 1917. Reprinted in Albert Fried, ed., *A Day of Dedication: The Essential Writings & Speeches of Woodrow Wilson* (New York: Macmillan, 1965), 301–9.

44. See Thomas Knock, *To End All Wars: Woodrow Wilson and the Quest for a New World Order* (New York: Oxford University Press, 1992), 55, 95–98; Rochester, *American Liberal Disillusionment*, 26, 38–47; David Kennedy, *Over Here: The First World War and American Society* (Oxford: Oxford University Press, 1980), 42, 50; Alan Dawley, *Changing the World: American Progressives in War and Revolution* (Princeton: Princeton University Press, 2003), 122–23, 136.

45. On how Wilson heightened expectations, see Dawley, *Changing the World*, chap. 7.

46. Warren Cohen, *The American Revisionists: The Lessons of Intervention in World War I* (Chicago: University of Chicago Press, 1967), 233; Raymond J. Sontag, *A Broken World* (New York: Harper and Row, 1971).

47. Knock, *To End All Wars*, 211, 239, 252.

48. Ralph B. Levering, *The Public and American Foreign Policy, 1918–1978* (New York: Morrow, 1978), 42.

49. Cohen, *American Revisionists*, 233; Selig Adler, *Uncertain Giant* (New York: Macmillan, 1967), 2–3.

50. Colin Dueck, "Ideas and Alternatives in American Grand Strategy, 1918–1921," manuscript, Princeton University, 2000, points out that this phenomena led to the withdrawal of support from Wilson, not just from the Left but also the Center and Right.

51. Knock, *To End All Wars*, 185–89; Cohen, *American Revisionists*, 234–40.

52. Robert Osgood, *Ideals and Self-Interest in America's Foreign Relations* (Chicago: University of Chicago Press, 1953), 307; Knock, *To End All Wars*, 148–60; Robert David Johnson, *The Peace Progressives and American Foreign Relations* (Cambridge: Harvard University Press, 1995), 87–103.

53. Roberts, "Anglo-American Theme," 353.

54. Knock, *To End All Wars*, 263–64, discussion of the votes indicates there were some 42–43 senators in favor of the League without reservations, another 38 with reservations, and 13 irreconcilably opposed.

55. See Robert Dallek, *Franklin D. Roosevelt and American Foreign Policy, 1932–1945* (New York: Oxford University Press, 1979), 101–3; Adler, *Uncertain Giant*, 39–40; Ernest May, "Lessons" of the Past: The Use and Misuse of History in American Foreign Policy* (New York: Oxford University Press, 1973), 4–5.

56. Lodge favored a more narrow commitment to French security, but this was not the choice of others including Wilson and probably the general public as seen in the 1921 *Literary Digest* poll of editors. Knock, *To End All Wars*, 265–68; Ninkovich, *Modernity and Power*, 65.

57. Roberts, "Anglo-American Theme," 351.

58. Many are critical of Wilson, e.g., Knock, *To End All Wars*, and Lloyd E. Ambrosius, *Woodrow Wilson and the Diplomatic Tradition: The Treaty Fight in Perspective* (New York: Cam-

bridge University Press, 1979). Dueck, "Ideas and Alternatives," offers a richer view of Wilson's agency and sees ideas as allowing some outcomes and not others via agenda setting and coalition building. See too G. John Ikenberry, *After Victory* (Princeton: Princeton University Press, 2001), 119.

59. See Knock, *To End All Wars*, 265–68; Ninkovich, *Modernity and Power*, 65; Ambrosius, *Woodrow Wilson and the Diplomatic Tradition*, 250.

60. See Leffler, *Elusive Quest*, 39; Michael Leigh, *Mobilizing Consent: Public Opinion and American Foreign Policy, 1937–1947* (Westport, Conn.: Greenwood, 1976), 109.

61. Ninkovich, *Modernity and Power*, 96.

62. Had the results of World War I been more positive, there may have been more pressure on the two sides to reach accommodation on change.

63. Charles W. Smith Jr., *Public Opinion in America* (New York: Prentice-Hall, 1939), 518, as quoted in Levering, *Public and American Foreign Policy*, 39.

64. Manfred Jonas, *Isolationism in America, 1935–1941* (Chicago: Imprint Publications, 1990), 32–69, 118–20.

65. Dallek, *Franklin D. Roosevelt and American Foreign Policy*, 147–53.

66. David Kennedy, *Freedom from Fear: The American People in Depression and War, 1929–1945* (Oxford: Oxford University, 1999), 406.

67. George Gallup, *The Gallup Polls: Public Opinion, 1935–1971* (New York: Random House, 1972), 54, 65. This data, and public opinion in general, is not the same as "collective ideas" because it is an aggregate of individual beliefs and may lack institutionalization in symbols, discourse, and bureaucratic procedures. It does, however, give us some clue to the movement of individual opinion that in the right conditions can lead to collective change.

68. Jonas, *Isolationism in America*, 168–71.

69. Among others, see Osgood, *Ideals and Self-Interest in America's Foreign Relations*, 112–13, and Jonas, *Isolationism in America*, 204–13.

70. The support for the Neutrality Acts was driven by a desire for noninvolvement as well as for a means to penalize aggressors. See Bear Braumoeller, "The Myth of American Isolationism," manuscript, http://www.people.fas.harvard.edu/bfbraum/MythOfUSIsol.pdf (4/28/04). That it was such an indirect signal suggests the power of separatist thinking prevented more direct penalties.

71. Benjamin Page and Robert Shapiro, *The Rational Public* (Chicago: University of Chicago Press, 1992), 183; Gallup, *Gallup Polls*, 259.

72. Gallup, *Gallup Polls*, 54, 253; Jerome Bruner, *Mandate from the People* (New York: Duell Sloan Pearce, 1944), 15–16.

73. Barbara Reardon Farnham, *Roosevelt and the Munich Crisis: A Study of Political Decision-Making* (Princeton: Princeton University Press, 1997), 6; Kennedy, *Freedom from Fear*, 419–20.

74. Robert A. Divine, *Second Chance: The Triumph of Internationalism in America during World War II* (New York: Athenium, 1967), 291; Dallek, *Franklin D. Roosevelt and American Foreign Policy*, 200–201.

75. See Ronald Steel, *Walter Lippmann and the American Century* (Boston: Little, Brown, 1980), 314; John M. Muresianu, *War of Ideas: American Intellectuals and the World Crisis, 1938–1945* (New York: Garland, 1988), 127.; Jonas, *Isolationism in America*, 217–18; Brian McKercher, *Transition of Power: Britain's Loss of Global Preeminence to the United States, 1930–1945* (Cambridge: Cambridge University Press, 1999), 293–94; David Reynolds, "1940: Fulcrum of the Twentieth Century?" *International Affairs* 66 (1990).

76. Bruner, *Mandate from the People*, 22.

77. Kennedy, *Freedom from Fear*, 474–75.

78. Arthur H. Vandenberg Jr., *The Private Papers of Senator Vandenberg* (Boston: Houghton Mifflin, 1952), 1.

79. This example comes from Bear F. Braumoeller, *Isolationism in International Relations* (PhD diss., University of Michigan, 1998), 269, who concludes (158) that isolationism died a year and a half before Pearl Harbor.

80. Pearl Harbor caused the agreement number to drop from 35 percent to 19 percent. Gallup, *Gallup Polls*, 189, 272; Bruner, *Mandate from the People*, 15–16.

81. See Waldo H. Heinrichs, *Threshold of War: Franklin D. Roosevelt and American Entry into World War II* (New York: Oxford University Press, 1988), on the activities that the United States had underway that pointed it toward war in Europe before Pearl Harbor.

82. Ninkovich, *Modernity and Power*, 115–19; Kennedy, *Freedom from Fear*, 421. For challenges to the notion that there was an actual threat, see Bruce Russett, *No Clear and Present Danger: A Skeptical View of the U.S. Entry into World War II* (New York: Harper Torchbooks, 1972), and John A. Thompson, "Another Look at the Downfall of 'Fortress America'," *Journal of American Studies* 26, no. 3 (1992).

83. Gaddis, *United States and the Origins of the Cold War*, 1.

84. Dallek, *Franklin D. Roosevelt and American Foreign Policy*, 313.

85. See Melvyn P. Leffler, *A Preponderance of Power: National Security, the Truman Administration, and the Cold War* (Stanford: Stanford University Press, 1992), 19–20, 23, 499; Thomas G. Patterson, *On Every Front: The Making and Unmaking of the Cold War*, rev. ed. (New York: W. W. Norton, 1992), 101–2; May, "*Lessons*" of the Past.

86. Leigh, *Mobilizing Consent*, 115.

87. Gallup, *Gallup Polls*, 405, 497.

88. See Cole, *Roosevelt and the Isolationists*, 514–28; Gaddis, *United States and the Origins of the Cold War*, 2, 23, 18–20; Leffler, *Preponderance of Power*, 499; Robert A. Pollard, *Economic Security and the Origins of the Cold War* (New York: Columbia University Press, 1985), 2, 7–9; Divine, *Second Chance*, 47.

89. Leffler, *Preponderance of Power*, 10–13, 19–23, 499; May, "*Lessons*" of the Past; John Lewis Gaddis, *The Long Peace: Inquiries into the History of the Cold War* (New York: Oxford University Press, 1987), 21–25; Ninkovich, *Modernity and Power*, charts the origins of this line of argument to Wilson himself.

90. William Fox, "Geopolitics and International Relations," in *On Geopolitics: Classical and Nuclear*, ed. Ciro E. Zoppo and Charles Zorgbibe (Boston: Martinus Nijhoff, 1985), 28.

91. Divine, *Second Chance*; Kuehl and Dunn, *Keeping the Covenant*; Inderjeet Parmar, "Engineering Consent: The Carnegie Endowment for International Peace and the Mobilization of American Public Opinion, 1939–1945," *Review of International Studies* 26, no. 1 (2000).

92. See Jonas, *Isolationism in America*. FDR, schooled in Wilson's failure, remained concerned about the strength of isolationists especially in the Republican Senate. See Gaddis, *United States and the Origins of the Cold War*, 28; Dallek, *Franklin D. Roosevelt and American Foreign Policy*, 419. The weakness of isolationist sentiments (vis-à-vis internationalism) that continued to exist into the 1950s is seen in the equivocal public positions taken by such ardent isolationists as Senator Robert Taft (R-Ohio)—reminiscent of FDR in the 1930s. See Patterson, *On Every Front*, 475–80.

93. This might be contrasted with a situation where there are many alternative ideas with different behavioral injunctions or even a small set that have diametrically opposed injunctions.

94. Nicholas John Cull, *Selling War: The British Propaganda Campaign against American Neutrality in World War II* (New York: Oxford University Press, 1990), esp. 198–200; Susan A. Brewer, *To Win the Peace: British Propaganda in the United States during World War II* (Ithaca: Cornell University Press, 1997), 235–42.

95. See, for example, Divine, *Second Chance*; Cole, *Roosevelt and the Isolationists*, 12–13.

96. Osgood, *Ideals and Self-Interest*; George Kennan, *American Diplomacy, 1900–1950* (Chicago: University of Chicago Press, 1951). See too Edward H. Buehrig, *Woodrow Wilson and the Balance of Power* (Bloomington: Indiana University Press, 1955).

97. See, e.g., John Thompson, "The Exaggeration of American Vulnerability: The Anatomy of a Tradition," *Diplomatic History* 16, no. 1 (1992).

98. Dallek, *Franklin D. Roosevelt and American Foreign Policy*, 18–20.

99. Raymond Moley, *The First New Deal* (New York: Harcourt, Brace and World, 1966), 35–38, 45. Stephen Schuker, *American "Reparations" to Germany, 1919–1933: Implications for the Third-World Debt Crisis* (Princeton: Princeton University, Princeton Studies in International Finance, 1988), 102–4, makes the case that Roosevelt was more of a nationalist in his first term than a Republican would have been.

100. See, for example, Walter Isaacson and Evan Thomas, *The Wise Men: Six Friends and the World They Made* (New York: Simon and Schuster, 1986).

101. For different variants of this argument see Leffler, *Elusive Quest*, 368; Braeman, "Power and Diplomacy"; Costigliola, *Awkward Dominion*, 9–10; David Lake, *Entangling Relations: American Foreign Policy in Its Century* (Princeton: Princeton University Press, 1999); John J. Mearsheimer, *The Tragedy of Great Power Politics* (New York: Norton, 2001), 252–57.

102. Mearsheimer, *Tragedy of Great Power Politics*, 252.

103. Stephen Walt, *The Origins of Alliance* (Ithaca: Cornell University Press, 1987); Harrison Wagner, "What Was Bipolarity?" *International Organization* 47, no. 1 (1993). John Lewis Gaddis, *We Now Know: Rethinking Cold War History* (New York: Oxford, 1997), stresses Soviet actions as the cause of the cold war. Melvyn P. Leffler, "The Cold War: What Do 'We Now Know'?" *American Historical Review* 104, no. 2 (1999): 501–24, points our attention to U.S. actions as well.

104. Wilson only explained intervention as a response to the threat of a German victory after the United States had entered the war. See Ninkovich, *Modernity and Power*, 47–48, 51–53, 55, esp. n. 47. There is evidence that Wilson was motivated in part by the balance of power—but he was not concerned so much about Germany as an immediate security threat as he was that German militarism, if successful, would somehow force the United States to become a militarist state. He was also worried that the collapse of Germany would leave a void that ceded too much control to France and Russia on the Continent. Link, *Wilson*, ix, 410–11; Arthur S. Link, *Woodrow Wilson: Revolution, War, and Peace* (Arlington Heights, Va.: Harlan Davidson, 1979), 13; Ernest R. May, *The World War and American Isolation, 1914–1917* (Cambridge: Harvard University Press, 1959), 426–29; Kennan, *American Diplomacy*, 66, 72, likewise argued that the United States should have cut a deal before the balance collapsed.

105. Ninkovich, *Modernity and Power*, 14–15. Lodge mixed clear realist logic with moral concerns. See John A. Garraty, *Henry Cabot Lodge: A Biography* (New York: Alfred A. Knopf, 1953), 305–7; Widenor, *Henry Cabot Lodge*, 68–77, 80–84, 91–92, 274–76.

106. Quote from Morgenthau, "Mainsprings of American Foreign Policy," 848. See too Henry Kissinger, *Diplomacy* (New York: Simon and Schuster, 1994), 50; Walter Lippmann, *U.S. Foreign Policy: Shield of the Republic* (Boston: Little, Brown, 1943); Osgood, *Ideals and Self-Interest*, 11; Norman Graebner, *Ideas and Diplomacy: Readings in the Intellectual Tradition of American Foreign Policy* (New York: Oxford University Press, 1964), 488; Buehrig, *Woodrow Wilson and the Balance of Power*.

107. Link, *Wilson*, ix, 410–11; Link, *Woodrow Wilson*, 13; May, *World War and American Isolation*, 426–29. This moralism might also be seen as being shaped by self-interest. See Gordon N. Levin Jr., *Woodrow Wilson and World Politics* (New York: Oxford University Press, 1968).

108. Michaela Hönecke, *"Know Your Enemy": American Interpretations of National Socialism, 1933–1945* (PhD diss., University of North Carolina, Chapel Hill, 1998), 54–56.

109. David Kahn, "The United States Views Germany and Japan in 1941," in *Knowing One's Enemies: Intelligence Assessment before the Two World Wars*, ed. Ernest May (Princeton: Princeton University Press, 1984), 478–79, 487, 501.

110. Thompson, "Another Look at the Downfall of 'Fortress America,'" esp. 405–8. The United States did undertake an array of defense mobilization actions. See Heinrichs, *Threshold of War*.

111. See Kennan, *American Diplomacy*, 225–30; Divine, *Second Chance*; Pollard, *Economic Security*, 4, 244.

112. See Pollard, *Economic Security*, 20–23; Marc Trachtenberg, *A Constructed Peace: The Making of the European Settlement, 1945–1963* (Princeton: Princeton University Press, 1999), 152–55.

113. David Reynolds, *From Munich to Pearl Harbor: Roosevelt's America and the Origins of the Second World War* (Chicago: Ivan R. Dee, 2001), esp. 183–84.

114. On threats, see Walt, *Origins of Alliance*.

115. On the threat, see Braeman, "Power and Diplomacy," 348–58; Leffler, *Elusive Quest*, 32–33, 164–65, 363–64; Eliot Cohen, "The Strategy of Innocence? The United States, 1920–1945," in *The Making of Strategy: Rulers, States, and War*, ed. Williamson Murray, MacGregor Knox, and Alvin Bernstein (Cambridge: Cambridge University Press, 1994), 441.

116. Steven Casey, *Cautious Crusader: FDR, American Public Opinion, and the War against Nazi Germany* (New York: Oxford University Press, 2001), 24; Jonas, *Isolationism in America*, 273–74.

117. On constraints imposed by "domestic politics" and "opinion" that affected decision makers (e.g., in the Hoover administration), see Leffler, "Political Isolationism," 450–52, 455, 457; Braeman, "Power and Diplomacy," 361, 363.

118. Leffler, *Elusive Quest*, x; Leffler, "Political Isolationism," 416–20.

119. See Dale Copeland, *Origins of Major War* (Ithaca: Cornell University Press, 2000), on anticipatory behavior.

120. Ninkovich, *Modernity and Power*, 52, 55, 66–67, 102. Ninkovich argues that Wilson generally did not use geopolitical logic to sell the League because it would have conflicted with his idealistic justification for entering the war. He doubts that such logic would have carried the day anyway due to "deep-seated foreign policy habits."

121. As quoted in Rochester, *American Liberal Disillusionment*, 66–67.

122. Roberts, "Anglo-American Theme," 353, 362–63. Ninkovich, *Wilsonian Century*, 94–95, concludes that "had Americans thought seriously of restoring a balance of power, they would have been more sympathetic to France."

123. See Michael Howard, *The Continental Commitment: The Dilemma of British Defence Policy in the Era of the Two World Wars* (London: Maurice Temple Smith, 1972); Kindleberger, *World in Depression*; Paul Kennedy, *The Rise and Fall of Great Powers* (New York: Random House, 1987), 328.

124. Lake, *Entangling Relations*, highlights this element.

125. See Adler, *Uncertain Giant*, 12; Alan Dobson, *Anglo-American Relations in the Twentieth Century* (New York: Routledge, 1995), 55; Ambrosius, *Woodrow Wilson and the Diplomatic Tradition*, 214; Leffler, *Elusive Quest*, 25–26, 81, 160, 163; Kennedy, *Over Here*, 325; Knock, *To End All Wars*, 80. David Reynolds, *The Creation of the Anglo-American Alliance: A Study in Competitive Cooperation* (London: Europa Publications, 1981), lays out the tensions in the relationship. The U.S. government played a relatively limited role in European reconstruction efforts as well after World War I—a sharp contrast with World War II. See Anne Orde, *British Policy and European Reconstruction after the First World War* (New York: Cambridge University Press, 1990), 57–64, 330–32.

126. Mearsheimer, *Tragedy of Great Power Politics*, 379. Of course the issue is why the United States has not pulled out of Europe since the end of the cold war, when there is no emerging hegemon. This same logic suggests the interwar period was one that should have brought U.S. intervention.

127. Mahan's and Mackinder's views did get a reading and had some influence before this period, but they did not dominate collective thinking. See, e.g., John Lamberton Harper, *American Visions of Europe: Franklin D. Roosevelt, George F. Kennan, and Dean Acheson* (New York: Cambridge University Press, 1994), 39–40.

128. Fox, "Geopolitics and International Relations," 20–23; Stanley Hoffmann, "An American Social Science: International Relations," *Daedalus* 106, no. 3 (1977): 41–60; Leffler, *Preponderance of Power*, 10–12, 23. Mahan's geopolitical ideas did, of course, appear earlier, but they favored free riding on British naval power. Britain's power after World War I was suspect, however, suggesting the need for U.S. commitment.

129. Geoffrey Parker, *Western Geopolitical Thought in the Twentieth Century* (London: Croom Helm, 1985), 102–19; Geoffrey R. Sloan, *Geopolitics in United States Strategic Policy, 1890–1987* (New York: St. Martin's, 1988), esp. 80–126; Alan K. Henrikson, "The Map as an 'Idea': The Role of Cartographic Imagery during the Second World War," *American Cartographer* 2, no. 1 (1975).

130. Lake, *Entangling Relations*, offers a version of this argument.

131. One journalist noted that the effect of the sinking of the *Lusitania* in 1915 was so great that, ten years after the fact, people remembered where they were and what they were doing when it occurred. Knock, *To End All Wars*, 60.

132. The telegram had an important influence both on President Wilson and on the public, dominating headlines for days. Knock, *To End All Wars*, 116–17; Link, *Wilson*, 354.

133. Nils Gustav Lundgren, "Bulk Trade and Maritime Transport Costs: The Evolution of Global Markets," *Resources Policy* 22 (1996): 5–32, 7–8; Lake, *Entangling Relations*, 100–101.

134. Cooper, *Vanity of Power*, 23–24.

135. Sloan, *Geopolitics in United States Strategic Policy*, 106.

136. Isolationists, such as Charles Lindbergh, of course offered this view, but some geopoliticians who favored engagement, such as Nicholas Spykman, also accepted it. See Thompson, "Exaggeration of American Vulnerability," 30–35.

137. Lake, *Entangling Relations*, 99–100. Unopposed amphibious operations were not problematic. Allan R. Millett, "Assault from the Sea: The Development of Amphibious Warfare between the Wars—the American, British, and Japanese Experiences," in *Military Innovation in the Interwar Period*, ed. Williamson Murray and Allan R. Millett (New York: Cambridge University Press, 1996), 52. The difficulty of opposed landings might also have been used in favor of engagement in Europe to avoid such a need in the event intervention was again needed.

138. For a survey of such arguments, see Justus Doenecke, *Anti-Interventionism: A Bibliographical Introduction to Isolationism and Pacifism from World War I to the Early Cold War* (New York: Garland, 1987).

139. See Peter Trubowitz, *Defining the National Interest: Conflict and Change in American Foreign Policy* (Chicago: University of Chicago Press, 1998), 100. Accounts that focus on the rise of internationally oriented industrial and financial interest groups include Thomas Ferguson, "From Normalcy to New Deal: Industrial Structure, Party Competition, and American Public Policy in the Great Depression," *International Organization* 38, no. 1 (1984): 41–94; Peter Gourevitch, *Politics in Hard Times* (Ithaca: Cornell University Press, 1996); and Frieden, "Sectoral Conflict."

140. See Frieden, "Sectoral Conflict," 64, 68, 83, on the sectoral shifts that occurred due to the Depression. Trubowitz, *Defining the National Interest*, 167, points to key shifts in sectional interests in 1932, but there was no collective change until after the Second World War.

141. Jonas, *Isolationism in America*, 17–21.

142. Schuker, *American "Reparations" to Germany*, 102–4. For example, the 1934 Reciprocal Trade Agreements Act led to new trade agreements with only twenty countries between 1934 and 1939. The most important trade agreement of the period was the Anglo-American agreement of 1938—one that was provoked in part by the Czech crisis after march 1938 and the concessions that event inspired on the British side. The Roosevelt administration meanwhile seemed motivated by securing its economic and political position in its hemisphere and not getting dragged into the European storm. See McKercher, *Transition of Power*, 258–60, 265.

143. Frieden, "Sectoral Conflict," 88.

144. Other demographic changes, such as urbanization and immigration, also played a role as demonstrated by Trubowitz, *Defining the National Interest*, 115.

145. Divine, *Second Chance*; Robert D. Shulzinger, *The Wise Men of Foreign Affairs: The History of the Council on Foreign Relations* (New York: Columbia University Press, 1984). For a recent piece that speaks to this effect, see Parmar, "Engineering Consent."

146. Louis Hartz, *The Liberal Tradition in America: An Interpretation of American Political Thought since the Revolution* (New York: Harcourt Brace, 1955); Halle, *Dreams and Reality*; Stanley Hoffmann, *Gulliver's Troubles; or, The Setting of American Foreign Policy* (New York: McGraw-Hill, 1968); John G. Ruggie, *Constructing the World Polity: Essays on International Institutionalization* (New York: Routledge, 1998), 73–3, 217–19, has recently argued that the adoption of multilateralism by the United States reflected its founding principles as a community open to all.

147. Klingberg, "Historical Alternation of Moods"; Hoffmann, *Gulliver's Troubles*; Samuel P. Huntington, "Paradigms of American Politics: Beyond the One, Two, and the Many," *Political Science Quarterly* 89, no. 1 (1974).

148. Hartz, *Liberal Tradition in America*. The same critique applies to Hartz's argument that the absence of a feudal experience in the United States has produced its sense of "absolutist liberalism," which has led it to keep its distance from other countries. Yet at times the United States also adopts a "messianic" interventionism. The question of course would be how to a priori explicate when one of the two orientations will dominate. See too Mlada Bukovansky, "American Identity and Neutral Rights from Independence to the War of 1812," *International Organization* 51, no. 4 (1997): 217–18.

149. Michael Roskin, "From Pearl Harbor to Viet Nam: Shifting Generational Paradigms and Foreign Policy," *Political Science Quarterly* 89 (1974): 563–88.

150. See Ole Holsti, *Public Opinion and American Foreign Policy* (Michigan: University of Michigan Press, 1996), 156–66, for further skepticism toward generational arguments.

151. Vietnam, for example, caused some changes in U.S. foreign policy thinking but not a fundamental reorientation like that during World War II. Pressure for change was brought on by an A4 "Do something!" scenario, where losses resulted from adherence to an orthodoxy favoring external political-military commitments. What is notable, however, is that few people in the Vietnam debate argued for a disengagement from international society. That is, the event was never seen as a challenge to America's engagement and commitment to other major powers and international society in general. Instead it was viewed as a signal that the United States needed to draw some lines on where it would commit in peripheral areas.

152. Ann-Marie Burley, "Regulating the World: Multilateralism, International Law, and the Projection of the New Deal Regulatory State," in *Multilateralism Matters*, ed. John G. Ruggie (New York: Columbia University Press, 1993), 130; Ruggie, "International Regimes, Transactions, and Change," 379–415. Charles S. Maier, "The Politics of Productivity: Foundations of American Economic Policy after World War II," in *Between Power and Plenty: Foreign Economic Policies of Advanced Industrial States*, ed. Peter Katzenstein (Madison: University of Wisconsin Press, 1977), offers a form of this argument in foreign economic policy—that is, that the domestic emphasis on productivity and growth to overcome social and political divisions at home would also serve as the basis for the reconstruction of Germany and Japan and a more harmonious international order after World War II. See also Akira Iriye, "Culture and Power: International Relations as Intercultural Relations," *Diplomatic History* 3, no. 2 (1979): 120–22.

153. See, e.g., Robert Higgs, *Crisis and Leviathan: Critical Episodes in the Growth of American Government* (New York: Oxford University Press, 1987).

154. See Knock, *To End All Wars*, x, 187, 255–56; Rochester, *American Liberal Disillusionment*, 2, 60–64, 88–89, 97.

Chapter 4. Germany, from Outsider to Insider

1. E.g., Dan Reiter, *Crucible of Beliefs* (Ithaca: Cornell University Press, 1996). On the broad-ranging effects of war on policy change, see Arthur Marwick, *War and Social Change in the Twentieth Century: A Comparative Study of Britain, France, Germany, Russia, and the United States* (New York: Macmillan, 1974); Charles Tilly, *The Formation of National States in Western Europe* (Princeton: Princeton University Press, 1975); and Gregory J. Kasza, "War and Comparative Politics," *Comparative Politics* 28, no. 3 (1996).

2. Konrad Jarausch and Michael Geyer, *Shattered Past: Reconstructing German Histories* (Princeton: Princeton University Press, 2003), 173, note that one of the central issues in German foreign policy for the past two hundred years "can be restated as inserting a German national state into the established order by negotiation or confrontation."

3. Peter Gay, *Weimar Culture: The Outsider as Insider* (New York: Norton, 2001 [1968]); Henry Cord-Meyer, *The Long Generation: Germany from Empire to Ruin, 1913–1945* (New York: Walker, 1973), 9; Marshall M. Lee and Wolfgang Mihalka, *German Foreign Policy, 1917–1933: Continuity or Break?* (Dover, N.H.: Berg, 1987), 34; Richard Bessell, "Introduction: Themes in the History of Weimar Germany," in *Social Change and Political Development in Weimar Germany*, ed. Richard Bessell and E. J. Feuchtwanger (London: Croom Helm, 1981), 12.

4. Richard Bessell, *Germany after the First World War* (Oxford: Clarendon Press, 1993), 6, 38–39, 95–97, 224, 229; Martin Gilbert, *First World War* (London: Weidenfeld and Nicolson, 1994), map 28.

5. Fritz Fischer, *War of Illusions: German Policies from 1911 to 1914*, trans. Marian Jackson (New York: W. W. Norton, 1975); Fritz Fischer, *From Kaiserreich to Third Reich: Elements of Continuity in German History, 1871–1945*, trans. Roger Fletcher (Boston: Allen and Unwin, 1986); Hans-Ulrich Wehler, *The German Empire, 1871–1918*, trans. Kim Traynor (Leamington Spa, U.K.: Berg, 1985), 97–99; Eckart Kehr, *Economic Interest, Militarism, and Foreign Policy*, trans. Grete Heinz (Berkeley: University of California Press, 1977), 22–49; Thomas A. Kohut, *Wilhelm II and the Germans: A Study in Leadership* (New York: Oxford University Press, 1991), 194–98, provides

a nice summary of these arguments along with their critics; Jack Snyder, *Myths of Empire* (Ithaca: Cornell University Press, 1991), 66–111, covers much of this in his own "log-rolling" synthesis.

6. Charles Cogan, "Integrated Command . . . or Military Protectorate," *Diplomatic History* 26, no. 2 (2002): 309.

7. Liah Greenfield, *Nationalism: Five Roads to Modernity* (Cambridge: Harvard University Press, 1992), 360.

8. Alfred Vagts, *A History of Militarism* (Westport, Conn.: Greenwood, 1981), 17. Vagts also highlights Japan as being as extreme as Germany. Aristotle Kallis, "Expansionism in Italy and Germany between Unification and the First World War: On the Ideological and Political Origins of Fascist Expansionism," *European History Quarterly* 28, no. 4 (1998), sees strong similarities between German and Italian ideas before World War I.

9. Paul Kennedy, *The Rise of Anglo-German Antagonism, 1860–1914* (London: Allen and Unwin, 1980), 384.

10. Brian Bond and Martin Alexander, "Lidell Hart and De Gaulle: The Doctrines of Limited Liability and Mobile Defense," in *Makers of Modern Strategy: From Machiavelli to the Modern Age*, ed. Peter Paret (Princeton: Princeton University Press, 1986), 616–17.

11. Holger H. Herwig, "Of Men and Myths," in *The Great War and the Twentieth Century*, ed. Jay Winter, Geoffrey Parker, and Mary R. Habeck (New Haven: Yale University Press, 2000), 300.

12. But did Germany have any other options? Possibly. For example, in the interwar period, Germany could have secured its well–being through alliances or the more cooperative *politik* represented by at least some of Stresemann's rhetoric, instead of through armed expansion. If threatened by the West, the Soviet Union would appear an ally; if threatened by the East, the anticommunism of Britain and France would suffice to cement a bond. But such a path was hardly considered. Other options were available; they just were not given much weight in light of the dominant mind-set.

13. Hedley Bull, *The Challenge of the Third Reich* (New York: Oxford University Press, 1986), 7–13.

14. Hedley Bull, *The Anarchical Society: A Study of Order in World Politics*, 2nd ed. (New York: Columbia University Press, 1995), 181–82.

15. A Nazi-dominated postwar order would have been much different than the international society of preceding eras. The import of German victory in World War I may have been less disruptive, although it still would have challenged the balance-of-power principles of the post-Westphalian international order.

16. Adolf Hitler, *Table Talk, 1941–44*, trans. Norman Cameron and R. H. Stevens (London: Weidenfeld and Nicolson, 1953), 66.

17. Louis L. Snyder, *Roots of German Nationalism* (Bloomington: Indiana University Press, 1978), 55–73; John C. G. Röhl, *From Bismarck to Hitler: The Problem of Continuity in German History* (London: Longman, 1970), xiii; Ian Kershaw, *The Hitler Myth: Image and Reality in the Third Reich* (Oxford: Oxford University Press, 1987), 14.

18. Wehler, *German Empire*, 156.

19. Kallis, "Expansionism in Italy and Germany."

20. Bismarck tried to placate demands for a preventive war against Russia in the late 1880s through a hard-line economic policy of tariffs and by refusing Russia access to German credit markets. The result was to push Russia into France's arms—an equally undesired outcome. Wehler, *German Empire*, 189–92. See too Jack Snyder, *The Ideology on the Offensive: Military Decision Making and the Disasters of 1914* (Ithaca: Cornell University Press, 1984), 84.

21. Woodruff D. Smith, *The Ideological Origins of Nazi Imperialism* (New York: Oxford University Press, 1986), 18–19, 52–112; Geoff Eley, *Reshaping the German Right: Radical Nationalism and Political Change after Bismarck* (New Haven: Yale University Press, 1980), 5–6, 14–16, 68–70, 95–98, 351–52.

22. Smith, *Ideological Origins*, 18–19; and Henry Cord-Meyer, *Mitteleuropa in German Thought and Action, 1815–1945* (The Hague: Nijhoff, 1955), discuss the development of these ideas. See too Kallis, "Expansionism in Italy and Germany."

23. Smith, *Ideological Origins*, 200–206; Jörg Brechtefeld, *Mitteleuropa and German Politics: 1848 to the Present* (New York: St. Martin's, 1996), 8.

24. Brechtefeld, *Mitteleuropa and German Politics*. Some promoted racist elements of these ideas as well—e.g., the need to defend German culture against the "Slavic hordes" and Polish and German Jews.

25. Richard Weikart, "The Origins of Social Darwinism in Germany, 1859–1895," *Journal of the History of Ideas* 54 (1993): 469–88, 471.

26. Even Max Weber in an 1895 speech argued for more *"Ellbogenraum* [elbow room]" as the key to the continuing welfare of "our national species." One of the stronger statements came from Gen. Friedrich von Bernhardi in his 1911 work "Germany and the Next War," where state conflict was depicted as part of man's biology and nature just as it was in Darwin's survival of the fittest. Bernhardi linked this struggle to the need to give priority to the state (over individualism) and its accumulation of power. Weber, "Die Nationalstaat und die Volkswirtsschaftspolitik," in *Gesammelte Politische Schriften*, 2nd ed. (Tübingen: Mohr [Paul Siebeck], 1958), 4, as cited in Weikart, "Origins of Social Darwinism in Germany," 482; Friedrich von Bernhardi, *Germany and the Next War*, trans. Allen H. Powles (New York: Charles A. Eron, 1914), 18–28; Kennedy, *Over Here*, 310–11; H. W. Koch, "Social Darwinism as a Factor in the New Imperialism," in *The Origins of the First World War: Great Power Rivalry and German War Aims*, ed. H. W. Koch (Basingstoke: Macmillan, 1972).

27. Walter Consuelo Langsam, "Nationalism and History in the Prussian Elementary Schools under William II," in *Nationalism and Internationalism*, ed. Edward Mead Earle (New York: Columbia University Press, 1950), 241–60; Peter Lambert, "Paving the 'Peculiar Path': German Nationalism and Historiography since Ranke," in *Imagining Nations*, ed. Geoffrey Cubitt (New York: Manchester University Press, 1998).

28. George G. Iggers, *The German Conception of History: The National Tradition of Historical Thought from Herder to the Present* (Middletown, Conn.: Wesleyan University Press, 1968), 4–12; Gay, *Weimer Culture*, 90.

29. Roger Chickering, *Imperial Germany and a World without War: The Peace Movement and German Society, 1892–1914* (Princeton: Princeton University Press, 1975), 385–86.

30. Eley, *Reshaping the German Right*, 347; Gay, *Weimer Culture*, 89–92.

31. Thimme to Karl Thimme, October 14, 1914, as quoted in Lambert, "'Paving the Peculiar Path,'" 99.

32. Chickering, *Imperial Germany and a World without War*, 181.

33. Ibid., 34, 163, 180–81, 217, 286–89, 382–86, 415; Peter G. J. Pulzer, *Germany, 1870–1945: Politics, State Formation, and War* (New York: Oxford University Press, 1997), 80.

34. E.g., Röhl, *From Bismarck to Hitler*; Konrad Jarausch, "From Second to Third Reich: The Problem of Continuity in German Foreign Policy," *Central European History* 12, no. 1 (1979); Fischer, *From Kaiserreich to Third Reich*; Smith, *Ideological Origins of Nazi Imperialism*; Lee and Mihalka, *German Foreign Policy*.

35. Detlef Lehnert and Klaus Megerle, "Problems of Identity and Consciousness in a Fragmented Society," in *Political Culture in Germany*, ed. Dirk Berg-Schlosser and Ralf Rytlewski (New York: St. Martin's, 1993), 8.

36. See the coverage of speeches by these leaders in the *New York Times*, February 8, 1919, p. 1; April 12, 1919, p. 1; April 13, 1919, sec. 2, p. 5.

37. Peter Krüger, "German Disappointment and Anti-Western Resentment, 1918–1919," in *Confrontation and Cooperation: Germany and the United States in the Era of World War I, 1900–1924*, ed. Hans-Jürgen Schröder (Providence, R.I.: Berg, 1993), 326.

38. James Kurth, "The Political Consequences of the Product Cycle: Industrial History and Political Outcomes," *International Organization* 33, no. 1 (1979): 22–24; David Abraham, *The Collapse of the Weimar Republic: Political Economy and Crisis* (New York: Holmes and Meier, 1986).

39. Carl Strikwerda, "Response to 'Economic Integration and the European International System in the Era of World War I,'" *American Historical Review* 98, no. 4 (1993): 1140; Klaus Schwabe, "Germany's Peace Aims and the Domestic and International Constraints," in *The Treaty of Versailles: A Reassessment after 75 Years*, ed. Manfred F. Boemecke, Gerald D. Feldman, and Elisabeth Glaser (New York: Cambridge University Press, 1998), 59. Gerald D. Feldman,

Iron and Steel in the German Inflation, 1916–1923 (Princeton: Princeton University Press, 1977), 447–49, notes the failed effort by several steel interests along with Konrad Adenauer, then mayor of Cologne, to advance cooperation for both economic and political purposes.

40. Wolfram Wette, "Ideology, Propaganda, and Internal Politics as Preconditions of the War Policy of the Third Reich," in *Germany and the Second World War*, vol. I, *The Build-Up of German Aggression*, ed. Wilhelm Deist, Manfred Messerschmidt, Hans-Erich Volkmann, and Wolfram Wette (New York: Oxford University Press, 1990), 14.

41. Guntram Henrik Herb, *Under the Map of Germany: Nationalism and Propaganda, 1918–1945* (New York: Routledge, 1997), explores the flowering of this notion in the 1920s, before the rise of Hitler.

42. E.g., see Marvin L. Edwards, *Stresemann and the Greater Germany* (New York: Bookman Associates, 1963), 12 n. 1, 169; Gay, *Weimer Culture*, 27–28, 136; Henry A. Turner, "Continuity in German Foreign Policy: The Case of Stresemann," *International History Review* 1, no. 4 (1979); Peter Krüger, "Das doppelte Dilemma: Die Außenpolitik der Republik von Weimar zwischen Staatensystem and Innenpolitik," *German Studies Review* 22, no. 2 (1999); Annelise Thimme, *Gustav Stresemann: Eine Politische Biographie zur Geschichte der Weimarer Republik* (Hannover: O. Goedel, 1957). Jonathan Wright, *Gustav Stresemann: Weimar's Greatest Statesman* (New York: Oxford University Press, 2002), offers a balanced case that Stresemann pursued an integrative strategy even as he was highly leveraged by a domestic and international setting that made that difficult. Jonathan Wright, "Stresemann and Locarno," *Contemporary European History* 4, no. 2 (1995): 121, 131.

43. The military was asked if resistance was possible and it answered in the negative. Stresemann realized that without accommodating France, and placating the victorious powers in general, Germany's restoration of its 1914 borders and Great Power status could not be achieved. Lee and Mihalka, *German Foreign Policy*, 76, 80–84; Eberhard Kolb, *The Weimar Republic*, trans. P. S. Falla (Boston: Unwin Hyman, 1988), 58; Fischer, *From Kaiserreich to Third Reich*, 83–85.

44. Stresemann had not been a lifelong integrationist. In World War I, he had been a prominent proponent of annexation and a "Greater Germany" when German victory looked likely. Edwards, *Stresemann and the Greater Germany*; Röhl, *From Bismarck to Hitler*, xii; Henry A. Turner, *Stresemann and the Politics of the Weimar Republic* (Princeton: Princeton University Press, 1963), 12.

45. But even in the economic realm, the aim was dominance—not a notion of free trade liberalism, but political control through economic exchange. This was especially true regarding the smaller countries to the east and south. For example, Germany attempted to dominate the Polish economy through an economic boycott in 1925. Lee and Mihalka, *German Foreign Policy*, 91, 103.

46. "Through Toil and Sacrifice," speech at the convention of the German People's Party at Hannover, in Gustav Stresemann, *Essays and Speeches on Various Subjects* (Freeport, N.Y.: Books for Libraries Press, 1968), 210, 216.

47. Turner, *Stresemann and the Politics of the Weimar Republic*, 171–73, 210; Krüger, "Das doppelte Dilemma," 261–62; Klaus Hildebrand, *The Foreign Policy of the Third Reich* (Berkeley: University of California Press, 1973), 144.

48. Michael Geyer, "Professionals and Junkers: German Rearmament and Politics in the Weimar Republic," in *Social Change and Political Development in Weimar Germany*, ed. Richard Bessell and E. J. Feuchtwanger (London: Croom Helm, 1981), 107.

49. Larry Eugene Jones, *German Liberalism and the Dissolution of the Weimar Party System, 1918–1933* (Chapel Hill: University of North Carolina Press, 1988), 121, 149; Wright, "Stresemann and Locarno," 116–17, 124–25; Kolb, *Weimer Republic*, 62; Fischer, *From Kaiserreich to Third Reich*, 83–84.

50. Wette, "Ideology, Propaganda, and Internal Politics," 56–57. The Truppenamt, the General Staff of Weimar, laid out its plans to recover and enlarge Wilhelmian borders in 1926. The German foreign ministry also had expansionist aims. Manfred Messerschmidt, "Foreign Policy and Preparation for War," in *Germany and the Second World War*, 557, 563.

51. German participation in international organizations (e.g., the League of Nations) was

used both to reduce international resistance to German rearmament and to manage ethnic minority issues that might negatively affect the German aim of keeping German populations in other countries cohesive. These groups were seen as a useful stepping-stone to realization of revisionist claims and Germany's penetration and influence in Europe (Lee and Mihalka, *German Foreign Policy*, 92–93, 98–100). The German reaction to nascent ideas on European unity was cool at best. See Carl H. Pegg, *Evolution of the European Idea, 1914–1932* (Chapel Hill: University of North Carolina Press, 1983), 113; Peter M. R. Stirk, *A History of European Integration* (London: Pitner, 1996), 29.

52. Christopher M. Kimmich, *Germany and the League of Nations* (Chicago: University of Chicago Press, 1976), vii, 26–27, 104–5, 198–200, 206–7.

53. For these views see Stresemann's speeches from 1916 to 1926 as found in Stresemann, *Essays and Speeches*, esp. 68–75, 77, 111–15, 239, 258.

54. Wette, "Ideology, Propaganda, and Internal Politics," 61–71; Schwabe, "Germany's Peace Aims," 66–67.

55. Wette, "Ideology, Propaganda, and Internal Politics," 80–81.

56. Iggers, *German Conception of History*, 229–37; Stephan Berger, *The Search for Normality: National Identity and Historical Consciousness in Germany since 1800* (Providence, R.I.: Berghahn Books, 1997), 36; Jarausch and Geyer, *Shattered Past*, 41–45. Kehr left the country in the 1930s.

57. Gerhard L. Weinberg, *Germany, Hitler, and World War II: Essays in Modern German and World History* (Cambridge: Cambridge University Press, 1995), esp. 51; Kershaw, *Hitler Myth*, 123. For sometimes oblique references to such plans in speeches see Hitler's words in Max Domarus, *Hitler: Speeches and Proclamations, 1932–1945*, vol. 1, trans. Mary Fran Gilbert (Wauconda, Ill.: Bolchazy-Carducci, 1990), 109, 114, 211.

58. Wette, "Ideology, Propaganda, and Internal Politics," 96, 104.

59. Kershaw, *Hitler Myth*, 122; Weinberg, *Germany, Hitler, and World War II*, 75.

60. Ernest K. Bramsted, *Goebbels and National Socialist Propaganda, 1925–1945* (East Lansing: Michigan State University Press, 1965), 158; Weinberg, *Germany, Hitler, and World War II*, 30–34, 68.

61. Jeremy Noakes and Geoffrey Pridham, *Nazism, 1919–1945*, vol. 3, *Foreign Policy, War, and Racial Extermination* (Exeter: University of Exeter, 1988), 665; Weinberg, *Germany, Hitler, and World War II*, 37. Hitler consistently despaired of international institutions and internationalism of any sort (especially socialist) that distracted citizens from their loyalty to Germany. See speeches in Domarus, *Hitler*, e.g., 91, 94, 104–6, 111, 232, 324.

62. Kershaw, *Hitler Myth*, 4, 14; Hildebrand, *Foreign Policy of the Third Reich*, 135–36.

63. Wette, "Ideology, Propaganda, and Internal Politics," 81–82.

64. Deist et al., *Germany and the Second World War*, 732. Such "groups" behind Hitler's policy were not just narrow interests but could be found across almost all segments of society, suggesting that a collective mentality (not simply instrumental groups somehow manipulating policy) was involved.

65. See Hitler speeches, e.g., as found in Norman H. Baynes, *The Speeches of Adolf Hitler, April 1922–August 1939*, vol. 1–2 (Oxford: Oxford University Press, 1942), 1014, 1045–47, 1057; Domarus, *Hitler*, 324, 648, 656, 766, 778.

66. Ian Kershaw, *Hitler, 1889–1936: Hubris* (New York: W. W. Norton, 1999), 547; Gerhard Weinberg, *The Foreign Policy of Hitler's Germany: Diplomatic Revolution in Europe, 1933–1936* (Chicago: University of Chicago Press, 1970), 27, 36.

67. Speech of November 10, 1938 as found in Domarus, *Hitler*, 1245.

68. Weinberg, *Foreign Policy of Hitler's Germany*, 22–24.

69. Ibid., 42, 143–45, 149.

70. Of course, after the war, there was not one but two Germanys, each harnessed to an opposing side in the emerging cold war. East Germany was quickly subsumed under direct Soviet control. In West Germany, a similar development took place under the auspices of the Western powers. In the latter case, however, there was a greater (albeit still limited) degree of autonomy, one that makes the evolution of foreign policy ideas in the Federal Republic of Germany more interesting and the focus of what follows.

71. For recent discussions of this change see Peter J. Katzenstein, *Policy and Politics in West*

Germany: The Growth of a Semisovereign State (Philadelphia: Temple University Press, 1996); Andrei S. Markovits and Simon Reich, *The German Predicament: Memory and Power in the New Europe* (Ithaca: Cornell University Press, 1997), 34–40; John Duffield, *World Power Forsaken: Political Culture, International Institutions, and German Security Policy after Unification* (Stanford: Stanford University Press, 1998), 61–69; Thomas Banchoff, *The German Problem Transformed: Institutions, Politics, and Foreign Policy, 1945–1995* (Ann Arbor: University of Michigan Press, 1999).

72. Richard Merritt, *Democracy Imposed: U.S. Occupation Policy and the German Public, 1945–1949* (New Haven: Yale University Press, 1995), 93.

73. Karl W. Deutsch and Lewis Edinger, *Germany Rejoins the Powers: Mass Opinion, Interest Groups, and Elites in Contemporary German Foreign Policy* (Stanford: Stanford University Press, 1959), 154–56; Michael Ermarth, introduction to *America and the Shaping of German Society, 1945–1955*, ed. Michael Ermarth (Providence, R.I.: Berg, 1993), 14; Hans Woller, "Germany in Transition from Stalingrad (1943) to Currency Reform (1948)," in *America and the Shaping of German Society, 1945–1955*, ed. Michael Ermarth (Providence, R.I.: Berg, 1993), 32–33.

74. Konrad Jarausch, "1945 and the Continuities of German History: Reflections on Memory, Historiography, and Politics," in *Stunde Null: The End and the Beginning Fifty Years Ago*, ed. Geoffrey J. Gilles (Washington, D.C.: German Historical Institute, 1997), 17.

75. George L. Mosse, *Fallen Soldiers: Reshaping the Memory of the World Wars* (New York: Oxford University Press, 1990), 200–202, 212; John H. Herz, *From Dictatorship to Democracy: Coping with the Legacies of Authoritarianism and Totalitarianism* (Westport, Conn.: Greenwood, 1982), 33.

76. Deutsch and Edinger, *Germany Rejoins the Powers*, 29. The fact that Prussia was now in a different state (East Germany) was not irrelevant to the waning of militarism.

77. See Katzenstein, *Policy and Politics in West Germany*; Thomas U. Berger, *Cultures of Antimilitarism: National Security in Germany and Japan* (New York: Columbia University Press, 1998). See too Markovits and Reich, *German Predicament*, 34–40; Duffield, *World Power Forsaken*, 61–69; Merritt, *Democracy Imposed*, 363–66.

78. *The Bonn Constitution* (New York: Roy Benard, 1950), 13. This is not to say that all of Germany's revisionist tendencies were extinguished. The eastern lands were still an open question to Adenauer and his associates. See Hans-Peter Schwartz, *Konrad Adenauer: A German Politician and Statesman in an Age of War, Revolution, and Reconstruction*, vol. 1, *From the German Empire to the Federal Republic, 1876–1952*, trans. Louise Willmot (Providence, R.I.: Berghahn, 1995), 680.

79. Ernst B. Haas, *The Uniting of Europe: Political, Social, and Economic Forces, 1950–1957* (Stanford: Stanford University Press, 1958), 134; Thomas Alan Schwartz, *America's Germany: John J. McCloy and the Federal Republic of Germany* (Cambridge: Harvard University Press, 1991), 186–97. Katja Weber and Paul A. Kowert, "Language, Rules, and Order: The Westpolitik Debate of Adenauer and Schumacher," in *Language, Agency, and Power in a Constructed World*, ed. Francois Debrix (Armonk, N.Y.: M. E. Sharpe, 2003), 196–219; John Gillingham, *Coal, Steel, and the Rebirth of Europe, 1945–1955: The Germans and French from Ruhr Conflict to Economic Community* (New York: Cambridge University Press, 1991), 217–27, sees a new internationalism on the part of the German steel and coal industries immediately after World War II because they recognized their future depended on others, and, once back on their feet, because of the threat of a steel glut at the end of the 1940s.

80. Iggers, *German Conception of History*, 245, 246–68; Hartmut Lehmann and James Van Horn Melton, *Paths of Continuity: Central European Historiography from the 1930s to the 1950s*(Cambridge: Cambridge University Press, 1994), 11–14.

81. Berger, *Search for Normality*, 40–68; See too Lehmann and Melton, *Paths of Continuity*; Jarausch and Geyer, *Shattered Past*.

82. Jarausch, "1945 and the Continuities of German History," 21.

83. Wolfram Hanrieder, *Germany, America, Europe: Forty Years of German Foreign Policy* (New Haven: Yale University Press, 1989), 341–43; Berger, *Cultures of Militarism*, 119–20.

84. David Welch, *Germany, Propaganda, and Total War, 1914–1918: The Sins of Omission* (New Brunswick, N.J.: Rutgers University Press, 2000), 221–28; Bessell, *Germany after the First World War*, 38–42, 69–73.

85. Krüger, "German Disappointment and Anti-Western Resentment," 327; Sally Marks, "Smoke and Mirrors: in Smoke Filled Rooms and the Galerie Des Glaces," in *The Treaty of Ver-*

sailles: A Reassessment after 75 Years, ed. Manfred F. Boemeke, Gerald D. Feldman, Elisabeth Glaser (New York: Cambridge University Press, 1998), 348–49; Fritz Klein, "Between Compeique and Versailles: The Germans and the Way from a Misunderstood Defeat to an Unwanted Peace," in *Treaty of Versailles,* ed. Boemeke, Feldman, and Glaser; Röhl, *From Bismarck to Hitler,* 185; Stresemann, *Essays and Speeches,* 82.

86. These themes are found in speeches made in Berlin, July 31, 1914, August 4, 1914, and August 6, 1914, as found in Charles Gauss, ed., *The German Emperor as Shown in His Public Utterances* (New York: Charles Scribner's Sons, 1915), 323–29.

87. Although today it appears that Germany had offensive aims and bore significant responsibility for the war, German leaders at the time contended that Germany had been attacked, not the reverse. On Germany's responsibility for World War I, see Fischer, *War of Illusions,* and Dale Copeland, *Origins of Major War* (Ithaca: Cornell University Press, 2000), 56–78.

88. Martin Broszat, *Hitler and the Collapse of the Weimar Republic* (New York: Berg, 1987), 40. The exception was the far Left.

89. The SPD went along because they were caught up in the spirit of the times, feared for their popularity and that the government might abolish the party if it opposed the war, perhaps believed the war was defensive (at least initially), and may have hoped that war (through the destruction of czarism) would further domestic German reform. During the war there was conflict between annexationist and nonannexationist war aims factions. See Welch, *Germany, Propaganda, and Total War,* 18–19, 58–75, 352; F. L. Carsten, *War against War: British and German Radical Movements in the First World War* (Berkeley: University of California Press, 1982), 12–18.

90. E.g., in March of 1918 when Germany's defeat of Russia ended in the Treaty of Brest-Litovsk, the million acres of territory that Germany and Austria gained was justified as important to ensuring Germany's borders. Welch, *Germany, Propaganda, and War,* 222–23. Hein Goemans, *War and Punishment: The Causes of War Termination and the First World War* (Princeton: Princeton University Press, 2000), esp. 87–106, argues that German war aims increased as the prospects for victory declined.

91. As quoted in Anthony Lentin, "A Comment," in *The Treaty of Versailles,* ed. Boemecke, Feldman, and Glaser (New York: Cambridge University Press, 1998), 238.

92. Arnold Brecht, *The Political Education of Arnold Brecht: An Autobiography, 1884–1970* (Princeton: Princeton University Press, 1971), 164, 174; Krüger, "German Disappointment," 327; Schwabe, "Germany's Peace Aims," 60.

93. Lentin, "A Comment," 239; Schwabe, "Germany's Peace Aims," 48.

94. Niall Ferguson, "The Balance of Payments Question: Versailles and After," in *The Treaty of Versailles,* ed. Boemecke, Feldman, and Glaser, 403.

95. Broszat, *Hitler and the Collapse,* 47; see too Hajo Holborn, *Germany and Europe: Historical Essays* (Garden City, N.Y.: Doubleday, 1970), 208.

96. Gay, *Weimer Culture,* 16.

97. Quidde had authentic credentials—during the war he had antagonized the military by calling for a negotiated peace. See Jones, *German Liberalism,* 36.

98. Accommodation with the Allied powers as a policy and the people who supported it were discredited, even though accommodation was pursued as a temporary necessity. Schwabe, "Germany's Peace Aims," 60–64.

99. As quoted in the *New York Times,* May 15, 1919, p. 5.

100. Some view this as the beginning of the end of Weimar. See Schwabe, "Germany's Peace Aims," 64; Gordon Alexander Craig, *Germany, 1866–1945* (Oxford: Clarendon Press, 1978), 433.

101. Broszat, *Hitler and the Collapse,* 45–47.

102. Theodore A. Johnstone, *Dolchstoss: The Making of a Legend, 1890–1919* (PhD diss., University of Kansas, 1974), 263–64, 291. Jack Snyder, *From Voting to Violence: Democratization and Nationalist Conflict* (New York: Norton, 2000), 120, argues that mythmaking helped discredit Versailles. But the reverse relationship seems more powerful: the terms of Versailles, given expectations, allowed the myths to flourish.

103. On the origins of the legend, see Holger Herwig, "Clio Deceived: Patriotic Self-Censorship in Germany after the Great War," *International Security* 12, no. 2 (1987): 30–31.

104. Bessell, *Germany after the First World War,* 45–49, 69–73.

105. Klein, "Between Compeique and Versailles," 219.

106. Johnstone, *Dolchstoss*, 177, 182, 206–7, 251–52.

107. Bessell, *Germany after the First World War*, 84, 263.

108. Bernd Huppauf, "Langemarck, Verdun, and the Myth of the New Man in Germany after the First World War," *War and Society* 6, no. 2 (1988): 76.

109. Mosse, *Fallen Soldiers*, 78; Bessell, *Germany after the First World War*, 266.

110. See Geoff Eley, "The SPD in War and Revolution, 1914–1919," in *Bernstein to Brandt: A Short History of German Social Democracy*, ed. Roger Fletcher (London: Edward Arnold, 1987), 65–74.

111. His speeches before Versailles emphasized domestic order; after Versailles, they emphasized national unity in the face of the Versailles challenge. See Friedrich Ebert, *Schriften, Aufzeichnungen, Reden*, vol. 2 (Dresden: Carl Reisser Verlag, 1926).

112. See Heinrich August Winkler, "Eduard Bernstein as Social Critic of Weimar Germany," in *Bernstein to Brandt: A Short History of German Social Democracy*, ed. Roger Fletcher (London: Edward Arnold, 1987), 179–80.

113. On propaganda during the war see Welch, *Germany, Propaganda, and Total War*. On the spread of nationalist myths in Weimar see Snyder, *From Voting to Violence*, 121–28.

114. Schwabe, "Germany's Peace Aims," 42–43, 47–48.

115. A fight nonetheless ensued between Communists and others in the crowd. See Robert Weldon Whalen, *Bitter Wounds: German Victims of the Great War, 1914–1939* (Ithaca: Cornell University Press, 1984), 33.

116. Herwig, "Clio Deceived," 35.

117. Brockdorff-Rantzau's rejection of the terms at Versailles infuriated Wilson. See Klaus Schwabe, *Woodrow Wilson, Revolutionary Germany, and Peacemaking, 1918–1919: Missionary Diplomacy and the Realities of Power*, trans. Rita and Robert Kimber (Chapel Hill: University of North Carolina Press, 1985), 404.

118. Eric J. C. Hahn, "The German Foreign Ministry and the Question of War Guilt in 1918–1919," in *German Nationalism and the European Response, 1890–1945*, ed. Carol Fink, Isabel Hull, and MacGregor Knox (Norman: University of Oklahoma Press, 1985); Herwig, "Clio Deceived."

119. One was the longtime socialist Eduard Bernstein; see Winkler, "Eduard Bernstein," 179–80.

120. Charles S. Maier, *Recasting Bourgeois Europe: Stabilization in France, Germany, and Italy in the Decade after World War I* (Princeton: Princeton University Press, 1975), 304, 262, 272, 358.

121. See Peter Gourevitch, *Politics in Hard Times* (Ithaca: Cornell University Press, 1986), 140–47; Lee and Mihalka, *German Foreign Policy*, 113–14; Wette, "Ideology, Propaganda, and Internal Politics."

122. Krüger, "German Disappointment," 330–33.

123. Schwabe, *Woodrow Wilson, Revolutionary Germany, and Peacemaking*, 402–7.

124. Noakes and Pridham, *Nazism, 1919–1945*, 650. The United States rejected the French security guarantee discussed in conjunction with the Versailles treaty. Britain similarly was wary of any continental commitment.

125. For example, the Dawes plan split the nationalists. The foreign policy impact was more mixed. The Dawes plan, for example, did make Germany feel like less of an international outcast, but the funding also allowed for the extension of German control over eastern markets. See Jones, *German Liberalism*, 229; Maier, *Recasting Bourgeois Europe*, 481; Lee and Mihalka, *German Foreign Policy*, 65–71, 91.

126. Schwabe, *Woodrow Wilson, Revolutionary Germany, and Peacemaking*, 401, 407.

127. Carl Strikwerda, "Troubled Origins of European Economic Integration: International Iron and Steel and Labor Migration in the Era of World War I," *American Historical Review* 98, no. 4 (1993): 1129, testifies to the power of the national idea: "Industrialists saw the economic rationality of internationalism, but they cooperated just the same with nationalist programs."

128. Hans-Erich Volkmann, "The National Socialist Economy in Preparation for War," in *Germany and the Second World War*, vol. 1, *The Build-up of German Aggression*, ed. Mil-

itärgeschichtliches Forschungsamt (New York: Oxford University Press, 1990), 159, 167–69, 189; Wette, "Ideology, Propaganda, and Internal Politics," 80–81.

129. Wette, "Ideology, Propaganda, and Internal Politics," 124, 130–31, 133–47.

130. See Katzenstein, *Policy and Politics in West Germany*; Peter Katzenstein, *Cultural Norms and National Security: Police and Military in Postwar Japan* (Ithaca: Cornell University Press, 1996b), esp. chap. 7. See too Markovits and Simon, *German Predicament*, 34–40, and Duffield, *World Power Forsaken*, 61–69. In general, see Berger, *Cultures of Antimilitarism*; Banchoff, *German Problem Transformed*.

131. Eberhard Jäckel, *Hitler in History* (Hanover, N.H.: University Press of New England, 1984), 32–34.

132. Bramsted, *Goebbels and National Socialist Propaganda*, 158, 183–84.

133. Kershaw, *Hitler Myth*, 126–45.

134. Ibid., 130, 133; Noakes and Pridham, *Nazism, 1919–1945*, 721; William L. Shirer, *The Rise and Fall of the Third Reich: A History of Nazi Germany* (New York: Simon and Schuster, 1960), 540–41.

135. See David Kaiser, "Hitler and the Coming of War," in *Modern Germany Reconsidered*, ed. Gordon Martel (New York: Routledge, 1992), 180–84. Much of this wariness of war was in the military, but the opposition was not about the overall vision, but the timing and tactics of using force. See Copeland, *Origins of Major War*, chap. 5.

136. Peter Hoffmann, *The History of the German Resistance, 1933–1945*, trans Richard Barry (Montreal: McGill-Queen's University Press, 1996), 99; Kershaw, *Hitler Myth*, 137–40; Wette, "Ideology, Propaganda, and Internal Politics," 122, 141. It did, however, set off alarms for foreigners; see Mark Haas, *Ideology, Threat Perception, and Great Power Politics, 1789–1989* (Ithaca: Cornell University Press, 2005).

137. Bramsted, *Goebbels and National Socialist Propaganda*, 183–84, 233; Welch, *Germany, Propaganda, and Total War*, 92.

138. Noakes and Pridham, *Nazism 1919–1945*, 763–64. Hoffmann, *History of the German Resistance*, 255, notes that after Poland no general would take part in a putsch. Hitler had used this same tactic in 1938 when addressing journalists after the Munich settlement. See Domarus, *Hitler*, 1244–49.

139. Kershaw, *Hitler Myth*, 155.

140. Ibid., 176.

141. Ibid., 192. Bramsted, *Goebbels and National Socialist Propaganda*, 259.

142. Woller, "Germany in Transition," 13, 23–24, 31.

143. Kershaw, *Hitler Myth*, 173–76, 193, 202–7; David Welch, *The Third Reich: Politics and Propaganda* (New York: Routledge, 1993), 125.

144. Weinberg, *Germany, Hitler, and World War II*, 277.

145. Kershaw, *Hitler Myth*, 194.

146. Stalingrad was so important because, as Goebbels recognized, Hitler's reputation as a strategist, and the credibility of his strategy, were at stake. Bramsted, *Goebbels and National Socialist Propaganda*, 259–60.

147. J. Goebbels, *Der steile Aufsteig*, 16, as quoted in Bramsted, *Goebbels and National Socialist Propaganda*, 261.

148. Woller, "Germany in Transition," 24. Hoffmann, *History of the German Resistance*, 278, notes that after the defeat at Stalingrad a near revolutionary atmosphere emerged in Germany. Kershaw, *Hitler Myth*, 193.

149. Woller, "Germany in Transition," 31.

150. Wette, "Ideology, Propaganda, and Internal Politics," 125–55.

151. Ermarth, *America and the Shaping of German Society*, 5.

152. Donald Abenheim, *Reforging the Iron Cross: The Search for Tradition in the West German Armed Forces* (Princeton: Princeton University Press, 1988), xvi, 46, 291; Berger, *Cultures of Antimilitarism*, 24.

153. Weinberg, *Germany, Hitler, and World War II*, 318

154. H. R. Trevor-Roper, *The Last Days of Hitler*, 6th ed. (Chicago: University of Chicago Press, 1987), 225.

155. Some revanchist sentiment existed, even in these circumstances. Many, for example, maintained that Nazi ideas were right but were implemented in the wrong fashion. Germans were also inclined to believe that Nazism was as much the product of Versailles and the Depression (both shaped by Allied policies as well) as it was something for which the Germans were responsible. Deutsch and Edinger, *Germany Rejoins the Powers*, 15; Merritt, *Democracy Imposed*, 97; Joseph Foschepoth, "German Reaction to Defeat and Occupation," in *West Germany under Construction: Politics, Society, and Culture in the Adenauer Era*, ed. Robert G. Moeller (Ann Arbor: University of Michigan, 1997), 77–78.

156. Wolfram Hanrieder, *West German Foreign Policy, 1949–1963: International Pressure and Domestic Response* (Stanford: Stanford University Press, 1967), 94–95, Schwartz, *Konrad Adenauer*, 469–70, 500–501; Thomas Banchoff, "Historical Memory and German Foreign Policy: The Cases of Adenauer and Brandt," *German Politics and Society* 14, no. 2 (1996): 40–43; Banchoff, *German Problem Transformed*; Berger, *Cultures of Antimilitarism*, 56–66, argues there were three subcultures, dividing the Western group into two, a European faction and a pro-Atlantic/U.S. faction. While there were at times friction between these two emphases, there was also much overlap.

157. Hanrieder, *West German Foreign Policy*, 98–101; Berger, *Cultures of Antimilitarism*, 61–62, 66, Schwartz, *Konrad Adenauer*, 450–51.

158. Schwartz, *Konrad Adenauer*, 483, 487, 496, 499.

159. Hanrieder, *West German Foreign Policy*, 101; Schwartz, *America's Germany*, 78, 81, 243–44; Schwartz, *Konrad Adenauer*, 487.

160. Robert Moeller, ed., *West Germany under Construction: Politics, Society, and Culture in the Adenauer Era* (Ann Arbor: University of Michigan Press, 1997), 9–10.

161. Hanrieder, *West German Foreign Policy*, 56, 61; Jarausch, "1945 and the Continuities of German History," 19.

162. Michael L. Hughes, "Restitution and Democracy in Germany after Two World Wars," *Contemporary European History* 4, no. 1 (1995): 15.

163. Katherine Pence, "The Myth of a Suspended Present: Prosperity's Painful Shadow in 1950s East Germany," in *Pain and Prosperity: Reconsidering Twentieth-Century German History*, ed. Paul Betts and Greg Eghigian (Stanford: Stanford University Press, 2003), 137, 141–42; Ingrid Schenk, "Scarcity and Success: The East according to the West in the 1950s," in *Pain and Prosperity*, ed. Betts and Eghigian, 161, 176.

164. See Schwartz, *America's Germany*, 86, 295–96. Of course, the Allies could not control minds, and many of the civilian foreign ministry personnel from the prewar period remained. Herz, *From Dictatorship to Democracy*.

165. Moeller, *West Germany under Construction*, 20; Schwartz, *America's Germany*, 76.

166. McCloy was arguing for policies to revive German industry (i.e., against steel production limits favored by France in 1950). See Schwartz, *America's Germany*, 94; also 296.

167. Schwartz, *Konrad Adenauer*, 149, Foschepoth, "German Reaction to Defeat and Occupation," 83.

168. Schwartz, *America's Germany*, 186–97.

169. As Hanrieder, *Germany, America, Europe*, 318, sums up, "Bonn's Western policies had proven remarkably successful."

170. Berger, *Cultures of Antimilitarism*, 42–43.

171. Which Adenauer was quick to point out; see Schwartz, *America's Germany*, 78–81.

172. Berger, *Cultures of Antimilitarism*, 119–20. Berger (84–85, 94–95) also argues that concessions were made to the SPD as well in terms of reform of the military (and its militarism). Some of the neutralist emphases—such as on collective security versus Western alliance—emerged later—e.g., in German support for the Organization for Security and Cooperation in Europe.

173. Quoted in Carole Fink, Isabel V. Hull, and MacGregor Knox, eds., *German Nationalism and the European Response, 1890–1945* (Norman: University of Oklahoma Press, 1985), 3.

174. Kenneth Waltz, *Theory of International Politics* (Reading, Mass.: Addison-Wesley, 1979),

and John Mearsheimer, *The Tragedy of Great Power Politics* (New York: Norton, 2001) have offered different forms of polarity arguments.

175. Jarausch and Geyer, *Shattered Past*, 175: "The Second Reich, therefore, had to choose whether to be content with mere membership in the concert of great powers, solidified by cooperation, or to aspire to become its conductor, at the risk of provoking hostility."

176. Kennedy, *Rise of Anglo-German Antagonism*, 468. Likewise, Stig Förster, "Dreams and Nightmares: German Military Leadership and the Images of Future Warfare, 1871–1914," in *Anticipating Total War: The German and American Experiences, 1871–1914,* ed. Manfred F. Boemeke, Roger Chickering, and Stig Förster (Cambridge: Cambridge University Press, 1999), 367–68, argues that Germany was not prepared for a long war. Hence it might have more usefully prepared for a long war or could have pursued a détente policy much as Moltke (the elder) advised in 1890.

177. Copeland, *Origins of Major War*, 118–45.

178. Letter, Isaiah Bowman to Lionel Cyrtis of Balliol College, Oxford, November 2, 1939 (copy sent to Franklin Delano Roosevelt) as cited in Geoffrey Sloan, *Geopolitics in United States Strategic Policy, 1890–1987* (New York: St. Martin's, 1988), 111.

179. Gunther Hellmann, "Goodbye Bismarck? The Foreign Policy of Contemporary Germany," *Mershon International Studies Review* 40, no. 1 (1996). The German government's challenge to U.S. plans to attack Iraq occurred in collaboration with other European countries.

180. Snyder, *Myths of Empire*, 104–7, uses the term "blowback" to capture this effect. See too Roger Chickering, *We Men Who Feel Most German: A Cultural Study of the Pan-German League, 1886–1914* (Boston: Allen and Unwin, 1984), 301–4.

181. Quoted in Kohut, *Wilhelm II and the Germans*, 196. Eley, *Reshaping the German Right*, 6; Larry E. Jones and James Retallack, "German Conservatism Reconsidered," in *Between Reform, Reaction, and Resistance: Studies in the History of German Conservatism from 1789 to 1945,* ed. Larry Eugene Jones and James Retallack (Providence, R.I.: Berg, 1993), 11–12; David Blackbourne and Geoff Eley, *The Peculiarities of German History: Bourgeois Society and Politics in Nineteenth-Century Germany* (New York: Oxford University Press, 1984).

182. Gay, *Weimer Culture,* nicely contrasts the continuity in political personnel against the rise of new cultural elites in Weimar.

183. Maier, *Recasting Bourgeois Europe.*

184. Eley, *Reshaping the German Right,* 346.

185. Geyer, "Professionals and Junkers," 80.

186. See, e.g., Henry A. Turner, *German Big Business and the Rise of Hitler* (New York : Oxford University Press, 1985), esp. 11, 34; Feldman, *Iron and Steel,* 463–65; Gerald D. Feldman, *The Great Disorder: Politics, Economics, and Society in the German Inflation, 1914–1924* (New York: Oxford University Press, 1997), 314–15, 325–26, on the continued and in some respects enhanced influence of heavy industry after World War I. Conservatives were not uniformly opposed to the new regime. Some important industrial interests leaned toward greater international cooperation and integration, not autarky. Peter Fritsche, "Breakdown or Breakthrough? Conservatives and the November Revolution," in *Between Reform, Reaction, and Resistance: Studies in the History of German Conservatism from 1789 to 1945,* ed. Larry Eugene Jones and James Retallack (Providence: Berg, 1993); Strikwerda, "Troubled Origins"; Schwabe, "Germany's Peace Aims," 89.

187. Turner, *German Big Business,* 14, 27–31.

188. Ibid.; Abraham, *Collapse of the Weimar Republic,* takes issue with this view in some respects but agrees industry was late to the table and was essentially jumping on the bandwagon when it backed Hitler.

189. Thomas Childers, *The Nazi Voter: The Social Foundations of Fascism in Germany, 1919–1933* (Chapel Hill: University of North Carolina Press, 1983), esp. 262–70.

190. Kallis, "Expansionism in Italy and Germany," 444–45.

191. We might also blame excessive German expectations. Theologian Ernst Troeltsch named the months between the end of the fighting and when the treaty's terms became known as "the dreamland of the armistice." As cited in Fritsche, "Breakdown or Breakthrough?" 302.

Chapter 5. Overhaul of Orthodoxy in Tokugawa Japan and the Soviet Union

1. Kenneth Waltz, *Theory of International Politics* (Reading, Mass.: Addison-Wesley, 1979), 76–77, 127–28.

2. Such contact need not always be seen as a source of legitimacy. For example, Japanese who had contact with Westerners were sometimes seen as contaminated or disloyal, especially before the Meiji Restoration. The same was true of Soviet citizens in the pre-Gorbachev era.

3. Ronald P. Toby, "Leaving the Closed Country: New Models for Early Modern Japan," *Transactions of the International Conference of Orientalists in Japan* 35 (1990): 213–30; Marius B. Jansen, *The Making of Modern Japan* (Cambridge: Harvard University Press, Belknap Press, 2000), 78. See too Noel Perrin, *Giving Up the Gun: Japan's Reversion to the Sword, 1543–1879* (Boston: David R. Godine, 1988).

4. Hidemi Suganami, "Japan's Entry into the International Society," in *The Expansion of International Society*, ed. Hedley Bull and Adam Watson (Oxford: Clarendon Press, 1984).

5. Immanuel C. Y. Hsü, *China's Entrance into the Family of Nations: The Diplomatic Phase, 1858–1880* (Cambridge: Harvard University Press, 1960), 3–6; Takeshi Hamashita, "The Intraregional System in East Asia in Modern Times," in *Network Power: Japan and Asia*, ed. Peter Katzenstein and Takashi Shiraishi (Ithaca: Cornell University Press, 1997), 114–23.

6. Shortly thereafter Hideyoshi invaded Korea, a poorly managed campaign that was bitterly resisted by Korea with the help of China. The episode ended with the withdrawal of Japan after Hideyoshi's death in 1598. Jansen, *Making of Modern Japan*, 11–21, 68–69.

7. William G. Beasley, ed., *Select Documents on Japanese Foreign Policy, 1853–1868* (New York: Oxford University Press, 1955), 18–19, 22; Conrad Totman, *The Collapse of the Tokugawa Bakufu, 1862–1868* (Honolulu: University of Hawaii Press, 1979), xv–xvii.

8. Beasley, *Select Documents*, 3–4; Totman, *Collapse of the Tokugawa Bakufu*, 478; Conrad Totman, "From Sakoku to Kaikoku: The Transformation of Foreign Policy Attitudes," *Monumenta Nipponica* 35, no. 1 (1980): 5; Ronald Toby, *State and Diplomacy in Early Modern Japan: Asia in the Development of the Tokugawa Bakufu* (Princeton: Princeton University Press, 1984), 55, 104, 106, 230–31, 242–43; Jansen, *Making of Modern Japan*, 78.

9. These were the Shimbara and Amakusa revolts in 1637–38. Shinobu Seizaburō, ed. *Nihon gaikō shi: 1853–1872* (Nagano: Shinano Mainichi shimbunsha, 1974), 10. I am grateful to Hiro Yamamoto for his research assistance with Japanese language sources found in this chapter.

10. See Ronald Toby, "Reopening the Question of Sakoku: Diplomacy in the Legitimation of the Tokugawa Bakufu," *Journal of Japanese Studies* 3, no. 2 (1997): 323–64.

11. Toby, "Reopening the Question of Sakoku"; Toby, *State and Diplomacy*; Totman, "From Sakoku to Kaikoku," 5; Brett Walker, "Reappraising the Sakoku Paradigm: The Ezo Trade and the Extension of Tokugawa Political Space into Hokkaido," *Journal of Asian History* 30, no. 2 (1996).

12. Toby, *State and Diplomacy*, develops this theme in most depth.

13. The term "closed country" came into use only in the late 1700s. Toby, *State and Diplomacy*, 17, 230, 239–42; Marius B. Jansen, "The Meiji Restoration," in *The Cambridge History of Japan*, vol. 5, *The Nineteenth Century*, ed. Marius B. Jansen (Cambridge: Cambridge University Press, 1989), 3, 14; Christopher Howe, *The Origins of Japan's Trade Supremacy: Development and Technology in Asia from 1540 to the Pacific War* (Chicago: University of Chicago Press, 1996), 41.

14. Jansen, *Making of Modern Japan*, 266–67; William G. Beasley, "The Foreign Threat and the Opening of the Ports," in *The Cambridge History of Japan*, vol. 5, *The Nineteenth Century*, ed. Marius B. Jansen (Cambridge: Cambridge University Press, 1989), 272–73.

15. William G. Beasley, *The Meiji Restoration* (Stanford: Stanford University Press 1972), 90; Beasley, *Select Documents*, 23. Note that two daimyo that favored doing whatever the Bakumatsu decided are not counted. Beasley, *Meiji Restoration*, says sixty-one responses exist in the record. Jansen, *Making of Modern Japan*, 280, offers a count that indicates fighting is the dominant interpretation. There is no indication of the total number polled or responses received. Jansen states that the daimyo consulted their own senior advisors so the results likely reflect a "broad sector of the ruling class."

16. Beasley, *Select Documents*, 4–8.

17. Jansen, *Making of Modern Japan*, 273.

18. Beasley, "Foreign Threat," 278.

19. For example, in 1808 the English ship *Phaeton* entered Nagasaki Harbor and threatened to attack other ships there if it was not resupplied. The Japanese complied. Russian ships were also increasingly present. See Marius B. Jansen, "Japan in the Early Nineteenth Century," in *The Cambridge History of Japan*, vol. 5, *The Nineteenth Century*, ed. Marius B. Jansen (Cambridge: Cambridge University Press, 1989), 94–97.

20. He demanded that Japan provide as "a right and not to solicit as a favor those acts of courtesy which are due from one civilized nation to another." Roger Pineau, ed., *The Japan Expedition, 1852–1854: The Personal Journal of Commodore Matthew C. Perry* (Washington, D.C.: Smithsonian Institution, 1968), 92.

21. Jansen, *Making of Modern Japan*, 270–74.

22. Beasley, *Select Documents*, 27–28; Jansen, *Making of Modern Japan*, 283–84; Beasley, "Foreign Threat," 283.

23. Totman, *Collapse of the Tokugawa Bakufu*, xx.

24. Donald Keene, *Japanese Discovery of Europe, 1720–1830*, rev. ed. (Stanford: Stanford University Press, 1969); Bob Tadashi Wakabayashi, *Anti-Foreignism and Western Learning in Early Modern Japan* (Cambridge: Council on East Asian Studies, 1986); George M. Wilson, *Patriots and Redeemers in Japan: Motives in the Meiji Restoration* (Chicago: University of Chicago Press, 1992), 40–41. These thinkers differed on the aims of openness.

25. Howe, *Origins of Japan's Trade Supremacy*, 70–71.

26. See, e.g., Harold Bolitho, "The Tempo Crisis," in *The Cambridge History of Japan*, vol. 5, *The Nineteenth Century*, ed. Marius B. Jansen (Cambridge: Cambridge University Press, 1989).

27. Beasley, *Select Documents*, 10. On the rise of Confucian/emperor ideas see Jansen, "Meiji Restoration," 313–15, 330–31; Wakabayashi, *Anti-Foreignism*.

28. Beasley, *Select Documents*, 22–23, 37–38; L. M. Cullen, *A History of Japan, 1582–1941: Internal and External Worlds* (New York: Cambridge University Press, 2003), 192.

29. Beasley, "Foreign Threat," 272–74.

30. Jansen, "Meiji Restoration," 335.

31. E.g., the removal of the ban on Japanese shipbuilding was one of the first measures taken; Jansen, "Meiji Restoration," 336.

32. This view was embraced by a range of leaders and thinkers including Hotta Masayoshi, Sakuma Shozan, Yokai Shounan, and Katsu Kaishu. See Beasley, *Select Documents*, 7–8; Kenichi Matsumoto, *Nihon no kindai*, vol. 1, *Kaikoku, Ishin: 1853–1871* (Tokyo: Chuo Koron, 1998), 51.

33. Beasley, "Foreign Threat," 273–74; Walter LaFeber, *The Clash: A History of U.S.-Japan Relations* (New York: W. W. Norton, 1997), 17–18; Totman, "From Sakoku to Kaikoku," 11–12; see too Beasley, *Select Documents*, 23, 47.

34. Totman, "From Sakoku to Kaikoku," 10, 12–14; Jansen, *Making of Modern Japan*, 315–16.

35. Totman, "From Sakoku to Kaikoku," 12; Beasley, "Foreign Threat," 299–302.

36. Takashi Ishii, *Meiji Ishin no Kokusaiteki Kankyo* (Tokyo: Yoshikawa Koubundou, 1966), 44, 344–45, 459–60.

37. The Jōi ideology in Chōshū, for example, was weakened by the defeats of 1864. Akira Tanaka, *Meiji Ishin Seijishi Kenkyui* (Tokyo: Aoki Shoten, 1978), 178–79.

38. Beasley, *Select Documents*, 83.

39. "They had made foreign policy 'a stick to beat the Bakufu'." Beasley, *Select Documents*, 90.

40. Matsumoto, *Nihon no kindai*, vol. 1, *Kaikoku, Ishin*, 11.

41. See Totman, "From Sakoku to Kaikoku," 17–18; Jansen, *Making of Modern Japan*, 321; Cullen, *History of Japan*, 194.

42. Note the two different strands of Jōi philosophy—one encouraged opening. Shinobu, *Nihon gaikō shi*, 23–31, and Beasley, *Select Documents*, 7–8.

43. Donald Keene, *Emperor of Japan: Meiji and His World, 1852–1912* (New York: Columbia University Press, 2002), 139–40.

44. Suganami, "Japan's Entry," claims the last of the seclusion principles was revoked in 1866. Beasley, "Foreign Threat," 303; LaFeber, *Clash*, 29–30.

45. Beasley, *Select Documents*, 93.

46. See Stephen Vlastos, "Opposition Movements in Early Meiji, 1868–1885," in *The Emergence of Meiji Japan*, ed. Marius Jansen (Cambridge: Cambridge University Press, 1995).

47. There was a counterrevolutionary reaction to the new Meiji regime but relatively little of it was over foreign policy.

48. Vlastos, "Opposition Movements in Early Meiji," 221, 227, 263, 265; Akira Iriye, "Japan's Drive to Great-Power Status," in *The Emergence of Meiji Japan*, ed. Marius Jansen (Cambridge: Cambridge University Press, 1995), 282, 293–94.

49. Howe, *Origins of Japan's Trade Supremacy*, 70, argues that the Tokugawa system and its seclusion policy "had unsatisfactory economic effects: they impeded the integration of the national economy, which was a prerequisite for economies of scale and specialization, and they inhibited economic flexibility and the transfer to Japan of Western knowledge." See too Perrin, *Giving Up the Gun*. This point should not be overstated, as European powers were not all that involved in the Pacific until the early nineteenth century, and there may not have been much sacrificed in terms of trade benefits. Jansen, *Making of Modern Japan*, 94–95. Toby, *State and Diplomacy*, 228, argues that Japan's self-focused seclusion may have helped keep it independent, whereas other countries in the Chinese sphere fell under Western influence. Cullen, *History of Japan*, argues that sakoku had negligible or positive effects on Japanese development.

50. Jansen, "Japan in the Early Nineteenth Century," 90, 101, 106; Hirakawa Sukehiro, "Japan's Turn to the West," in *The Cambridge History of Japan*, vol. 5, *The Nineteenth Century*, ed. Marius B. Jansen (Cambridge: Cambridge University Press, 1989), 460; Wakabayashi, *Anti-Foreignism*. Cullen, *History of Japan*, makes the starkest case on this point; see, for example, pp. 9–10.

51. Japan's situation would have been difficult had it faced, for example, a conquest-minded United States not distracted by civil war. On general warnings, see J. Victor Koschman, *The Mito Ideology: Discourse, Reform, and Insurrection in Late Tokugawa Japan, 1790–1864* (Berkeley: University of California Press, 1987), 2–4; H. D. Harootunian, "Late Tokugawa Culture and Thought," in *The Cambridge History of Japan*, vol. 5, *The Nineteenth Century*, ed. Marius B. Jansen (Cambridge: Cambridge University Press, 1989), 232–33; Jansen, *Making of Modern Japan*, 262–64.

52. Watanabe Kazan as quoted in Harootunian, "Late Tokugawa Culture and Thought," 237–38.

53. Jansen, "Japan in the Early Nineteenth Century," 95–99.

54. Kudo Heisuke, a samurai of Sendai-Han, suggested in 1783 that Japan should establish a formal trading relationship with Russia. In 1786, Hayashi Shihei, a famous intellectual, wrote *Kaikoku Heidan*, a book that warned of the dangers from abroad and emphasized the need to improve defenses. In 1827, Sato Nobuhiro, a scholar, wrote *Keizai Youroku*, which urged the bakufu to start trading with foreign powers in order to achieve "rich nation, strong army." Most of these scholars were oppressed by the bakufu's harsh measures. See Shinobu, *Nihon gaikō shi*, 23–31; Sukehiro, "Japan's Turn to the West"; Wakabayashi, *Anti-Foreignism*.

55. Sukehiro, "Japan's Turn to the West," 462. Jansen, *Making of Modern Japan*, 262–63, 267–68.

56. Beasley, "Foreign Threat," 301; LaFeber, *Clash*, 8.

57. Vlastos, "Opposition Movements in Early Meiji," 227.

58. Totman, *Collapse of the Tokugawa Bakufu*, 446–61; Jansen, "Meiji Restoration," 332.

59. Jansen, *Making of Modern Japan*, 331.

60. Beasley, *Select Documents*, 14–15, 18, 36; Ishii, *Meiji Ishin no Kokusaiteki Kankyo*, 599.

61. Jansen, "Meiji Restoration," 314; Beasley, "Foreign Threat," 235, 282, 287; Totman, *Collapse of the Tokugawa Bakufu*, 444–46, 478; Totman, "From Sakoku to Kaikoku," 19.

62. Michio Kitahara, "The Rise of Four Mottoes in Japan," *Journal of Asian History* 20 (1986): 54–68, 59, 62–63.

63. Leon Trotsky, *My Life* (New York: Pathfinder Press, 1970), 341.

64. Stephen White and Stephen Revell, "Revolution and Integration in Soviet International

Diplomacy, 1917–1991," *Review of International Studies* 25, no. 4 (1999): 641–54, argue that in terms of the countries the USSR had relations with and the treaties signed, "the USSR had become a largely 'normal' participant in the international system before the end of communist rule."

65. Hannes Adomeit, *Imperial Overstretch: Germany in Soviet Policy from Stalin to Gorbachev* (Baden-Baden: Nomos Verlagsgesellschaft, 1998), 134, 156–57, and articles cited therein such as Richard Owen, "Chernenko Walling Out the West," *London Times*, June 28, 1984; Kevin Klose, "The New Soviet Isolationism: A Sorry Retreat," *International Herald Tribune*, May 26, 1984.

66. See, e.g., Richard Ned Lebow and Thomas Risse-Kappen, *International Relations Theory and the End of the Cold War* (New York: Columbia University Press, 1995); Matthew Evangelista, *Unarmed Forces: The Transnational Movement to End the Cold War* (Ithaca: Cornell University Press, 1995); Stephen G. Brooks and William C. Wohlforth, "Power, Globalization, and the End of the Cold War: Reevaluating a Landmark Case for Ideas," *International Security* 25, no. 3 (2000); Robert D. English, *Russia and the Idea of the West: Gorbachev, Intellectuals, and the End of the Cold War* (New York: Columbia University Press, 2000).

67. See, e.g., Steven Kull, *Burying Lenin: The Revolution in Soviet Ideology and Foreign Policy* (Boulder: Westview Press, 1992); Douglas Blum, "The Soviet Foreign Policy Belief System: Beliefs, Politics, and Foreign Policy Outcomes," *International Studies Quarterly* 37, no. 4 (1993); Janice Gross Stein, "Political Learning by Doing: Gorbachev as an Uncommitted Thinker and Motivated Learner," *International Organization* 48, no. 2 (1994); Jeffrey T. Checkel, *Ideas and International Political Change: Soviet/Russian Behavior and the End of the Cold War* (New Haven: Yale University Press, 1997); Robert G. Herman, "Identity, Norms, and National Security: The Soviet Foreign Policy Revolution and the End of the Cold War," in *The Culture of National Security: Norms, Identity, and World Politics*, ed. Peter Katzenstein (New York: Columbia University Press, 1996); Thomas Risse-Kappen, "Ideas Do Not Float Freely: Transnational Coalitions, Domestic Structures, and the End of the Cold War," *International Organization* 48, no. 2 (1994); Sarah E. Mendelson, *Changing Course: Ideas, Politics, and the Soviet Withdrawal from Afghanistan* (Princeton: Princeton University Press, 1998); Andrew Bennett, *Condemned to Repetition? The Rise, Fall, and Reprise of Soviet-Russian Military Interventionism, 1973–1996* (Cambridge: MIT Press, 1999); Evangelista, *Unarmed Forces*; English, *Russia and the Idea of the West*. William Wohlforth, *The Elusive Balance: Power and Perceptions during the Cold War* (Ithaca: Cornell University Press, 1993), does so more implicitly by highlighting perceptions of power. Most of these analyses focus more on individual psychology and action than on a structural approach that features the collective nature of ideas.

68. On the necessity of top-down change in the Soviet case, see Mikhail S. Gorbachev and Zdenek Mlynar, *Conversations with Gorbachev: On Perestroika, the Prague Spring, and the Crossroads of Socialism* (New York: Columbia University Press, 2002), 94.

69. This is not to suggest that there were no changes in Soviet views—indeed several alterations had taken place. Perhaps the most notable was Khrushchev's emphasis that war with capitalist countries need not be inevitable—even if it was a possibility. Soviet thinking consistently stressed the primacy of class conflict in interstate relations, the danger of war with capitalist countries, and the predatory nature of imperialism under capitalism. See, e.g., the discussion in Blacker, *Hostage to Revolution*, 14–17.

70. On the Soviet approach to international relations see, e.g., Allen Lynch, *The Soviet Study of International Relations* (Cambridge: Cambridge University Press, 1989). Also see Wohlforth, *Elusive Balance*, 53–53, 143–45, 188–92; R. Craig Nation, *Black Earth, Red Star: A History of Soviet Security Policy* (Ithaca: Cornell University Press, 1992), 36, 72; Checkel, *Ideas and International Political Change*, 56; English, *Russia and the Idea of the West*, 17–48; G. A. Arbatov, *The System: An Insider's Life in Soviet Politics* (New York: Times Books, 1992), 308; Coit D. Blacker, *Hostage to Revolution: Gorbachev and Soviet Security Policy, 1985–1991* (New York: Council on Foreign Relations Press, 1993), 14–17.

71. See especially Wohlforth, *Elusive Balance*, 188–92; Michael MccGwire, *Perestroika and Soviet National Security* (Washington, D.C.: Brookings Institution, 1991), 82–83; Margot Light, *The Soviet Theory of International Relations* (New York: St. Martin's, 1988), 276–90.

72. A. S. Chernyaev, *My Six Years with Gorbachev*, trans. Robert D. English and Elizabeth Tucker (University Park: Pennsylvania State University Press, 2000), 43.

73. Arbatov, *The System*, 307. See too Michael Ellman and Vladimir Kontorovich, "The Collapse of the Soviet System and the Memoir Literature," *Europe-Asia Studies* 49, no. 2 (1997): 265.

74. Quoted in William E. Odom, *The Collapse of the Soviet Military* (New Haven: Yale University Press, 1998), 95; Geoffrey Hosking, *The Awakening of the Soviet Union* (Cambridge: Harvard University Press, 1991), 12, writes, "In Soviet society . . . ideas, especially all-embracing systematic ideas, are worthy of respect as such and require no extrinsic justification." Kull, *Burying Lenin*, 6, argues that ideology was especially important in Russia because it lacked a Renaissance experience and the related processes of pluralization and secularization.

75. Chernyaev, *My Six Years with Gorbachev*, 98–99.

76. See, e.g., Wohlforth, *Elusive Balance*, 144, 209. These more minor shifts might be described as being within the dominant orthodoxy (in Kuhnian terms, "intraparadigm" change) rather than shifts of the dominant orthodoxy when compared with Gorbachev's revolution.

77. As quoted in English, *Russia and the Idea of the West*, 210.

78. This is the thesis in V. Kubalkova and A. A. Cruickshank, *Thinking New about Soviet "New Thinking"* (Berkeley: University of California Press, 1989), 103.

79. For more on the content of Gorbachev's new thinking see Robert Legvold, "The Revolution in Soviet Foreign Policy," *Foreign Affairs* 68, no. 1 (1989); Blum, "Soviet Foreign Policy Belief System"; Checkel, *Ideas and International Political Change*, 24–25; Kull, *Burying Lenin*, 25–37; Blacker, *Hostage to Revolution*, 63–66; MccGwire, *Perestroika and Soviet National Security*, 181–253.

80. See Celeste Wallander, "Lost and Found: Gorbachev's New Thinking," *Washington Quarterly* 25, no. 1 (2002).

81. Raymond Garthoff, *The Great Transition: American-Soviet Relations and the End of the Cold War* (Washington, D.C.: Brookings Institution, 1994), 758–61.

82. This was vividly illustrated later by the teenage pilot Mathias Rust's flight in 1987 from Hamburg, Germany, to Moscow's Red Square. Rust seems to have been a latter-day Perry in that his incursion encouraged further skepticism toward devoting so much of the economy to the military. If a small plane could not be detected and stopped, how might a more sophisticated penetration of planes or missiles be halted? There were of course many reasons why the plane was not stopped (e.g., the recent fallout from the shooting down of KAL 007). Still, the Rust affair absorbed several days of the Politburo's attention and led to an upheaval in the officer ranks. See Odom, *Collapse of the Soviet Military*, 107–10; Chernyaev, *My Six Years with Gorbachev*, 119.

83. On status as a motivation for Soviet new thinking see Deborah Larson and Alexei Shevchenko, "Shortcut to Greatness: New Thinking and the Revolution in Soviet Foreign Policy," *International Organization* 57 (2003).

84. Chernyaev, *My Six Years with Gorbachev*, 44–45. Ponomarev might also have mentioned that the Soviet Union was a co-victor of World War II. See Nina Tumarkin, *The Living and the Dead: The Rise and Fall of the Cult of World War II in Russia* (New York: Basic Books, 1994).

85. Chernyaev, *My Six Years with Gorbachev*, 32, 56. Gorbachev, in a speech to an internal Soviet audience, noted the Soviet Union's "obsession with S.D.I." Mikhail S. Gorbachev, *Memoirs* (New York: Doubleday, 1996), 56. On the conventional aspect see Phillip A. Petersen and Notra Trulock III, "A 'New' Soviet Military Doctrine: Origins and Implications," *Strategic Review* 16, no. 3 (1988), or Jeffrey W. Legro, "The Military Meaning of the New Soviet Doctrine," *Parameters* 14 (1989). Neither "Star Wars" nor Ronald Reagan was responsible for the new thinking revolution in the Soviet Union, according to Arbatov, *The System*, 321–22; English, *Russia and the Idea of the West*, 13–14; Archie Brown, *The Gorbachev Factor* (Oxford: Oxford University Press, 1997), 227–29; Evangelista, *Unarmed Forces*, 14–15, 240–45; MccGwire, *Perestroika and Soviet National Security*, 386–87; and Garthoff, *Great Transition*, 775.

86. Raymond Garthoff, *Détente and Confrontation* (Washington, D.C.: Brookings Institution, 1985), 710–13; Sidney I. Ploss, *Moscow and the Polish Crisis: An Interpretation* (Boulder: Westview, 1986); English, *Russia and the Idea of the West*, 160–63.

87. Mendelson, *Changing Course*, 109. See Kull, *Burying Lenin*, on the third world in general.

88. Wohlforth, *Elusive Balance*, e.g., chap. 8.

89. Nation, *Black Earth, Red Star*, 284.

90. Lynch, *Soviet Study of International Relations*, xxii.

91. Wohlforth, *Elusive Balance*, 227.

92. George W. Breslauer, *Gorbachev and Yeltsin as Leaders* (New York: Cambridge University Press, 2002), 75.

93. On economic problems see William Easterly and Stanley Fischer, "The Soviet Economic Decline," *World Bank Economic Review* 9, no. 3 (1995). On the "window of opportunity" analogy developed in the Soviet case, see Checkel, *Ideas and International Political Change*. For earlier opportunities for ideational change in the Soviet case see Checkel, *Ideas and International Political Change*, 43–45, and Wohlforth, *Elusive Balance*, 228–29.

94. Wohlforth, *Elusive Balance*, 225–26.

95. Bruce Parrot, *Politics and Technology in the Soviet Union* (Cambridge, Mass." MIT Press, 1983), 181–87; Easterly and Fischer, "Soviet Economic Decline," 347; Brown, *Gorbachev Factor*, 134.

96. Wohlforth, *Elusive Balance*, 220–29; McGwire, *Perestroika and Soviet National Security*, 115–73.

97. Gorbachev and Mlynar, *Conversations with Gorbachev*, 37.

98. Alexander Yanov, *The Drama of the Soviet 1960s: A Lost Reform* (Berkeley: Institute of International Studies, University of California, Berkeley, 1984), 1. Soviet visitors to the West were often ushered (usually at their request) to commercial establishments such as supermarkets, department stores, and electronics stores. The visitors not only witnessed the difference in prosperity and technology, they also filled suitcases with these goods, which were put on display, given, sold, or traded to still larger numbers of family, friends, and guests at home.

99. Gorbachev, *Memoirs*, 102–3.

100. Arbatov, *The System*, 212; Brown, *Gorbachev Factor*, 134; Brooks and Wohlforth, "Power, Globalization, and the End of the Cold War"; and Easterly and Fischer, "Soviet Economic Decline," on data.

101. Wohlforth, *Elusive Balance*, 241–43, 251.

102. Easterly and Fischer, "Soviet Economic Decline," 7.

103. Thane Gustafson, *Crisis amid Plenty: The Politics of Soviet Energy under Brezhnev and Gorbachev* (Princeton: Princeton University Press, 1989), 20, 40; Stephen Kotkin, *Armageddon Averted: The Soviet Collapse, 1970–2000* (New York: Oxford University Press, 2001), 15–17; English, *Russia and the Idea of the West*, 146; Chernyaev, *My Six Years with Gorbachev*, 91, 108–10.

104. Arbatov, *The System*, 216. Gorbachev accused Brezhnev of masking the economic problems the country faced through oil exports, and of not using hard currency profits for effective modernization. See Gustafson, *Crisis amid Plenty*, 56.

105. Andrei Kortunov, "The Soviet Disintegration: Did the West Play a Role?" in *The Fall of the Soviet Empire*, ed. Anne De Tinguy (Boulder: East European Monographs; New York: Distributed by Columbia University Press, 1997), 357.

106. Wohlforth, *Elusive Balance*, 210, 271.

107. Garthoff, *Détente and Confrontation*, 710–13; English, *Russia and the Idea of the West*, 57–59; Arbatov, *The System*, 83, 101–3, 93–94.

108. Wohlforth, *Elusive Balance*, 229.

109. Breslauer, *Gorbachev and Yeltsin*, 75.

110. Chernenko may have been elected simply as a result of the precedent of the number-two official becoming general secretary. Chernenko insisted on Gorbachev as number two, against some resistance. See E. K. Ligachev, *Inside Gorbachev's Kremlin: The Memoirs of Yegor Ligachev*, trans. Catherine A. Fitzpatrick et al. (New York: Pantheon Books, 1993), 30–31.

111. Chernyaev, *My Six Years with Gorbachev*, 22.

112. Ligachev, *Inside Gorbachev's Kremlin*, 69, 74–76, 80.

113. Gorbachev, *Memoirs*, 236, 239; Chernyaev, *My Six Years with Gorbachev*, 21, 29.

114. Gorbachev initially followed a somewhat tough line in international affairs in such areas as defense spending and Afghanistan. See Ellman and Kontorovich, "Collapse of the Soviet System," 267, 269; MccGwire, *Perestroika and Soviet National Security*, 253; Hosking, *Awakening of the Soviet Union*, 139–41; Brooks and Wohlforth, "Power, Globalization, and the End of the Cold War," 20–21.

115. On different possible alternatives, see Kull, *Burying Lenin*, vii–viii, 25–86; Garthoff, *Great Transition*, 773–74; Evangelista, *Unarmed Forces*, 258; English, *Russia and the Idea of the West*, 3, 19, 194; Kotkin, *Armageddon Averted*, 2; Larson and Shevchenko, "Shortcut to Greatness," 82–84; Breslauer, *Gorbachev and Yeltsin*, 45.

116. Breslauer, *Gorbachev and Yeltsin*, 31–32, 46.

117. *Ibid.*, 43.

118. English, *Russia and the Idea of the West*, 2, 9–12, 49–192, 198–99; Evangelista, *Unarmed Forces*, 116; Arbatov, *The System*, 87; Robert G. Kaiser, *Why Gorbachev Happened: His Triumphs and His Failure* (New York: Simon and Schuster, 1991), 87; Daniel C. Thomas, *The Helsinki Effect: International Norms, Human Rights, and the Demise of Communism* (Princeton: Princeton University Press, 2001), 223–24, 282.

119. See English, *Russia and the Idea of the West*, 2081–116, and memoirs.

120. John B. Dunlop, *The Rise of Russia and the Fall of the Soviet Empire* (Princeton: Princeton University Press, 1993), 68.

121. Checkel, *Ideas and International Political Change*, 69.

122. English, *Russia and the Idea of the West*, 186–90.

123. A key example is the Nina Andreyeva letter in March 1988 that criticized new thinking and promoted a return to the old views. Ligachev himself voiced old thinking truisms about foreign policy in the pages of *Pravda* in August 1988. See Chernyaev, *My Six Years with Gorbachev*, 153, 171. On resistance to new thinking and vacillations between old and new rhetoric in the 1988–1990 period, see Kull, *Burying Lenin*, 50–56.

124. Brooks and Wohlforth, "Power, Globalization, and the End of the Cold War," 15, 20–21; Ellman and Kontorovich, "Collapse of the Soviet System," 273.

125. Breslauer, *Gorbachev and Yeltsin*, 77.

126. This is largely the story told in depth by Evangelista, *Unarmed Forces*. See too English, *Russia and the Idea of the West*, 104–6, 150–54, 168–69; Risse-Kappen, "Ideas Do Not Float Freely"; Yale Richmond, *Cultural Exchange and the Cold War: Raising the Iron Curtain* (University Park: Pennsylvania State University Press, 2003). Indeed, Thatcher's favorable imprimatur may have helped Gorbachev become general secretary. Garthoff, *Great Transition*, 192–93. U.S. government actions also affected internal Soviet idea dynamics. See Evangelista, *Unarmed Forces*, 116–21; Chernyaev, *My Six Years with Gorbachev*, 202.

127. Yanov, *Drama of the Soviet 1960s*, 81–82, 104–6, argues that had the West supported Khrushchev, he and his reform efforts might have made more progress in the early 1960s.

128. See Breslauer, *Gorbachev and Yeltsin*, 48–50, 69–70.

129. See, for example, Ellman and Kontorovich, "Collapse of the Soviet System," 263; Stein, "Political Learning by Doing"; Garthoff, *Great Transition*, 77–71, 769, 778; Breslauer, *Gorbachev and Yeltsin*, 236–37, attributes the content of new thinking to Gorbachev the man.

130. Ellman and Kontorovich, "Collapse of the Soviet System," 270.

131. Ligachev, *Inside Gorbachev's Kremlin*, 131. See Kubalkova and Cruickshank, *Thinking New*, 28, on pre-Gorbachev new thinking ideas.

132. Stein, "Political Learning by Doing."

133. Ligachev, *Inside Gorbachev's Kremlin*, 74–75; see too 69, 76, 80.

134. There were some negative reactions in the opposite direction in response to the inability of Gorbachev's forces to meet the expectations his mutual security program generated. Even when Gorbachev's external popularity remained high, internally he suffered, as did his new ideas, because of the lack of results. At this point Western support of Gorbachev may have hurt, not helped, his position. For example, when Gorbachev received the Nobel Peace Prize against a backdrop of deteriorating domestic conditions, he was ridiculed at home for the prize. See Garthoff, *Great Transition*, 782; Evangelista, *Unarmed Forces*, 239; Brooks and Wohlforth, "Power, Globalization, and the End of the Cold War," 20–21; Kaiser, *Why Gorbachev Happened*, 419; Chernyaev, *My Six Years with Gorbachev*, 301.

135. See Brooks and Wohlforth, "Power, Globalization, and the End of the Cold War"; Kenneth A. Oye, "Explaining the End of the Cold War: Morphological and Behavioral Adaptations to the Nuclear Peace?" in *International Relations Theory and the End of the Cold War*, ed. Richard Ned Lebow and Thomas Risse-Kappen (New York: Columbia University Press, 1995).

136. Brooks and Wohlforth, "Power, Globalization, and the End of the Cold War;" and "From Old Thinking to New Thinking in Qualitative Research," *International Security* 26, no. 4 (2002).

137. Hence, it is misguided to analytically try to assess which mattered most probabilistically. On this issue see English, "Power, Ideas, and New Evidence on the Cold War's End: A Reply to Brooks and Wohlforth," *International Security* 26, no. 4 (2002): 70–92; and Brooks and Wohlforth, "Power, Globalization, and the End of the Cold War."

138. Why the Brezhnev regime was so energetic in hyping expectations is a question that deserves further study—and may relate to Brezhnev's personal influence.

139. Jack Snyder, *Myths of Empire* (Ithaca: Cornell University Press, 1991). Jack Snyder, "Myths, Modernization, and the Post-Gorbachev World," in *International Relations Theory and the End of the Cold War*, ed. Richard Ned Lebow and Thomas Risse-Kappen (New York: Columbia University Press, 1995), posits that change in this case was due to the demands of intensive development, the emergence of a constituency for new thinking, and a legitimizing concept. Daniel Deudney and G. John Ikenberry, "The International Sources of Soviet Change," *International Security* 16 (1991–92), cite the constraining influence of nuclear weapons and the pacific promises of liberal democracies to account for why the Soviet Union did not turn to aggression to address its problems.

140. Risse-Kappen, "Ideas Do Not Float Freely"; Evangelista, *Unarmed Forces*, 8.

141. For example, English, "Power, Ideas, and New Evidence on the Cold War's End," and Brooks and Wohlforth, "From Old Thinking to New Thinking," debate exactly who, and how many, individuals opposed new thinking, but neither offers a logic linking individual views to outcomes. For example, even if a majority of elites favored an alternative different than new thinking, it is not clear how such a preference would translate into outcomes in a democracy, let alone an autocracy.

Chapter 6. The Next Century

1. Arthur Stinchcomb, *Constructing Social Theories* (New York: Harcourt, Brace, 1968), 108–29; Stephen D. Krasner, "Are Bureaucracies Important?" *Foreign Policy* 7, no. 4 (1972): 164; Ruth Berins Collier and David Collier, *Shaping the Political Arena: Critical Junctures, the Labor Movement, and Regime Dynamics in Latin America* (Princeton: Princeton University Press, 1991), 35–36.

2. This reaction may reflect the fact that neither Germans nor foreigners believed that "peace" was an enduring feature of German thinking in the 1930s.

3. Ivo Daalder and James Lindsay, *America Unbound: The Bush Revolution in Foreign Policy* (Washington, D.C.: Brookings Institution Press, 2003), quote at 40; Philip Zelikow, "The Transformation of National Security," *National Interest* (spring 2003), 17–28; Fischer quote from *Der Spiegel*, March 24, 2003, http://www.spiegel.de/spiegel/english/0,1518,242042,00.html. Those who see more continuity amid the change include John Lewis Gaddis, *Surprise, Security, and the American Experience* (Cambridge: Harvard University Press, 2004), and Melvyn P. Leffler, "Think Again: Bush's Foreign Policy," *Foreign Policy* 144 (September–October 2004).

4. Both of these assumptions of course can be debated. My own review of public opinion, presidential rhetoric (in State of the Union addresses), and multilateral behavior as measured by trends in institutional involvement suggests relatively little change in U.S. thinking (which has always included a certain unilateral streak) at least through 2001. This continuity is especially striking given the large surge in relative U.S. power in the 1990s. See the basic data found in Steven Kull and I. M. Destler, *Misreading the Public: The Myth of a New Isolationism* (Washington, D.C.: Brookings Institution Press, 1999); Vox Populi, http:www.vox-populi.org/digest/america_role1.html (accessed 1/17/04); Pew Research Center, http://people-press.org/other polls/; World Views, http://www.worldviews.org. State of the Union addresses can be accessed online at http://www.presidency.ucsb.edu/site/docs/sou.php. Data on U.S. multilateral behavior is available in John G. Ikenberry, "Is American Multilateralism in Decline?" *Perspectives on Politics* 1, no. 3 (2003); see too David Caron, "Between Empire and Commu-

nity—The United States and Multilateralism, 2001–2003: A Mid-Term Assessment," *Berkeley Journal of International Law* 21 (2003).

5. See, for example, John G. Ikenberry, *After Victory* (Princeton: Princeton University Press, 2001).

6. John J. Mearsheimer, "Back to the Future: Instability in Europe after the Cold War," *International Security* 15, no. 4 (1990); Kenneth N. Waltz, "The Emerging Structure of International Politics," *International Security* 18, no. 2 (1993).

7. The evidence of the more recent period, mostly since 9/11, is more mixed, raising the possibility that the predictions were not wrong, but that it took longer for systemic pressures and incentives to work themselves out. Yet, as with the interwar period, we still would want to explain the important lag in state reactions to power conditions.

8. In order to solidify this image, a group called the Cold War Veterans Association has formed and is attempting to establish a "Cold War Victory Day" (some ten states have signed up) as well as a "National Cold War Memorial." See Cold War Veterans, http://www.cold warveterans.com.

9. The minority view is that the "victory" can be attributed to the hard-line approach of one administration—that of Ronald Reagan. Yet Reagan worked largely within the long-term orthodoxy. See Ikenberry, *After Victory*, 220–21, and chapter 5 above.

10. See, e.g., Michael E. Brown, et al., eds., *America's Strategic Choices* (Cambridge, Mass.: MIT Press, 1997), on the debates. In terms of lack of traction, see the fate of the draft of the Defense Planning Guidance for the Fiscal Years 1994–1999 in 1992, which did suggest changes. See David Armstrong, "Dick Cheney's Song of America—Drafting a Plan for Global Dominance," *Harper's* (October 2002).

11. According to Paul Wolfowitz, deputy secretary of defense, "If you had to pick the ten most important foreign policy things for the United States over the last 100 years [September 11] would surely rank in the top ten if not number one." Deputy Secretary Wolfowitz interview with Sam Tannenhaus of *Vanity Fair*, May 9, 2003. Transcript available at http://www .defenselink.mil/transcripts/2003/tr20030509-depsecdef0223.html (5/5/04).

12. E.g., Emily Rosenberg, "September 11, through the Prism of Pearl Harbor," *Chronicle of Higher Education*, December 5, 2003, B14–15.

13. John Lewis Gaddis, "A Grand Strategy of Transformation," *Foreign Policy* (November–December 2002): 50.

14. See "Remarks by the President at 2002 Graduation Exercise of the United States Military Academy West Point, New York, June 1, 2002," http://www.whitehouse.gov/news/releases/2002/06/20020601-3.html; *National Security Strategy of the United States of America 2002*, http://www.whitehouse.gov/nsc/nss.html, introduction and p. 1.

15. Some believe the turn toward unilateralism and a reliance on U.S. military power began during the Clinton administration. See, e.g., Stewart Patrick, "America's Retreat from Multilateral Engagement," *Current History* 99 (December 2000); Gwen Prins, ed., *Understanding Unilateralism in American Foreign Relations* (London: Royal Institute of International Affairs, 2000). Ikenberry, "Is American Multilateralism in Decline?" and Caron, "Between Empire and Community," make part of the case for continuity to 2001.

16. See *National Security Strategy of the United States of America 2002*. Richard Haass referred to the orientation as "a la carte multilateralism." See Thom Shanker, "White House Says the U.S. Is Not a Loner, Just Choosy," *New York Times*, July 31 2001, A1.

17. See Gaddis, "A Grand Strategy of Transformation"; Melvyn Leffler, "9/11 and the Past and Future of American Foreign Policy," *International Affairs* 79, no. 5 (2003); Robert Jervis, "Understanding the Bush Doctrine," *Political Science Quarterly* 118, no. 3 (2003).

18. Andrew Hurrell, "There Are No Rules (George W. Bush): International Order after September 11," *International Relations* 16, no. 2 (2002); Edward Rhodes, "The Imperial Logic of Bush's Liberal Agenda," *Survival* 45, no. 1 (2003). The United Kingdom has of course pursued a policy more supportive of the United States.

19. See Robert Kagan, "A Tougher War for the U.S. Is One of Legitimacy," *New York Times*, January 24, 2004.

20. While some of the same thinking that motivates Bush has precedents in the thinking of some in, and certain actions of, the Clinton administration, the combination of the elements and their forceful statement as national policy was never considered viable before 9/11.

21. As cited in Daalder and Lindsay, *America Unbound*, 79.

22. Daalder and Lindsay, *America Unbound*, 130.

23. Armstrong, "Dick Cheney's Song of America"; Jervis, "Understanding the Bush Doctrine," 368; Leffler, "9/11," 1053–54.

24. See *National Security Strategy of the United States of America 2002*, introduction.

25. *National Security Strategy of the United States of America 2002*, 15; Daalder and Lindsay, *America Unbound*, 40–47.

26. See John J. Mearsheimer and Stephen Walt, "An Unnecessary War," *Foreign Policy* (January–February 2003); Todd S. Purdum and Patrick E. Tyler, "Top Republicans Break with Bush on Iraq Strategy," *New York Times*, August 16, 2002.

27. E.g., Theodore Roosevelt's views did not endure, Wilson's were thwarted (at the time) as well, whereas Franklin Roosevelt tried, with little success, to point the United States toward change before the no-engagement orthodoxy had been undermined.

28. This is the thrust of *National Security Strategy of the United States of America 2002* in terms of the growing attraction of U.S. values ("true for every person in every society") and the benevolence of the United States ("we do not use our strength for unilateral advantage"). Hence others will welcome U.S. leadership. See too "Remarks by the President at 2002 Graduation Exercise."

29. Some believed that even if other countries were opposed, they would not be able to impose costs anyway. Daalder and Lindsay, *America Unbound*, 73.

30. To date, however, the results are mixed in both of the two main areas. Some gains have been made in security (Afghanistan, Libya) while significant uncertainties remain (Iraq, broader Islamic radicalism). In terms of great power relations, perceived U.S. hubris has had negative effects on Atlantic relations. Sino-American ties, on the other hand, have improved, as have U.S. relations with Great Britain—at least at the government-to-government level.

31. "Moderate" republicans—many from the Bush 41 administration—are among the strongest critics of American supremacy; these include such people as Brent Scowcroft and Lawrence Eagleberger. See, e.g., Purdum and Tyler, "Top Republicans Break with Bush on Iraq Strategy."

32. The split between conservative internationalists, such as Theodore Roosevelt and Henry Cabot Lodge, and liberals, such as Wilson, contributed to the collapse of American participation in the League of Nations. In the current context analysts identify a similar divide between unilateral and multilateral proponents, one that points to the fraying of the Atlantic Pact coalition. See David Fromkin, "Rival Internationalisms: Lodge, Wilson, and the Two Roosevelts," *World Policy Journal* 13, no. 2 (1996).

33. American opinion on foreign policy appears sensitive to world opinion. See "U.S. Public Beliefs on Iraq and the Presidential Election, The PIPA/Knowledge Networks Poll," April 22, 2004, http://www.pipa.org/OnlineReports/Iraq/IraqReport4_22_04.pdf.

34. See, for example, issues of *The American Conservative* in 2003 and 2004.

35. One could also imagine some elements of the Bush revolution being layered on to basic Atlantic Pact ideas.

36. See Ann Kent, "China's International Socialization: The Role of International Organizations," *Global Governance* 8, no. 3 (2002); Alastair Iain Johnston, "Is China a Status Quo Power?" *International Security* 27, no. 4 (2003); Qin Yaqing, "National Identity, Strategic Culture, and Security Interest: Three Hypotheses on the Interaction between China and International Society," *SIIS Journal* 1 (2003), http://www.siis.org.cn/english/journal/en20031-2/qinyaqing.htm.; Alastair Iain Johnston, "Beijing's Security Behavior in the Asia-Pacific: Is China a Dissatisfied Power?" in *Rethinking Security in East Asia: Identity, Power, and Efficiency*, ed. Allen Carlson, Peter Katzenstein, and J. J. Suh (Stanford: Stanford University Press, 2004).

37. Hongying Wang, "Multilateralism in Chinese Foreign Policy," in *China's International Relations in the 21st Century: Dynamics of Paradigm Shifts*, ed. Weixing Hu, Gerald Chan, and

Daojiong Zha (Lanham, Md.: University Press of America, 2000), argues integration is relatively shallow.

38. Such themes are common in speeches from the 1970s. See for example, the general secretary's speeches at the tenth (1973) and eleventh (1978) party congresses.

39. The five principles, which have been included in the Chinese constitution, are (1) mutual respect for sovereignty and territorial integrity; (2) nonaggression; (3) noninterference; (4) equality and mutual benefit; (5) peaceful coexistence.

40. Jiang Zemin's "Report to the 16th National Congress of the Chinese Communist Party," November 8, 2002. China's "reassurance diplomacy" in Southeast Asia suggests a mode of cooperative leadership not easily equated with domination or balancing behavior, but it is nonetheless compatible with extant norms. See Evan S. Medeiros and M. Taylor Fravel, "China's New Diplomacy," *Foreign Affairs* 82, no. 6 (2003).

41. Jiang Zemin's "Report to the 14th National Congress of the Chinese Communist Party," October 12, 1992, as reprinted in *Beijing Review* (October 26–November 1, 1992), 28: "Hegemonism and power politics—that is, the monopoly and manipulation of international affairs by a few countries—will not be tolerated."

42. Michael Pillsbury, *China Debates the Future Security Environment* (Washington, D.C.: National Defense University Press, 2000); Qin Yaqing, "A Response to Yong Deng: Power Perception and the Cultural Lens," *Asian Affairs: An American Review* 28, no. 3 (2001), 158.

43. Samuel Barkin, "The Evolution of the Constitution of Sovereignty and the Emergence of Human Rights Norms,"*Millennium* 27, no. 2 (1998); Rodger A. Payne and Nayef H. Samhat, *Democratizing Global Politics: Discourse Norms, International Regimes, and Political Community* (Albany: State University of New York Press, 2004).

44. Suisheng Zhao, "Introduction: China's Democratization Reconsidered," in *China and Democracy: Reconsidering the Prospects for a Democratic China*, ed. Suisheng Zhao (New York: Routledge, 2000), 11–12; Ian Johnson, "The Death and Life of China's Civil Society," *Perspectives on Politics* 1, no. 3 (2003).

45. As Robert Gilpin, *War and Change in World Politics* (Princeton: Princeton University Press, 1981), 187, posits: "As its relative power increases, a rising state attempts to change the rules governing the system." See too Fareed Zakaria, "Realism and Domestic Politics: A Review Essay," *International Security* 17, no. 1 (1992); Kim Woosang and James D. Morrow, "When Do Power Shifts Lead to War?" *American Journal of Political Science* 36, no. 4 (1992); A. F. K. Organski and Jacek Kugler, *The War Ledger* (Chicago: University of Chicago Press, 1980). Applied to China, see Denny Roy, "Hegemon on the Horizon? China's Threat to East Asian Security," *International Security* 19 (1994), 159–60. For different strategies of managing such a situation, see Randall Schweller, "Managing the Rise of Great Powers: History and Theory," in *Engaging China: The Management of a Rising Power*, ed. Alastair Iain Johnston and Robert Ross (New York: Routledge, 1999).

46. See Indra De Soysa, John R. Oneal, and Yong-Hee Park, "Testing Power-Transition Theory Using Alternative Measures of National Capabilities," *Journal of Conflict Resolution* 41, no. 4 (1997).

47. For other examples, see Stephan Walt, *The Origins of Alliance* (Ithaca: Cornell University Press, 1987); Jack Snyder, *Myths of Empire* (Ithaca: Cornell University Press, 1991); Arthur Stein and Richard Rosecrance, eds., *The Domestic Bases of Grand Strategy* (Ithaca: Cornell University Press, 1993); Charles A. Kupchan, *The Vulnerability of Empire* (Ithaca: Cornell University Press, 1994).

48. The use of "peaceful rise" as a concept appeared to wane after the spring of 2004, and it is unclear if Hu Jintao will reembrace it in the wake of Jiang Zemin's fall 2004 retirement from the Military Commission. See Robert L. Suettinger, "The Rise and Descent of 'Peaceful Rise'," *China Leadership Monitor* 12 (fall 2004), http://www.chinaleadershipmonitor.org/20044/rs .pdf.

49. For a brief illustration of these dynamics at work in continuity and changes in Chinese ideas since the late Qing era, see Jeffrey W. Legro, "Contingencies of Ideapolitik: The Rise of China and International Order," paper presented at the annual meeting of the American Political Science Association, Chicago, September 2004.

50. David Lampton, *Same Bed, Different Dreams: Managing U.S.-China Relations, 1989–2000* (Berkeley: University of California Press, 2001), 251–53.

51. Erica Strecker Downs and Philip C. Sanders, "Legitimacy and the Limits of National-ism: China and the Diaoyu Islands," *International Security* 23 (winter 1998–99), argue that China has valued economic development ahead of nationalist goals.

52. "Report to the 16th National Party Congress." See too Joseph Fewsmith, "The Sixteenth National Party Congress: The Succession That Didn't Happen," *China Quarterly* 173 (2002).

53. Xinbo W., "Four Contradictions Constraining China's Foreign Policy Behavior," *Journal of Contemporary China* 10, no. 27 (2001).

54. Carl Riskin and Azizur Rahman Khan, *Inequality and Poverty in China in the Age of Glob-alization*(New York: Oxford University Press, 2000); Nicholas R. Lardy, *Integrating China into the Global Economy* (Washington, D.C.: Brookings Institution, 2002); Eric Eckholm, "Leaner Facto-ries, Fewer Workers Bring More Labor Unrest to China," *New York Times*, March 19, 2002, p. 1.

55. For example, the 1999 NATO bombing of the Chinese embassy in Belgrade fueled na-tionalism and strengthened opponents of opening. Zheng Yongnian, "Nationalism, Globalism, and China's International Relations," in *China's International Relations in the 21st Century: Dy-namics of Paradigm Shifts,* ed. Weixing Hu, Gerald Chan, and Daojiong Zha (Lanham, Md.: Uni-versity Press of America, 2000); Peter Hayes Gries, *China's New Nationalism: Pride, Politics, and Diplomacy* (Berkeley: University of California Press, 2004).

56. Gerald Segal, "Does China Matter?" *Foreign Affairs* 78, no. 5 (1999); Paul Krugman, "Myth of Asia's Miracle," *Foreign Affairs* 73, no. 6 (1994). For the argument that Chinese chal-lenges to the status quo need not be based on rising power but on specific capabilities in spe-cific scenarios, see Thomas Christensen, "Posing Problems without Catching Up: China's Rise and Challenges for U.S. Security Policy," *International Security* 25 (2001).

57. Even seasoned China specialists have difficulty assessing the nature and strength of competing coalitions. E.g., Thomas Christensen, "The Party Transition: Will It Bring a New Maturity in Chinese Security Policy?" *China Leadership Monitor #5* (2003), 4–6, http://www .chinaleadershipmonitor.org/20031/tc.html.

58. "Report to the 14th National Party Congress."

59. Johnston, "China's Civil Society," discusses some of the factions. See too Yan Xuetong, "The Rise of China in Chinese Eyes," *Journal of Contemporary China* 10, no. 26 (2001): 35.

60. E.g., the appeal to in group–out group biases—see Gries, *China's New Nationalism*, 27, 140–49.

61. Yan, "The Rise of China in Chinese Eyes," 35.

62. Lanxin Xiang, "Washington's Misguided China Policy," *Survival* 43, no. 3 (2001); David Shambaugh, "China or America: Which Is the Revisionist Power?" *Survival* 43, no. 3 (2001).

63. On paradigms, see Colin Elman and Miriam Fendius Elman, eds., *Progress in Interna-tional Relations Theory: Appraising the Field* (Cambridge: MIT Press, 2003).

64. A different approach found in Andrew Moravcsik, *The Choice for Europe: Social Progress and State Power from Messina to Maastricht* (Ithaca: Cornell University Press, 1988), treats the different paradigms as possible alternatives in explaining each individual element of the broader rationalist framework.

65. Neta Crawford, *Argument and Change in World Politics: Ethics, Decolonization, and Hu-manitarian Intervention* (New York: Cambridge University Press, 2002).

66. See Judith Goldstein, *Ideas, Interests, and American Trade Policy* (Ithaca: Cornell Univer-sity Press, 1993); Mark Blyth, *Great Transformations: Economic Ideas and Institutional Change in the Twentieth Century* (New York: Cambridge University Press, 2002).

67. Cf. Timur Kuran, "Now Out of Never: The Element of Surprise in the East European Revolution 1989," *World Politics* 44, no. 1 (1991), and Susanne Lohmann, "Dynamics of Infor-mational Cascades: The Monday Demonstrations in Leipzig, East Germany, 1989–91," *World Politics* 47, no. 1 (1994), and neglect of the role of Gorbachev's signal in the events that followed.

68. Matthew Evangelista, *Unarmed Forces: The Transnational Movement to End the Cold War* (Ithaca: Cornell University Press, 1999), 341–49.

69. See, e.g., Margaret Keck and Kathryn Sikkink, *Activists beyond Borders* (Ithaca: Cornell University Press, 1998); Sidney Tarrow, *Power in Movement: Social Movements and Contentious*

Politics, 2nd ed. (Cambridge: Cambridge University Press, 1998); Crawford, *Argument and Change.*

70. See James Fearon and Alexander Wendt, "Rationalism v. Constructivism: A Skeptical View," in *Handbook of International Relations,* ed. Walter Carlsnaes, Thomas Risse, and Beth Simmons (London: Sage Publications, 2002).

71. And, unlike individual ideas, we do not have to "add them up" to see how they affect national policy.

72. Close observers of Germany in the interwar period were able to distinguish the inconsistencies in these measures under Hitler. See Michaela Hönecke, *"Know Your Enemy": American Interpretations of National Socialism, 1933–1945* (PhD diss., University of North Carolina, Chapel Hill, 1998).

73. This example comes from Thomas A. Birkland, *After Disaster: Agenda-Setting, Public Policy, and Focusing Events* (Washington, D.C.: Georgetown University Press, 1997), 43–44.

74. Keck and Sikkink, *Activists beyond Borders;* Richard Price, "Transnational Civil Society Targets Land Mines," *International Organization* 52, no. 3 (1998); Thomas Risse, Steven C. Ropp, and Kathryn Sikkink, *The Power of Human Rights: International Norms and Domestic Change* (New York: Cambridge University Press, 1999); Evangelista, *Unarmed Forces;* Daniel C. Thomas, *The Helsinki Effect: International Norms, Human Rights, and the Demise of Communism* (Princeton: Princeton University Press, 2001).

75. Francis Fukuyama, *The End of History and the Last Man* (New York: Free Press, 1992), identifies and laments such a possibility; *National Security Strategy of the United States of America 2002* celebrates it.

76. See Thomas L. Friedman, *The Lexus and the Olive Tree: Understanding Globalization* (New York: Farrar, Straus, 1999); Anthony Giddens, *Runaway World: How Globalization Is Reshaping Our Lives* (New York: Routledge, 2000).

77. See the issues of the journal *Review of International Studies* in the past decade and the "English School" website, http://www.leeds.ac.uk/polis/englishschool.

Appendix 1. The Transformation of Economic Ideas

1. See, e.g., John Odell, *U.S. International Monetary Policy: Markets, Power, and Ideas as Sources of Change* (Princeton: Princeton University Press, 1982); Peter Katzenstein, *Small States in World Markets: Industrial Policy in Europe* (Ithaca: Cornell University Press, 1985); Peter Hall, *Governing the Economy: The Politics of State Intervention in Britain and France* (New York: Oxford University Press, 1985); Peter Hall, *The Political Power of Economic Ideas* (Princeton: Princeton University Press, 1989); Emanuel Adler, *The Power of Ideology: The Quest for Technological Autonomy in Argentina and Brazil* (Berkeley: University of California Press, 1987); Paul Egon Rohrlich, "Economic Culture and Foreign Policy," *International Organization* 41, no. 1 (1987); Kathryn Sikkink, *Ideas and Institutions: Developmentalism in Brazil and Argentina* (Ithaca: Cornell University Press, 1991); Judith Goldstein, *Ideas, Interests, and American Trade Policy* (Ithaca: Cornell University Press, 1993); Frank Dobbin, "The Social Construction of the Great Depression: Industrial Policy during the 1930s in the United States, Britain, and France," *Theory and Society* 22, no. 1 (1993); Frank Dobbin, *Forging Industrial Policy: The United States, Britain, and France in the Railway Age* (Cambridge: Cambridge University Press, 1994); Kathleen R. McNamara, *The Currency of Ideas: Monetary Politics in the European Union* (Ithaca: Cornell University Press, 1998); Mark Blyth, *Great Transformations: Economic Ideas and Institutional Change in the Twentieth Century* (New York: Cambridge University Press, 2002).

2. Peter Katzenstein, *Between Power and Plenty: Foreign Economic Policies of Advanced Industrial States* (Madison: University of Wisconsin Press, 1978); G. John Ikenberry, *Reasons of State: Oil Politics and the Capacities of American Government* (Ithaca: Cornell University Press, 1988).

3. E.g., see Margaret Weir and Theda Skocpol, "State Structures and the Possibilities for Keynesian Responses to the Great Depression in Sweden, Britain, and the United States," in *Bringing the State Back In,* ed. Peter B. Evans, Dietrich Rueschemeyer, Theda Skocpol (Cam-

bridge: Cambridge University Press, 1985); Peter Gourevitch, *Politics in Hard Times* (Ithaca: Cornell University Press, 1986).

4. Blyth, *Great Transformations,* is particularly good on the problems of "exogenous shock" as an explanation for change.

5. E.g., see Harold L. Wattel, *The Policy Consequences of John Maynard Keynes* (Armonk, N.Y.: M. E. Sharpe, 1985), and Hall, *Political Power.*

6. Germany certainly retained a "strong state" to ensure a level playing field in the economy and in part as a reaction to the feeling that parochial interests had hijacked the state under Weimar. Dudley Dillard, "The Influence of Keynesian Thought on German Economic Policy," in *Policy Consequences of John Maynard Keynes,* ed. Wattel; Christopher S. Allen, " 'Ordo-Liberalism' Trumps Keynesianism," in *Monetary Union: The European Union as a Neo-Liberal Project,* ed. Bernard Moss (London: Palgrave, 2005), 200–209, http://www.arches.uga.edu/csallen/allen_ moss.pdf (1/20/05); Herbert Giersch, Karl-Heinz Paque, and Holger Schmieding, *The Fading Miracle: Four Decades of Market Economy in Germany* (New York: Cambridge University Press, 1992); Christopher Allen, "The Underdevelopment of Keynesianism in the Federal Republic of Germany," in *The Political Power of Economic Ideas: Keynesianism Across Nations,* ed. Peter A. Hall (Princeton: Princeton University Press, 1989).

7. Weir and Skocpol, "State Structures," 139. Although Keynes's thesis was most fully presented in his 1936 book, the general notions had been circulating earlier.

8. As with internationalism, the fact that the United States, the dominant global power, followed and advocated Keynesian views helped to propagate them. Hall, *Political Power,* 386–89.

9. Allen, "Underdevelopment of Keynesianism," 288; Allen, "Ordo-Liberalism," 219–20. Peter A. Johnson, *The Government of Money: Monetarism in Germany and the United States* (Ithaca: Cornell University Press, 1998), 55–57, notes considerable support for Keynes's ideas among economists, especially in the SPD faction after the war. Still, SPD resistance to ordo-liberalism, which emphasized the supply side and the social market economy, declined in the 1950s.

10. This is the puzzle identified and explored by Dobbin, "Social Construction of the Great Depression."

11. Dobbin, "Social Construction of the Great Depression," 5.

12. Ibid., 6. Weir and Skocpol, "State Structures," 131–32, find a similar result for Sweden.

13. Dobbin, "Social Construction of the Great Depression," 49.

14. Goldstein, *Ideas, Interests, and American Trade Policy,* 126, 134–35.

15. Ibid., 11.

16. The tariff may not have been seen as a break with tradition at the time as it was sold as being in line with the traditional focus on fair trade. Goldstein, *Ideas, Interests, and American Trade Policy,* 82, 94–95, 118–23, 131; Alfred Eckes, *Opening America's Market: U.S. Foreign Trade Policy since 1776* (Chapel Hill: University of North Carolina Press, 1995), 88, 112.

17. Note here the link to nationalism as in other cases.

18. Sikkink, *Ideas and Institutions,* 29–30, 41–42, 51, 242. My argument does less well in explaining the difference between the particular forms of ISI that Argentina and Brazil adopted. Developmentalism itself collapsed in the 1970s due to excessive expectations and meager results. See ibid., 67, 245.

19. Rohrlich, "Economic Culture," 80–90. These beliefs remained durable even through the later depression that Gourevitch covers. Thus the degree of embeddedness of an "economic culture" also seems to affect the nature of the shock needed to dislodge it.

20. Gourevitch, *Politics in Hard Times,* argues as follows" Crisis → Delegitimization of Old Orthodoxy → Debate and Experimentation → New Orthodoxy or Reassertion of Old.

21. Gourevitch, *Politics in Hard Times,* 62–63, 234.

22. See Peter Gourevitch, "International Trade, Domestic Coalitions, and Liberty: Comparative Responses to the Crisis of 1873–1896," *Journal of Interdisciplinary History* 8, no. 3 (1977).

23. Gourevitch, *Politics in Hard Times,* 115. The impact of the depression also differed because the countries inevitably occupied different niches in the international economy.

24. See Weir and Skocpol, "State Structures." For an application of this logic to the Swedish

and German Social Democratic parties in the first half of the twentieth century, see Sheri Berman, *The Social Democratic Moment: Ideas and Politics in the Making of Interwar Europe* (Cambridge: Harvard University Press, 1998).

25. One could refer to certain groups winning because they were more powerful, but this begs the question of how to identify interest group power independent of the outcomes observed.

26. Peter Hall, "Policy Paradigms, Social Learning, and the State," *Comparative Politics* 25, no. 3 (1993): 291.

27. A similar lack of replacement ideas is linked to continuity in Swedish economic policies in the 1920s and in the 1990s. See Blyth, *Great Transformations,* 101–4, 237–38.

28. Hall, "Policy Paradigms," 287.

29. McNamara, *Currency of Ideas,* 20–21, 63–66, 144–52. See too Blyth, *Great Transformations.*

Appendix 2

1. The 1916 and 1933 addresses either had too little to code or did not discuss foreign affairs; I assigned them a value that is an average of the year before and after.

Index

Acheson, Dean, 114
Adenauer, Konrad, 18, 86, 99, 108, 185; champions integration, 112–15; policy successes of, 120–21
Adler, Emanuel, 20
Afghanistan, 148, 171
Allied High Command, 99
aloofness, U.S. *See* foreign policy ideas, U.S., no entanglement
Al-Qaeda, 31
alternative explanations, 17–19, 43–46, 72–83, 137–41, 156–60. *See also* domestic politics; identity; leaders, impact of; political structure; psychology; strategic circumstances
alternative ideas. *See* replacement ideas
American Supremacy. *See* foreign policy ideas, U.S.
Andropov, Yuri, 151, 153, 155, 159
Angell, Norman, 92
Anschluss, 95
Arbatov, Georgi, 145
armed expansion. *See* foreign policy ideas, German
Atlantic Pact. *See* foreign policy ideas, U.S.
Aussenpolitik, 87
Austria, 95
Austro-Prussian War, 90

Bakumatsu Japan. *See* Japan
balance of power, 11, 63, 75, 163. *See also* strategic circumstances
Barbarossa, 110
Bayesian updating, 25, 27
Berlin Airlift, 115

Berman, Sheri, 7
Bethmann-Hollweg, Theobold von, 90, 92
Bhutan, 9
Bismarck, Otto von, 90, 117
Bolsheviks, 61, 185
Bowman, Isaiah, 115
Bracher, Karl Dietrich, 100
Braeman, John, 74
Breslauer, George, 148, 151, 152
Bretton Woods agreement, 94
Brezhnev, Leonid: death of and change, 151–52; foreign policy failures of, 148; hypes expectations in Soviet Union, 149, 163, 182; ignores power, 174; promotes correlation-of-forces, 145, 147
Britain. *See* Great Britain
British Royal Navy, 36
Brockdorff-Rantzau, Ulrich von, 93, 103, 106
Brooks, Stephen, 156
Bruning, Heinrich, 96
Buchanan, Patrick, 172
Bull, Hedley, 2, 89
Bülow, Bernard von, 92, 118
Burley, Ann-Marie, 82
Burma, 127
Bush, George Herbert Walker (41), 167, 169
Bush, George Walker (43): comparison with other presidents, 170, 182; 9/11 and, 169–70; potential foreign policy revolution of, 3, 166–72

Canada, 9
Carnegie Endowment for International Peace, 69

Carter, Jimmy, 147, 164
case selection, 46–47
Century Group, 69
Charter Oath, Meji, 136
Chernenko, Konstantin, 151, 155, 159
Chernyaev, Anatoli, 145
Chickering, Roger, 93
China, Peoples Republic of (PRC): founding ideas of, 173; and geopolitics, 174–75; integrationism and, 173–74; and Japan, 9, 125, 127, 128; possible change in grand strategy, 1, 23, 175–78; rise and ideas, 3, 173–74; and United States, 173–74, 178, 186. *See also* China *and* Chinese *under other entries*
Chinese Communist Party, 173, 174, 176
Chōshū, 134–36, 140–41
Clinton, William J., 169
closed country. *See* foreign policy ideas, Japanese
Cobb, Frank, 61
collapse, of old ideas, 14–16, 29–35, 163
collapse scenarios: "Do Something!" 33, 34, 50, 65, 101, 126–27, 194, 221n151; "If it ain't broke," 33, 34, 109, 134, 150, 193; "Old Faithful," 33, 131, 167; "Told you so," 33, 50, 134, 167, 193
collective ideas: as fundamental influence on international relations, 24–28; constructivism and, 19–21; content of, 8–10; continuity and change in, 10, 13–17, 14, 22, 24, 29–39, 41, 44–46, 50, 122, 125; defined, 4; dominant, 5, 8, 16, 42, 46, 47, 181–84; effect on their own transformation, 3, 13, 32, 50, 65, 79, 144, 161, 179; and expectations, 4, 40, 41; as focal point, 28, 37; and globalization, 180–81; human biology, 5; ideal types and international society, 9–10; identity and, 20–21; individual ideas and, 4–5, 19, 26–27, 42; interaction with other factors, 13–14, 28, 39–41, 46, 75, 113, 164, 165; levels, 4–7; policy implications, 21, 22, 182–87; and states, 5–6; synonyms for, 7. *See also* economic ideas, foreign policy ideas; integrationism; replacement ideas; revisionism; separatism; synthetic explanation
collective ideation problems, 14–15, 19, 28–29, 31, 82, 158, 162
collective memory, 6, 36
Committee to Defend America by Aiding the Allies, 69
Common Sense, 67
consolidation, of new ideas, 14–16, 35–38, 163, 164
consolidation scenarios: "Counterrevolution," 36, 101, 103; "Long live change,"
36–37, 65, 70, 194; "Try Harder" 36, 127, 165
constructivism, 2–3, 17, 19–21, 182–83
Coolidge, Calvin, 57
Copeland, Dale, 116
correlation of forces. *See* foreign policy ideas, Soviet
Council on Foreign Relations, 69
"Counterrevolution." *See* consolidation scenarios
Cuba, 56, 168

Dartmouth Conference, 154
Dawes Plan, 57, 107
DeGaulle, Charles, 88
Dehio, Ludwig, 100
Delbrück, Hans, 96
democratization, 3, 71, 171, 178
Deng Xiaoping, 173
Denmark, 90
Deshima Island, 125, 128, 133
disarmament, 57, 103
Dobbins, Frank, 7
domestic politics, 2, 45–46, 162, 179; and China, 176–78; and Germany, 85, 112–15, 119–21; and Japan, 130, 140–41; and the Soviet Union, 152, 157–58; and the United States, 72, 79–81
dominant ideas. *See* collective ideas
"Do Something!" *See* collapse scenarios
Durkheim, Emile, 5
Dutch scholars, 133

Ebert, Friedrich, 93, 103, 105
economic development, 176, 190, 193
economic ideas, 189–92, 195, 197
economic nationalism and internationalism, 80, 172
Eisenhower, Dwight D., 59, 74
Ellingson, Stephen, 7
English, Robert, 153
English School, 186
Erzberger, Matthias, 113
Eschenburg, Theodor, 100
Espionage Act (1917), 63
European Monetary System, 196
European Steel and Coal Community, 115
events. *See* expectations and consequences; external shocks
expectations and consequences: in China, 175–76; in Germany, 86, 87, 101–3, 109–12, 120; and idea change, 15, 29–35, 40, 41, 46, 163, 184; in Japan, 131–37; in national economic policies, 191, 193, 196; in the Soviet Union, 144, 147–49, 154, 156–59; in the United States, 61–64, 66–68

export-led growth (ELG), 194

external shocks: change and, 11–15, 23, 28, 34, 46; economic crises as, 189–90, 193, 195; end of cold war as, 169; 9/11 as, 166, 168–69; Pearl Harbor attack as, 67–68; Perry's visit as, 122, 130; *Stunde Null* as, 85–86, 100–111; world wars as, 12, 23, 46

Fillmore, Millard, 132

Fisher, Fritz, 100

focal point, ideas as, 27, 38, 154

Foran, John, 37

Foreign Policy Association, 69

foreign policy ideas, 1, 4, 10, 13, 82; American Supremacy, 166–72; Atlantic Pact, 166–72, 186; Chinese, 173–75; German, 84–85, 90–93, 96, 99, 101, 112, 120; German, armed expansion, 84–85, 92, 94, 98, 101, 106–9, 112, 116, 120, 185–86; German, neutrality, 85, 108, 112, 117; Japan, closed country, 127, 131–41, 159; Japan, open country, 127, 133, 136, 159, 185; Japanese, 122–27, 136, 137; Soviet, correlation of forces (old thinking), 143, 144–50, 153–55, 159, 164, 182; Soviet, mutual security (new thinking), 1, 16, 19, 47, 122, 124, 142–46, 152–57, 165, 185–86; U.S., 49–50, 60, 63– 65, 71, 83, 166; U.S. no-entanglement, 7, 12, 49–51, 66, 162, 172, 199 *See also* economic ideas; integrationism; internationalism; isolationism; revisionism; *entries for individual nations*

France, 9, 37, 76, 88, 92, 106, 109, 116, 168; in Far East, 130–31, 133; insecurity after World War I, 87, 104, 107, 121; after World War II, 99

Franco-Prussian War, 90

Frieden, Jeffry, 45, 80

Gaddis, John Lewis, 168

Gallipoli, 78

generations and change, 81–82

geopolitical thinking, 44; China and, 174; Germany and, 84–85, 115–17; United States and, 69–70, 75, 77

German Democratic Republic (GDR or East Germany), 114

"German miracle," 191

German Peace Society, 103

Germany: change to integration, 12–13, 99, 108–15; continuity of armed expansion, 46, 84–87, 93–94, 101–8, 186; economic ideas of, 191, 195–96, founding ideas, 88, 90–91; historians in, 90, 92, 96, 100; ideas passed over, 84–85, 116–17; and League of Nations, 95; opposition to Hitler, 97–98, 108–9; peace movement in, 92–93, 98; and Versailles, 18, 102–6, 120. *See also* Germany *and* German *under other entries*

Gilbert, Margaret, 5

globalization, 180–81, 185–87

Goebbels, Joseph, 111

Goldstein, Judith, 8

Gorbachev, Mikhail, 1, 16, 18, 19, 47, 163, 165, 185; foreign policy revolution of, 142–44, 157–58, 160; impact as leader, 155–56; new thinking and, 122, 124, 145–46, 149, 152–54; and the Soviet system, 181–82

Gourevitch, Peter, 45

grand strategy, 7–8; contemporary U.S. debates and, 166–67; as explanation, 17–18. *See also* foreign policy ideas

Great Britain, 3, 116, 121; influence on United States, 39, 70, 164–65; interwar period policies, 70, 73, 76, 87, 92, 98; involvement in Japan, Far East, 125, 130–32, 135; after World War II, 99

Great Depression, 2, 17, 18, 37, 58, 71; and economic ideas, 190–94; effect on Germany, 96, 97, 106–7, 113; effect on United States, 49–51, 80–81, 82

Grenada, 168

Grishin, Viktor, 152, 155

Haggard, Stephan, 38

Harding, Warren G., 57

Harris, Townsend, 132

Hayashi, Ōen, 139–40

Herwig, Holger, 88

Herzfeld, Hans, 100

Hindenburg, Paul von, 104

Hitler, Adolf, 18, 94, 104, 108, 164, 183; failures of and change, 110–12; favors revisionism, 86, 89, 96–98, 106, 117, 119; impact on United States, 70–71; racist ideology of, 87, 97; successes of, 109–10, 121

Hofer, Walter, 100

Holland, 125, 128, 129, 133, 139

Hu Jintao, 175

ideapolitik, 22, 182–86

ideas. *See* collective ideas

identity: as a collective idea, 7; constructivism and, 2, 20–21; continuity and change in, 19–21; and Germany, 88–89, 99, 100; and Japan, 124, 141–42, 159; and national ideas, 20–21, 26; organizational culture and, 6; and the Soviet Union, 124, 159; and the United States, 49, 72, 81–83

"If it ain't broke." *See* collapse scenarios

imperialism, 56, 62, 71

import substitution industrialization (ISI), 194

Independent Social Democratic Party of Germany, 93
individuals, role of. *See* leaders
industrial culture, 192
industrial strategy, 190–91
Institute for Western Learning, 139
institutions. *See* organizational culture; political structure
integrationism, 1, 9, 161; China and, 9, 173–77; Germany and, 86–88, 95–96, 99, 101–2, 108, 120–21, 165; as ideal type, 9–10, 169; Japan and, 13, 125, 126, 132, 142, 158, 159; Soviet Union and, 122, 124, 146, 153, 155, 156, 158, 159, 165; United States and, 49, 52, 57, 59, 70, 83, 166, 167, 169. *See also* internationalism, foreign policy ideas, *individual country entries*
interest groups. *See* domestic politics
international circumstances. *See* strategic circumstances
international engagement. *See* internationalism
internationalism: definition and measurement of, 52, 199; in current U.S. policy, 171–72; as interwar replacement idea, 50, 56, 58, 61, 63, 80, 185; switch to in World War II, 55, 58, 66–71, 74, 79, 80, 162, 170, 186
international order. *See* international society
International Physicians for the Prevention of Nuclear War, 154
international society, 2, 8, 9, 12, 21, 40, 51, 122, 185–86; China and, 173–74, 178; Germany and, 84–85, 87, 89, 93, 120, 181; Japan and, 126, 128, 131, 132, 142, 158; Soviet Union and, 142–43, 146, 152–53, 155, 157–58; United States and, 49, 53, 56, 59, 83, 166, 168, 170, 178
international system, 1, 3, 42, 89, 181
Iraq, 170, 171, 182
isolationism: as distinct from non-engagement, 51; in Japan, 46, 128–29; and U.S. policy in the interwar period, 1, 56, 58, 80; in the United States during and after WWII, 59, 61, 68, 70. *See also* foreign policy ideas; separatism
Italy, 66, 68, 153

Japan: *bakufu* of, 127, 128, 130, 133–35, 140; change to integration, 125–26, 130–31, 135–37; comparison with Soviet Union, 122–25, 158–60; continuity of separatism, 126, 130–36; discarded ideas of, 130, 138–40; limited contact with West, 122–24, 128–30, 158–59; social turmoil in, 125,

133–34, 137; and United States, 40, 122, 124, 133, 142. *See also* Japan *and* Japanese *under other entries*
Jefferson, Thomas, 55
Jervis, Robert, 5, 19, 38
Jiang Zemin, 176, 177
Johnston, Alastair Iain, 8
"Joi!" ("Expel the Barbarians!"), 134–37, 140–41
Junkers, 119
justification. *See* leaders, rhetoric and

kaikoku. *See* foreign policy ideas, Japan, open country
Katenstein, Peter, 108
Kaufman, Robert, 38
Kehr, Eckart, 96
Keil Revolt, 101
Kennan, George, 73
Kennedy, Paul, 88, 116
Kershaw, Ian, 110
Keynes, John Maynard, 104
Khrushchev, Nikita, 142, 143, 148, 149, 153, 154
Kissinger, Henry, 73
Korea, 127, 128, 129
Kosygin, Alexsey, 149
Kruger, Peter, 107
Kuhn, Thomas, 31–32
Kupchan, Charles, 8

Langemarck myth, 105, 111
leaders, impact of, 4, 7–8, 16, 18–19, 45–46, 185; Chinese, 175–76; German, 94–96, 120; Japanese, 124, 140; Soviet, 154–56, 160 rhetoric and, 16, 31, 39, 182; U.S., 70–71, 81, 182. *See also specific individual leaders*
League of Nations, 2, 51, 57, 70, 76, 170; and German foreign policy, 93, 95, 103; and lack of U.S. commitment, 61–65, 75
League of Nations Association, 69
League to Enforce Peace, 62
Lebensraum, 91, 97, 110
Leffler, Melvyn, 74
legitimacy, 89, 177
Lend-Lease Aid, 67
Lenin, V. I., 142, 146
Lenz, Max, 96
liberalism, 2, 17–19. *See also* domestic politics
Ligachev, Yegor, 152, 155
Lindbergh, Charles, 67
Linz, Juan, 37
Lippmann, Walter, 27, 67, 76
Lithuania, 88
Locarno Pact, 94–95, 106
Lodge, Henry Cabot, 62, 63, 78

London Economic Conference, 80
"Long live change." *See* consolidation scenarios
Lowell, Abbot Lawrence, 62
Ludendorff, Erich, 104
Lynch, Allen, 148

Machtstaat, 90, 99
macroeconomic policy, 190
Mareks, Ernst, 96
Marshall Plan, 114
Marx, Karl, 6
Marxism-Leninism, 145, 151, 186
May, Ernest, 7–8
McCloy, John, 114
Mearsheimer, John, 72, 77, 167
Meiji Restoration. *See* Japan
Meinecke, Friedrich, 92, 100
methodology, 22–23, 41–48
Mexico, 40, 78
militarism, 56–57, 87, 90, 93, 96, 120
Mitteleuropa, 91–92, 164
monetarism, 195–96
Monroe, James, 55
Monroe Doctrine, 76
Moore, Barrington, 29
Morgenthau, Hans, 73
Morgenthau Plan, 114
Moscow Institute of World Economy and International Relations (IMEMO), 153
multilateralism, 3, 33, 63, 168, 171
Munich Crisis, Agreement, 6, 109, 110
mutual security. *See* foreign policy ideas, Soviet

Nagasaki, 125, 128
Napoleon Bonaparte, 37, 89
national ideas. *See* collective ideas; economic ideas; foreign policy ideas
national identity. *See* identity
nationalism, 88, 90, 108
Nation, Craig, 148
National War Labor Board, 62
Naumann, Friedrich, 92
Neutrality Acts, 50, 66, 73, 80
New Republic, 67
new thinking. *See* foreign policy ideas, Soviet
9/11 attacks, 16, 168–69, 173, 178, 180
9/11 Commission, 30
no entanglement. *See* foreign policy ideas, U.S.
norms: adherence to, 32; agency and, 31; American Supremacy and, 168; China and, 173, 174, 178; constructivism and, 20; imperialism and, 10; international society and, 2, 9, 13, 51; Japan and; 137, 185; leaders rhetoric and, 52; Russia and, 143; sovereignty and, 168, 178
Norris, George W., 61
North, Douglass, 26
North Atlantic Treaty Organization (NATO), 77, 100, 167
North Korea, 9
North Vietnam, 140
Nicaragua, 168

Oda Nobunaga, 128
off–shore balancing, 172
Okubo Toshimichi, 135
"Old Faithful." *See* collapse scenarios
old thinking. *See* foreign policy ideas, Soviet
OPEC, 150
open country. *See* foreign policy ideas, Japanese
Opium Wars, 132–33
organizational culture, states and, 5, 7

Panama, 168
Papen, Franz von, 96
Pearl Harbor, 66, 67, 69, 140, 169, 174
Perry, Matthew, 16, 122, 125, 130–34, 136, 142, 159
Pershing missile, 147
Philippines, 56
Poland, 95, 109, 148
policy implications, 182–87
Ponomarev, Boris, 147
political structure, 157–58, 181–82
Portugal, 125
Posen, Barry, 7
power. *See* strategic circumstances
preventive use of force, 3, 168
Progressives, 62–64, 71
protectionism, 192–94
psychology, as an explanation, 2, 18–19, 26, 29–30
public opinion, 5, 66–67
Pugwash movement, 154

Quidde, Ludwig, 103

Rathenau, Walter113
reach of technology. *See* strategic circumstances
Reagan, Ronald, 147, 153, 164
realism, 2, 17–18, 21, 44, 45, 67, 180. *See also* strategic circumstances
Reciprocal Trade Agreements, 80
Red Army, 110, 111
regional interests. *See* domestic politics
Reichstag, 102

Reichswehr, 95, 97
Reizler, Kurt, 92
replacement ideas, 1, 16, 36, 40–44, 162–63,
    182, 185; in China, 3, 173, 177; in Germany,
    93, 112–13; in Japan, 123, 127, 133–34, 141;
    in national economic policy, 191, 193, 196;
    in the Soviet Union, 123, 152, 154, 158–59;
    in the United States, 60, 61, 63–65, 68–70,
    81, 169–72
revisionism, 9, 186; and China, 3, 173–74; as
    ideal type, 9–10, 169; and Napoleonic
    France, 9; and Germany, 1, 9, 89, 95, 109;
    and the Soviet Union, 142–43; and the
    United States, 9, 169, 178
rhetoric. *See* leaders
Ritter, Gerhard, 100
Rogowski, Ronald, 45
Roman Empire, 166
Romanov, Grigory, 152
Roosevelt, Franklin Delano (FDR), 18, 27, 51,
    61, 78, 81, 90, 185; and current U.S. policy,
    169–70; isolationist posture of, 58–60, 75;
    response to threats, 68, 70–71; and shift to
    internationalism, 66, 76
Roosevelt, Theodore, 56, 63, 73, 170
Root, Elihu, 62
Roskin, Michael, 81
Rothfels, Hans, 100
Ruggie, John, 82
Ruhr, French occupation of, 106
Ruhr industrialists, 100, 112, 114
Rumsfeld, Donald, 25
Russia, 142, 156, 168, 185; and Japan, 125,
    130–31; and World War I, 101, 102, 116. *See
    also* Soviet Union
Russo-Japanese War, 137
Ryukyu Islands, 128, 129
Ryzhkov, Nikolai, 152

Sagan, Scott, 34
Saigo Takamori, 136
sakoku. *See* foreign policy ideas, Japanese,
    closed country
Salewski, Michael, 118
Satsuma, 134–36, 140–41
Schafer, Dietrich, 96
Scheidemann, Phillip, 93
Schelling, Thomas, 27
Schleicher, Kurt von, 96
Schleswig-Holstein, 90
Schumacher, Kurt, 100, 108, 112–13, 117
Schuman Plan, 114
Scott, James, 29
Searle, John, 5
seclusion, of Japan. *See* foreign policy ideas,
    Japanese, closed country

sectoral conflict. *See* domestic politics
Sedition Act, 63
Seeckt, Hans von, 95
Sekigahara, Battle of, 128
separatism, 9; as ideal type, 9–10, 169; and
    Tokugawa Japan, 9, 16; and the United
    States, 9, 57, 59, 63, 66, 158. *See also* foreign
    policy ideas
Shaknazarov, Georgi, 145
shock. *See* external shock
Siam, 127
Sino-Japanese War, 137
Sino-Soviet split, 148
Skocpol, Theda, 7
Smith, Charles, 65
Smith, Woodruff, 91
Snyder, Jack, 45, 157
Social Darwinism, 91
Social Democratic Party (SDP), 108; and in-
    terwar German politics, 85–86, 96, 102–5,
    120; post–World War II German politics,
    100, 112–15
social facts, 5
socialist internationalism, 93, 145
"Sonno!" (Revere the Emperor), 133–37, 140
Sovetskaya Rossiya, 153
Soviet Communist Party, 145, 155
Soviet Union: change to new thinking in, 1,
    13, 16, 18, 23, 47, 122–25, 147–51, 163; and
    China, 151; continuity in 1960s, 144,
    148–49, 151, 154; discarded ideas of,
    152–54; founding ideas of, 9, 142, 145;
    ideas literature and, 143–44; oil crisis and,
    150–51; as threat to Germany, 84, 110–11,
    116–17; as threat to United States, 70, 74,
    77, 79, 147. *See also* Russia; Soviet Union
    and Soviet *under other entries*
Spanish Civil War, 66
Spykman, Nicholas, 77
SS-20 missiles, 147
stab-in-the back myth, 102, 104, 106
Stalin, Joseph, 142, 145, 146, 148, 153
Stalingrad, Battle of, 110, 121
"Star Wars," 147
State of the Union Addresses, 52–55, 89,
    200–201
Stein, Janice Gross, 155
strategic circumstances, 4, 17, 44; and China,
    174; and Germany, 17, 40, 89–90, 115–17,
    120; inadequacy as sole cause, 18, 19, 141,
    157, 161–62; and Japan, 138–40; and the So-
    viet Union, 156–58; synthetic explanation
    and, 13–14, 16–17, 40; and the United
    States, 17, 56, 63, 72–79, 167, 170
Stresemann, Gustav, 19, 89, 94–96, 98, 106, 17,
    120

synthetic explanation, 4, 13–14, 24, 38, 40–41, 46, 161–62, 179–80; the German case, 115–21; the Japanese case, 141–42; the Soviet case, 156–58; the U.S. case, 72–83

Taft, Robert, 59
Taft, William Howard, 56, 62
Taiwan, 173, 174, 176
Taylor, Charles, 5
terrorism, 35, 169–72, 185, 186
Thimme, Friedrich, 92
Threats. *See* strategic circumstances
Tibet, 173
Tirpitz, Alfred von, 92
Tokugawa Bakufu (Shogunate). *See* Japan
Tokugawa Ieyasu, 128
"Told you so." *See* collapse scenarios
Toyotomi Hideyoshi, 128
transnational influence, 39, 46, 164–65, 185; in Germany, 87, 92, 107, 120–21; in Japan, 122, 130, 159; in the Soviet Union, 122, 124, 154, 159; in United States, 39, 70
tribute system (China), 125, 127
Tripartite Pact, 80
Troeltsch, Ernst, 92
Trotsky, Leon, 142
Trubowitz, Peter, 45
"Try Harder." *See* consolidation scenarios
Tsushima Islands, 128

United Nations, 74
United States: change after 9/11, 3, 166–72; change in World War II, 12, 52–53, 58–60, 65–70, 163; and China, 173–75, 178; continuity after World War I, 8–12, 52–53, 56–58, 60–65; economic ideas of, 190–94; founding ideas of, 55–56; future grand strategy of, 169–72; generations and policy in, 81–82; and Germany, 87, 98, 101, 107, 114, 121, 165, 185; and Japan, 122, 130, 132, 142; shocks and, 15, 23, 46, 166, 168; social purpose of, 82. *See* United States *and* U.S. *under other entries*

Vagt, Alfred, 88
Vandenberg, Arthur, 67
Versailles, Treaty of, 16, 88, 89, 114, 155, 171; impact on German politics, 86, 94–98, 101–7, 119–21; U.S. repudiation of, 63–63
Vietnam, 81

Waltz, Kenneth, 72, 123, 167
war guilt myth, 102, 104–6

War Industries Board, 62
Washington, George, Farewell Address, 55
Weber, Max, 2, 5
Weigert, Hans, 77
Weimar Republic. *See* Germany
Weinberg, Gerhard, 97
Weir, Margaret, 7
Weltpolitik, 91–92, 117
Wen Jiabao, 175
Westphalia, Treaty of, 89
Wette, Wolfram, 94
White Rose Movement, 110
Wilhelm II, Kaiser, 86, 92, 102, 112
Wilhelmine Germany (Kaiserreich). *See* Germany
William II, King of Holland, 132
Wilson, Woodrow, 51, 90, 172; decision to intervene and domestic politics, 61–64, 73, 75–76, 82–83; "Fourteen Points" and Germany, 103, 106–7; and Versailles Treaty/League of Nations, 63–65; World War I and shift to internationalism, 56–57; World War I undermines policies of, 62–64, 70–71, 163, 170, 172, 182
Wirth, Joseph, 106
Wohlforth, William, 148, 149, 151, 156
Woller, Hans, 110
World Trade Center Attacks, 35
World Trade Organization (WTO), 173, 176, 177
World War I, 2, 3, 12, 17, 18, 23, 46; caused by German expansionism, 90–93; continuity of German policy after, 15–16, 85–87, 94–98, 109, 119–21; continuity of U.S. policy after, 12, 49–51, 171–72, 175, 185–86; effects compared with World War II, 50, 65, 67, 72, 113–15, 162–66; strategic setting after the war, 76–77; U.S. decision to intervene in, 61–62; and U.S. disillusionment, 62–65, 182–83, 111
World War II, 1, 2, 3, 17, 18, 23, 40, 46, 116, 142, 153; impact on German foreign policy, 16, 98–100, 110–15, 120–21; German revisionism and, 97–98; U.S. internationalism and, 12–13, 49–51, 52, 58–61, 65–71, 171, 185–86; U.S. intervention in, 66–68

Yakovlev, Alexander, 146
Yeltsin, Boris, 152
Young Plan, 57, 107

Zimmerman telegram, 61, 77–78

Reputation and International Politics by Jonathan Mercer

Undermining the Kremlin: America's Strategy to Subvert the Soviet Bloc, 1947–1956 by Gregory Mitrovich

The Remnants of War by John Mueller

Report to JFK: The Skybolt Crisis in Perspective by Richard E. Neustadt

The Sacred Cause: Civil-Military Conflict over Soviet National Security, 1917–1992 by Thomas M. Nichols

Liberal Peace, Liberal War: American Politics and International Security by John M. Owen IV

Bombing to Win: Air Power and Coercion in War by Robert A. Pape

A Question of Loyalty: Military Manpower in Multiethnic States by Alon Peled

Inadvertent Escalation: Conventional War and Nuclear Risks by Barry R. Posen

The Sources of Military Doctrine: France, Britain, and Germany between the World Wars by Barry Posen

Dilemmas of Appeasement: British Deterrence and Defense, 1934–1937 by Gaines Post Jr.

Calculating Credibility: How Leaders Assess Military Threats by Daryl G. Press

Crucible of Beliefs: Learning, Alliances, and World Wars by Dan Reiter

Eisenhower and the Missile Gap by Peter J. Roman

The Domestic Bases of Grand Strategy edited by Richard Rosecrance and Arthur Stein

Societies and Military Power: India and Its Armies by Stephen Peter Rosen

Winning the Next War: Innovation and the Modern Military by Stephen Peter Rosen

Vital Crossroads: Mediterranean Origins of the Second World War, 1935–1940 by Reynolds Salerno

Fighting to a Finish: The Politics of War Termination in the United States and Japan, 1945 by Leon V. Sigal

Divided Union: The Politics of War in the Early American Republic by Scott A. Silverstone

Corporate Warriors: The Rise of the Privatized Military Industry by P. W. Singer

Alliance Politics by Glenn H. Snyder

The Ideology of the Offensive: Military Decision Making and the Disasters of 1914 by Jack Snyder

Myths of Empire: Domestic Politics and International Ambition by Jack Snyder

The Militarization of Space: U.S. Policy, 1945–1984 by Paul B. Stares

Balancing Risks: Great Power Intervention in the Periphery by Jeffrey W. Taliaferro

The Nixon Administration and the Making of U.S. Nuclear Strategy by Terry Terriff

The Ethics of Destruction: Norms and Force in International Relations by Ward Thomas

Causes of War: Power and the Roots of Conflict by Stephen Van Evera

Mortal Friends, Best Enemies: German-Russian Cooperation after the Cold War by Celeste A. Wallander

The Origins of Alliances by Stephen M. Walt

Revolution and War by Stephen M. Walt

The Tet Offensive: Intelligence Failure in War by James J. Wirtz

The Elusive Balance: Power and Perceptions during the Cold War by William Curti Wohlforth

Deterrence and Strategic Culture: Chinese-American Confrontations, 1949–1958 by Shu Guang Zhang